Kevin Hoffman
Robert Foster

Microsoft®
SharePoint® 2007
Development

UNLEASHED

SAMS | 800 East 96th Street, Indianapolis, Indiana 46240 USA

Microsoft® SharePoint® 2007 Development Unleashed

ISBN-13: 978-0-672-32903-6
ISBN-10: 0-672-32903-4

Library of Congress Cataloging-in-Publication Data

Hoffman, Kevin.
  Microsoft SharePoint 2007 development unleashed / Kevin Hoffman, Robert Foster.
    p. cm.
  ISBN 0-672-32903-4
  1. Intranets (Computer networks) 2. Web servers. I. Foster, Robert Hill. II. Title.

TK5105.875.I6H63 2007
004.6'8—dc22
                        2007012474

Printed in the United States of America

First Printing: May 2007

Trademarks

Warning and Disclaimer

Bulk Sales

Sams Publishing offers excellent discounts on this book when ordered in quantity for bulk purchases or special sales. For more information, please contact

U.S. Corporate and Government Sales
1-800-382-3419
corpsales@pearsontechgroup.com

For sales outside of the U.S., please contact

International Sales
international@pearsoned.com

Editor-in-Chief
Karen Gettman

Acquisitions Editor
Neil Rowe

Development Editor
Mark Renfrow

Managing Editor
Gina Kanouse

Project Editor
Betsy Harris

Copy Editor
Karen Annett

Proofreader
Kathy Bidwell

Technical Editor
Kenneth Cox

Publishing Coordinator
Cindy Teeters

Interior Designer
Gary Adair

Cover Designer
Gary Adair

Compositor
Bronkella Publishing

 This Book Is Safari Enabled

The Safari® Enabled icon on the cover of your favorite technology book means the book is available through Safari Bookshelf. When you buy this book, you get free access to the online edition for 45 days. Safari Bookshelf is an electronic reference library that lets you easily search thousands of technical books, find code samples, download chapters, and access technical information whenever and wherever you need it.

To gain 45-day Safari Enabled access to this book:

· Go to http://www.samspublishing.com/safarienabled
· Complete the brief registration form
· Enter the coupon code EVG3-UDMF-7VXJ-ZUFZ-DGHR

If you have difficulty registering on Safari Bookshelf or accessing the online edition, please e-mail customer-service@safaribooksonline.com.

Contents at a Glance

Introduction 1

1 Collaborative Application Markup Language (CAML) Primer 5

Part I **Programming with the SharePoint Object Model**

2 Introduction to the SharePoint Object Model 15

3 Programming with Features and Solutions 25

4 Working with Sites and Webs 35

5 Managing SharePoint Lists 47

6 Advanced List Management 59

7 Handling List Events 69

8 Working with Document Libraries and Files 83

9 Working with Meetings 97

Part II **Enterprise Content Management**

10 Integrating Business Data 109

11 Creating Business Data Applications 121

12 Working with User Profiles 135

13 Building Workflows 147

Part III **Programming SharePoint Web Parts**

14 ASP.NET Server Control Primer 163

15 Introduction to Web Parts 173

16 Developing Full-Featured Web Parts 191

17 Building Web Parts for Maintaining SharePoint 2007 Lists 205

18 Building Connected Web Parts 217

19 Debugging and Deploying Web Parts 229

Part IV   **Programming the SharePoint 2007 Web Services**

20   Using the Document Workspace Web Service 241

21   Using the Imaging Web Service 255

22   Using the Lists Web Service 273

23   Using the Meeting Workspace Web Service 291

24   Working with User Profiles and Security 307

25   Using Excel Services 321

26   Working with the Web Part Pages Web Service 337

27   Using the Business Data Catalog Web Services 347

28   Using the Workflow Web Service 359

29   Working with Records Repositories 369

30   Additional Web Services 377

     Index 387

Table of Contents

Introduction   **1**

1   **Collaborative Application Markup Language (CAML) Primer**   **5**

The CAML Language 5

Querying a List 8

Using the U2U CAML Query Builder 11

Summary 12

Part I   **Programming with the SharePoint Object Model**

2   **Introduction to the SharePoint Object Model**   **15**

First Look at the Object Model 15

Development Scenarios and Sample Applications 17

Developing Applications on the Server 17

Developing Web Parts 18

Developing Remote Applications 18

Setting Up Your Development Environment 18

Setting Up a Local Development Environment 19

Setting Up a Remote Development Environment 20

Creating Your First Object Model Application 21

Deploying Your Application 22

Summary 23

3   **Programming with Features and Solutions**   **25**

Overview of Features and Solutions 25

Programming with Features 26

Enumerating Features and Feature Definitions 27

Activating and Deactivating Features 29

Using Feature Properties 30

Installing and Removing Feature Definitions 31

Programming with Solutions 31

Installing and Removing Solutions 32

Enumerating Solutions 32

Controlling Solution Deployment 34

Summary 34

4   Working with Sites and Webs   **35**

Understanding Webs and Sites 35

Using the SPSite Class 36

   Creating Sites 39

   Accessing Site Information 41

   Updating Sites 42

Using the SPWeb Class 42

   Creating Webs 44

   Accessing Web Information 45

   Updating Webs 46

Summary 46

5   Managing SharePoint Lists   **47**

List Management Basics 47

Enumerating Lists 48

Enumerating List Contents 51

Adding, Removing, and Updating Lists 53

Manipulating List Items 56

Using Lookup Types in Lists 58

Summary 58

6   Advanced List Management   **59**

Accessing BDC Data in Lists 59

Querying List Items with CAML 62

Creating Parent/Child Relationships in a Single List 64

Summary 68

7   Handling List Events   **69**

Introduction to List Event Handlers 69

Creating Event Receivers 70

   Creating List Event Receivers 70

   Creating List Item Event Receivers 73

Deploying Event Receivers 77

   Deploying Event Receivers Programmatically 77

   Deploying Event Receivers with Features 77

   Deploying Event Receivers with Content Types 81

Summary 81

8   Working with Document Libraries and Files   83

Document Library Basics 83
Working with the Document Library Object Model 84
    Building a Document Library Explorer Sample 86
Working with Versioning 91
    Checking Files Out 91
    Checking Files In 91
Manipulating Folders and Files 94
Summary 95

9   Working with Meetings   97

Managing Meeting Workspace Sites 97
    Creating a Meeting Workspace 97
    Deleting a Meeting Workspace 99
Accessing Existing Meetings 99
Managing Meetings 102
    Creating Meetings 102
    Modifying Meetings 104
    Deleting Meetings 104
    Handling Attendee Responses 105
Working with Events 105
Summary 106

Part II   Enterprise Content Management

10   Integrating Business Data   109

Introduction to the Business Data Catalog 109
    Authentication 110
    BDC Pros and Cons 111
Configuring a New Business Data Application 111
Using the Business Data Web Parts 114
Searching for Business Data Entities 117
Using Entity Actions 117
Using Business Data Columns in Custom Lists 118
Summary 119

11   Creating Business Data Applications   121

Using the Business Data Catalog Administration API 121
Using the Business Data Catalog Runtime API 124
    Querying Metadata 124
    Using a Specific Finder 126

Using a Filter Finder...128
Using a Wildcard Finder...130
Executing Methods Directly...131
Creating BDC-friendly Applications..132
Building BDC-compatible Web Services..............................132
Exposing Relational Data to SharePoint............................133
Summary..133

12   Working with User Profiles   135

Accessing User Profiles with the Object Model.......................135
Retrieving User Profiles...135
Retrieving Profile Properties..137
Modifying a User Profile..140
Retrieving Recent Changes...140
Configuring the User Profile Store with the Object Model.....142
Creating a User Profile...143
Creating a User Profile Property.......................................143
Creating Advanced User Profile Properties......................144
Changing the Separator Value for Multi-valued Properties........144
Manipulating Memberships..145
Viewing Commonalities Among Profiles............................145
Summary..146

13   Building Workflows   147

Workflow as a Solution..147
SharePoint Workflows..148
Workflow Objects..149
Building the Workflow..150
Designing the Forms...151
Modeling the Workflow in Visual Studio 2005..................153
Coding the Workflow..155
Deploying the Workflow..156
Summary..159

Part III   Programming SharePoint Web Parts

14   ASP.NET Server Control Primer   163

Contrasting Server Controls and User Controls.......................163
Building Your First Server Control...166
Extending Server Controls..168
Summary..172

15   Introduction to Web Parts   **173**

Introduction to the ASP.NET 2.0 Web Part Infrastructure 173
Primer on Creating ASP.NET 2.0 Web Parts 178
   Creating an ASP.NET 2.0 Web Part 178
   Testing the Web Part 181
Integrating Server Controls and Web User Controls 183
Using the HelloWorld WebPart Control with SharePoint 185
   ASP.NET Web Parts Versus SharePoint Web Parts 185
   SharePoint Integration 185
Summary 189

16   Developing Full-Featured Web Parts   **191**

Web Part Properties 191
   Customizing Web Parts with Properties 191
Picking Property Values from a List 195
Interactive Web Parts 196
   Handling Postback 203
   Including JavaScript 204
Summary 204

17   Building Web Parts for Maintaining SharePoint 2007 Lists   **205**

Web Parts and SharePoint Lists 205
The SharePoint List Example 205
Accessing a List 206
Updating List Data 209
Summary 215

18   Building Connected Web Parts   **217**

Building the Provider 217
   Creating the Data Interface 218
   Creating the Provider Web Part 218
Building the Consumer 221
Connecting Web Parts 223
Summary 227

19   Debugging and Deploying Web Parts   **229**

Debugging Web Parts 229
   The Developer's Machine Configuration 229
   Debugging 230

Deploying Web Parts 235
    Adding a Setup Project to Your Solution 235
    Configuring Setup Application 236
    Compile Setup Application (Creates an .msi File) and
    Deploy the Components 237
Summary 238

Part IV   Programming the SharePoint 2007 Web Services

20   Using the Document Workspace Web Service   241
Overview of Document Workspaces 241
Managing Document Workspace Sites 242
    Validating Document Workspace Site URLs 242
    Creating and Deleting Document Workspace Sites 242
Managing Document Workspace Data 244
    Getting DWS Data 244
    Getting DWS MetaData 246
Working with Folders 248
Locating Documents in a Workspace 251
Managing Workspace Users 253
Summary 253

21   Using the Imaging Web Service   255
Overview of Picture Libraries 255
Introducing the Imaging Web Service 256
Locating Picture Libraries and Images 257
    Enumerating Picture Libraries 258
    Obtaining Picture Library List Items 258
    Getting Items by ID 260
    Obtaining Item XML Data 260
Managing Photos 261
    Uploading Photos 261
    Downloading Photos 262
    Renaming Photos 263
    Deleting Photos 263
    Creating Folders 263
Building a Practical Sample: Photo Browser 264
Summary 272

22 Using the Lists Web Service   **273**

Overview of the SharePoint Lists Web Services 273

Performing Common List Actions 274

    Retrieving Lists and List Items 274

    Updating Lists 278

    Updating, Deleting, and Creating List Items 281

    Retrieving Parent/Child List Data 283

Working with Revision Control 286

Querying List Data 286

Working with Views 288

    Creating a View 288

    Deleting a View 289

    Getting View Collections and Details 289

Summary 289

23 Using the Meeting Workspace Web Service   **291**

Overview of Meeting Workspaces 291

    Creating a Meeting Workspace Site 292

Managing Meeting Workspaces 293

    Listing Available Meeting Workspaces 293

    Creating a Workspace 295

    Deleting a Workspace 296

    Changing Workspace Details 297

Managing Meetings 298

    Creating Meetings 298

    Removing Meetings 300

    Updating Meetings 301

    Restoring Meetings 302

Managing Meeting Attendance 302

Accessing Meeting Workspace Lists 304

Summary 305

24 Working with User Profiles and Security   **307**

What's New with User Profiles in MOSS 2007 307

Working with User Profiles 308

Working with the User Group Service 314

Summary 319

25   Using Excel Services   **321**

    Introduction to Excel Services 321
        Workbook Management 322
        Centralized Application Logic 322
        Business Intelligence 322
    Excel Services Architecture 323
        Excel Web Access 324
        Excel Calculation Services 324
        Excel Web Services 325
    Using the Excel Services Web Service 325
        Setting Excel Services Trusted Locations 326
        Canonical "Hello World" Sample, Excel Services Style 326
        Developing a Real-World Excel Services Client Application 328
    Creating a Managed Excel Services User-Defined Function 332
    Summary 336

26   Working with the Web Part Pages Web Service   **337**

    Overview of the Web Part Pages Web Service 337
    Adding and Updating Web Parts 339
    Querying Web Part Pages 344
        Using the GetWebPart Method 344
        Getting Safe Assembly Details 345
    Summary 346

27   Using the Business Data Catalog Web Services   **347**

    Overview of the Business Data Catalog 347
    Using the Business Data Catalog Web Service 348
    Using the BDC Field Resolver Web Service 355
    Summary 357

28   Using the Workflow Web Service   **359**

    Overview of Workflows in SharePoint 2007 359
    Introduction to the Workflow Web Service 360
    Performing Workflow Tasks with the Web Service 360
        Getting Workflow Data for an Item 361
        Getting To-Dos for an Item 362
        Modifying To-Do Items 365
        Claiming or Releasing Tasks 366
        Getting Templates for an Item 366
        Getting Workflow Task Data 367
        Starting a Workflow 367
    Summary 368

29   Working with Records Repositories   369

Overview of Records Repositories 369

Using Records Repositories 370

  Using the Records Center Site Definition 370

  Using a Custom Records Center 372

  Submitting Files via Workflows 373

  Programmatically Submitting Files Using the SPFile Class 373

  Querying an Official File Web Service 374

Creating Your Own Records Repository 375

  SubmitFile 375

  GetServerInfo 376

Summary 376

30   Additional Web Services   377

Using the Spell Checker Web Service 377

Using the Alerts Web Service 379

Using the Versions Web Service 383

Summary 385

Index   387

About the Authors

Kevin Hoffman wrote his first line of code more than 21 years ago. When he received his first computer, a Commodore VIC-20, he became addicted immediately and has been writing code and learning as much about programming and the art of software development ever since. He has worked in many industries writing applications for the .NET Framework since the original 1.0 release, and, more recently, has been involved in development for the .NET Framework 3.0 and SharePoint 2007. He is currently a Research Developer for Liquidnet Holdings, one of the largest global institutional equities brokers, working on many varied technologies, including the .NET Framework and SharePoint 2007.

Rob Foster is an enterprise architect in Nashville, Tennessee. He began writing code at the age of 10 when he purchased his first computer, a Tandy TRS-80 Color Computer 2, with money that he received for his birthday. He graduated from Middle Tennessee State University with a BBA in Computer Information Systems and holds several certifications, including MCSD, MCSE, MCDBA, and MCT. In 2000 with the PDC bits in hand, Rob founded the Nashville .NET Users Group (http://www.nashdotnet.org), which is a charter member of INETA. He has been writing and designing .NET applications since version 1.0, as well as has been implementing SharePoint solutions since SharePoint 2001. In his spare time, Rob enjoys writing books and articles relating to SharePoint and .NET. Rob lives in Murfreesboro, Tennessee, with his wife, Leigh, and two sons, Andrew and Will.

Dedication

I would like to dedicate this book to my wife and daughter. The sacrifices that my family has made while I have been writing books have been immense. Without their support, I never would have been able to finish the first book, let alone the last. They have been more than patient with my late-night coding sessions, frustrated all-day chapter binges, and all-around writer's block crankiness. They helped me through it all, and this book is as much a work of their patience and support as it is of my hands.

—Kevin Hoffman

I would like to dedicate this book to my wife, Leigh, and my boys, Andrew and Will. Leigh, words can't express how grateful I am to have had so much support and positive reinforcement from you through this whole process—all while being pregnant for most of the duration of the writing phase. You do it all and never complain when I have to buckle down and write yet another chapter. Thank you so much for everything that you do—you are the greatest!

—Rob Foster

Acknowledgments

I would like to acknowledge my coauthor, Rob Foster. People like him have made coding fun again when the looming shadow of burnout has been hovering near. I've worked with a lot of coauthors and worked with even more developers in my career, and it's been an absolute joy working with Rob on this book.

—Kevin Hoffman

I would like to acknowledge my coauthor, Kevin Hoffman. After meeting Kevin for the first time, we became instant friends. His wit and sense of humor got me through a lot of late nights coding and cranking out chapters when I was having writer's block or just simply didn't feel like writing. I know that if I have a question about technology (and often times questions about life), he will always have an inspirational and thoughtful answer for me. Kevin, I have been a long-time fan of your work and have thoroughly enjoyed working with you on this book.

—Rob Foster

We Want to Hear from You!

As the reader of this book, *you* are our most important critic and commentator. We value your opinion and want to know what we're doing right, what we could do better, what areas you'd like to see us publish in, and any other words of wisdom you're willing to pass our way.

As a senior acquisitions editor for Sams Publishing, I welcome your comments. You can email or write me directly to let me know what you did or didn't like about this book—as well as what we can do to make our books better.

Please note that I cannot help you with technical problems related to the topic of this book. We do have a User Services group, however, where I will forward specific technical questions related to the book.

When you write, please be sure to include this book's title and author as well as your name, email address, and phone number. I will carefully review your comments and share them with the author and editors who worked on the book.

Email: feedback@samspublishing.com

Mail: Neil Rowe
         Senior Acquisitions Editor
         Sams Publishing
         800 East 96th Street
         Indianapolis, IN 46240 USA

For more information about this book or another Sams Publishing title, visit our website at www.samspublishing.com. Type the ISBN (excluding hyphens) or the title of a book in the Search field to find the page you're looking for.

Introduction

When many people first encounter Microsoft Office SharePoint Server (MOSS), they are often confused. Out of the box, a lot of people have trouble figuring out what it does and what it's for. The most important thing to realize about SharePoint is that it isn't intended to be a complete, off-the-shelf, shrink-wrapped product. Rather, MOSS is a *development platform*, upon which powerful and compelling portal applications can be built.

This book provides developers with a thorough, in-depth guide to the internals of writing code for the SharePoint *platform*. SharePoint programming can be divided into four main categories: programming the object model, programming the web services, programming the Web Parts, and programming the enterprise content.

Programming the SharePoint object model involves writing code that physically resides on one of the front-end servers in a SharePoint web farm. Web services expose powerful SharePoint functionality to applications that do *not* reside on the same server as SharePoint, such as smart clients and other remote servers. Web Parts are components that can be dropped onto Web Part pages within a SharePoint site, which provide valuable displays for various types of data and functionality. Finally, enterprise content programming involves working with the Business Data Catalog.

The following is a description of the chapters included in this book:

▶ **Chapter 1: Collaborative Application Markup Language (CAML) Primer**—This chapter provides an introduction to the Collaborative Application Markup Language (CAML), an Extensible Markup Language (XML) dialect used throughout SharePoint for defining content, manipulating searches and search results, and much more.

▶ **Part I: Programming with the SharePoint Object Model**

    ▶ **Chapter 2: Introduction to the SharePoint Object Model**—This chapter provides an introduction to writing server-side code that interfaces directly with the SharePoint application programming interface (API).

    ▶ **Chapter 3: Programming with Features and Solutions**—Features and Solutions are powerful new concepts in this version of SharePoint that allow developers to create reusable packages that can be easily installed and deployed throughout a farm. This chapter shows you how to write code to manipulate and query Features and Solutions.

    ▶ **Chapter 4: Working with Sites and Webs**—This chapter provides an introduction to programming with the main units of hierarchy within SharePoint—webs and sites.

    ▶ **Chapter 5: Managing SharePoint Lists**—Virtually every piece of data contained within SharePoint is contained as a list item in a list. As a result, knowing how to program against lists is a vital developer skill and this chapter provides a thorough introduction to managing lists and list items.

▶ **Chapter 6: Advanced List Management**—This chapter builds on the previous chapter and provides additional information and samples on working with lists and list items.

▶ **Chapter 7: Handling List Events**—This chapter illustrates how to write code that will respond to events that take place on lists and list items. Previous versions of SharePoint limited this functionality to only document libraries, and this chapter shows you how to harness the new power of list events.

▶ **Chapter 8: Working with Document Libraries and Files**—Document libraries provide a powerful way to store documents, photos, slide shows, and any other type of file. This chapter shows you how to write code to query and manipulate document libraries, folders, and the files contained within them.

▶ **Chapter 9: Working with Meetings**—Meetings are a powerful aspect of the collaboration functionality provided by SharePoint. This chapter gives you thorough coverage of how to work with the object model to manipulate and query meetings and meeting workspaces.

▶ **Part II: Enterprise Content Management**

▶ **Chapter 10: Integrating Business Data**—This chapter provides an overview of how to integrate external business data into your SharePoint application.

▶ **Chapter 11: Creating Business Data Applications**—This chapter details how to create an application that can expose its data to a SharePoint application via the Business Data Catalog.

▶ **Chapter 12: Working with User Profiles**—User profiles are an important concept in the enterprise deployment and configuration of SharePoint, and have seen much improvement in this new release. This chapter provides details on how to work with user profiles as a developer.

▶ **Chapter 13: Building Workflows**—Integration with the Windows Workflow Foundation is a critical piece of new functionality in MOSS 2007, and this chapter details how to create workflows that can be used for enterprise content management either through Visual Studio or through the SharePoint Designer.

▶ **Part III: Programming SharePoint Web Parts**

▶ **Chapter 14: ASP.NET Server Control Primer**—Before you can grasp the intricacies of building SharePoint Web Parts, you need to know how they work and what makes them possible. SharePoint Web Parts are specialized versions of ASP.NET Web Parts, which are ASP.NET server controls. This chapter provides an overview of the ASP.NET web controls that make Web Parts possible.

▶ **Chapter 15: Introduction to Web Parts**—This chapter provides an overview of building SharePoint Web Parts.

▶ **Chapter 16: Developing Full-Featured Web Parts**—This chapter expands on the foundation provided by the previous chapter and gets into more detail on how to create truly powerful and compelling Web Parts.

▶ **Chapter 17: Building Web Parts for Maintaining SharePoint 2007 Lists**—Lists are a key part of the data storage facility provided by SharePoint and one of the most common tasks of SharePoint Web Parts is interacting with SharePoint lists—the subject of this chapter.

▶ **Chapter 18: Building Connected Web Parts**—One of the most powerful features of Web Parts is their ability to provide and consume data through connections. This chapter shows you how to build connected Web Parts.

▶ **Chapter 19: Debugging and Deploying Web Parts**—After you know how to build Web Parts and how to write the code, you need to debug and deploy those Web Parts and harden them for a production environment. This chapter provides you with the information you need to debug and deploy your Web Parts.

▶ **Part IV: Programming the SharePoint 2007 Web Services**

▶ **Chapter 20: Using the Document Workspace Web Service**—This chapter illustrates how to use web services to interact with document workspaces and related data.

▶ **Chapter 21: Using the Imaging Web Service**—This chapter illustrates how to use the Imaging Web Service provided by SharePoint, including creating a sample photo browser client application.

▶ **Chapter 22: Using the Lists Web Service**—This chapter details how to interact with lists and list items remotely using the Lists Web Service.

▶ **Chapter 23: Using the Meeting Workspace Web Service**—This chapter provides an overview of interacting with meeting workspaces using the Meeting Workspaces Web Service.

▶ **Chapter 24: Working with User Profiles and Security**—User profiles and security are an important aspect of SharePoint development, and this chapter illustrates how to work with user profiles, security groups, and permissions using web services.

▶ **Chapter 25: Using Excel Services**—This chapter covers the use of Excel Services in SharePoint 2007. Excel Services is a powerful new feature of SharePoint 2007 that allows for centralized storage and management of spreadsheets. This web service allows for session-based query and manipulation of server-side spreadsheets.

▶ **Chapter 26: Working with the Web Part Pages Web Service**—This chapter covers manipulating Web Part Pages via web services. This web service exposes functionality that lets applications remotely manipulate Web Parts and Web Part pages, such as installing, hiding, removing, and changing properties for Web Parts.

▶ **Chapter 27: Using the Business Data Catalog Web Services**—This chapter covers utilizing some of the functionality of the Business Data Catalog from remote client applications via Web Services.

▶ **Chapter 28: Using the Workflow Web Service**—This chapter discusses the Workflow Web Service, which exposes functionality for initiating workflows, changing workflow properties, and manipulating workflow tasks.

▶ **Chapter 29: Working with Records Repositories**—This chapter deals with the Official File Web Service. Records repositories allow for the storage of files and their associated metadata in a read-only location that can satisfy compliance regulations and audit rules.

▶ **Chapter 30: Additional Web Services**—This chapter provides details on several other web services that might be handy for developers.

In addition, you can download example code for this book from www.samspublishing.com.

CHAPTER 1

Collaborative Application Markup Language (CAML) Primer

IN THIS CHAPTER

▸ The CAML Language

▸ Querying a List

▸ Using the U2U CAML Query Builder

The Collaborative Application Markup Language (CAML) is used in SharePoint to query lists and help with the creation and customization of sites. After you start digging deeper, programming is almost a required skill set that can help you easily get data from SharePoint. This chapter shows you how to create CAML queries to extract data from lists.

The CAML Language

The CAML language has been associated with SharePoint since the first version, SharePoint 2001, and SharePoint Team Services. It is based on a defined Extensible Markup Language (XML) document that will help you perform a data manipulation task in SharePoint. It is easy to relate a list to CAML if you compare it to a database table and query. When querying a database, you could get all of the records back from the table and then find the one that you want, or you can use a Structured Query Language (SQL) query to narrow the results to just the records in which you are interested. CAML helps you to do just this.

A CAML query must be a well-formed XML document that is composed of the following elements:

```
<Query>
        <Where>
                <!--Comparison Operators here-->
                <Eq>
                        <FieldRef Name="insertFieldNameHere" />
                        <Value Type="insertDataTypeHere">insertValueHere</Value>
                </Eq>
        </Where>
        <OrderBy>
                <FieldRef Name="insertFieldNameHere" />
                <FieldRef Name="insertFieldNameHere" />
        </OrderBy>
</Query>
```

This simple CAML query definition defines a filter where a field equals a specified value using the Eq element. In addition, one or many FieldRef elements can be specified inside the OrderBy element to sort by one or many columns.

In the preceding example, a CAML query can define one or many of the comparison operators listed in Table 1.1 that will be used to further filter the data that the query returns.

TABLE 1.1   CAML Comparison Operators

Begins With	Begins with a Given Text Value
Contains	Contains a given text value
Eq	Equal to
Geq	Greater than or equal to
Gt	Greater than
Leq	Less than or equal to
Lt	Less than
Neq	Not equal to
DateRangesOverlap	Compares dates in recurring events to determine if they overlap
IsNotNull	Is not null
IsNull	Is null

You must supply all of these elements with a FieldRef child element. The FieldRef element specifies the SharePoint-specific name of the column that is being evaluated. In addition, almost all of the query elements (with the exception of IsNotNull and IsNull) require that you also specify a Value child element. This is where you will specify what value to evaluate the specified FieldRef element against.

Unfortunately, SharePoint doesn't always intuitively name each of the `FieldRefs` that you need to reference. The following code is an example that you can use to extract the `FieldRef` name from a list by using a console application and the Microsoft Office SharePoint Server 2007 application programming interface (API):

```
using System;
using System.Collections.Generic;
using System.Text;
using Microsoft.SharePoint;

namespace SharePointUtils
{
    class Program
    {
        static void Main(string[] args)
        {
            string siteUrl = args[0];
            string listName = args[1];
            string viewName = args[2];
            SPSite site = new SPSite(siteUrl);
            SPWeb web = site.OpenWeb();
            SPList employeesList = web.Lists[listName];
            SPQuery query = new SPQuery(employeesList.Views[viewName]);
            System.Diagnostics.Debug.WriteLine(query.ViewXml);
            Console.WriteLine(query.ViewXml);
            Console.ReadLine();
        }
    }
}
```

NOTE

As you are developing in SharePoint 2007, you will soon find yourself building a set of utilities or tools that you keep handy to help you write code. The `FieldRef` extraction utility is an example of one of these useful tools.

The code is very simple and the output is very usable when you start writing CAML queries. Three arguments are required for the site uniform resource locator (URL), list name, and view name, respectively. Objects are created for the site, the web, and the list. Notice that an instance of `SPQuery` is also created. The `SPQuery` object is used to get the SharePoint-specific field names (or `FieldRefs`) from the view. Figure 1.1 illustrates the All Items view from a custom list called Employees. Note that to get the code to work correctly, you will need to recreate the Employees custom list on your site.

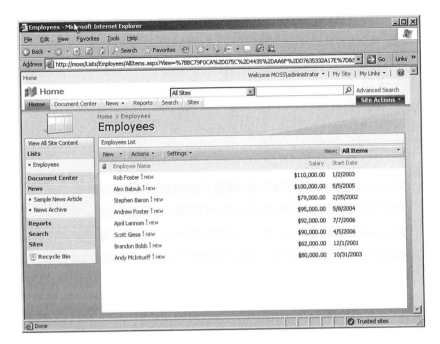

FIGURE 1.1   Employees—All Items view.

When you execute the preceding code against the All Items view of the Employees custom list, the results listed in Figure 1.2 are output to the console window.

FIGURE 1.2   FieldRef Extraction Utility Output.

The list's fields are defined with `FieldRef` elements. For example, the three fields that are displayed in Figure 1.1, Employee Name, Salary, and Start Date, are actually represented in SharePoint as "LinkTitle", "Salary", and "Start_x0020_Date", respectively.

The next section shows you how to use the `FieldRefs` to write a CAML query that will return results from the Employees list.

Querying a List

After you have identified the `FieldRefs` that you want to filter your query by, actually querying a list is quite simple. Taking into account the Employees list, you might want to create a query that displays all employees with a start date before January 1, 2003. The following is an example of a CAML query that will filter records by those with a start date beginning before January 1, 2003:

```
<Query>
   <OrderBy>
      <FieldRef Name="Title" />
   </OrderBy>
   <Where>
      <Lt>
         <FieldRef Name="Start_x0020_Date" />
         <Value Type="DateTime">2003-01-01T00:00:00Z</Value>
      </Lt>
   </Where>
</Query>
```

This query does two things. First, it specifies how the data is sorted when values are returned by using the OrderBy element. Notice that the results will be ordered by Title, which is actually the Employee Name field. Next, a Where element is defined that will specify the filter, which is similar in functionality to a SQL WHERE clause. The Where element defines an Lt (less than element), which contains a FieldRef element and a Value element. The FieldRef element is the column in the list and the Value element represents the data type and value that is being compared.

The following is a code excerpt that will execute the CAML query defined previously:

```
using System;
using System.Collections.Generic;
using System.Text;
using Microsoft.SharePoint;

namespace SharePointUtils
{
    class CAMLQuery
    {
        static void Main(string[] args)
        {
            string siteName = args[0];
            string listName = args[1];
            string viewName = args[1];
            SPSite site = new SPSite(siteName);
            SPWeb web = site.OpenWeb();
            SPList employeesList = web.Lists[listName];
            SPQuery query = new SPQuery(employeesList.Views[viewName]);
            query.Query = "<Query><OrderBy><FieldRef Name=\"Title\"
 /></OrderBy><Where><Lt><FieldRef Name=\"Start_x0020_Date\" /><Value
 Type=\"DateTime\">2003-01-01T00:00:00Z</Value></Lt></Where></Query>";
```

```
        SPListItemCollection filteredEmployees = employeesList.GetItems(query);
        foreach (SPListItem i in filteredEmployees)
        {
            System.Diagnostics.Debug.WriteLine(i["Title"].ToString() + " " +
➥i["Salary"].ToString() + " " + i["Start_x0020_Date"].ToString());
        }
        Console.ReadLine();
    }


  }
}
```

The code to perform the query is identical to the first code example in the chapter with the exception of setting the Query property of the SPQuery object named query. This is where you set the value of the CAML query that will be used to filter the data. The results are returned by using the GetItems method of the SPList object and an instance of the SPListItemCollection class. This collection is then iterated and the values are output to the debug window. The following is an example of the results that are returned by the CAML query:

```
Brandon Bobb 62000 12/1/2001 12:00:00 AM
Rob Foster 110000 1/1/1999 12:00:00 AM
Stephen Baron 79000 1/25/2002 12:00:00 AM
```

Though the number of records in the list is limited, the results are filtered to three records. Now what if you want to filter the list further? CAML has And and Or elements that can be used in conjunction with the Where element. The following is an example of a CAML query that filters by start dates before January 1, 2003 AND salaries lower than $80,000:

```
<Query>
   <OrderBy>
      <FieldRef Name="Title" />
   </OrderBy>
   <Where>
      <And>
         <Lt>
            <FieldRef Name="Start_x0020_Date" />
            <Value Type="DateTime">2003-01-01T00:00:00Z</Value>
         </Lt>
         <Lt>
            <FieldRef Name="Salary" />
            <Value Type="Currency">80000</Value>
         </Lt>
      </And>
   </Where>
</Query>
```

Naturally, this filters the sample list data to the following two records:

```
Brandon Bobb 62000 12/1/2001 12:00:00 AM
Stephen Baron 79000 1/25/2002 12:00:00 AM
```

As you can see, CAML queries are very easy to construct and execute. The next section highlights a free downloadable utility that you can use to easily construct and test your CAML queries.

Using the U2U CAML Query Builder

The U2U CAML Query Builder tool is a free download from U2U that you can use to create and test your CAML queries. It is a very useful tool that will save you a lot of time and effort while you are writing CAML queries. It can be downloaded from http://www.u2u.info/SharePoint/U2U%20Community%20Tools/Forms/AllItems.aspx.

Figure 1.3 illustrates the tool, which is referencing the Employees list that was discussed earlier in this chapter.

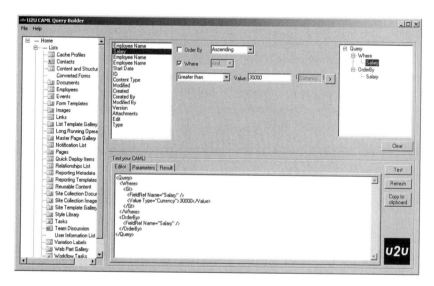

FIGURE 1.3   U2U CAML Query Builder.

Notice that after you select your list, the list's columns are populated in a ListBox control. From there, you can select each column and then provide some information about how the query should be filtered. In Figure 1.1, the CAML query is filtering by all records where the Salary column is greater than $30,000.

It is also equally as easy to pretest your CAML query before you actually write any code. You can do this by clicking the Test button. Figure 1.4 illustrates the results that are returned by the CAML query that was generated.

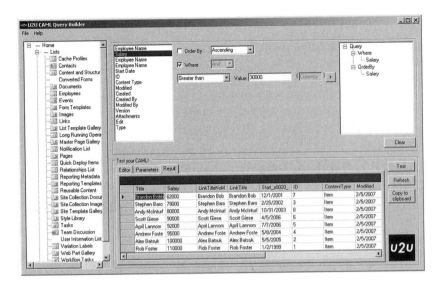

FIGURE 1.4   U2U CAML Query Builder (Results).

Summary

CAML is a very powerful language that you need to add to your SharePoint skill set. This chapter provided details on how to use CAML to query lists and filter data based on specified criteria. This will help you improve performance of your Web Parts and other code that will interact with any type of list-based data.

PART I

Programming with the SharePoint Object Model

IN THIS PART

CHAPTER 2	Introduction to the SharePoint Object Model	15
CHAPTER 3	Programming with Features and Solutions	25
CHAPTER 4	Working with Sites and Webs	35
CHAPTER 5	Managing SharePoint Lists	47
CHAPTER 6	Advanced List Management	59
CHAPTER 7	Handling List Events	69
CHAPTER 8	Working with Document Libraries and Files	83
CHAPTER 9	Working with Meetings	97

Introduction to the SharePoint Object Model

IN THIS CHAPTER

▶ First Look at the Object Model

▶ Development Scenarios and Sample Applications

▶ Setting Up Your Development Environment

▶ Creating Your First Object Model Application

▶ Deploying Your Application

Quite possibly one of the most important facts to remember about Microsoft Office SharePoint Server (MOSS) is that it is an application framework as much as it is an application on its own. As a result, both Windows SharePoint Services (WSS) and MOSS expose a rich and powerful managed application programming interface (API).

This chapter introduces you to the object model exposed by this API, shows you how to set up your development environment for working with this object model, and walks you through creating your first application targeting the SharePoint object model. You need a version of Visual Studio 2005 and network connectivity to a SharePoint server (either physical or on a Virtual PC) to compile and execute the code in this chapter and all subsequent chapters in the portion of the book dealing with the SharePoint object model.

First Look at the Object Model

SharePoint itself is functionally segmented by Windows SharePoint Services and Microsoft Office SharePoint Server. Within each of these separate but complementary products there are several namespaces that house the object model with which you'll be working. MOSS is responsible for such things as farm-enabled search, Excel Services, the Business Data Catalog, Single Sign-On, and other centralized portal-style activities. Virtually all activity that takes place within the context of a team site (regardless of template) is the purview of WSS. WSS is technically part of Windows Server

2003 R2, whereas MOSS is a product that installs on top of that to add additional enterprise portal functionality. The `Microsoft.Office.Server` namespace is the root namespace of all Office Server objects and `Microsoft.SharePoint` is the root namespace for all WSS objects.

Figure 2.1 illustrates some of the key classes contained in each of these namespaces, as well as to which functional area they belong. The namespace of each group of classes is shown in parentheses next to the functional area. For example, all list-related functionality is handled within the `Microsoft.SharePoint` namespace.

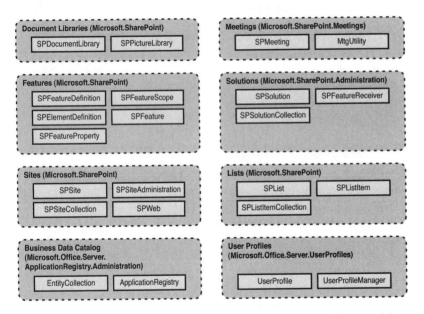

FIGURE 2.1   Illustration of key classes in the SharePoint object model, segmented by functional area.

Don't worry if you haven't seen any of these class names before—the next several chapters in the book are devoted entirely to the functional areas shown in Figure 2.1. By the time you are done with these chapters, all this will have become second nature to you. The following is a list of the functional areas of the object model that are covered in the upcoming chapters:

▶ **Features and Solutions**—As you will see in Chapter 3, "Programming with Features and Solutions," Features and Solutions allow you to create small, deployable packages of functionality that can be reused among multiple sites and site templates.

▶ **Site administration and enumeration**—Chapter 4, "Working with Sites and Webs," shows you how to iterate through site collection hierarchies, create and edit existing sites, and manipulate site collections.

▶ **List management**—Of all the tasks a programmer can do with SharePoint, working with lists is probably the one most commonly performed task. It is so common, in fact, that there are three chapters (5, 6, and 7) dedicated to working with lists and handling list events.

▶ **Document libraries**—Document libraries are a special type of list designed to store documents. Chapter 8, "Working with Document Libraries and Files," shows you how to work with document libraries, picture libraries, and files in general using the SharePoint object model.

▶ **Meetings**—Meeting workspaces are a special type of team collaboration site. Chapter 9, "Working with Meetings," shows you how to programmatically manipulate meetings and meeting workspaces.

▶ **Business Data Catalog**—The Business Data Catalog is an extremely powerful and important new feature of MOSS 2007. Chapter 10, "Integrating Business Data," shows you how to integrate enterprise data into SharePoint, and Chapter 11, "Creating Business Data Applications," shows you how to create applications designed to expose their business data to SharePoint.

▶ **User profiles**—Chapter 12, "Working with User Profiles," provides a detailed discussion of how to work with user profiles using the SharePoint API.

Development Scenarios and Sample Applications

Now that you have a general idea of what the object model looks like and how it is divided, you might be wondering why you would be using the object model instead of web services and what kinds of applications you might be able to create using the object model.

Developing Applications on the Server

You will see it stated over and over again throughout this book that SharePoint is much more than just an application, it is an application framework. That essentially means that SharePoint doesn't truly shine until you begin extending its reach and influence and integrating it with other applications and solutions.

To use the SharePoint API, your code must reside on one of the machines in a SharePoint application server farm. Your code can still work with other sites in the farm from any other site in the farm, but you cannot, for example, work with the SharePoint API from a machine on which MOSS or WSS is not installed.

Because of the fact that SharePoint runs on Windows Server 2003 and is frequently deployed in a data center environment, applications written to run on SharePoint servers are *almost always* administrative in nature. It is a rare case when a user will find reason to be logged on to the console of a Windows Server 2003 machine to interact with a SharePoint API application for a nonadministrative purpose.

Some examples of tools that can be written using the SharePoint API that reside directly on SharePoint servers might include data migration applications, applications that operate on batches of information, scheduled maintenance applications, or even system monitoring tools that examine specific aspects of a large installation or farm.

Developing Web Parts

Another reason you might find yourself creating code that utilizes the SharePoint object model is if you are creating Web Parts. Web Parts are componentized, self-contained packages of user interface that can be dropped into place on SharePoint Web Part pages to provide discrete sets of functionality to users. Later in the book, an entire section is devoted to programming Web Parts. Unless the Web Part you are creating will be working entirely with information not contained within SharePoint, you will need to be familiar with the SharePoint API to create it. Later chapters in this book provide in-depth coverage of Web Part programming.

Developing Remote Applications

The other extremely common usage scenario for SharePoint is to consume SharePoint data and functionality remotely from a client application running outside the SharePoint farm. This can be done for any number of reasons such as storing lists on SharePoint that provide data for a public-facing ASP.NET application, creating a Windows Forms application for a technical support help desk that consumes data from a SharePoint site created with a Help Desk site template, or any of hundreds of other possibilities.

The only practical way to consume SharePoint data and functionality from a remote client is to use the SharePoint web services. These web services are discussed in chapters 20 through 30. Despite the rich functionality provided by the web services, you might still want to expose specific SharePoint functionality contained in the object model in your own custom web service so that clients can consume your custom service instead of the stock services that ship with SharePoint. The object model is not designed to support Remoting. If you need to expose a portion of the object model that you can't easily access with one of the stock web services, you should create your own web service rather than attempting to use Remoting.

Setting Up Your Development Environment

Making sure you have a good development environment is essential to your ability to write easy-to-maintain, reliable, stable code for SharePoint.

The first tool you will need is Visual Studio 2005. If you are an MSDN subscriber, you should have access to multiple versions of Visual Studio 2005. If you don't have access to any of the licensed versions of Visual Studio 2005 but you are still interested in writing SharePoint code, you can download Visual C# 2005 Express Edition for free from http://msdn.microsoft.com/vstudio/express/visualcsharp/download/.

After installing Visual Studio 2005 (or Visual C# 2005 Express Edition), you should be able to use Visual Studio to create standard Windows Forms and console applications.

SharePoint 2007 also makes extensive use of the Windows Workflow Foundation, which is part of the .NET Framework 3.0. If you want to whet your appetite for workflow programming, you can also download the .NET Framework 3.0 runtime components and the Visual Studio 2005 extensions for the Windows Workflow Foundation.

You have an option of installing your development environment directly on the SharePoint server or setting up the development environment on another workstation. There are pros and cons to each option that are discussed in their respective forthcoming sections.

Setting Up a Local Development Environment

The biggest advantage to the local development environment is the debugger. With Visual Studio 2005 installed directly on the Windows Server 2003 machine, it becomes extremely easy to write the code, build the code, and debug the code all in a single sweep without having to do any painstaking deployment.

Unfortunately, as programmers, we often find ourselves on the other side of Information Technology (IT) and/or security restrictions that prevent us from running compilers and other development tools on servers. It is for this reason that developers will often have their own Windows Server 2003 installations that are rough approximations of the target environment so that they can have the benefits of coding locally without running the risk of damaging a live production server.

> **CAUTION**
>
> Even if there are no IT restrictions or security policy restrictions in place telling you not to run Visual Studio 2005 on a live SharePoint server, pragmatism and some good common sense should tell you to avoid this scenario whenever possible. If the cost of using multiple servers for development and production is prohibitive, consider using Virtual PCs or Virtual Servers as development environments and keep production environments pristine.

After Visual Studio 2005 is installed, you need to be able to create applications that reference the appropriate SharePoint Assemblies.

Open Visual Studio and create a new console application called `LocalDevelopmentSample`. You can put it anywhere you want, but Visual Studio defaults to creating a new solution in your `My Documents\Visual Studio\Projects` folder.

Right-click the project and select Add Reference. Click the Browse tab and select the following directory:

```
C:\program files\common files\microsoft shared\web server extensions\12\isapi
```

Obviously, if you installed your copy of SharePoint in an alternate location or on a different disk/partition, this path will be slightly different for you.

Figure 2.2 shows the Add Reference dialog box pointing at this directory.

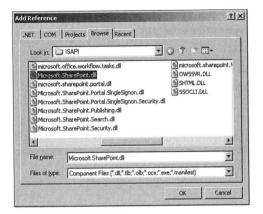

FIGURE 2.2   Adding a reference to a SharePoint Assembly.

Select the `Microsoft.SharePoint.dll` Assembly and add a reference to it. Make sure that the `Copy Local` property is set to `true` (you do not want your application referencing the actual Assemblies used by the server).

At this point, you can skip to the "Creating Your First Object Model Application" section if you plan on developing locally with both Visual Studio and SharePoint in the same environment, or you can continue reading the next section, "Setting Up a Remote Development Environment."

Setting Up a Remote Development Environment

A remote development environment, at least as far as SharePoint development is concerned, is a development environment that is not on a SharePoint server. The question, then, is how do you add a reference to the SharePoint Assemblies if your copy of Visual Studio 2005 isn't on the SharePoint server?

The answer is simple: *cheat*. Well, maybe it's not quite cheating, but it sounds more exciting than *copy the files*. You cannot run or test your application in your development environment, so you only need the bare minimum that will get your code to compile. To do that, you just copy the Assemblies from the following directory to a safe location somewhere on your development machine:

```
[drive]:\program files\common files\microsoft shared\
web server extensions\12\isapi
```

For this example, just copy the `Microsoft.SharePoint.dll` Assembly. As you progress through this section, you will learn which Assemblies are required for the various functional areas of the object model. After the file has been copied from your server, you can add a reference to it from your remote development machine, as shown in Figure 2.3.

FIGURE 2.3   Adding a reference to a SharePoint Assembly on a Windows XP development machine.

Now that you have a reference to a SharePoint Assembly in your application, you're ready to write some code.

Creating Your First Object Model Application

The first thing that your code needs to do is establish site context. The site context is the link between your code and the SharePoint site collection hierarchy. This context is represented by the SPContext class. This class is the doorway through which all of your code must step to do *anything* with the SharePoint object model.

Establishing site context is done differently between Web Parts and console/WinForms applications. You will see how to establish site context in the upcoming Web Parts programming chapters (Chapters 14 through 19), so what is shown here is how to establish site context in a console or Windows Forms application (this also applies to a Windows Presentation Foundation application).

Add a few lines of code so that your Program.cs file contains the code shown in Listing 2.1. Throughout the book, you may see references to the server names of the lab environment of the authors (such as win2k3r2lab). As you enter the code for samples throughout the book, please change the name of the server and other relative URLs to match those of your development environment.

LISTING 2.1   Program.cs to Test SharePoint Assembly Reference

```
using System;
using Microsoft.SharePoint;
using System.Collections.Generic;
using System.Text;
namespace LocalDevelopmentSample
{
```

LISTING 2.1   Continued

```
class Program
{
    static void Main(string[] args)
    {
        SPSite rootCollection = new SPSite("http://win2k3r2lab");
        Console.WriteLine(
         "Root collection found at Url {0} is part of Web Application {1}",
         rootCollection.Url, rootCollection.WebApplication.Name);
        Console.ReadLine();
    }
}
}
```

The SPSite constructor used in the preceding code obtains a reference to the site collection contained at the given uniform resource locator (URL). You can access the web application to which a given site collection belongs using the WebApplication property, which is of type Microsoft.SharePoint.Administration.SPWebApplication.

If you are running your development environment directly on the SharePoint server, you can simply press F5 on your keyboard to run your application; you should see output similar to the following text (the URL of your server will probably be different than win2k3r2lab):

```
Root collection found at Url
http://win2k3r2lab is part of Web Application SharePoint (80)
```

SharePoint (80) is the default name of the web application that was created during the standalone (no farm) installation on that particular server.

If your code resides on a remote server, you'll need to deploy your application before you can test it.

Deploying Your Application

For a Windows Forms or console application, deploying your application follows the standard deployment methods available to all .NET Framework applications. You can simply copy the application and its dependencies (you don't need to copy the SharePoint dynamic link libraries [DLLs]) or you can create a ClickOnce deployment package.

Figure 2.4 shows one possible deployment progression from your development workstation to production that involves a separate build machine that might be the target of automated nightly builds. In addition, there is a staging machine, on which a QA team might perform testing against the most recent build, and a production machine, which is the target of the final, verified deployment.

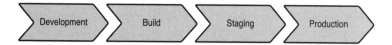

FIGURE 2.4   Large deployment scenario involving both build and stage environments.

Figures 2.5 and 2.6 show progressively smaller deployment chains. Going directly from the development machine to production, as shown in Figure 2.6, is *not* recommended. The complex, highly integrated nature of SharePoint practically demands integration testing of every application or component deployed to a SharePoint server.

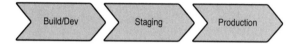

FIGURE 2.5   Deployment scenario involving a combined build/development machine and a staging server.

FIGURE 2.6   Impractical scenario involving deploying to production directly from a developer workstation.

Summary

The SharePoint API gives developers the ability to control virtually every aspect of SharePoint through managed code. It is an extensive object model that covers a wide variety of functionality from Features and Solutions to site administration and user profile management. The next several chapters provide you with in-depth coverage of these functional areas. Using the information in this chapter and your new SharePoint development environment, you should be able to follow along with the samples and start mastering the SharePoint API.

CHAPTER 3

Programming with Features and Solutions

IN THIS CHAPTER

▶ Overview of Features and Solutions

▶ Programming with Features

▶ Programming with Solutions

Features and Solutions are two new aspects of Windows SharePoint Services (WSS) and Microsoft Office SharePoint Server (MOSS) that make it dramatically easier to customize sites and site templates. This chapter focuses on illustrating how to work with site Features, Feature definitions, and Solutions using the SharePoint object model.

For an introduction to the concepts behind Features and Solutions as well as information on how to build your own Features and Solutions, refer to the *Microsoft SharePoint 2007 Unleashed* book (ISBN: 0672329476) that contains the best administrator's reference available for SharePoint.

Overview of Features and Solutions

Features provide the ability for sites to reuse functionality that exists in other sites without requiring the tedious task of copying and pasting complex Extensible Markup Language (XML) code from one template to another.

By installing Feature definitions at the farm level, Features can then be activated at any site within the farm. This allows reusable pieces of functionality to be created and deployed without modifying site templates, and it allows site templates to be far less complex than they used to be by referring to Features instead of directly embedding mountains of complex XML.

Using Features, you can do everything from adding a link to the Site Settings page to creating a complete, fully functioning Project Management suite that can be added to any SharePoint site.

Solutions allow you to package Features in a cabinet (.cab) file and define important metadata about those Features. After a Solution is installed on a server in the farm, you can then use SharePoint's Solution management features to automate the deployment of that Solution to other sites within the farm. This kind of hands-off deployment of reusable pieces of SharePoint functionality has never been possible in SharePoint before and developers are sure to love how easy it is to deploy new functionality in this version of SharePoint.

Programming with Features

SharePoint includes a robust object model for working with Features that allows developers to enumerate installed and activated Features, to turn Features on and off, and to control the installation or removal of Features.

The object model for Features includes the following key classes:

- SPFeatureCollection/SPFeature—Refers to a Feature state at a given site hierarchy level. The presence of an SPFeature instance within a property of type SPFeatureCollection indicates that the Feature is *active* at that level.

- SPFeaturePropertyCollection/SPFeatureProperty—Represents a single property on a Feature or a collection of those properties.

- SPFeatureScope—Represents an enumeration of the possible scopes in which Features can be activated. Possible values are: Farm, WebApplication, Site, and Web.

- SPFeatureDefinition—Represents the basic definition of a Feature, including its name, scope, ID, and version. You can also store and retrieve properties of a Feature. Note that Feature properties apply globally to a single Feature definition, not to instances of Features activated throughout the farm.

- SPFeatureDependency—Represents a Feature upon which another Feature depends.

- SPElementDefinition—Represents a single element that will be provisioned when the Feature is activated.

Feature collections can be accessed from the following properties on their respective classes:

- Features on Microsoft.SharePoint.Administration.SPWebApplication

- Features on Microsoft.SharePoint.Administration.SPWebService

- FeatureDefinitions on Microsoft.SharePoint.Administration.SPFarm

- Features on Microsoft.SharePoint.SPSite

- Features on Microsoft.SharePoint.SPWeb

- ActivationDependencies on Microsoft.SharePoint.Administration.SPFeatureDefinition

The next few sections of this chapter provide many examples of programming with the Features portion of the SharePoint application programming interface (API).

Enumerating Features and Feature Definitions

It is important to recognize the difference between a Feature and a Feature definition. A Feature definition, as far as the object model is concerned, is an abstraction around the Feature manifest contained in a Feature directory in the Features directory. Feature definitions are installed at the farm (or server, if there is no farm) level.

A Feature is an instance of a Feature definition. Features can be activated or deactivated, and they exist at the various levels of scope such as the site or web level.

To enumerate the list of Feature definitions that are currently installed within a farm (which includes single-server farms and standalone servers, which are another form of single-server farms), you need to use an instance of the SPFarm class and access the FeatureDefinitions property. To enumerate the list of *active* Features on a given site, you need to enumerate the Features property on the appropriate SPWeb or SPSite class instance. You might be tempted to iterate through the collection contained in the Features property and look for something like an Active property. However, *the only SPFeature instances that appear in the Features property are those features that are* active *in the current scope.*

Creating an instance of the SPFarm class might seem a little tricky at first. Rather than obtaining it through a context provided by the Web Part manager or from a site uniform resource locator (URL), you need to pass a connection string that points to the farm's configuration database to the constructor. The connection string should look familiar to anyone with ADO.NET experience connecting to SQL server, because it is just a SQL server connection string.

The code in Listing 3.1 shows how to create an instance of the SPFarm class, create an instance of the SPSite class, and use the two of those to enumerate the list of installed Feature definitions and determine which of those definitions are active on the given site. This code is for a Windows Forms application that adds the name and enabled status of each Feature definition to a ListView control. If you plan to copy this code and test it, be sure to add a reference to the Microsoft.SharePoint.dll Assembly.

LISTING 3.1   Enumerating Feature Definitions and Features

```
using System;
using System.Collections.Generic;
using System.ComponentModel;
using System.Data;
using System.Drawing;
using System.Text;
using Microsoft.SharePoint;
using Microsoft.SharePoint.Administration;
using System.Windows.Forms;
```

LISTING 3.1   Continued

```csharp
namespace FeatureEnumerator
{
public partial class Form1 : Form
{
  private SPSite _rootCollection;

public Form1()
{
    InitializeComponent();
}

private string GetFeatureEnabled(SPFeatureDefinition featureDefinition)
{
    foreach (SPFeature feature in _rootCollection.Features)
    {
        if (feature.Definition.Id == featureDefinition.Id)
            return "Yes";
    }
    return "No";
}

private void button1_Click(object sender, EventArgs e)
{
    featureList.Enabled = true;
    featureList.Items.Clear();
    string dbConn = @"server=localhost\OfficeServers;initial
➥catalog=SharePoint_Config_66140120-a9bf-4191-86b6-
➥ec21810ca019;IntegratedSecurity=SSPI;";

    _rootCollection = new SPSite(siteUrl.Text);
    SPFarm farm = SPFarm.Open(dbConn);
    statusLabel.Text = "Site Feature Status (" +
      farm.FeatureDefinitions.Count.ToString() +
        " Feature Definitions Installed)";

    foreach (SPFeatureDefinition featureDefinition in farm.FeatureDefinitions)
    {
        ListViewItem lvi = new ListViewItem(featureDefinition.DisplayName);
        if (featureDefinition.Hidden)
            lvi.ForeColor = Color.Gray;
        lvi.Tag = featureDefinition.Id;
        lvi.SubItems.Add(GetFeatureEnabled(featureDefinition));
        featureList.Items.Add(lvi);
```

LISTING 3.1   Continued

```
    }


}



}
}
```

This Windows Forms application is shown in Figure 3.1.

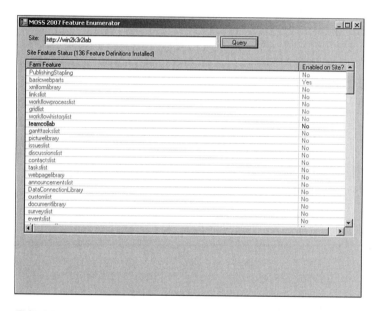

FIGURE 3.1   Feature Enumerator Windows Forms application.

The true power of Features should become immediately obvious as soon as you start using this tool to examine the list of active and inactive features on various sites. Most of the key functionality provided by SharePoint 2007 is implemented using Features. Previous versions of SharePoint did not provide anywhere near the amount of flexibility, customization, and enhancement capability that Features provide.

Activating and Deactivating Features

It follows that if the SPFeatureCollection instance represented by the Features property of a site or web object contains the list of active Features, then adding and removing to and from that collection should activate and deactivate Features. In fact, that is exactly how it works with one small exception: You cannot add or remove SPFeature or SPFeatureDefinition instances; you can only add or remove globally unique identifiers (GUIDs).

Before you start writing code that activates and deactivates Features, you should definitely create a test site that you don't mind destroying. Deactivating hidden features can have drastic consequences on the ability of your site to function properly. However, knowing what those consequences are can certainly provide deeper understanding of the Features system and time spent tinkering with Features is definitely time well spent.

To deactivate a Feature, simply remove it from the Features collection of the current site or web object:

```
currentSite.Features.Remove(new Guid("… guid of feature to remove …"));
```

Conversely, activating an installed Feature on a site or web object is accomplished simply by adding the Feature's GUID to the Features collection:

```
currentSite.Features.Add(new Guid(".. guid .."));
```

Keep in mind that an exception will be thrown if you attempt to activate a Feature that cannot be activated at the current scope.

Using Feature Properties

Every Feature installed in SharePoint maintains its own property bag.

> **NOTE**
>
> For those of you who don't know, a **property bag** is a special kind of name-value collection that first reared its head back in the days of Site Server and Commerce Server. For most developers, it remains a point of contention as to whether the head of a property bag is ugly or not.

Features and Feature definitions both have properties exposed through the Properties property, which is of type SPFeaturePropertyCollection—a collection of SPFeatureProperty objects. Regardless of whether you access the Properties property of a site Feature instance or of a Feature definition, the result will be the same. That is, you can think of Feature properties as static, global data that belongs to the definition itself but can also be accessed from an activated Feature SPFeature object.

The following code snippet illustrates how to enumerate through the properties associated with a given Feature (or Feature definition):

```
foreach (SPFeatureProperty property in myFeature.Properties)
{
    Console.WriteLine("{0} : {1}", property.Name, property.Value);
}
```

You don't have to worry about typecasting or conversion because the only value type acceptable to a property bag is System.String. Adding a new property to an existing Feature or Feature definition is quite simple:

```
SPFeatureProperty prop = new SPFeatureProperty("myProp", "myValue");
myFeature.Properties.Add(prop);
```

That's all there is to it—you don't need to explicitly call any methods to commit that change to SharePoint. It is just as easy to remove a property from a Feature:

```
SPFeatureProperty prop = myFeature.Properties[0];
myFeature.Properties.Remove(prop);
```

A few of the Features that are installed with SharePoint make use of properties such as the workflow features. You can use properties to do tremendously powerful things. You can think of the property bag assigned to each Feature as either a place for global configuration settings or for global state management for the Feature, or both.

Installing and Removing Feature Definitions

To install a Feature definition, you need to make use of one of the overloads of the Add method on the SPFeatureDefinitionCollection class:

- Add(SPFeatureDefinition)—Adds a new Feature definition based on the properties of the SPFeatureDefinition instance passed to the method.

- Add(relative path to manifest, GUID of solution)—Adds a new Feature definition that resides in the location indicated by the first parameter with the given solution ID.

- Add(relative path to manifest, GUID of solution, force)—Adds a new Feature definition that resides in the location indicated by the first parameter with the given solution ID and forces a reinstallation of the Feature.

The following code is a simple example of installing a new Feature in a farm (remember that to get an instance of the SPFarm class, you need the connection string of the farm's configuration database):

```
SPFeatureDefinitionCollection installedFeatures = theFarm.FeatureDefinitions;
installedFeatures.Add("newfeature", new Guid("- feature GUID -"));
```

Conversely, to uninstall a Feature, simply remove it from the collection. You can remove the Feature based on the relative path to the Feature manifest or the Feature's GUID:

```
installedFeatures.Remove(new Guid("- feature GUID -"));
```

Programming with Solutions

Solutions are the means by which collections of Features are installed on SharePoint farms and deployed to servers within those farms. After being installed on a farm, Solutions can be deployed to any server within that farm automatically using the web-based Solution management interface.

Installing and Removing Solutions

If you don't want to use the stsadm.exe command-line tool, or you simply can't for some reason, you can still programmatically manipulate the list of Solutions available for deployment within a farm.

As shown earlier in the chapter, any time you need to work with the SPFarm class, you need to pass a configuration database connection string to the constructor:

```
string dbConn = @"server=localhost\OfficeServers;initial
➥catalog=SharePoint_Config_66140120-a9bf-4191-86b6-
➥ec21810ca019;IntegratedSecurity=SSPI;";


_rootCollection = new SPSite(siteUrl.Text);
SPFarm farm = SPFarm.Open(dbConn);
```

After you have a reference to the farm, you can then access the list of installed Solutions in the farm with the Solutions property. To install a Solution, just add it to the Solutions collection. To uninstall a Solution, simply remove it from the collection.

The SPSolution class cannot be instantiated directly with a constructor. Instead, you have two options when adding to the Solutions collection. You can pass the Solution filename as a parameter, or you can pass the Solution filename and a locale identifier (a UInt32, such as 1033):

```
farm.Solutions.Add("myapplication.cab");
farm.Solutions.Add("myapplication.cab", 1033);
```

When removing a Solution, you can either pass the name of the Solution as a parameter, or you can pass the GUID of the Solution:

```
farm.Solutions.Remove(new Guid("..."));
```

The Add and Remove methods of the Solutions collection correspond directly to the functionality provided by the stsadm.exe commands "-o addsolution" and "-o deletesolution".

Enumerating Solutions

When working with Solutions, you might want to take a look at the list of Solutions currently installed in the farm. From this list, you can then control the deployment status (shown in the next section) of the Solution or inspect the various properties of the Solutions. The following code is a simple illustration of how to examine the list of installed Solutions in a farm:

```
Console.WriteLine("Solution:\tCAS Policy\tGAC Assembly\tWeb Resource\n");
foreach (SPSolution solution in farm.Solutions)
{
    Console.WriteLine("{0}:\t{1}\t{2}\t{3}",
```

```
        solution.DisplayName,
        solution.ContainsCasPolicy,
        solution.ContainsGlobalAssembly,
        solution.ContainsWebApplicationResource);
    foreach (SPServer deployedServer in solution.DeployedServers)
    {
        Console.WriteLine("\t\tDeployed to {0}", deployedServer.DisplayName);
    }
}
```

Table 3.1 describes many of the properties of the SPSolution class.

TABLE 3.1   SPSolution Properties

Property	Description
Added	Indicates whether a language-neutral Solution package has been added to the Solution
ContainsCasPolicy	Indicates whether the Solution contains a Code Access Security policy
ContainsGlobalAssembly	Indicates whether the Solution installs Assemblies into the GAC
ContainsWebApplicationResource	Indicates whether the Solution contains any application-specific resources
Deployed	Indicates whether the Solution has been deployed to one or more locations within the farm
DeployedServers	Indicates the list of servers to which the Solution has been deployed
DeployedWebApplications	Indicates the list of web applications to which the Solution has been deployed
DeploymentState	Indicates the current state of deployment for the Solution
Id	Indicates the GUID of the Solution
IsWebPartPackage	Indicates whether the Solution is a Web Part package
LastOperationDetails	Represents the details of the last operation performed while deploying the Solution
LastOperationEndTime	Indicates the time the last operation completed
LastOperationResult	Indicates the results of the last operation during deployment
Name	Indicates the name of the Solution
Properties	Indicates the property bag containing custom properties for the Solution
SolutionFile	Indicates the file associated with the Solution
SolutionId	Indicates the ID of the Solution as indicated by the Solution's manifest file

Controlling Solution Deployment

Controlling Solution deployment really boils down to two different methods on the SPSolution class: Deploy and Retract. The Deploy method deploys a Solution to the given location, whereas the Retract method removes the Solution from the given location while still remaining installed within the farm.

The deploy methods take the following arguments:

- ▶ dt—The date and time when the deployment should take place

- ▶ globalInstallWPPackDlls—A Boolean indicating whether to install the dynamic link libraries (DLLs) in the GAC (for Web Part packages only)

- ▶ force—A Boolean indicating whether the Solution can be redeployed

You can also optionally supply a collection of SPWebApplication instances to further refine the deployment. The Retract() method schedules a job for when the Solution should be retracted and can optionally take a list of web applications from which to retract the solution.

Summary

Features and Solutions are two of the most powerful new additions to SharePoint 2007. As a developer, you will probably be spending a considerable amount of time creating and manipulating Features and Solutions. This chapter included details on how to manipulate Features and Solutions programmatically using the SharePoint object model. At this point, you should not only be able to create your own Features and Solutions, but you should also be able to install, manipulate, and deploy them programmatically. For more information on the administration and maintenance of features unrelated to writing code, consult the SharePoint documentation or the Sams Publishing book, *Microsoft SharePoint 2007 Unleashed* (ISBN: 0672329476).

CHAPTER 4

Working with Sites and Webs

IN THIS CHAPTER

▸ Understanding Webs and Sites

▸ Using the SPSite Class

▸ Using the SPWeb Class

When users interact with SharePoint, the majority of that interaction is done through the SharePoint concepts of sites and webs. It is often confusing for both developers and users to determine the difference between site collections, sites, web collections, and webs.

This chapter takes you through the SPSite and SPWeb classes and shows you how to create and delete both site collections and webs as well as how to interact with sites and webs.

Understanding Webs and Sites

Within SharePoint, there are two different concepts: a web and a site. The site, as far as SharePoint is concerned, is actually a site collection. The SPSite class models a collection of websites and the SPSiteCollection contains the list of all root-level site collections on a virtual server. Each site collection consists of one or more root websites. You cannot have a site collection that doesn't have a root website. For example, if you use the object model to create a site collection and you indicate that the template for that site collection should be a Team site, what you have actually done is created a site collection *and* a root website (an SPWeb instance) that was provisioned from the Team Site template.

As long as you remember that the SPSite class is the model for a collection of SPWeb objects, you shouldn't get lost. To get at the list of site collections on a given web application, you simply reference the Sites property of an instance of the SPWebApplication class.

Websites and Web Applications

It can be incredibly easy to get confused between sites, webs, web applications, and site collections. The farm is the topmost level in the hierarchy. Below the farm, you have web applications represented by the SPWebApplication class, which typically correspond to an IIS application pool. Below that, you have a collection of site collections contained in the SPSiteCollection class. Finally, you have site collections represented by the SPSite class and individual websites represented by the SPWeb class.

In a default installation of SharePoint, the root site collection (instance of the SPSite class) contains several stock webs (instances of the SPWeb class). They are Home, Document Center, News, Reports, Search Center, and Sites.

Using the SPSite Class

The SPSite class represents a collection of sites contained on a virtual server, which includes the top-level (root) site and all its subsites. Each SPSite object can be found within the Sites property of an SPWebApplication class.

This section covers the basic properties and methods of the SPSite class, followed by code samples of the SPSite class in action—including creating, deleting, and updating site collections. For the complete listing of all properties and methods, consult the online SharePoint Software Development Kit (SDK) found on MSDN (http://msdn2.microsoft. com/en-us/library/aa905858.aspx).

Table 4.1 covers the commonly used properties of the SPSite class.

TABLE 4.1   Common SPSite Properties

Property	Description
AllowRssFeeds	Gets a Boolean value indicating whether the site supports publication of list data in the form of RSS feeds
AllowUnsafeUpdates	Indicates whether updates can be committed to the database using a GET request without requiring security validation; applies mostly to Web Parts and Web Part pages
AllWebs	Gets the collection of websites contained within the site collection, including the root site and subsites
Audit	Gets a reference to the SPAudit instance associated with the site
CatchAccessDeniedException	Gets a Boolean value controlling whether the site catches permission failures
CertificationDate	Gets the time stamp indicating when the site collection was set for automatic deletion
ContentDatabase	Gets the SPContentDatabase instance representing the content database used for all site content
CurrentChangeToken	Gets the SPChangeToken instance for the site

TABLE 4.1   Continued

Property	Description
DeadWebNotificationCount	Gets the number of notifications that have been sent indicating that websites within the site collection have not been used within a certain time period
Features	Gets the list of features installed for the site (SPFeatureCollection)
HostHeaderIsSiteName	Gets a Boolean value indicating whether the site name is used as the host header for Internet Information Services (IIS) uniform resource locator (URL) rewriting
IISAllowsAnonymous	Gets a Boolean value indicating whether IIS allows anonymous access for the site
Impersonating	Gets a Boolean value indicating whether impersonation is active for the site
LastContentModifiedDate	Gets the time stamp (in UTC) indicating when the last content modification on the site took place
LastSecurityModifiedDate	Gets the time stamp (in UTC) indicating when the last security modification on the site took place (such as permissions change or user add/remove)
Owner	Controls the owner of the site collection
Port	Indicates the port number on which the virtual server for the site collection is listening
PortalUrl	Controls the URL to the portal site
Protocol	Gets the protocol for the site collection (HTTP or HTTPS)
ReadLocked	Gets a Boolean value indicating whether the site has been locked and cannot be read
ReadOnly	Gets a Boolean value indicating whether the site cannot be modified
RecycleBin	Gets a reference to the Recycle Bin for the site collection (SPRecycleBinItemCollection)
RootWeb	Gets a reference to the topmost SPWeb instance for the site collection
SearchServiceInstance	Gets an SPServiceInstance object indicating the search service used for the site collection
SecondaryContact	Gets or sets the secondary contact (SPUser) for the site collection
ServerRelativeUrl	Gets the server-relative URL for the root web of the site collection
SyndicationEnabled	Gets or sets whether syndication is enabled on the site
UpgradeRedirectedUri	Gets the uniform resource identifier (URI) of the new site after being updated to the newest version of SharePoint
Url	Gets the fully qualified URL of the root web of the site collection
Usage	Indicates usage statistics about the site collection, such as storage and bandwidth; an extremely handy property of type SPUsageInfo

4

TABLE 4.1   Continued

Property	Description
WebApplication	Gets the parent web application for the site collection
WorkflowManager	Gets the workflow manager (SPWorkflowManager) for the site collection
WriteLocked	Indicates whether the site has been locked and will not accept content modifications
Zone	Gets the URL zone (Intranet, Internet, and so on) of the site collection

Table 4.2 highlights some of the most commonly used methods of the SPSite class.

TABLE 4.2   Common SPSite Methods

Method	Description
CheckForPermissions	Compares a reusable Access Control List (ACL) with a permission mask
Close	Closes the site collection and frees resources
ConfirmUsage	Indicates whether the site collection is in use
Delete	Deletes the site collection
Dispose	Releases resources associated with the site collection instance
DoesUserHavePermissions	Indicates whether the current user has the permissions indicated by a permission mask on the supplied reusable ACL
Exists	Tests for the existence of a site collection; a static member
GetCatalog	Returns a list template gallery, site template gallery, or Web Part gallery based on the given SPListTemplateType parameter
GetCustomListTemplates	Returns the custom list templates for the site
GetCustomWebTemplates	Returns site templates for the site collection based on a locale ID
GetRecycleBinItems	Returns a list of items in the Recycle Bin for the site collection
GetRecycleBinStatistics	Returns the Recycle Bin statistics
GetWebTemplates	Returns the collection of site templates available for the site collection
MakeFullUrl	Converts a server-relative URL into a fully qualified URL, including protocol and port
OpenWeb	Returns a website (SPWeb) from the site collection
SelfServiceCreateSite	Creates a site collection via self-service site creation
StorageManagementInformation	Returns information about storage management for the site collection in a DataTable object

Creating Sites

Site creation is done by calling the Add() method on an SPSiteCollection class instance. There are multiple overloads that allow you to supply progressively more information to create the new site collection.

To create a new site collection, you need some basic information such as the URL of the new site, the name of the site, the site description, and its locale identifier (default is 1033 for U.S. English). You can also supply an optional web template ID string to control the type of site collection you are creating.

The following code illustrates creating a new site collection (SPSite instance) at the URL http://win2k3r2lab/sites/NewTestSite:

```
using System;
using System.Collections.Generic;
using System.Text;
using Microsoft.SharePoint;
using Microsoft.SharePoint.Administration;

namespace SiteCreation
{
class Program
{
    static void Main(string[] args)
    {
        SPSite site = new SPSite("http://win2k3r2lab");
        SPWebApplication webApplication = site.WebApplication;

        webApplication.Sites.Add("/sites/TestNewSite",
            "New Test Site",
            "This is a new site added programmatically",
            1033,
            "STS#0",
            @"WIN2K3R2LAB\Administrator",
            "Administrator",
            "anon@anon.com");

        Console.WriteLine("New site created.");

        Console.ReadLine();
    }
}
}
```

After executing the above code for your own lab server, go ahead and open a new browser window at the new site to see that it has been created with the values you supplied.

When executing code like this in a production application, you might want to run the code in a background thread. The process of creating and provisioning a new site collection can take a very long time, even on a relatively traffic-free server.

Most of this code is pretty self-explanatory. The only really tricky parts are figuring out the web template ID, and remembering that you need the preceding slash on the server-relative URL. If you don't include the preceding slash, you might run into errors complaining that a site already exists at the URL of the root site. To help you determine which template ID you need to create your site, take a look at Tables 4.3 and 4.4.

TABLE 4.3   Stock/Default Web Template IDs

Template ID	Description
STS#0	Team site
STS#1	Blank site
STS#2	Document workspace
MPS#0	Basic meeting workspace
MPS#1	Blank meeting workspace
MPS#2	Decision meeting workspace
MPS#3	Social meeting workspace
MPS#4	Multipage meeting workspace
WIKI#0	Wiki
BLOG#0	Blog

TABLE 4.4   Additional Web Template IDs

Template ID	Description
BDR#0	Document center—A central document management location for an enterprise
OFFILE#0 OFFILE#1	Records center—A central location in which records managers can define routes for incoming files
CMSPUBLISHING#0	Publishing site
BLANKINTERNET#0	Publishing site—A site for publishing web pages on a schedule with workflow features enabled
BLANKINTERNET#1	Press releases site
BLANKINTERNET#2	Publishing site with workflow—A publishing site for web pages using approval workflows
SPSNHOME#0	A site for publishing news and articles
SPSREPORTCENTER#0	Report center—A site for creating, managing, and delivering web pages, dashboards, and Key Performance Indicators (KPIs)
SPSPORTAL#0	A starter hierarchy for an intranet divisional portal
PROFILES#0	A profile site that includes page layouts with zones
BLANKINTERNETCONTAINER#0	Publishing portal—a site collection preconfigured for revision-controlled, secure content creation and publication

TABLE 4.4   Continued

Template ID	Description
SPSMYSITEHOST#0	My Site host—keep in mind that only one of these can be provisioned per Shared Services Provider
SRCHCENTERLITE#0	Search center—A site designed to deliver the search query and results experience
SRCHCENTERLITE#1	Search center—A superset of the previous; does not appear in navigation bars

After executing the previous code to create a new site, a site similar to the one shown in Figure 4.1 is created.

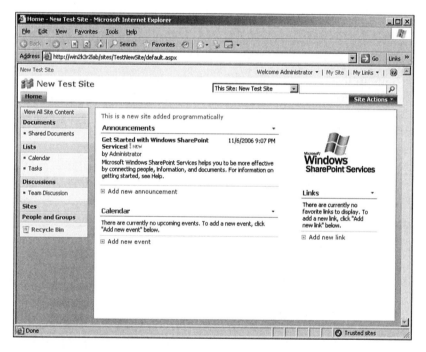

FIGURE 4.1   Creating a new site collection programmatically.

Accessing Site Information

Table 4.1 provides a list of some of the most commonly used properties on the SPSite class. You can obtain a reference to a site collection in a couple of different ways.

The easiest method is to use the site collection constructor with a fully qualified URL of the site collection's root web:

```
SPSite mySite = new SPSite("http://win2k3r2lab/sites/NewTestSite");
```

You can also obtain a reference to a site by finding the site in the web application's `Sites` collection:

```
SPSite mySite = myWebApplication.Sites["New Test Site"];
```

Updating Sites

Site collection updating is a bit misleading. There are very few properties that you can modify on the site collection itself. For example, if you created a new site by using the previous code, such as the one shown in Figure 4.1, you might notice that you can't change any of the properties such as the site title or description on the `SPSite` instance.

Instead, you need to get an instance of the `SPWeb` class for the root web of the site collection (which was created by default when you created a new site collection). Working with the `SPWeb` class is discussed in the next section.

Using the SPWeb Class

The `SPWeb` class represents an instance of a single website. It is often confusing to developers because the root web of a site collection (which is created when a site collection is created) is an instance of the `SPWeb` class. As shown in Tables 4.5 and 4.6, the `SPWeb` class provides most of the functionality of single websites, whereas the `SPSite` class is designed to deal with site collections.

TABLE 4.5   Common `SPWeb` Properties

Property	Description
Alerts	Indicates the collection of alerts for the site
AllowAnonymousAccess	Indicates whether the website allows anonymous access
AllowRssFeeds	Indicates whether the website allows RSS feeds to expose list data
AllowUnsafeUpdates	Carries the same meaning as the property on the SPSite class
AllProperties	Gets a hash table containing metadata for the website
AllUsers	Gets a collection of user objects that are either site members or members of a group that belongs to the web
AlternateCssUrl	Controls the URL of an alternate style sheet to be used for the web
AlternateHeader	Controls the URL for an alternate ASPX header for the web
AnonymousState	Indicates the level of anonymous access allowed for users of the website
Audit	Gets the SPAudit instance for the website
AuthenticationMode	Indicates the authentication mode used for the website (Forms, None, Passport, or Windows)
Author	Indicates the user who created the website
AvailableContentTypes	Gets the list of all content types available for the website
ContentTypes	Gets the collection of content types in use on the website
Created	Indicates when the website was created

TABLE 4.5   Continued

Property	Description
CurrentUser	Indicates the current user of the site
Description	Controls the description of the site
DocTemplates	Gets the collection of document templates for the site
EventReceivers	Gets the collection of event receivers for the website
Features	Gets the collection of Features available for activation on the website
Files	Gets the collection of all files in the root of the website
Folders	Gets the collection of all top-level folders on the website
Groups	Gets the collection of all cross-site groups for the website
ID	Gets the globally unique identifier (GUID) for the website
IsRootWeb	Indicates whether the website is a root web
Language	Indicates the LCID (Locale Identifier; for example, 1033 for the default of US-English) of the website
Lists	Gets all lists contained within the website
ListTemplates	Gets all list templates available for list creation within the website
Locale	Controls the website's locale
MasterUrl	Controls the URL of the ASP.NET 2.0 Master Page for the website
Name	Controls the name of the website
Navigation	Gets an object representing the navigation bar on the website
ParentWeb	Gets the SPWeb instance of the parent website (if applicable)
PortalMember	Gets a Boolean value indicating whether the website is a member of a portal
PortalName	Gets the name of the portal site to which the website belongs (if any)
PortalSubscriptionUrl	Gets the URL used for portal alert notifications
PortalUrl	Gets the URL to the associated portal site
PresenceEnabled	Controls whether online presence information is displayed for users of the site
RecycleBin	Gets the Recycle Bin for the site
RootFolder	Gets the root folder of the website
ServerRelativeUrl	Returns the server-relative URL of the site
Site	Returns the parent SPSite instance to which this website belongs
SiteLogoUrl	Controls the URL of the logo image for the site
Theme	Returns the name of the theme currently assigned to the site
Title	Gets the title of the site
Url	Gets the fully qualified URL for the site
Webs	Gets a collection of SPWeb objects representing a collection of websites beneath the current site
WorkflowTemplates	Gets a list of workflow templates associated with the site

4

TABLE 4.6   Common SPWeb Methods

Method	Description
ApplyTheme	Applies a theme to the current website
ApplyWebTemplate	Applies a site definition or site template object to the current website
Close	Closes the site and frees up associated resources
Delete	Deletes the website
GetCatalog	Functions the same as the method on the SPSite class
GetChanges	Gets a list of changes made to the website
GetDocDiscussions	Gets a list of document discussions for the given directory on the website
GetFile	Returns an SPFile instance for the given file GUID or URL
GetFolder	Returns an instance of the SPFolder class for the folder with the given GUID or URL
GetList	Returns an SPList instance for the specified list identifier
GetListFromUrl	Returns a list given the list's URL
GetListItem	Returns an instance of the SPListItem class for the specified list item
GetListsOfType	Returns all lists of the given type (indicated by an SPBaseType enumeration value)
GetRecycleBinItems	Gets the contents of the website's Recycle Bin
GetSiteData	Performs a query for list items across multiple lists—data can be spread across multiple sites in the same site collection
GetUsageData	Returns a DataTable containing site usage information
SaveAsTemplate	Saves the current website as a template
SearchDocuments	Searches through all documents contained in the site for a given string
SearchListItems	Searches through all list items contained in the site for a given string
Update	Commits changes made to the site since instantiation or the last call to Update

Creating Webs

Creating a new web involves calling the Add() method on any SPWebCollection instance. To add a new web to the root web of a site collection (for instance, the "New Test Site" site collection created in the preceding sample), you obtain a reference to that site and then call the Add() method on the AllWebs property, as shown in the following code that adds a blog as a subweb of the parent site collection:

```
using System;
using System.Collections.Generic;
using System.Text;
using Microsoft.SharePoint;
```

```
namespace WebCreation
{
class Program
{
static void Main(string[] args)
{
    SPSite parentSite =
      new SPSite("http://win2k3r2lab/sites/TestNewSite");

    SPWebTemplateCollection webTemplates =
       parentSite.GetWebTemplates(1033);
    SPWebTemplate blogTemplate = webTemplates["BLOG#0"];

    SPWeb blogWeb = parentSite.AllWebs.Add(
        "blog",
        "Test Site Blog",
        "This is the blog for the new site",
        1033,
        blogTemplate,
        false,
        false);

}
}
}
```

Note that when you're creating a new site collection, you use a server-relative URL, which requires a preceding forward slash and when creating a new website, you use a site-relative URL, which *cannot* start with a forward slash. It is an important distinction that can save you some debugging hassles if you remember it.

Running the preceding code creates a new blog site such as the one shown in Figure 4.2.

Accessing Web Information

You can obtain a reference to an SPWeb instance either by obtaining it through an indexer property on an SPWebCollection instance:

```
SPWeb myWeb = parentSite.AllWebs["blog"];
```

or by calling the OpenWeb() method on a site collection:

```
SPWeb myWeb = parentSite.OpenWeb("blog");
```

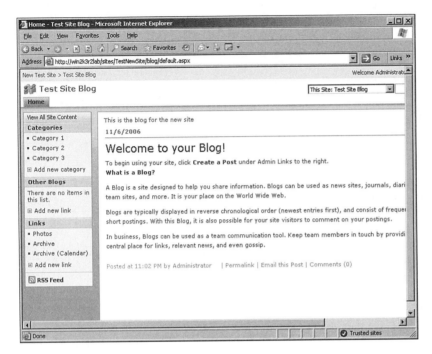

FIGURE 4.2   Programmatically created blog website.

Updating Webs

Committing changes made to an SPWeb instance are only saved after you call the Update() method. There are some properties on a website that cannot be changed after the site has been created. Take a look at Table 4.4 and the MSDN SDK for a full list of which properties can and cannot be modified. The following code illustrates how to change the title of the blog site created in the preceding code sample:

```
SPSite parentSite = new SPSite("http://win2k3r2lab/sites/TestNewSite");
SPWeb blogWeb = parentSite.OpenWeb("blog");
blogWeb.Title = "Modified Blog Site";
blogWeb.Update();
```

Summary

Working with sites and webs is actually a fairly simple process. The most difficult part of the development process is remembering which properties and methods are available on the SPSite and SPWeb classes. This chapter provided a thorough reference for both of these classes. This chapter also provided code samples illustrating how you can write code that examines and manipulates properties on sites and webs.

After reading this chapter, you should feel confident in your ability to create new sites and webs, locate existing sites and webs, and update existing sites and webs.

CHAPTER 5

Managing SharePoint Lists

IN THIS CHAPTER

▶ List Management Basics

▶ Enumerating Lists

▶ Enumerating List Contents

▶ Adding, Removing, and Updating Lists

▶ Manipulating List Items

▶ Using Lookup Types in Lists

Of all the different kinds of classes available to the developer within the SharePoint application programming interface (API), the ones that you will encounter most often will most likely be lists and list items (SPList and SPListItem, respectively). This chapter provides you with an introduction to the basics of reading and writing lists and list items. Knowing how to work with lists will give you the necessary foundation to move on to more advanced list topics as well as to more complex data types. The next two chapters provide more advanced list topics such as querying lists using CAML queries and creating event sinks and listeners for list events.

There are a lot of tables in this chapter showing the various properties and methods of some of the core, list-related classes. Lists are one of the keystones of SharePoint development and every SharePoint developer should have a firm grasp of how to work with lists.

List Management Basics

This section of the chapter provides you with an overview of the basics of list management, including sample code. When working with lists in SharePoint, you will be performing some or all of the following actions:

▶ Enumerating lists—Traversing, displaying, or filtering the collection of lists that belong to a given SPWeb class instance

▶ Enumerating list contents—Examining the list items that belong to a given list

▶ Adding and removing lists

▶ Adding or removing list items

Enumerating Lists

Enumerating lists is a simple task of enumerating through any `SPListCollection` instance. After you have the `SPList` instance, it's just a matter of wading through the many properties on the `SPList` class. Some of the most commonly used properties of this class are described in Table 5.1.

TABLE 5.1   Major `SPList` Properties

Property	Description
AlertTemplate	Gets the `SPAlertTemplate` for the list
AllowContentTypes	Gets a Boolean value indicating whether the list allows content types
AllowDeletion	Indicates whether the list can be deleted; note this applies to the list, not to the items
AllowEveryoneViewItems	Indicates whether the list items in this list are unprotected—anyone can see them
AllowMultiResponses	For survey list types, indicates whether users can supply multiple responses
AllowRssFeeds	Gets a Boolean value indicating whether the list exposes its data via Really Simple Syndication (RSS, an XML news publication dialect)
Audit	Gets a reference to an SPAudit instance controlling the auditing activity for the list
BaseTemplate	Gets a list definition on which the current list is based
BaseType	Gets the list's base type (an SPBaseType instance)
CanReceiveEmail	Indicates whether the list can receive incoming emails, allowing the email to be posted as a new item (for example, the Discussion Board)
ContentTypes	Gets a list of content types associated with the list
ContentTypesEnabled	Indicates whether content types are enabled for the list
Created	Gets the creation time stamp for the list
CurrentChangeToken	Gets the current change token in the change log for the list
DefaultItemOpen	Indicates whether items should be opened in the browser or a client application for the list
DefaultView	Gets the default view for the list
DefaultViewUrl	Gets the uniform resource locator (URL) to the default view of the list
Description	Gets the description of the list
Direction	Indicates the reading order for the list ("ltr" or "rtl" or "none")
DraftVersionVisibility	Controls which users can see draft (minor) versions of items
EmailAlias	Sets or gets the alias name for the list (does not include server name!) for use with incoming email

TABLE 5.1   Continued

Property	Description
EnableAttachments	Gets a Boolean value indicating whether attachments are allowed on list items
EnableFolderCreation	Indicates whether folders and subfolders can be created within the list
EnableMinorVersions	Indicates whether minor (draft) versions are allowed for revision tracking on list items within the list
EnableModeration	Indicates whether content approval is required before publication
EnableVersioning	Indicates whether version numbers are tracked for items contained within the list
Event [Receivers/SinkAssembly/ SinkClass/SinkData]	Enables and supports event reception and handling
Fields	Gets the collection of fields in the list
Folders	Gets the list of folders in the list
Forms	Gets the list of forms used when creating, editing, displaying, and deleting list items
Hidden	Indicates whether the list is hidden; a lot about the internal workings of SharePoint can be gleaned from examining its hidden lists
ImageUrl	Indicates the relative URL for the list image
ItemCount	Indicates the number of items contained in the list
Items	An SPListItemCollection that contains all the files (including those in subfolders) in a document library
LastItemDeletedDate	Indicates the time stamp of last item deletion
LastItemModifiedDate	Indicates the time stamp of last item modification
Lists	Gets the parent collection of lists to which the current list belongs
MajorVersionLimit	Indicates the major version maximum value
MajorWithMinorVersionsLimit	Indicates the major version maximum value when minor versions are enabled
MobileDefaultViewUrl	Indicates the default view URL of the mobile form factor display
MultipleDataList	Gets a Boolean value indicating that the list serves multiple instances of data, such as multiple instances of a meeting
NoCrawl	Gets a Boolean value indicating whether the contents of the list should appear in search results
ParentWeb	Indicates the parent web in which the list resides (SPWeb instance)
ParentWebUrl	Indicates the URL of the parent web
PropertiesXml	Gets a CAML fragment specifying property values for the list

5

TABLE 5.1   Continued

Property	Description
RootFolder	Indicates the topmost folder in the list
SchemaXml	Gets the CAML schema for the list
SendToLocationName	Gets the name of the "Send To" location
SendToLocationUrl	Gets the URL of the repository for the Send To menu option
Title	Gets the title of the list
Version	Gets the Version number of the list (not of the list items within it)
Views	Gets the collection of views for the list
WorkflowAssociations	Gets the list of workflows associated with the list

The following code enumerates through all of the lists contained in a sample SharePoint site, displaying a few of the properties of each list:

```
using System;
using System.Collections.Generic;
using System.Text;
using Microsoft.SharePoint;

namespace EnumLists
{
class Program
{
    static void Main(string[] args)
    {
        SPSite site = new SPSite("http://win2k3r2lab/Budget Test Site");
        SPWeb web = site.AllWebs[0];
        foreach (SPList list in web.Lists)
        {
            Console.WriteLine("{0}{1} - {2} items.",
                list.Hidden ? "*" : "",
                list.Title, list.ItemCount);
            Console.WriteLine("Created by {0}", list.Author.Name);
            Console.WriteLine("{0}", list.Description);
            Console.WriteLine
("----------------------------------------------------");
        }
        Console.WriteLine("\n{0} lists found.", web.Lists.Count);
        Console.ReadLine();
    }
}
}
```

The preceding code displays all the lists in the site found at the URL http://win2k3r2lab/ Budget Test Site. If the list is hidden, an asterisk is displayed before the list title and the item count.

Keep in mind that a lot of things that you might not expect to be lists (such as the Calendar that comes with default Team Sites) are lists. SharePoint accomplishes virtually all data storage tasks with lists, so knowing how to find and manipulate them is key to being a successful SharePoint developer.

Enumerating List Contents

Getting the items that belong to a list is as simple as accessing the list's Items property. This is a collection of SPListItem objects. What you do with the list item after you have a reference to it is limited only by the properties and methods on the list item. Table 5.2 shows some of the common properties of the SPListItem class.

TABLE 5.2   Common SPListItem Properties

Property	Description
Attachments	The list of attachments associated with the list item (SPAttachmentCollection instance)
Audit	The SPAudit instance associated with the list item
ContentType	The content type associated with the list item
CopyDestinations	A list of destinations to which the list item can be copied
DisplayName	The display name of the list item
Fields	The list of fields that belong to the list item
File	If in a document library, the file that corresponds to the list item
Folder	The folder in which the list item resides
HasPublishedVersion	This property indicates if this list item has been published at least once with a major version
ID	The unique (integer) identifier for the list item
ListItems	The parent collection of list items to which this list item belongs
Name	The name of the list item
ParentList	The parent list to which the item belongs
Properties	The name-value collection (hash table) of the list item's properties
Tasks	The workflow tasks associated with the list item
Title	The title of the list item
UniqueId	The globally unique identifier (GUID) of the list item
Url	The URL that will take a browser directly to the list item
Versions	The version history (SPListItemVersionCollection instance) of the list item
Web	The SPWeb instance on which the list item resides
Workflows	The workflows that are associated with the list item
Xml	The data for this list item in XMLDATA format as a string

If you want the full and complete list of properties for the SPListItem class as well as detailed reference information on each property, consult the Windows SharePoint Services v3 Software Development Kit (SDK), which you can download from Microsoft.

The following code is modified from the preceding example to enumerate the lists on a given site and (for each list) to display the title of every list item belonging to that list:

```
using System;
using System.Collections.Generic;
using System.Text;
using Microsoft.SharePoint;

namespace EnumLists
{
class Program
{
static void Main(string[] args)
{
    SPSite site = new SPSite("http://win2k3r2lab/Budget Test Site");
    SPWeb web = site.AllWebs[0];
    foreach (SPList list in web.Lists)
    {
        Console.WriteLine("{0}{1} - {2} items.",
            list.Hidden ? "*" : "",
            list.Title, list.ItemCount);
        Console.WriteLine("Created by {0}", list.Author.Name);
        Console.WriteLine("{0}", list.Description);
        foreach (SPListItem item in list.Items)
        {
            Console.WriteLine("\t{0}", item.Title);
        }
        Console.WriteLine("-------------------------------------------------------");
    }
    Console.WriteLine("\n{0} lists found.", web.Lists.Count);
    Console.ReadLine();
}
}
}
```

Note that if you run this code against a top-level site collection instead of a team site, you might run into some errors. (Many internal lists on top-level site collections have list items with null titles.)

This just displays the list item's Title property. To check the completed status of a task list item, or the value of a custom column that you created on a list, you can use the [] accessor on the list item to directly access the values associated with that item, as shown in Listing 5.1. If you are unsure of which fields belong to which list, you can always inspect the list's Fields property.

LISTING 5.1   Accessing List Item Values

```
using System;
using System.Collections.Generic;
using System.Text;
using Microsoft.SharePoint;

namespace EnumListItems
{
    class Program
    {
        static void Main(string[] args)
        {
            SPSite rootSite = new SPSite("http://win2k3r2lab");
            SPWeb web = rootSite.AllWebs["Budget Test Site"];

            SPList taskList = web.Lists["Tasks"];
            foreach (SPListItem item in taskList.Items)
            {
                Console.WriteLine(
                  "--- {0}:\n\tStatus:{1}\n\tProgress:{2}%\n\tDue Date:{3}",
                    item.Title,
                    item["Status"],
                    (double)item["PercentComplete"] * 100,
                    item["DueDate"]);
            }

            Console.ReadLine();
        }
    }
}
```

Adding, Removing, and Updating Lists

The pattern for adding and removing virtually any kind of object within SharePoint is fairly consistent. To add a new instance of something to the system, you generally need to call the Add() method on the container into which you will be placing the new item. Removing objects works the same way by calling the Remove() method on the source container.

When working with lists, that source container is any instance of SPListCollection. As you have already seen, there is a property called Lists on the SPWeb class that contains a collection of lists on that SharePoint web. When you call one of the Add() overloads, you will not only add the list to the collection (and, therefore, the website), but you will also get back an instance of SPList that you can manipulate if you choose.

The code in Listing 5.2 illustrates list manipulation by creating a new list, updating a list, and deleting a list.

LISTING 5.2   List Manipulation

```
using System;
using System.Collections.Generic;
using System.Text;
using Microsoft.SharePoint;

namespace ListManipulation
{
    class Program
    {
        static void Main(string[] args)
        {
            SPSite rootSite = new SPSite("http://win2k3r2lab");
            SPWeb rootWeb = rootSite.AllWebs["Budget Test Site"];


            SPListTemplate sourceTemplate = rootWeb.ListTemplates["Tasks"];

            Guid newListGuid = rootWeb.Lists.Add("Custom Task List",
                "Custom Task List", sourceTemplate);
            Guid secondNewListGuid = rootWeb.Lists.Add("Second Task List",
                "Second Task List", sourceTemplate);

            SPList newList = rootWeb.Lists[newListGuid];
            SPList secondNewList = rootWeb.Lists[secondNewListGuid];

            secondNewList.Delete();
            newList.Description = "Modified Custom Task List";
            newList.Update();

            Console.WriteLine("List manipulations complete.");


            Console.ReadLine();


        }
    }
}
```

As shown in Figure 5.1, the preceding code created a new list called "Custom Task List," and the one that was created and subsequently deleted does not appear.

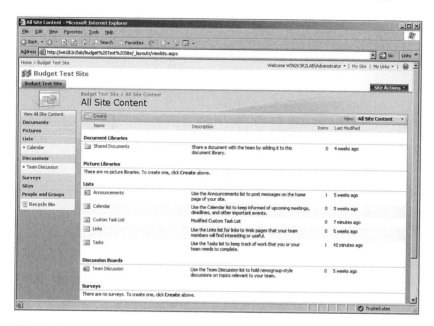

FIGURE 5.1   Site content after list manipulation.

Table 5.3 shows most of the commonly used methods on the SPList class that will help you write code for creating and manipulating lists.

TABLE 5.3   Common SPList Methods

Method	Description
AddWorkflowAssociation	Associates the current list with a workflow
BreakRoleInheritance	Separates the list permissions from its container
Delete	Deletes the list
DoesUserHavePermissions	Checks to see if the user has the given permissions on that list
GetChanges	Gets changes made to the list from the change log
GetItemById	Retrieves a list item from the list based on its numeric ID
GetItemByUniqueId	Retrieves a list item from the list based on the item's GUID
GetItems	Retrieves an optionally filtered list of items from the list
GetView	Retrieves a specific view of the list
RenderAsHtml	Renders the list contents in Hypertext Markup Language (HTML)
SaveAsTemplate	Saves the list's metadata (and possibly its data as well) as a template
Update	Commits changes made to the list since the last update
WriteRssFeed	Writes the RSS feed for the list to a given stream

Manipulating List Items

Manipulating list items is just as easy as manipulating lists. The item indexer property that allows you to access the various fields (columns) in the list for displaying also allows modification.

The code in Listing 5.3 shows how to create new list items, update the items, and delete existing items.

LISTING 5.3   Manipulating List Items

```
using System;
using System.Collections.Generic;
using System.Text;
using Microsoft.SharePoint;
using Microsoft.SharePoint.Utilities;

namespace ListItemManipulation
{
class Program
{
static void Main(string[] args)
{
    SPSite rootSite = new SPSite("http://win2k3r2lab");
    SPWeb web = rootSite.AllWebs["Budget Test Site"];

    SPList taskList = web.Lists["Custom Task List"];

    SPListItem newTask = taskList.Items.Add();
    newTask["Title"] = "Finish SharePoint 2010 Unleashed";
    newTask["DueDate"] = SPUtility.CreateISO8601DateTimeFromSystemDateTime
➥(DateTime.Now.AddDays(30));
    newTask["PercentComplete"] = 0.1;
    newTask.Update();

    newTask = taskList.Items.Add();
    newTask["Title"] = "This will be deleted.";
    newTask.Delete();

    taskList.Update();

    Console.WriteLine("List item manipulation completed.");
    Console.ReadLine();
}
}
}
```

Note that when setting the `DueDate` field of the list, the
`CreateISO8601DateTimeFromSystemDateTime` method of the `SPUtility` class was called to
convert a `System.DateTime` value into a string recognizable by SharePoint as a valid
date/time in the correct format.

Figure 5.2 shows the contents of the list "Custom Task List" after the preceding code is
executed.

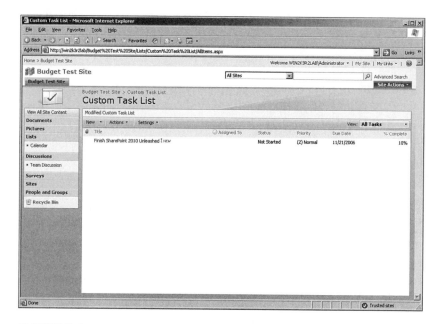

FIGURE 5.2   List item manipulation results.

Table 5.4 shows some of the most commonly used methods on the `SPListItem` class that
provide the developer with a wide range of functionality and flexibility.

TABLE 5.4   Common `SPListItem` Methods

Method	Description
BreakRoleInheritance	Separates the permissions on the list item from its container
Copy	Copies a list item from one list to another, both indicated by URLs
Delete	Deletes a list item
DoesUserHavePermissions	Checks to see if the user has permissions on the list item
GetFormattedValue	Retrieves an "easy-to-render" value for the list item
Update	Updates a list item
UpdateOverwriteVersion	Updates the list item overwriting the current version of the item

Using Lookup Types in Lists

Lookup data is slightly more difficult to deal with than standard data types in SharePoint lists. When you create a lookup column, you give the user the ability to select the value from a drop-down list provided by the contents of another list. For example, you might want to add a `Project` column to a custom task list to allow users to associate a task with a project.

When you examine the contents of a lookup column in a list, you might see a string that looks like this:

```
1;#Super-Important Project
```

This is the standard format of a lookup column and should look familiar to anyone who has done much list-based programming with SharePoint in the past.

To set the value of a lookup column, you need only supply the ID of the list item in the remote list to which you want to associate the item. For example, if "Super-Important Project" has an internal ID of 1, you would set the project of a custom task item to "Super-Important Project" as follows:

```
currentItem["Project"] = "1";
```

When reading the contents of a lookup column, you can separate the ID from the string value simply by splitting the string on the ";" character and stripping the leading "#" from the string. In the case where multiple values are allowed, multiple occurrences of the "ID;#string" phrase will appear—also separated with the ";#" character sequence.

Summary

When writing code for SharePoint, you will almost certainly encounter situations in which you need to read from or write to lists—either standard lists or custom lists. In either case, this chapter has provided you with a basic overview of the fundamentals of list enumeration, list item enumeration, list manipulation, and list content enumeration. You should be able to use this foundation to proceed to the next two chapters, which provide specialized and advanced list management topics—"Advanced List Management" and "Handling List Events."

CHAPTER 6

Advanced List Management

IN THIS CHAPTER

▶ Accessing BDC Data in Lists

▶ Querying List Items with CAML

▶ Creating Parent/Child Relationships in a Single List

The list item is the core piece of data upon which all of SharePoint rests. You would be hard pressed to find any functionality in all of Microsoft Office SharePoint Server (MOSS) or Windows SharePoint Services (WSS) that doesn't rely directly or indirectly on list items in some way. Chapter 5, "Managing SharePoint Lists," provided an introduction to the list and list item and how to manipulate them programmatically.

This chapter provides information on some more advanced list management topics, such as accessing Business Data Catalog data within a list, querying and filtering list items using the Collaborative Application Markup Language (CAML), and, finally, creating a single list that models a parent/child relationship using content types.

Accessing BDC Data in Lists

The Business Data Catalog (BDC), as you will discover throughout this book, is a feature of SharePoint that allows you to access data in remote Line of Business (LOB) applications. By supplying metadata information about the external application, you can tell SharePoint how to properly index data from that application.

Another incredibly powerful thing you can do with BDC applications is to create columns in lists that are actually lookup columns into tables in the external application. This means that you can, for example, create a column in a SharePoint list called Defect that is actually a lookup into a defect tracking system that is integrated with SharePoint through the Business Data Catalog.

When you create a list with these columns, you might think that you need to treat these columns differently. The code in Listing 6.1 shows how accessing data contained within an external system via the BDC is completely transparent to the client code. The sample in Listing 6.1 accesses the Customer table within the AdventureWorks sample database by reading columns in a custom list that are actually lookup values contained in the remote database.

LISTING 6.1   Accessing BDC Data Within Lists

```
using System;
using System.Collections.Generic;
using System.Text;
using Microsoft.SharePoint;

namespace ListBdcLookup
{
class Program
{
static void Main(string[] args)
{
    SPSite site = new SPSite("http://win2k3r2lab/");
    SPWeb web = site.AllWebs["Budget Test Site"];
    SPList bdcList = web.Lists["List with BDC Lookup"];
    foreach (SPListItem item in bdcList.Items)
    {
        Console.WriteLine("Item {0}", item.Title);
        foreach (SPField field in item.Fields)
        {
            Console.WriteLine("\t{0} ({1}) : {2}",
                field.Title, field.InternalName,
                item[field.Id]);
        }
    }

    // test directly accessing members from BDC lookups
    SPListItem firstItem = bdcList.Items[0];
    Console.WriteLine(firstItem["Customer"]);
    // access field using friendly name
    Console.WriteLine(firstItem["Customer: LastName"]);
    // access field using internal name
    Console.WriteLine(firstItem["Customer_x003a__x0020_LastName"]);

    Console.ReadLine();
}
}
}
```

When the preceding code is executed, assuming there is a custom list named "List with BDC Lookup" that contains lookup columns into the AdventureWorks sample database, the output will look similar to the following. (For information on how to create custom lists and manipulate the Business Data Catalog, you might want to look at *Microsoft SharePoint 2007 Unleashed* [ISBN: 0672329476], the SharePoint 2007 administration book from Sams Publishing.)

```
Item Sample Item
        Content Type ID (ContentTypeId) : 0x01003113BF4CD09F074AAA9063904B6BCA76

        Title (Title) : Sample Item
        Approver Comments (_ModerationComments) :
        File Type (File_x0020_Type) :
        Customer (Customer) : Aaron
        Customer_ID (Customer_ID) : __bg4100130073001300830083008300
        Customer: LastName (Customer_x003a__x0020_LastName) : Chen
        ID (ID) : 1
        Content Type (ContentType) : Item
        Modified (Modified) : 12/12/2006 10:39:33 AM
        Created (Created) : 12/12/2006 10:39:33 AM
        Created By (Author) : 1;#WIN2K3R2LAB\Administrator
        Modified By (Editor) : 1;#WIN2K3R2LAB\Administrator
        Has Copy Destinations (_HasCopyDestinations) :
        Copy Source (_CopySource) :
        owshiddenversion (owshiddenversion) : 1
        Workflow Version (WorkflowVersion) : 1
        UI Version (_UIVersion) : 512
        Version (_UIVersionString) : 1.0
        Attachments (Attachments) : False
        Approval Status (_ModerationStatus) : 0
        Edit (Edit) :
        Title (LinkTitleNoMenu) : Sample Item
        Title (LinkTitle) : Sample Item
        Select (SelectTitle) : 1
        Instance ID (InstanceID) :
        Order (Order) : 100
        GUID (GUID) : {62AA933B-6918-405A-BC07-1A0172432530}
        Workflow Instance ID (WorkflowInstanceID) :
        URL Path (FileRef) : /Budget Test Site/Lists/List with BDC Lookup/1_.000

        Path (FileDirRef) : 1;#Budget Test Site/Lists/List with BDC Lookup
        Modified (Last_x0020_Modified) : 2006-12-12 10:39:33
        Created (Created_x0020_Date) : 2006-12-12 10:39:33
        Item Type (FSObjType) : 0
        Effective Permissions Mask (PermMask) : 0x7ffffffffffffffff
        Name (FileLeafRef) : 1_.000
```

```
Unique Id (UniqueId) : e81a3434-933b-4ff6-bde2-20b65ea10fc1
ProgId (ProgId) :
ScopeId (ScopeId) : {3070AEB5-A178-47B7-AE4F-E8A7E86F7E82}
HTML File Type (HTML_x0020_File_x0020_Type) :
Edit Menu Table Start (_EditMenuTableStart) : 1_.000
Edit Menu Table End (_EditMenuTableEnd) : 1
Name (LinkFilenameNoMenu) : 1_.000
Name (LinkFilename) : 1_.000
Type (DocIcon) :
Server Relative URL (ServerUrl) :
  /Budget Test Site/Lists/List with BDC Lookup/1_.000
Encoded Absolute URL (EncodedAbsUrl) :
    http://win2k3r2lab/Budget%20Test%20Site/
      Lists/List%20with%20BDC%20Lookup/1_.000
File Name (BaseName) : 1_
Property Bag (MetaInfo) :
Level (_Level) : 1
Is Current Version (_IsCurrentVersion) : True
```

Aaron
Chen
Chen

Not only does the preceding output illustrate that accessing BDC-stored data is completely transparent to the programmer, but it also shows all of the various properties that are common to every list item within SharePoint.

Querying List Items with CAML

The Collaborative Application Markup Language (CAML), pronounced "Camel," is used within SharePoint for everything from site definitions to defining and invoking complex search queries, list views, and item filters. For more information on the CAML syntax, consult the MSDN documentation online or download the WSS v3.0 Software Development Kit (SDK) from Microsoft Downloads.

Listing 6.2 shows how to use a CAML query, which is basically an Extensible Markup Language (XML) fragment that defines the criteria that each element in the resultset must match.

LISTING 6.2   Using a CAML Query to Filter Items

```
using System;
using System.Collections.Generic;
using System.Text;
using Microsoft.SharePoint;


namespace CamlQuery
```

LISTING 6.2   Continued

```
{
class Program
{
    static void Main(string[] args)
    {
        string camlQuery =
            "<Query>" +
            "<Where>" +
            "<Eq>" +
            "<FieldRef Name=\"Customer_x003a__x0020_LastName\" />" +
            "<Value Type=\"Text\">Chen</Value>" +
            "</Eq>" +
            "</Where>" +
            "</Query>";

        SPSite site = new SPSite("http://win2k3r2lab");
        SPWeb testWeb = site.AllWebs["Budget Test Site"];
        SPList bdcList = testWeb.Lists["List with BDC Lookup"];

        SPQuery query = new SPQuery();
        query.Query = camlQuery;
        SPListItemCollection filteredItems =
            bdcList.GetItems(query);

        Console.WriteLine("Found {0} items in query.",
          filteredItems.Count);
        foreach (SPListItem item in filteredItems)
        {
            Console.WriteLine("Found customer: {0} {1}",
                item["Customer"],
                item["Customer: LastName"]);
        }

        Console.ReadLine();

    }
}
}
```

When the preceding code is executed against some sample data from the AdventureWorks database, it displays the following output:

```
Found 1 items in query.
Found customer: Aaron Chen
```

CAML queries can get extremely complex very quickly depending on the type of query you are performing. A variety of third-party tools are available on the Internet that you can download to assist you in defining CAML queries. One such tool is the U2U CAML Query Builder, which is shown in Figure 6.1.

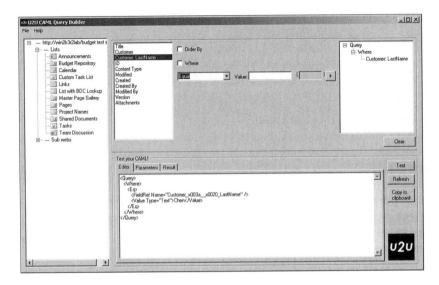

FIGURE 6.1   U2U tool for building CAML queries.

You can download this tool from http://www.u2u.info/SharePoint/ U2U%20Community%20Tools/Forms/AllItems.aspx.

Creating Parent/Child Relationships in a Single List

Content types are an extremely powerful new feature of SharePoint 2007. They allow administrators to define properties and functionality that are common to documents and list items that belong to the same content type. This provides for functionality such as defining a common set of properties and actions for things like whitepapers, expense reports, PDFs, and much more.

One interesting thing you can do with content types is to create a content type that inherits from the master content type of "Folder". This allows you to create a folder within a list (SharePoint 2007 allows folders in all lists now, not just document libraries!) that can have its own set of properties.

Using the combination of folders, items contained within folders, and content types, you can create a parent/child hierarchy of items contained within a single list that doesn't even require the use of lookup columns.

If you have ever tried to accomplish parent/child hierarchies with SharePoint 2003 lists, you know that it was difficult and tedious and required creating lookup columns that linked the child items to the parent items, but the hierarchy was still flimsy and not easily discernable from the context of looking at the lists.

Now, you can create a hierarchy in which the parent is a folder and the children are simply items contained within that folder. This is an extremely natural "Container" style approach to related data that a lot of developers find extremely appealing.

To see how this works, the first step is to create some content types. Figure 6.2 shows a screenshot of the Order Parent type, a content type that inherits from the Folder content type that will be used to store orders for customers. Each folder will represent a single order. As you can see, additional properties about the order can be created as columns on the content type.

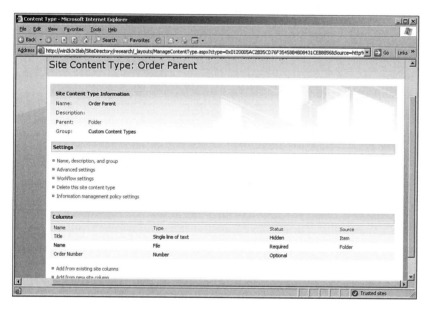

FIGURE 6.2   The Order Parent content type.

After you have the parent content type in place, you need to create a content type for the children. In the case of the Order Item content type (see Figure 6.3), it is a custom content type that inherits from the basic List Item content type. Note that there is no column in this content type that links to a parent—all of the parent/child association is done implicitly by items being contained within an order folder.

With those content types in place, you can easily create new items that are orders or order items, as shown in Figure 6.4. This type of scenario is ideal for lists that might be used as the backing store for help-desk support applications, issue-tracking applications, and many other applications that use traditional parent/child data relationships.

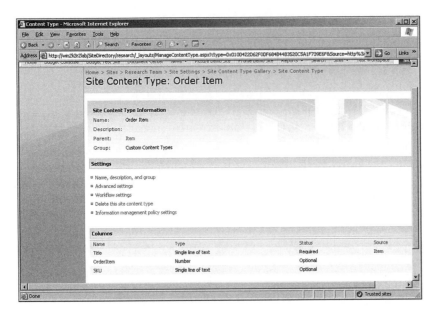

FIGURE 6.3   The Order Item content type.

FIGURE 6.4   The New Item menu with content types.

With some sample data stored in a list that supports the Order Parent and Order Item content types, you can write some code that looks similar to Listing 6.3 to traverse a hierarchical list of items.

LISTING 6.3   Writing Code to Traverse a Hierarchical List

```
using System;
using System.Collections.Generic;
using System.Text;
using Microsoft.SharePoint;

namespace ListHierarchy
{
class Program
```

LISTING 6.3   Continued

```
{
static void Main(string[] args)
{
    SPSite site = new SPSite("http://win2k3r2lab");
    SPWeb web = site.AllWebs["SiteDirectory/research"];
    SPList parentList = web.Lists["Hierarchy Demo"];

    foreach (SPListItem order in parentList.Folders)
    {
        Console.WriteLine("Order        : {0}",order["Name"]);
        Console.WriteLine("Order Number : {0}", order["Order Number"]);

        SPQuery orderItemsQuery = new SPQuery();
        orderItemsQuery.Folder = order.Folder;
        SPListItemCollection orderItems =
          parentList.GetItems(orderItemsQuery);
        foreach (SPListItem orderItem in orderItems)
        {
            Console.WriteLine("\tLine Item {0}: {1} {2}",
                orderItem["OrderItem"],
                orderItem["SKU"],
                orderItem["Title"]);
        }
    }
    Console.ReadLine();
}
}
}
```

Note that the way that the preceding code obtained a list of all items that belong to a given folder was by using an empty instance of the SPQuery class and specifying the folder. By default, if you do not specify a filtering query, the SPQuery object will return all list items. If you indicate a folder and still leave the query empty, the object will return a list of all items that are contained within that folder.

When the code is executed against some sample data, it produces the following output:

```
Order        : First Order
Order Number : 1001
        Line Item 1: MP3100 MP3 Player
        Line Item 2: 1011002 Alarm Clock
Order        : Second Order
Order Number : 2
        Line Item 1: 1039202 Bottled Water
```

Summary

Lists and list items are not only the core way of storing data within SharePoint, but they are absolutely unavoidable if you are a developer. Very few SharePoint development tasks do not involve lists or list items. This chapter provided an overview of some of the more advanced things that can be done with lists and list items.

CHAPTER 7

Handling List Events

IN THIS CHAPTER

▶ Introduction to List Event Handlers

▶ Creating Event Receivers

▶ Deploying Event Receivers

One of the first facts that a SharePoint developer learns is that SharePoint is built on a foundation of lists. Virtually every piece of data contained within SharePoint is contained within a list of some form or another.

One of the extremely powerful new features in SharePoint is the ability to create event receivers for *any list type*. In previous versions of SharePoint, the only lists that had this functionality were document libraries, and even then the functionality was fairly limited.

An event receiver is a piece of managed code that is launched in response to an event that takes place within SharePoint. These events can be triggered in response to changes to list items, creation of new lists, new list items, list items being deleted, and much more. These event handlers can allow you to write extremely powerful applications that integrate directly with SharePoint lists.

This chapter shows you how to create event receivers as well as how to deploy them programmatically, via Features and via content types.

Introduction to List Event Handlers

List event handlers are made possible through the concept of event receivers. An event receiver is a .NET Framework class, contained in a strong-typed Assembly that must be installed in the Global Assembly Cache (GAC). This class is then instantiated by SharePoint and when events for which the class has been registered are fired, event handlers on the event receiver class are then invoked.

This all works through the SPItemEventReceiver class, which contains all of the plumbing necessary to subscribe and respond to list item events. Similarly, events on lists themselves are handled through the `SPListEventReceiver` class. To create your own event receivers, you just need to create classes that derive from either the `SPItemEventReceiver` class or the `SPListEventReceiver` class. Both of these classes inherit from the abstract base class `SPEventReceiverBase`.

Creating Event Receivers

In previous versions of SharePoint, the only way to create code that responded to events on lists was to create classes that implemented an interface. There were also problems in attempting to obtain a valid security context with which to access the SharePoint object model from inside an event handler. The worst part of SharePoint's prior list event handling implementation is that it only allowed you to define event handlers for document libraries. No other list type within SharePoint supported managed code event handlers.

With the 2007 version of SharePoint, you create event receivers. These receivers are actually classes that derive from a base class. To write code that responds to a given event, you simply override the method on the base class that corresponds to the event for which your code will be listening.

Not only can you create event receivers for list items such as when an item changes or is created, but you can also create event receivers for lists, such as when list fields (columns) are added or removed.

The procedure for creating your own event receivers is a four-step process:

1. Create a class that inherits from `SPListEventReceiver` or from `SPItemEventReceiver`.

2. Sign the class library to give it a strong name.

3. Deploy the class library to the Global Assembly Cache.

4. Deploy the event receiver Assembly with a Feature, with a content type, or with code.

The following two sections illustrate how to create event receivers for lists and for list items. The final section of the chapter covers the process of deploying event receivers.

Creating List Event Receivers

List events occur when the metadata of the list itself has been modified. For example, you can write code that will respond when fields are added to or removed from the list. As with most event receivers, you can create a handler either for the *post* event (occurs after the event has already taken place) or the *during* event (occurs before the event changes are made permanent).

Each list event receiver method takes a single argument of type `SPListEventProperties`. This object allows your code to obtain information about the event, the context in which the event is executing, and allows you to optionally signal to SharePoint that the event should be canceled. Table 7.1 contains a list of the properties of this class.

TABLE 7.1   `SPListEventProperties` Properties

Property	Description
Cancel	A value indicating whether the event should be canceled (set by your receiver)
ErrorMessage	The error message to be displayed when an event is canceled
EventType	The type of event that was received
Field	The field affected by the event
FieldName	The name of the field affected by the event
FieldXml	The XML definition of the field affected by the event
List	A reference to the list affected by the event
ListId	The globally unique identifier (GUID) of the list affected by the event
ListTitle	The title of the list affected by the event
ReceiverData	A string containing custom data about the event (from the receiver configuration)
SiteId	The GUID of the site collection in which the event was fired
Status	A value indicating the status of the event (SPEventReceiverStatus instance)
UserDisplayName	The display name of the user that triggered the event
UserLoginName	The login name of the user that triggered the event
Web	A reference to the individual web in which the event occurred
WebId	The GUID of the web in which the event occurred
WebUrl	The uniform resource locator (URL) of the web in which the event occurred

Table 7.2 contains a list of events to which your code can respond.

TABLE 7.2   List Events

Event	Description
FieldAdded	Event fired after a field has been added
FieldAdding	Event fired before a field is added
FieldDeleted	Event fired after a field is removed
FieldDeleting	Event fired before a field is removed
FieldUpdated	Event fired after a field is updated
FieldUpdating	Event fired before a field is updated

To create a simple list event handler, start by creating a new class library in Visual Studio 2005. Right-click the project and select Properties. Click the Signing tab and select the <New...> option from the dropdown list for strong name keys and then fill out the Create Strong Name Key dialog box to sign the Assembly with a new key. You will see the new key (a file with the extension .snk) appear in the solution.

Next, add a class to the class library called ListMetaLogger. It should inherit from the base class SPListEventReceiver.

Listing 7.1 shows a class that logs activity on list metadata to a text file on disk.

LISTING 7.1   A Sample List Event Receiver Class

```
using System;
using System.IO;
using System.Collections.Generic;
using System.Text;
using Microsoft.SharePoint;

namespace ListMetaLogger
{
public class ListMetaLogger : SPListEventReceiver
{
    public override void FieldAdded(SPListEventProperties properties)
    {
        LogEvent(properties, "FieldAdded");
    }

    public override void FieldAdding(SPListEventProperties properties)
    {
        LogEvent(properties, "FieldAdding");
    }

    public override void FieldDeleting(SPListEventProperties properties)
    {
        LogEvent(properties, "FieldDeleting");
    }

    public override void FieldDeleted(SPListEventProperties properties)
    {
        LogEvent(properties, "FieldDeleted");
    }

    public override void FieldUpdated(SPListEventProperties properties)
    {
        LogEvent(properties, "FieldUpdated");
```

LISTING 7.1   Continued

```
    }

    public override void FieldUpdating(SPListEventProperties properties)
    {
        LogEvent(properties, "FieldUpdating");
    }

    private void LogEvent(SPListEventProperties properties, string eventName)
    {
        StreamWriter sw = File.AppendText(@"C:\listeventlog.txt");
        StringBuilder sb = new StringBuilder();
        sb.AppendFormat("[{0}] {1} Event Occurred:\n",
            DateTime.Now.ToString(), eventName);
        sb.AppendFormat("\tList : {0}", properties.ListTitle);
        sb.AppendFormat("\t{0} - Field {1}",
            properties.EventType.ToString(), properties.FieldName);

        sw.WriteLine(sb.ToString());
        sw.Close();
    }
}
}
```

When deployed against a Task list (deployment of event receivers is covered later in this chapter) and a user adds a column to the list, the contents of listeventlog.txt might look like this:

```
[10/29/2006 2:03:30 PM] FieldAdding Event Occurred:
        List : Tasks    FieldAdding - Field Test_x0020_Column_x0020_2
[10/29/2006 2:03:30 PM] FieldAdded Event Occurred:
        List : Tasks    FieldAdded - Field Test_x0020_Column_x0020_2
```

It is worth noting that the field name property is URL encoded. This means that when the user created a new field called "Test Column 2," SharePoint converted the internal field name to Test_x0020_Column_x0020_2. The spaces are converted into their hexadecimal equivalent: 0x0020.

Creating List Item Event Receivers

Event receivers for list items work in exactly the same fashion as list event receivers. The only difference between the two is that the events and event properties with list item event receivers are related to list items and not list metadata.

Table 7.3 shows the list of properties available to event receivers when passed an instance of the SPItemEventProperties class.

TABLE 7.3   SPItemEventProperties Properties

Property	Description
AfterProperties	An SPItemEventDataCollection instance consisting of name/value pairs indicating the state of the list item as it appears after the event takes place
AfterUrl	The URL of the item after the event occurred
BeforeProperties	A name/value pair collection indicating the state of the list item before the event took place
BeforeUrl	The URL of the item before the event took place
Cancel	A Boolean indicating whether the item event should be canceled
Context	An SPEventContext instance containing information related to the context in which the event occurred
CurrentUserId	The numeric ID of the user that triggered the event
ErrorMessage	The error message to be displayed in case an error occurred (when Cancel is true)
EventType	The type of event that occurred
ListId	The GUID of the list in which the event occurred
ListItem	A reference to the list item for which the event took place
ListItemId	The integer ID of the list item associated with the event
ListTitle	The title of the list in which the event occurred
ReceiverData	The custom receiver data as defined by the receiver's registration configuration
RelativeWebUrl	The server-relative URL of the website in which the event took place
SiteId	The GUID of the site collection in which the event took place
Status	The status of the handling event (CancelNoError, CancelWithError, Continue)
UserDisplayName	The display name of the user that triggered the event
UserLoginName	The login name of the user that triggered the event
Versionless	A Boolean indicating whether the item does not track versions
WebUrl	The absolute URL of the website in which the event took place
Zone	The URL zone (for example, Local, Intranet) of the site in which the event took place

Several more events are available for list items than for list metadata because there are far more significant events in the life cycle of list data than in list metadata. Table 7.4 contains a list of list item events to which your code can respond.

TABLE 7.4   List Item Events

Event	Description
ItemAdded	Occurs after an item is added
ItemAdding	Occurs before an item is added to the list
ItemAttachmentAdded	Occurs after an attachment is added to an item
ItemAttachmentAdding	Occurs before an attachment is added to an item
ItemAttachmentDeleted	Occurs after an attachment is deleted from an item
ItemAttachmentDeleting	Occurs before an attachment is removed from an item
ItemCheckedIn	Occurs after an item is checked in
ItemCheckedOut	Occurs after an item is checked out
ItemCheckingIn	Occurs before an item is checked in
ItemCheckingOut	Occurs before an item is checked out
ItemDeleted	Occurs after an item is deleted
ItemDeleting	Occurs before an item is deleted
ItemFileConverted	Occurs after a file is converted
ItemFileMoved	Occurs after a file is moved
ItemFileMoving	Occurs before a file is moved
ItemUncheckedOut	Occurs after an item's last changes are undone (uncheckout)
ItemUncheckingOut	Occurs before an item's last changes are undone (uncheckout)
ItemUpdated	Occurs after an item is updated
ItemUpdating	Occurs before an item is updated

Listing 7.2 shows a sample class that logs item events to a text file.

LISTING 7.2   Sample List Item Event Receiver

```
using System;
using System.IO;
using System.Collections.Generic;
using System.Text;
using Microsoft.SharePoint;

namespace EventLogger
{
public class ListEventLogger : SPItemEventReceiver
{
public override void ItemAdded(SPItemEventProperties properties)
{
    WriteTextToLog(string.Format("[{0}] Item Added : {1}",
      properties.ListItem.Title, DateTime.Now.ToString()));
}
```

LISTING 7.2   Continued

```
public override void ItemDeleted(SPItemEventProperties properties)
{
    WriteTextToLog(string.Format("[{0}] Item Deleted : {1}",
      properties.ListItem.Title, DateTime.Now.ToString()));
}

public override void ItemUpdated(SPItemEventProperties properties)
{
    WriteTextToLog(string.Format("[{0}] Item Updated : {1}",
        properties.ListItem.Title, DateTime.Now.ToString()));
}

private void WriteTextToLog(string text)
{
    StreamWriter logFile = File.AppendText(@"C:\listlog.txt");
    logFile.Write(text + "\n");
    logFile.Close();
}
}
}
```

One aspect of list item event receivers (and to a lesser extent, list event receivers) that is extremely powerful is the ability to actually stop an event from taking place. If your code responds to the ItemUpdating event and sets the Cancel property of the properties object to true, the *list item update will not take place*. This allows you to custom code your own constraints on creating, updating, and deleting list items above and beyond what might be available natively within SharePoint.

So far, the sample code has just illustrated how to execute code unrelated to SharePoint (logging text information to disk) in response to an event. The vast majority of event receivers will also want to be able to access the SharePoint object model when handling an event. In addition to having access to the list item and the list when an item event occurs, you can also obtain a reference to the site collection in which the event occurred using the following code:

```
SPSite eventSite = new SPSite(properties.SiteId);
SPWeb eventWeb = eventSite.OpenWeb(properties.RelativeWebUrl);
```

With access to the SPSite and SPWeb instances for the website in which the event occurred, you can write code that performs more powerful actions. For example, you might want to create a new announcement every time a user creates a new entry in a given list. Using the previous two lines of code, you can obtain a reference to the Announcements list on the site and add new entries in the ItemAdded event receiver method.

Deploying Event Receivers

You can deploy event receivers in three different ways:

- Deploying programmatically
- Deploying via Features
- Deploying with Content types

Regardless of how you deploy the event receivers, the class library that you created that contains the event receiver class must be strongly named (signed with a key) and must also be installed in the Global Assembly Cache (GAC).

Deploying Event Receivers Programmatically

If you want your event receivers to only be associated with a single instance of a list rather than with all lists of a certain template ID (Table 7.5 in the next section shows all the built-in template IDs), you can write some code to manually register your event receivers with a given list.

The following code snippet shows how to associate an event receiver class and Assembly with a specific list by calling the Add method on the EventReceivers collection. Once the new receiver has been created, you need to give it the fully qualified assembly name that points to the code you have written and deployed as well as provide a sequence number and indicate the type of event to which the receiver responds.

```
SPWeb webSite = new SPSite("http://win2k3r2lab").OpenWeb();
SPList theList = webSite.Lists["Tasks"];
SPEventReceiverDefinition newReceiver = theList.EventReceivers.Add();
newReceiver.Class = "Receiver.ReceiverClass";
newReceiver.Assembly =
"Receiver,Version=1.0.0.0,Culture=neutral,PublicKeyToken=abc123abc123abc";
newReceiver.Sequence = 5000;
newReceiver.Type = SPEventReceiverType.ItemUpdated;
newReceiver.Update();
```

Deploying Event Receivers with Features

The problem with deploying event receivers by manually writing code that installs the receiver against a specific instance of a list is that you don't get much reuse benefit from that receiver.

When developing SharePoint Solutions that include code that responds to list events, those event receivers are often part of a Feature definition. When including an event receiver in a Feature definition, you can indicate the type of list for which your code will be listening for events by specifying the list's template ID in the Feature definition itself.

Listings 7.3 and 7.4 show the `Feature.xml` and `Elements.xml` files that configure a Feature that contains a list item event receiver.

LISTING 7.3   Feature.xml

```
<Feature Scope="Web"
    Title="List Item Event Logger"
    Id="{EF0917F4-5ED8-40b1-9A37-585BCDE9DB63}"
    xmlns="http://schemas.microsoft.com/sharepoint/">
    <ElementManifests>
        <ElementManifest Location="Elements.xml"/>
    </ElementManifests>
</Feature>
```

LISTING 7.4   Elements.xml

```
<Elements xmlns="http://schemas.microsoft.com/sharepoint/">
<Receivers ListTemplateId="107">
<Receiver>
<Name>EventLogger</Name>
<Type>ItemAdded</Type>
<SequenceNumber>10000</SequenceNumber>
<Assembly>EventLogger, Version=1.0.0.0, Culture=neutral,
➥PublicKeyToken=5d1d751131e0aacf</Assembly>
<Class>EventLogger.ListEventLogger</Class>
<Data></Data>
<Filter></Filter>
</Receiver>
<Receiver>
<Name>EventLogger</Name>
<Type>ItemUpdated</Type>
<SequenceNumber>10000</SequenceNumber>
<Assembly>EventLogger, Version=1.0.0.0, Culture=neutral,
➥PublicKeyToken=5d1d751131e0aacf</Assembly>
<Class>EventLogger.ListEventLogger</Class>
<Data></Data>
<Filter></Filter>
</Receiver>
<Receiver>
<Name>EventLogger</Name>
<Type>ItemDeleted</Type>
<SequenceNumber>10000</SequenceNumber>
<Assembly>EventLogger, Version=1.0.0.0, Culture=neutral,
➥PublicKeyToken=5d1d751131e0aacf</Assembly>
<Class>EventLogger.ListEventLogger</Class>
```

LISTING 7.4   Continued

```
<Data></Data>
<Filter></Filter>
</Receiver>
</Receivers>
</Elements>
```

After you have the `Feature.xml` and `Elements.xml` files, you can deploy them into your SharePoint `Template\Features` directory. After they are in the directory, use the following `stsadm.exe` command to install the Feature:

```
Stsadm -o installfeature -filename FeatureDirectory\Feature.xml
```

Use the following `stsadm.exe` command to activate the Feature on your website (make sure you change the relative directory paths and URLs to match your configuration):

```
Stsadm -o activatefeature -filename FeatureDirectory\Feature.xml -url
➥"http://server/web site"
```

After you install and activate the Feature, you *must* run `iisreset` for SharePoint to start making use of the newly registered event receivers.

When the Feature is installed and activated, you can verify this using the Site Features page, as shown in Figure 7.1.

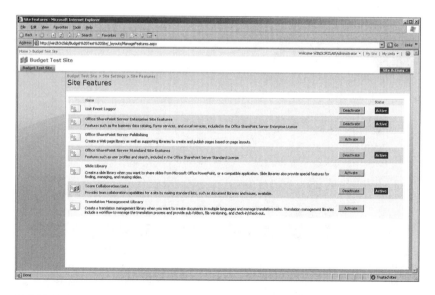

FIGURE 7.1   Site Features list after installing event handler feature.

You might have noticed that in the `Elements.xml` file you had to specify the list template ID as a raw number. Table 7.5 provides a list of template IDs and the built-in SharePoint list types to which they correspond.

TABLE 7.5   Built-In SharePoint List Templates

Template ID	Description
100	Generic list
101	Document library
102	Survey
103	Links list
104	Announcements list
105	Contacts list
106	Events list
107	Tasks list
108	Discussion board
109	Picture library
110	Data Sources list
111	Site Template Gallery
113	Web Part Gallery
114	List Template Gallery
115	XML Form Library (InfoPath)
120	Custom grid for list
200	Meeting Series list
201	Meeting Agenda list
204	Meeting Decisions list
207	Meeting Objectives list
210	Meeting text box
211	"Things to Bring" Meeting list
212	Meeting Workspace Pages list
300	Portal Sites list
1100	Issue Tracking list
2002	Personal document library
2003	Private document library

NOTE

Unfortunately, you cannot listen for multiple list template IDs within the same Feature. If the Solution you are delivering involves listening for events on multiple list template IDs, you should create a Solution with multiple Features, where each Feature contains event receivers for a single list template ID.

Deploying Event Receivers with Content Types

Deploying event receivers with content types follows the same pattern as deployment with Features. First, you must create the strongly named, signed Assembly and place it in the GAC of the destination server. If you are deploying to a farm, *the event receiver Assembly must be in the GAC of every front-end server*. After the Assembly has been deployed, it is just a matter of creating a content type with a Feature and using the procedure for Feature-based event receiver deployment discussed in the preceding section.

Summary

One of the most powerful new abilities given to SharePoint developers with the new version of SharePoint is the ability to write code that responds to events on any list, not just document libraries. This chapter provided an illustration of how to write list event receivers, list item event receivers, and how to deploy those event receivers. You can even use the information in this chapter to create event receivers for events that take place at the site scope.

Responding to list events and deploying that code programmatically or via Solutions, Features, and content types give you tremendous power and flexibility when building your SharePoint-based solutions.

CHAPTER 8

Working with Document Libraries and Files

IN THIS CHAPTER

▶ Document Library Basics

▶ Working with the Document Library Object Model

▶ Working with Versioning

▶ Manipulating Folders and Files

Document management is one of SharePoint's key features. Many organizations that use Microsoft Office SharePoint Server (MOSS) might choose to ignore the vast majority of SharePoint's features but will still utilize its document management facilities.

SharePoint includes incredibly powerful features for storing, indexing, manipulating, versioning, and retrieving documents. As with just about every other aspect of SharePoint, you can utilize all of this power within your applications or your Web Parts. This chapter provides a description of the various ways in which you can write code to access and manipulate documents within SharePoint—everything from checking files in and out to navigating a nested hierarchy of folders and files within a document library.

Document Library Basics

A document library is really just a list with some added functionality on top. Many developers assume that document libraries aren't very powerful because they are just specialized lists. Although it is true that they are specialized lists, document libraries are also extremely powerful and flexible and your code can benefit greatly from being able to treat document libraries like standard lists when the need arises.

The first thing that developers might find helpful about document libraries is that the entire object model for lists and list items applies to document libraries and documents, respectively. You can treat a document as an instance of SPListItem and you can treat a document library as an instance of SPList.

If you don't need that kind of generic access, you can access document libraries with the SPDocumentLibrary class and you can manipulate files with the SPFile class.

Uploading a document to a document library causes SharePoint to store the document's raw data internally within Microsoft SQL Server. This means that you can use the application programming interface (API) to get at the document itself rather than having to hunt around on shared drives for files.

SharePoint lists (which include document libraries) can be version controlled, and the SPFile class provides multiple methods for dealing with version control. All of these powerful features are explored throughout this chapter.

Working with the Document Library Object Model

The SharePoint object model has robust support for document libraries. That support is provided by several key classes:

▶ SPFileCollection

▶ SPFile

▶ SPDocumentLibrary

▶ SPListItem

▶ SPFolderCollection

▶ SPFolder

Classes such as SPFile and SPFolder provide a great deal of functionality as well as many properties that can be used to examine a considerable amount of information pertaining to files and folders.

Tables 8.1 and 8.2 provide an overview of some of the most commonly used properties on the SPFile and SPFolder classes.

TABLE 8.1   Common SPFile Properties

Property	Description
Author	Lists the user who created the document
CheckedOutBy	Gets the user who currently has the file checked out
CheckedOutDate	Gets the date/time that the file was checked out; note that this property will throw an exception if the file is not checked out
CheckInComment	Gets the comment used when the file was checked into the document library
CheckOutExpires	Gets the time stamp for when a short-term check-out expires
CheckOutStatus	Gets the status of the check-out (LongTerm, LongTermOffline, None, ShortTerm)

TABLE 8.1   Continued

EventReceivers	Gets a list of event receivers defined for the file
Exists	Indicates whether the file exists
IconUrl	Gets the uniform resource locator (URL) of the icon associated with the file
InDocumentLibrary	Gets a Boolean value indicating whether the file is in a document library
IsIRMed	Gets a Boolean value indicating whether Information Rights Management is enabled for the file
Item	Gets the SPListItem instance corresponding to the file
Length	Gets the length (size) of the file in bytes; if the file is a Web Part page, the size excludes Web Parts in the page
LengthByUser	For Web Part pages, indicates the size of the file (page) per user
Level	Gets the publication level of the item (Checkout=255, Draft=2, Published=1)
MajorVersion	Gets an integer indicating the file's major version number; always '1' for unversioned files
MinorVersion	Gets an integer indicating the file's minor version number; always '0' for unversioned files
Name	Indicates the name of the file
ParentFolder	Indicates the folder in which the file resides
Properties	Provides access to the metadata for the file
ServerRedirected	Gets a Boolean value indicating whether users are redirected to server-side rendering of the file when the appropriate client application is not installed or the user does not have access to the file
ServerRelativeUrl	Gets the server-relative URL for the file
SourceLeafName	Gets the leaf name of the parent document for the file
SourceUIVersion	Gets the version number of the parent document for the file
TimeCreated	Gets the time stamp indicating when the file was created; this is not necessarily the same as the time when the file was uploaded into the document library
TimeLastModified	Gets the time stamp indicating the last time the file was modified; this is different than the last time the item metadata changed
Title	Gets the file's display name/title
TotalLength	Gets a value indicating the file size in bytes of the file, including any associated Web Parts for a Web Part page; use this property to get the most inclusive file size
UIVersion	Gets the version number of the file; this corresponds roughly to the old numeric version index from SharePoint 2003 lists
UIVersionLabel	Gets a string showing how the file version is displayed to users
UniqueId	Gets the file's globally unique identifier (GUID)
Url	Indicates the site-relative URL of the file
Versions	Gets a collection of version objects representing the file's version history

8

TABLE 8.2   Common `SPFolder` Properties

Property	Description
Audit	Gets the auditing object associated with the folder (`SPAudit`)
ContainingDocumentLibrary	Gets the document library that contains the folder, if applicable
Exists	Gets a Boolean value indicating whether the folder exists
Files	Gets the collection (`SPFileCollection`) of files contained within the folder
Item	Gets the `SPListItem` instance that corresponds to the folder
Name	Gets the name of the folder
ParentFolder	Gets the parent folder of the folder; if the folder is a top-level folder in a document library, this actually indicates the document library itself
ParentListId	Gets the ID for the folder's parent list
ParentWeb	Gets the `SPWeb` in which the folder resides
Properties	Gets the metadata for the folder
ServerRelativeUrl	Gets the server-relative URL for the folder
SubFolders	Gets an `SPFolderCollection` instance containing the subfolders beneath the current folder
UniqueId	Gets the GUID of the folder
Url	Gets the site-relative URL of the folder
WelcomePage	Gets (or sets) the URL indicating where users will be redirected when they browse to the folder

Building a Document Library Explorer Sample

The best way to get a feel for how all of the document, file, and folder classes relate to each other is to look at a hands-on example. This section walks you through building a sample document library explorer. This application illustrates how to get a list of document libraries on a site, how to recursively obtain a list of all folders within the library, and how to retrieve a list of all files contained within a given folder.

To get started, create a new Windows Forms application and make sure you add a reference to the `Microsoft.SharePoint.dll` Assembly.

Add a text box called `siteName`, a text box called `siteUrl`, and a button called `exploreButton`. Then add a TreeView (`folderTree`) and a ListView (`documentList`). With that in place, modify the code behind the form to match the code in Listing 8.1. You'll need to double-click the Explore button to create a click-handler stub and create an event-handler stub for the TreeView's `AfterSelect` property.

LISTING 8.1   Form1.cs (Document Library Explorer)

```csharp
using System;
using System.Collections.Generic;
using System.ComponentModel;
using System.Data;
using System.Drawing;
using System.Text;
using System.Windows.Forms;
using Microsoft.SharePoint;

namespace DocLibBrowser
{
public partial class Form1 : Form
{
SPWeb sourceWeb;
SPDocumentLibrary selectedLib;

public Form1()
{
    InitializeComponent();
}

private void exploreButton_Click(object sender, EventArgs e)
{
    SPSite sourceSite = new SPSite(siteUrl.Text);
    sourceWeb = sourceSite.AllWebs[siteName.Text];

    DocLibPicker picker = new DocLibPicker(sourceWeb);
    if (picker.ShowDialog() == DialogResult.OK)
    {
        selectedLib = picker.SelectedLibrary;
        folderTree.Nodes.Add(selectedLib.Title);
        foreach (SPListItem folderItem in selectedLib.Folders)
        {
            System.Diagnostics.Debug.WriteLine("Top-level folder found : " +
                folderItem.Name);
            if (folderItem.Folder.ParentFolder.Name.ToUpper() ==
                selectedLib.Title.ToUpper()) // weed out non-top-level nodes
                PopulateTree(folderItem, folderTree.Nodes[0]);
        }

    }
}
```

8

LISTING 8.1   Continued

```
private void PopulateTree(SPListItem folderItem, TreeNode rootNode)
{
    SPFolder realFolder = folderItem.Folder;
    TreeNode newNode = new TreeNode(folderItem.Name);
    newNode.Tag = realFolder;
    rootNode.Nodes.Add(newNode);
    foreach (SPFolder subFolder in realFolder.SubFolders)
    {
        PopulateTree(subFolder.Item, newNode);
    }
}

private void folderTree_AfterSelect(object sender, TreeViewEventArgs e)
{
    documentList.Items.Clear();
    if (e.Node.Level > 0) // not root node
    {
        SPFolder folder = (SPFolder)e.Node.Tag;
        System.Diagnostics.Debug.WriteLine("Folder clicked " +
          folder.Name);
        foreach (SPFile file in folder.Files)
        {
            ListViewItem lvi = new ListViewItem(file.Name);
            lvi.SubItems.Add(file.MajorVersion.ToString() + "." +
              file.MinorVersion.ToString());
            lvi.SubItems.Add(file.Author.Name);
            documentList.Items.Add(lvi);
        }
    }
}
}
}
```

An interesting thing to note in Listing 8.1 is that the Folders property of the SPDocumentLibrary class actually returns an SPListItemCollection instead of an SPFolderCollection. It's not that big of an inconvenience, however. When using an instance of an SPListItem, you can use the Folder property to get back an instance of the corresponding folder. Conversely, when using an instance of SPFolder, you can get at the corresponding list item with the Item property.

Take a look at the lines of code in Listing 8.1 that loop through the contents of the Folders collection on the selectedLib.Folders collection. Notice that there is logic in there to make sure that only items that belong directly to the root folder appear. This is because the `Folders` collection of a document library actually contains *all* of that library's folders, regardless of their position within the hierarchy. This can be a help or a hindrance, depending on what you need to accomplish.

Add a second form called `DocLibPicker.cs` to the project. On the form, add a ListBox called `docLibList` and a button called `selectButton`. Add three columns to `docLibList`: File Name, Version, and Author. Double-click the selectButton to create an event handler. If you don't feel like going through all those steps manually, you can always get the code directly from the code download for this book.

Listing 8.2 shows the code for the dialog box that presents the user with a list of document libraries from which they can choose. This illustrates the inheritance hierarchy that allows you to use the `is` and `as` operators with the `SPList` and `SPDocumentLibrary` classes.

LISTING 8.2   `DocLibPicker.cs` (Document Library Explorer)

```
using System;
using System.Collections.Generic;
using System.ComponentModel;
using System.Data;
using System.Drawing;
using System.Text;
using System.Windows.Forms;
using Microsoft.SharePoint;

namespace DocLibBrowser
{
public partial class DocLibPicker : Form
{
SPWeb sourceWeb;
List<SPDocumentLibrary> docLibs;

public DocLibPicker(SPWeb _source)
{
    InitializeComponent();
    docLibs = new List<SPDocumentLibrary>();
    sourceWeb = _source;

    foreach (SPList theList in sourceWeb.Lists)
    {
        if (theList is SPDocumentLibrary)
        {
            docLibs.Add(theList as SPDocumentLibrary);
            docLibList.Items.Add(theList.Title);
        }
    }
```

LISTING 8.2   Continued

```
}

private void selectButton_Click(object sender, EventArgs e)
{
    this.Close();
}

public SPDocumentLibrary SelectedLibrary
{
    get
    {
        return docLibs[docLibList.SelectedIndex];
    }
}
}
}
```

Figure 8.1 shows this application in action.

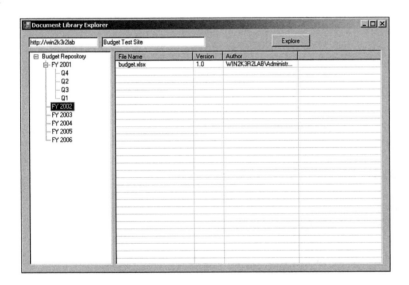

FIGURE 8.1   Document Library Explorer application.

The sample Document Library Explorer application shows how you can navigate folder hierarchies within document libraries, tell the difference between regular lists and document libraries, and how to get a listing of files belonging to a given folder.

Working with Versioning

Versioning only applied to document libraries in previous versions of SharePoint. In the new version, any list item anywhere within SharePoint can be versioned. Not only do all items now have versioning support, they all have support for both major and minor version numbers—another new addition with MOSS 2007.

One of the most common reasons behind a company's need for a document management solution is the need for document revision control. Using traditional source code control systems to manage document revisions often fails miserably when applied to regular documents. SharePoint is optimized for document revision control.

Checking Files Out

There are two overloads to the CheckOut() method on the SPFile class:

▶ CheckOut()—This is the default method for checking files out. It simply changes the file's status to checked out. Note that if you want to check a file out, you need to have a valid security context. This means that the security context under which the CheckOut() method executes is also the user who will show up in the file's CheckedOutBy property.

▶ CheckOut(Boolean, string)—The Boolean indicates whether the file should be checked out locally, and the string parameter is a UTC-formatted date/time stamp indicating the time and date the item was last modified.

Checking Files In

Checking files in to SharePoint is just as easy as checking them out. You can check files in with the following two overloads of the CheckIn() method:

▶ CheckIn(string)—This method checks a file in to SharePoint with the specified comment. Even though check-in comments are optional within the SharePoint UI, you must still include a comment with this method call.

▶ CheckIn(string, SPCheckinType)—This method checks a file in to SharePoint with the specified comment and indicates the type of check-in. By default, check-ins are minor revision check-ins, but you can override that with the SPCheckinType enumeration: MajorCheckIn, MinorCheckIn, or OverwriteCheckIn. Make sure you use the last option only when you're sure that's what you need because it will overwrite the current version in SharePoint.

The code in Listing 8.3 illustrates how to locate a file, check it out, make changes, and then check the file back in to SharePoint.

LISTING 8.3   Versioning Demonstration Code

```
using System;
using System.Collections.Generic;
using System.Text;
using Microsoft.SharePoint;

namespace VersioningExample
{
class Program
{
static void Main(string[] args)
{
    SPSite site = new SPSite("http://win2k3r2lab");
    SPWeb web = site.AllWebs["Budget Test Site"];

    SPList docLib = web.Lists["Budget Repository"];


    SPFolder folder = docLib.RootFolder;
    SPFile theFile =
        folder.Files["Budget Repository/sample text file.txt"];
    Console.WriteLine("About to make changes to {0}", theFile.Name);

    // once we have the file reference, check it out, make changes
    // and check it back in.

    theFile.CheckOut();
    theFile.SaveBinary(
        ASCIIEncoding.Default.GetBytes(
        "This file has been modified programmatically."));
    theFile.Update();
    theFile.CheckIn("File was modified programmatically.");

    Console.ReadLine();


}
}
}
```

Although it might make sense that the root folder of a document library would be located in the first element of the Folders property of the document library, that isn't the case. Remember that the Folders property contains all folders belonging to the document library regardless of their hierarchy level. As such, you need to use the RootFolder property of the document library to get the SPFolder instance that corresponds to the document library's root folder.

Figure 8.2 shows the version history for the sample text file modified in Listing 8.3 after executing the application a few times.

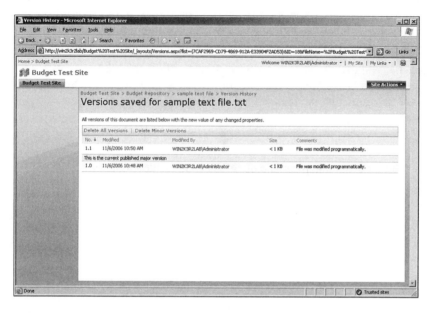

FIGURE 8.2   Version history for sample text file.

Figure 8.3 shows the contents of the latest version of the file—the string that was passed as a parameter to the SaveBinary() method of the SPFile object.

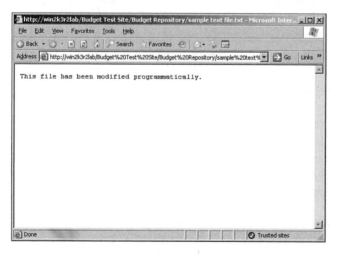

FIGURE 8.3   Contents of a programmatically modified file in a document library.

Manipulating Folders and Files

SharePoint allows virtually any list to have folders and subfolders and you can even create content types for folders within lists. Despite the ubiquity of folders in SharePoint lists, the most common use for folders is to organize files within document and picture libraries (a picture library is a specialized form of a document library).

A small sample of what you can do with folders and files was illustrated in Listing 8.3. Tables 8.3 and 8.4 provide a good reference list of some of the more commonly used methods on the SPFolder and SPFile classes.

TABLE 8.3   Common SPFolder Methods

Method	Description
CopyTo	Copies the folder and all of its contents into the new folder at a given URL
Delete	Deletes the folder
MoveTo	Moves the folder (and all contents) to a new folder at the given URL
Recycle	Moves the folder to SharePoint's Recycle Bin
Update	Commits changes made to the folder

TABLE 8.4   Common SPFile Methods

Method	Description
Approve	Approves a file that has been submitted for content approval
CheckIn	Checks the file in
CheckOut	Checks the file out
Convert	Transforms the file
CopyTo	Copies the file to the given URL
Delete	Deletes the file
Deny	Denies a file submitted for content approval
GetConversionState	Indicates the transform state of the file
GetConvertedFile	Gets the file created by transformation
MoveTo	Moves the file to the given location
OpenBinary	Returns an array of bytes representing the actual file
OpenBinaryStream	Returns a stream that points to the raw file bytes
Publish	Submits the file for content approval
Recycle	Sends the file to the SharePoint Recycle Bin
SaveBinary	Saves the contents of a byte array into SharePoint's storage for the file
TakeOffline	Takes the most current approved file offline
UndoCheckOut	Cancels pending changes made since the last checkout and sets the file back to its prior (checked-in) state
UnPublish	Removes the file from the content approval queue
Update	Commits changes made to the file

Summary

Document libraries are the foundation of the document management functionality within SharePoint. This chapter covered the basics of document libraries, working with version-controlled documents, modifying documents, and navigating through nested hierarchies of folders within document libraries.

Using the information contained in this chapter, you should be well equipped to perform virtually any task that involves a document library, folder, or file.

CHAPTER 9

Working with Meetings

IN THIS CHAPTER

▶ Managing Meeting Workspace Sites

▶ Accessing Existing Meetings

▶ Managing Meetings

▶ Working with Events

Microsoft Office SharePoint Server (MOSS) provides a powerful foundation that provides for collaboration around the concept of meetings. Meeting Workspaces provide websites dedicated to supporting and maintaining meetings, meeting information, attendee lists, minutes, meeting-related documents, and much more.

Meetings themselves take place within Meeting Workspaces and can either be recurring or stored as single-instance events. As developers themselves, the authors of this book obviously think that the most important aspect of SharePoint meetings is that you can control every aspect of meetings programmatically using the SharePoint object model and web services (web services and meetings are discussed in Chapter 23, "Using the Meeting Workspace Web Service").

Managing Meeting Workspace Sites

A Meeting Workspace is just a special web template that comes with all default SharePoint installations. With that knowledge in hand, you can use your knowledge of manipulating sites and webs (SPSite and SPWeb classes, respectively) to manipulate Meeting Workspaces. The following two sections show how to create and delete Meeting Workspaces.

Creating a Meeting Workspace

As discussed in Chapter 4, "Working with Sites and Webs," you can create a Meeting Workspace by adding a new website to a parent SPWebCollection instance. For example, to add a Meeting Workspace to a site collection, you would add it to the site's AllWebs property. To add a Meeting

Workspace as a subweb beneath another website (SPWeb instance), you just need to add the new workspace to the website's Webs property, which is of type SPWebCollection.

Listing 9.1 shows a simple console application that creates a new Meeting Workspace web.

LISTING 9.1   Creating a New Meeting Workspace

```
using System;
using System.Collections.Generic;
using System.Text;
using Microsoft.SharePoint;

namespace MwsCreate
{
class Program
{
static void Main(string[] args)
{
    SPSite rootSite = new SPSite("http://win2k3r2lab");
    SPWeb budgetWeb = rootSite.AllWebs["Budget Test Site"];
    SPWebTemplateCollection availTemplates =
        budgetWeb.GetAvailableWebTemplates(1033);
    SPWebTemplate mwsTemplate = availTemplates["MPS#0"];

    budgetWeb.Webs.Add(
        "statusMeeting06",
        "Status Meeting",
        "Recurring Meeting to discuss FY 2006 Budget Status",
        1033,
        mwsTemplate,
        false,
        false);
}
}
}
```

You should notice a couple of interesting things about this code. The first is that you must obtain a reference to an SPWebTemplate to create a new website based on that template. Second, the uniform resource locator (URL) of a new website is site-relative, and as such does not use a preceding forward slash.

The preceding sample creates a new Meeting Workspace to manage meetings related to the FY 2006 budget status and makes the new Meeting Workspace a subweb of the budget Team Site, as shown in Figure 9.1.

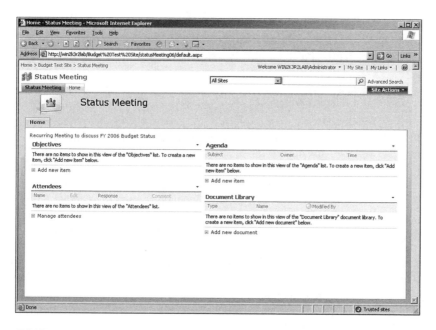

FIGURE 9.1   The new meeting workspace.

If you plan to follow along with the code throughout the rest of the chapter, you should execute the code from Listing 9.1 (modified for your environment, of course) so that you will have a Meeting Workspace with which to experiment for the rest of the chapter.

Deleting a Meeting Workspace

Deleting a Meeting Workspace follows the same pattern as deleting any other instance of the SPWeb class. You can delete a web in two different ways. The first method is to call the Delete method on the SPWeb object itself. The second method is to call Delete on an instance of SPWebCollection and pass in the URL of the web to delete.

Accessing Existing Meetings

It might be extremely tempting to use the SPMeeting class in the Microsoft.SharePoint.Meetings namespace to gain access to the properties of a meeting instance or meeting recurrence, but, unfortunately, that doesn't work. As you will see later in the chapter, the primary use for the SPMeeting class is to provide a shortcut to creating new meeting instances on existing Meeting Workspace sites.

To get at the real data that supports a Meeting Workspace and all meeting instances within that workspace, you need to dig down into the lists on the Meeting Workspace site, some of which are hidden and only directly accessible programmatically.

Table 9.1 provides a description of the lists that are automatically created as a part of every new Meeting Workspace. Some types of Meeting Workspaces come with more information, but Table 9.1 represents the basic set of lists that comes with each Meeting Workspace.

TABLE 9.1   Default Lists in a Meeting Workspace

List	Description
Agenda	List that contains the agenda items for all meetings within the Meeting Workspace. The Instance ID column is used to separate agendas from different instances.
Attendees	List that contains the attendee data for the attendees for meetings in the workspace. The Instance ID column is used to separate attendees from different instances.
Document Library	Document library that is used for document storage for a recurring meeting or individual instances of meetings.
Master Page Gallery	List that contains the Master Page Gallery for the Meeting Workspace site.
Meeting Series	List that contains the data for the meeting instances themselves, as well as recurrence information for a workspace that revolves around a recurring meeting rather than instances of individual meetings.
Objectives	List that stores meeting objectives that is also filtered by meeting instance ID.
Workspace Pages	List that contains Web Part pages for meetings in the workspace.

Meetings themselves, whether individual meetings or recurring meetings, are stored in the Meeting Series list on the Meeting Workspace.

Keep in mind that the Meeting Series list is hidden, and you cannot see it from within SharePoint—even if you are an administrator and click the View All Site Content button on the navigation bar. Table 9.2 provides a detailed list of some of the more commonly used columns in the Meeting Series list.

TABLE 9.2   Useful Columns in the Meeting Series List

Column	Description
Title	The title of the list item representing a meeting instance or recurrence
Modified	The time stamp of the last modification date
InstanceID	The instance ID to which the list item belongs; virtually all data within a Meeting Workspace is filtered by instance ID
Order	A number by which the meeting series can be easily sorted; numbers are auto-assigned in hundreds (for example, 100, 200, 300) to allow room for changes and additions between meetings
GUID	A globally unique identifier (GUID) for the meeting instance
Created	A time stamp indicating when the meeting was created

TABLE 9.2   Continued

Column	Description
UniqueId	A unique ID for the meeting instance, also a GUID; is not the same value as the GUID column
EventType	The type of event
RecurrenceID	The recurrence ID for the meeting instance
EventDate	The date/time the event starts
EndDate	The date/time the event ends
Duration	The duration of the event
Location	The location of the meeting
RecurrenceData	An Extensible Markup Language (XML) fragment indicating the recurrence information for recurring meetings
TimeZone	If specified, the number of the time zone for the meeting time stamps; if no time zone is specified, the server time zone is assumed
fAllDayEvent	A Boolean value indicating whether the meeting is an all-day event
fRecurrence	A Boolean value indicating whether the meeting is a recurring meeting
Organizer	A string (delimited as ID;#Name) indicating the user designated as the meeting organizer
EventUrl	If the meeting is associated with an event on a SharePoint calendar, this indicates the URL of the calendar as well as the name of the calendar in which the meeting resides (for example, "http://server/sites/site/Lists/ Calendar, Project Schedule")

Meetings appear in the Meeting Series list in two different styles. When the meeting isn't recurring, each list item in the list represents a distinct occurrence of the meeting with a unique date and time. When the meeting is recurring, the first item in the list contains information on how often and on what day and time the meeting occurs. As users navigate through the Meeting Workspace and click on new instances, items are created in the list for that particular occurrence. Individual meetings have simple, auto-incremented instance IDs, such as 1, 2, 3, and so on. Recurring meetings have numeric instance IDs that correspond to the date on which the meeting is to occur, such as 20061012 or 20061013.

CAUTION

Obtaining data from recurring meetings can be tricky. You might encounter situations in which your code attempts to access a list item for a meeting occurrence that has not yet been provisioned in the Meeting Series list. To ensure that the individual instance has been created, you can make a dummy web request to the instance's home page, for example:

http://server/sites/mymeeting/default.aspx?InstanceID=20061012

Managing Meetings

Meeting management involves the creation, cancellation, and updating of meetings. Some of these tasks are pretty straightforward and other tasks, such as updating an existing meeting, might not be immediately obvious. This section shows you how to create, update, and cancel meetings.

Creating Meetings

Creating a new meeting involves calling the Add method on the SPMeeting class. Given experience with the SharePoint application programming interface (API), you might be tempted to try to create a new instance of the SPMeeting class with a default constructor. Unfortunately, this doesn't work. To obtain a reference to an SPMeeting object, you need to call the GetMeetingInformation method on an instance of a Meeting Workspace site.

The code in Listing 9.2 illustrates how to obtain a reference to a Meeting Workspace's SPWeb instance and how to use that reference to get an SPMeeting object, which can then be used to create a new meeting.

LISTING 9.2   Creating a New Meeting Instance Within a Meeting Workspace

```
using System;
using System.Collections.Generic;
using System.Text;
using Microsoft.SharePoint;
using Microsoft.SharePoint.Utilities;
using Microsoft.SharePoint.Meetings;

namespace MeetingCreate
{
class Program
{
static void Main(string[] args)
{
    SPSite rootSite = new SPSite("http://win2k3r2lab");
    SPWeb budgetWeb = rootSite.AllWebs["Budget Test Site"];
    SPWeb mwsWeb = budgetWeb.Webs["statusmeeting06"];
    short meetingCount = 0;

    SPMeeting meeting = SPMeeting.GetMeetingInformation(mwsWeb);

    Console.WriteLine("Meeting count is {0} for instance {1}",
        meeting.MeetingCount, meeting.InstanceId);

    meeting.Add(
        "alothien@gmail.com",
        Guid.NewGuid().ToString(),
```

LISTING 9.2   Continued

```
        1,
        "20061108T110100Z",
        "Status Check Meeting",
        "Conference Room Alpha",
        "20061109T180000Z",
        "20061109T190000Z",
        false, out meetingCount);

    Console.WriteLine("Meeting created.");
    Console.ReadLine();
}
}
}
```

The Add method can either take the text version of an iCalendar format file, or it can take the individual arguments, as shown in Listing 9.2. The version illustrated takes the following arguments:

- ▶ organizer—The email address of the person organizing the meeting. If this email address does not match the email of the security context of the user making the method call, that user must be a valid scheduling delegate or SharePoint will throw an exception.

- ▶ uid—A unique ID (GUID) string to be used for the new meeting.

- ▶ sequence—A numeric sequence number used for ordering multiple updates.

- ▶ dateStamp—A specially formatted string indicating the time stamp for when the meeting was created.

- ▶ title—The title of the meeting.

- ▶ location—The location of the meeting.

- ▶ dateStart—The time stamp for when the meeting starts.

- ▶ dateEnd—The time stamp for when the meeting ends.

- ▶ nonGregorian—A Boolean value indicating whether the meeting time stamps are in a non-Gregorian calendar.

- ▶ [out] nMeetingCount—The meeting count for the workspace.

When looking at the code in Listing 9.2, take note of the format of the parameters for the meeting's start and end time. First, the times are in the Greenwich mean time (GMT) time zone, and they use a format where the date comes first in the format *YYYYMMDD*, followed by a *T*, followed by the time in the format *HHMMDD*, followed by a *Z*. If you do not use this time stamp format, SharePoint will throw an exception and reject the attempt to create the new meeting.

For more complex meeting occurrences such as recurring meetings, you might find it easier to supply the iCalendar format text instead of discrete parameters, as shown in Listing 9.2.

Modifying Meetings

Modifying an instance of a meeting can be done in a number of ways. You could always try the brute force method and modify the Meeting Series list itself. However, you can use the SPMeeting.Update method to make changes to a meeting.

The following is a list of parameters to the SPMeeting.Update method:

- ▶ uid—This is the persistent GUID for the calendar entry

- ▶ sequence—A sequence number used for organizing multiple updates

- ▶ dateStamp—A time stamp indicating the date and time that the change was made

- ▶ title—The title (or subject) of the meeting

- ▶ location—The location of the meeting

- ▶ dateStart—The date/time the meeting starts

- ▶ dateEnd—The date/time the meeting ends

- ▶ nonGregorian—A Boolean value indicating whether the time stamps are in a non-Gregorian calendar

After a meeting has been created using the Add method, you can use the GUID for the meeting to make changes to the start time, end time, meeting location, and subject.

Deleting Meetings

Deleting a meeting is accomplished using the Cancel method on the SPMeeting class. Meetings are canceled on a per-recurrence basis, so you will need to know the instance ID you are canceling. For recurring meetings, the instance ID is a number that represents the date of the meeting such as 20061115 for a meeting that occurs on November 15, 2006. For individual meetings, the instance ID is simply a sequential number starting with 1. The Cancel method has the following arguments:

- ▶ uid—The GUID of the meeting

- ▶ recurrenceID—The recurrence ID of the meeting to be canceled

- ▶ sequence—A number used for sequencing multiple updates

- ▶ dateStamp—A date stamp used for when the deletion occurred

- ▶ cancelMeeting—A Boolean value indicating whether the meeting should be deleted

Even if the meeting is associated with a calendar event, and you remove the calendar event, the meeting instance will still exist on the Meeting Workspace site.

Handling Attendee Responses

As with most other meeting-related data, you can either access the lists directly (which some people find far easier than using the SPMeeting class) or you can utilize the appropriate methods on the SPMeeting class. The preferred method is to use the SetAttendeeResponse method on the SPMeeting class. This method takes the following arguments:

- ▶ attendeeId—The email address of the attendee in question

- ▶ uid—The persistent GUID for the calendar component

- ▶ recurrenceId—The recurrence ID for the meeting

- ▶ sequence—A number used to arrange multiple updates

- ▶ dateStamp—The date and time stamp for the modification of the calendar component

- ▶ response—The response from the user (Accepted, Tentative, or Declined)

Working with Events

You might have noticed that calendar events can be linked directly with instances of a meeting within a Meeting Workspace site. This can be accomplished by calling the LinkWithEvent method on the SPMeeting class. To make this method call, you need to have an instance of the SPWeb class representing the website containing the calendar, and you need an SPWeb instance representing the Meeting Workspace site to get a reference to the SPMeeting class via the GetMeetingInformation method.

The LinkWithEvent method takes the following arguments:

- ▶ eventWeb—The SPWeb instance of the website containing the calendar that will have an item linked to the meeting

- ▶ strEventListId—The list ID of the calendar list within the event web

- ▶ eventItemId—The item ID that will be linked to the meeting

- ▶ strEventWorkspaceLinkField—The field on the Meeting Workspace site with which the event will be linked

- ▶ strEventWorkspaceLinkURLField—The URL of the field on the Meeting Workspace site with which the event will be associated

After calling this method, you will see a link from the calendar item to the Meeting Workspace. In addition, there will be a Back to Calendar (or whatever the list name is called) link in the header display for the Meeting Workspace.

Summary

Meetings and Meeting Workspaces are a powerful feature of SharePoint and can add a tremendous amount of productivity to any enterprise or custom application. This chapter covered how to use the object model to access and manipulate Meeting Workspaces and meetings. After having read this chapter, you should feel comfortable using the meeting and Meeting Workspace components of SharePoint within your custom applications and within SharePoint itself.

PART II

Enterprise Content Management

IN THIS PART

CHAPTER 10 Integrating Business Data   109

CHAPTER 11 Creating Business Data
            Applications   121

CHAPTER 12 Working with User Profiles   135

CHAPTER 13 Building Workflows   147

Integrating Business Data

IN THIS CHAPTER

▶ Introduction to the Business Data Catalog

▶ Configuring a New Business Data Application

▶ Using the Business Data Web Parts

▶ Searching for Business Data Entities

▶ Using Entity Actions

▶ Using Business Data Columns in Custom Lists

The Business Data Catalog (BDC) is arguably one of the most powerful new features available in Microsoft Office SharePoint Server (MOSS) 2007. This chapter provides details on how to consume data provided by a BDC application, including entities, associations, custom column lookups, searching, browsing, and much more. After you have a firm grasp on what the BDC is and how to consume BDC data, you can move on to Chapter 11, "Creating Business Data Applications," which provides details on how to create your own BDC applications and expose your data to SharePoint via the BDC.

Introduction to the Business Data Catalog

SharePoint is often perceived as a point of integration or aggregation. This is the main reason why SharePoint Portal Server 2003 was used so much—it facilitated the publication of content and made it easy to gather multiple sites to create a cohesive portal.

As more and more consultants and developers began working with SharePoint, it became obvious that integrating content and data from non-SharePoint sources required tedious coding, testing, and deployment efforts often resulting in custom Web Part development or even in circumventing entire sections of SharePoint entirely.

The BDC provides a means by which developers and administrators can connect SharePoint to external data sources. Those external data sources can be integrated so tightly that entities from external Line of Business (LOB) applications can appear in search results, on user profiles, in Web Parts, and even as custom columns in lists.

The BDC is driven by several core types of information:

▶ **Entities**—An entity is a unit of data. This is typically a single row in a database table or a single element of information, such as a customer, a bug in a defect tracking system, an order, and so forth.

▶ **ID enumerators**—For SharePoint to use the BDC to properly index remote entities such as customers or orders, it needs to be able to enumerate the unique IDs of each entity. BDC application definitions provide definitions for ID enumerators.

▶ **Methods**—A method on a BDC entity is responsible for retrieving entity lists or retrieving related entities. These methods can be used to provide the user with the ability to filter the display and choose which columns are returned for each operation.

▶ **Associations**—Associations provide links between entities. These links can be one-to-many or many-to-many and go in either direction, giving the developer a lot of flexibility. These associations are used to go from one record (such as a Customer) to one or more related records (such as purchase history or a list of relatives).

The BDC is a shared service, which means it can be provided by any of the servers within a farm and you have to use the Shared Services administration console to configure the BDC. The Shared Services administration console can be reached by going to the SharePoint Central Administration website and clicking on the link for your Shared Services instance (often called SharedServices1 by default).

Authentication

Most external LOB applications require authentication to gain access to the data. Quite frankly, if they don't require authenticated access to their data, those applications might have other problems that SharePoint will never be able to solve.

The BDC supports multiple forms of authentication:

▶ Passthrough—The authentication mode quite literally passes credentials through from the front end (SharePoint) to the back end (LOB application identified via the BDC). In other words, authentication is done against whatever process under which the BDC is running.

▶ RevertToSelf—This authentication mode "reverts" whatever impersonation might be done by Internet Information Services (IIS) and authenticates against the BDC application using the identity of the IIS application pool itself.

▶ Single Sign-On (SSO)—This authentication mode uses the SSO subsystem for authentication to the BDC application.

▶ RdbCredentials—This authentication mode uses database credentials pulled from the SSO service to supply clear-text database credentials. In this case, make sure you're using Secure Sockets Layer (SSL) or some other means of obscuring the otherwise clear-text credentials.

▶ `WindowsCredentials`—This authentication mode uses manually supplied Windows credentials to authenticate against the BDC application.

BDC Pros and Cons

As a developer, you are often asked to make recommendations on systems as well as to develop against them. As such, you should know some of the things that the BDC does extremely well and some of the situations in which the BDC might not be a viable option for your solution.

The following are some of the benefits of the BDC:

▶ Integrate existing LOB applications with relative ease.

▶ Extend SharePoint's reach to aggregate and integrate multiple disparate systems throughout your enterprise into a single cohesive location.

▶ Allow external data to be searched and indexed in a meaningful way.

▶ Wherever external entities appear, you can define custom actions that might take you to the entity's host application (for example, launch your Defect Tracking system when looking at a bug within SharePoint).

▶ Data is read-only; SharePoint adopts the "one and only one data owner" approach and leaves the work of editing remote entities up to their native host application.

The following are some of the drawbacks of the BDC:

▶ **Authentication**—Although SharePoint provides multiple means of authentication, the most common LOB application authentication method is not supported. If the user credentials themselves are stored within the remote database or web service, SharePoint has no way of validating those credentials. This makes it *extremely* difficult to access large application data sets like those contained within third-party applications like SAP from within SharePoint.

▶ **Configuration**—As you will see in the next section of the chapter, configuration of the BDC is done entirely through very large, difficult-to-manipulate Extensible Markup Language (XML) files and there are currently no tools available to make this process any easier.

▶ **Data is read-only**—Although some people consider this a positive aspect, other developers might consider it a negative.

Configuring a New Business Data Application

Configuring a new BDC application involves creating an XML metadata file for the application and then uploading it to the SharePoint BDC application manager.

The schema for this BDC metadata file is somewhat complicated and hand-creating these XML files on your own is time consuming and error prone. Given the fact that there are currently no tools available for manipulating the BDC application definition XML files, your next best bet is to take the XML files from sample applications and modify them to suit your needs. The following XML snippet shows the first few elements and the last element of a BDC application definition file:

```
<?xml version="1.0" encoding="utf-8" standalone="yes" ?>
<LobSystem
    xmlns:xsi="http://www.w3.org/2001/XMLSchema-instance"
    xsi:schemaLocation="http://schemas.microsoft.com/office/2006/
➥03/BusinessDataCatalog BDCMetadata.xsd"
 Type="Database"
 Version="1.0.0.0"
 Name="BugSystem"
   xmlns="http://schemas.microsoft.com/office/2006/03/BusinessDataCatalog">
    <Properties>
     <Property Name="WildcardCharacter" Type="System.String">%</Property>
   </Properties>
   <LobSystemInstances>
     <LobSystemInstance Name="BugSystemInstance">
       <Properties>
         <Property Name="AuthenticationMode" Type="System.String"
➥>PassThrough</Property>
         <Property Name="DatabaseAccessProvider" Type="System.String"
➥>SqlServer</Property>
         <Property Name="RdbConnection Data Source"
➥Type="System.String">win2k3r2lab\officeservers</Property>
         <Property Name="RdbConnection Initial Catalog"
➥Type="System.String">CustomerData</Property>
         <Property Name="RdbConnection Integrated Security"
➥Type="System.String">SSPI</Property>
         <Property Name="RdbConnection Pooling"
➥Type="System.String">false</Property>
       </Properties>
     </LobSystemInstance>   </LobSystemInstances>
 ...
 ...
</LobSystem>
```

The business data application represented by the preceding configuration XML is a relational database application residing on the local SQL Server instance officeservers (the default instance name for the standalone installation of SharePoint) and uses the database named CustomerData and authenticates via Passthrough authentication. The details of the entity definitions, method instances, and associations were left out to keep the file readable within the context of this chapter. You can also tell from the XML file that the name of the business data application is BugSystem. Presumably it will have definitions for entities that deal with defect tracking.

Before continuing through the rest of the chapter, you should download and install the "AdventureWorks Cycles Database 2000" SQL 2000 database. This database is used as the basis for many of the figures in this chapter as well as much of the code written in the following chapter. You can download the AdventureWorks SQL database sample at the following uniform resource locator (URL):

http://go.microsoft.com/fwlink/?linkid=55253

A version of the AdventureWorks BDC XML application definition file is available with the code downloads for this book that defines a connection to the .mdf disk file under the officeservers local SQL instance (the default if you installed on a standalone server). If you are downloading the XML file on your own, make sure you edit the XML file with notepad and change the server name to the one appropriate for your environment.

To install the configuration for a new business data application, go to the SharePoint 3.0 Central Administration website and then go to the Shared Services administration console. Under the BDC heading, click Import Application Definition. You will be prompted to browse for an XML file; select the XML file that corresponds to the AdventureWorks 2000 sample application.

It could take a while to finish the application import process. When complete, you will be able to examine the list of entities and entity relationships. Figure 10.1 shows the overview of a newly configured application definition (the BugSystem application).

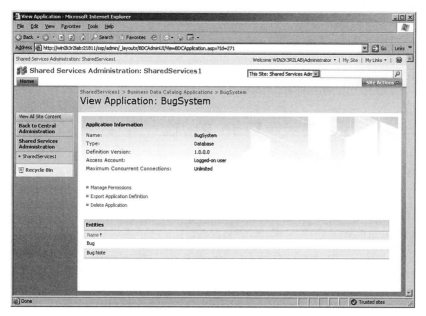

FIGURE 10.1   Overview of a newly configured business data application.

Figure 10.2 shows the entity profile home page for a business data application entity. In this case, it is the Bug entity. You can see that the Bug entity has the following properties: Created, CreatedBy, Description, ID, and Status. You can also see the relationship that links individual bugs with one-to-many bug notes. There is even an action definition (covered later in the chapter) called Search on Live.

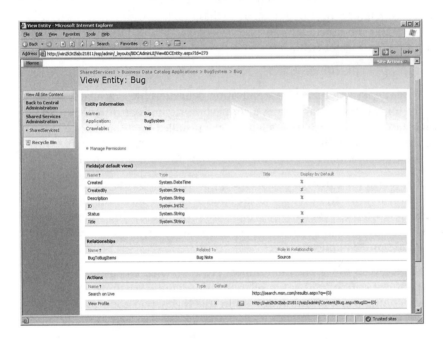

FIGURE 10.2   Viewing an entity profile.

After you have uploaded an application definition file that was provided to you by a third-party vendor or that you manually created yourself, you can start consuming business data contained within the remote application.

Using the Business Data Web Parts

Business Data Web Parts allow you to render the data contained within LOB applications defined and accessed by the BDC. The following is a list of the Web Parts that SharePoint provides for rendering and querying line of business data:

▶ **Business Data Item**—Renders a single business data entity

▶ **Business Data Item List**—Displays a list of business data entities

▶ **Business Data Actions**—Displays a list of actions that pertain to a business data item indicated by a row supplied by a connected Web Part

> ▶ **Business Data Item Builder**—Creates an item from parameters in the query string and provides it to other Web Parts on the page via Web Part connections

> ▶ **Business Data Related List**—Displays a list of entities related to an entity supplied by a connected Web Part

Using the BDC Web Parts is actually quite easy. Simply open up a page for editing and click the Add Web Part link at the top of a Web Part zone. From there, select one of the BDC Web Parts and add it to the page.

Figure 10.3 shows the Business Data List Web Part. It was associated with entities of type Bug. You can browse for an entity type easily using a browser window, which displays all of the entity types for all installed business data applications.

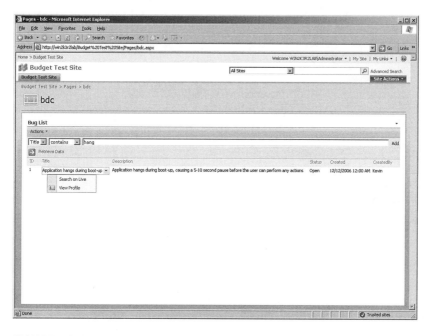

FIGURE 10.3   The Business Data List Web Part.

When the Business Data List Web Part appears on a Web Part page, it doesn't immediately render data. When you define the configuration XML, you can optionally define a set of filters. These filters provide queries and parameters that filter the entity data when the user clicks the Retrieve Data link.

10

The Business Data List Web Part is also a connectable Web Part. It exposes the currently selected row as an entity that can be supplied to other connected Web Parts on the same page. This means that when the user selects an entity from a Business Data List, child rows or related rows can be displayed in a Business Related Data List Web Part.

Figure 10.4 shows the context menus that allow you to connect a Business Data List and a Related Business Data List Web Part together using the ASP.NET 2.0 connected Web Part mechanism.

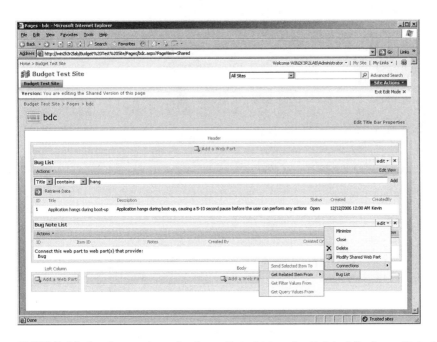

FIGURE 10.4   Connecting a Business Data List and a Related Business Data List.

After the Web Parts are connected and you click one of the records in the Business Data List, the Related Business Data List will automatically update itself to retrieve records related to the one provided by the source list. This can be done to traverse one-to-many relationships as well as many-to-many relationships.

Figure 10.5 shows an example of these connected Web Parts using the data from the AdventureWorks 2000 sample SQL database.

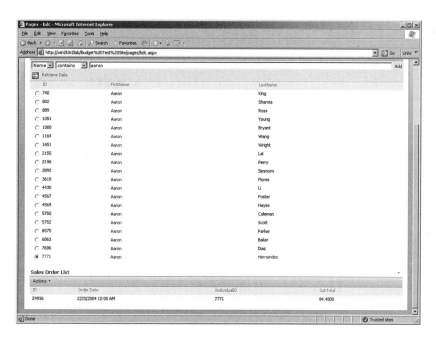

FIGURE 10.5   Connected Business Data Web Parts (AdventureWorks 2000 sample).

Searching for Business Data Entities

Business data application definitions provide for method types referred to as `Wildcard` methods. These methods are invoked by SharePoint when searches are performed against the system. When these searches are performed, SharePoint returns applicable business data entities mixed with native SharePoint data. This provides a unified search experience that allows entities from external databases to appear as though they were native SharePoint entities.

The SharePoint Software Development Kit (SDK) provides full documentation on the metadata schema required to define wildcard operations. Wildcard operations can be performed against both relational database applications and web service applications.

Using Entity Actions

Entity actions allow developers to define URLs that can be launched from a drop-down menu of actions related to a particular entity. Information from the entity itself (such as an ID) can be passed on that URL. One example of when this might be useful is if you have an existing defect tracking system and you are looking at a bug entity. You might want an action on that entity to take you to the host defect tracking web application to allow the user to make changes to the data.

Figure 10.3 shown earlier in this chapter contains an action with the text "Search on Live." This action redirects the current browser window to Windows Live Search, using the title of the entity as the search query string.

As long as the action you want to allow users to take can be expressed as a URL composed of data from the entity itself, you can create any action that does virtually anything—providing an incredible amount of flexibility and room for enhancement.

Using Business Data Columns in Custom Lists

In addition to just being able to render lists of business data entities and related entities, SharePoint allows you to do special business data lookups as columns within custom lists.

Assume you have your own internal customer management system and the standard SharePoint contact lists are insufficient. You might have data where you need to know the customer that is related to a single item in a list. In this situation, you could create a custom column that stores a reference to an individual customer. Anywhere a row in this list appears, you can also have a live link to the individual customer entity.

Figure 10.6 shows an example of how to create a column in a custom list that stores a reference to a Customer entity from the AdventureWorks sample database.

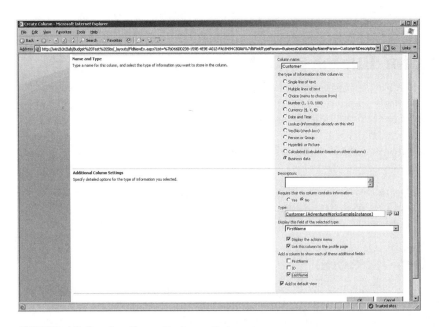

FIGURE 10.6   Creating a Business Data column.

Figure 10.7 shows what it looks like when a row in the custom list is displayed and the Business Data column is included in the view. Note how the customer is clickable and there is even a drop-down menu next to the customer that contains entity actions defined by the BDC application definition.

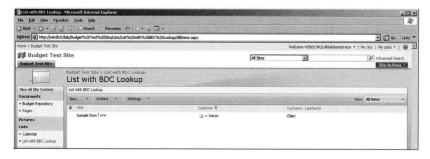

FIGURE 10.7   A Business Data column in action.

Summary

This chapter provided a walk-through of the basics of consuming and integrating LOB applications using the BDC. This is accomplished using a Business Data configuration file. You can find the one used for the AdventureWorks 2000 database in the file advworks_ bdc.xml with the code downloads for this chapter. Using BDC Web Parts, custom BDC columns, and wildcard searching and indexing, you can create powerful extension and integration points within SharePoint to extend SharePoint's reach and even extend the reach of the data contained within your external application. The next chapter focuses on the information you need to create applications that can be consumed by the BDC and how to use the BDC application programming interfaces (API).

CHAPTER 11

Creating Business Data Applications

IN THIS CHAPTER

▶ Using the Business Data Catalog Administration API

▶ Using the Business Data Catalog Runtime API

▶ Creating BDC-friendly Applications

Developing applications that expose themselves to the Business Data Catalog (BDC) as well as applications that can directly affect the BDC can be a large portion of a developer's tasks on the new version of SharePoint. This chapter provides an overview of creating, editing, and querying BDC application data using the BDC administration object model and querying BDC applications and viewing BDC application data using the BDC runtime object model. Finally, this chapter provides information on some of the things you can do within your own code to make your applications more BDC-friendly.

Using the Business Data Catalog Administration API

Chapter 10, "Integrating Business Data," mentioned that the Extensible Markup Language (XML) format for defining a BDC application was difficult and unwieldy. It also mentioned that there was a lack of tool support for defining BDC applications or for editing the XML file.

The XML file is actually just a shortcut. When you upload the XML file to SharePoint, SharePoint actually makes use of the BDC administration application programming interface (API) to configure the Business Data object model.

Using the BDC administration object model, you can create new Line of Business (LOB) system instances, entities, associations, and methods. You can also query existing metadata contained within the BDC, but those operations are slower using the administration object model than using the runtime object model, which is specialized for fast read-only access.

Developers perform three main tasks using the BDC administration object model:

▶ Creating a LOB system, entity, and method

▶ Creating access control lists (ACLs) for metadata objects

▶ Importing metadata into the BDC

You saw how to import metadata into the BDC using XML files and the SharePoint web-based graphical user interface (GUI) on the Shared Services website in Chapter 10. The sample contained in Listing 11.1 illustrates how to create a complete LOB system and entity. It uses the `Create` method of the `LobSystems` collection to create the LOB system and then creates a LOB system instance from that system.

LISTING 11.1   Creating a LOB System and Entity Using the Administration Object Model

```
using System;
using System.Collections.Generic;
using System.Text;
using Microsoft.SharePoint.Administration;
using Microsoft.Office.Server.ApplicationRegistry.Administration;
using Microsoft.Office.Server.Administration;
using Microsoft.Office.Server.ApplicationRegistry.Infrastructure;
using System.IO;
using System.Xml;

namespace BDCAdmin
{
class Program
{
static void Main(string[] args)
{
    SqlSessionProvider.Instance().SetSharedResourceProviderToUse
➥("SharedServices1");
    LobSystem system =
        ApplicationRegistry.Instance.LobSystems.Create(
          "BugSystemFromCode", true,
          "Microsoft.Office.Server.ApplicationRegistry.SystemSpecific.
➥Db.DbSystemUtility",
          "Microsoft.Office.Server.ApplicationRegistry.SystemSpecific.
➥Db.DbConnectionManager",
          "Microsoft.Office.Server.ApplicationRegistry.SystemSpecific.
➥Db.DbEntityInstance");
```

LISTING 11.1   Continued

```
    LobSystemInstance sysInstance =
        system.LobSystemInstances.Create("BugSystemFromCode", true);

    sysInstance.Properties.Add("AuthenticationMode",
        (Int32)Microsoft.Office.Server.ApplicationRegistry.SystemSpecific.
➥Db.DbAuthenticationMode.PassThrough);

    sysInstance.Properties.Add("DatabaseAccessProvider",
        (Int32)Microsoft.Office.Server.ApplicationRegistry.SystemSpecific.
➥Db.DbAccessProvider.SqlServer);

    sysInstance.Properties.Add("RdbConnection Data Source",
➥@"win2k3r2lab\officeservers");
    sysInstance.Properties.Add("RdbConnection Initial Catalog", "CustomerData");
    sysInstance.Properties.Add("RdbConnection Integrated Security", "SSPI");
    sysInstance.Properties.Add("RdbConnection Pooling", "false");

    sysInstance.Properties.Add("WildCardCharacter", "%");
    sysInstance.Update();

    Entity bugEntity = system.Entities.Create("Bug", true, 10000);
    bugEntity.Properties.Add("Title", "Title"); // title property in list is
➥title column in DB
    bugEntity.Identifiers.Create("BugID", true, "System.Int32");
    bugEntity.Update();

    Console.WriteLine("BugEntity created.");
    Console.ReadLine();
}
}
}
```

In addition to creating an entity, each entity can have methods for index retrieval that return a list of identifiers and methods for wildcard searching and browsing by title, and so on. The combination of entities, methods, and associations allows for data contained in an external source to be indexed, cataloged, and rendered within SharePoint. Figure 11.1 shows the contents of the BDC after programmatically creating a new LOB system, LOB system instance, and entity.

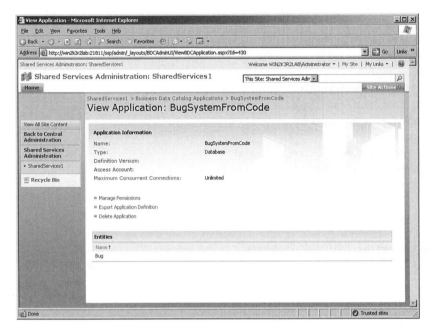

FIGURE 11.1   Entity information after creation.

Using the Business Data Catalog Runtime API

The BDC runtime API is another section of the object model that allows you to examine the contents of BDC application metadata as well as execute methods, locate entities, and much more. The metadata access is quicker than using the administration model because the metadata in the runtime version of the object model is read-only.

Using the BDC runtime API, you can accomplish anything that the BDC Web Parts can do. The following is a list of the most common coding scenarios for the BDC runtime API:

- ▶ Querying for a LOB system and entities
- ▶ Using a wildcard Finder
- ▶ Using a specific Finder
- ▶ Entity enumeration using Finders
- ▶ Direct method execution against entities

Querying Metadata

The first example, shown in Listing 11.2, illustrates using the key namespace in the BDC, `Microsoft.Office.Server.ApplicationRegistry`, to query the metadata for a LOB system application and its entities.

LISTING 11.2   Querying BDC Metadata Using the Runtime Object Model

```csharp
using System;
using System.Collections.Generic;
using System.Text;
using Microsoft.Office.Server.ApplicationRegistry.MetadataModel;
using Microsoft.Office.Server.ApplicationRegistry.Runtime;
using Microsoft.Office.Server.ApplicationRegistry.SystemSpecific;
using Microsoft.Office.Server.ApplicationRegistry.Infrastructure;
using Microsoft.SharePoint.Administration;
using Microsoft.Office.Server.Administration;
using System.Data;

namespace GetMetadata
{
class Program
{
static void Main(string[] args)
{
    SqlSessionProvider.Instance().SetSharedResourceProviderToUse(
      "SharedServices1");
    NamedLobSystemInstanceDictionary sysInstances =
       ApplicationRegistry.GetLobSystemInstances();
    Console.WriteLine("Installed LOB System Instances:");
    foreach (string name in sysInstances.Keys)
    {
        Console.WriteLine("\t" + name);
    }

    LobSystemInstance advWorksInstance =
       sysInstances["AdventureWorksSampleInstance"];
    LobSystem advWorksSystem = advWorksInstance.GetLobSystem();
    Console.WriteLine("\n" + advWorksSystem.ConnectionManagerType.ToString());
    Console.WriteLine(advWorksSystem.Name.ToString());
    Console.WriteLine(advWorksSystem.Id.ToString());

    NamedEntityDictionary entities = advWorksInstance.GetEntities();
    foreach (string key in entities.Keys)
    {
        Entity entity = entities[key];
        Console.WriteLine("Entity {0}, ID {1}", key, entity.Id);
    }
    Console.ReadLine();
}
}
}
```

The most important piece of working with any part of the BDC API is remembering to point your code at the right Shared Services provider. The BDC is a service provided to farms by an SSP (Shared Services Provider), and as such, any time you access the BDC, you need to indicate the SSP name, as follows:

```
SqlSessionProvider.Instance().SetSharedResourceProviderToUse(
    "SharedServices1");
```

Before you can enumerate entities or examine the metadata, you need to get a reference to the LobSystemInstance representing the registered BDC application. In the preceding code, the list of entities belonging to a given system instance is retrieved with the GetEntities method.

The output of the application contained in Listing 11.2 will look something similar to the following text (assuming you have the AdventureWorks sample installed):

```
Installed LOB System Instances:
        BugSystemInstance
        AdventureWorksSampleInstance
        BugSystemFromCode

Microsoft.Office.Server.ApplicationRegistry.SystemSpecific.Db.DbConnectionManager
AdventureWorksSample
339
Entity Product, ID 341
Entity SalesOrder, ID 372
Entity Customer, ID 392
```

After you have access to the metadata that constitutes the BDC application, the next thing you might want to do is gain access to the data itself. Although you can certainly use the BDC Web Parts for visual access to the data, there will probably be many times where you want to work with the BDC data directly. Using the BDC API to access remote data provides you with a datasource-agnostic means of accessing remote LOB systems and their data.

Using a Specific Finder

One of the ways in which the BDC allows you to access data is through the use of what is called a specific Finder. A specific Finder is an abstraction around the act of locating a single entity through the use of its unique identifier.

The code in Listing 11.3 shows how to make use of a specific Finder to locate an individual entity within an LOB system instance, but to gain access to its properties, data, and even associated entities.

LISTING 11.3   Locating an Entity and Associated Entities

```
using System;
using System.Collections.Generic;
using System.Text;
using Microsoft.Office.Server.ApplicationRegistry.MetadataModel;
using Microsoft.Office.Server.ApplicationRegistry.Runtime;
using Microsoft.Office.Server.ApplicationRegistry.SystemSpecific;
using Microsoft.Office.Server.ApplicationRegistry.Infrastructure;
using Microsoft.SharePoint.Administration;
using Microsoft.Office.Server.Administration;
using System.Data;

namespace SpecificFinder
{
class Program
{
static void Main(string[] args)
{
    SqlSessionProvider.Instance().SetSharedResourceProviderToUse(
        "SharedServices1");
    NamedLobSystemInstanceDictionary sysInstances =
        ApplicationRegistry.GetLobSystemInstances();
    LobSystemInstance advWorksInstance =
        sysInstances["AdventureWorksSampleInstance"];
    Entity custEntity = advWorksInstance.GetEntities()["Customer"];

    IEntityInstance entityInstance =
        custEntity.FindSpecific(740, advWorksInstance);

    Console.WriteLine("Customer Fields:");
    foreach (Field f in custEntity.GetSpecificFinderView().Fields)
        Console.WriteLine("{0}:{1}", f.Name,entityInstance[f]);

    IEntityInstanceEnumerator orderInstances =
        entityInstance.GetAssociatedInstances(
          custEntity.GetSourceAssociations()["CustomerToSalesOrder"]);

    while (orderInstances.MoveNext())
    {
        foreach (Field f in orderInstances.Current.ViewDefinition.Fields)
        {
            Console.WriteLine("\t{0}:{1}", f.Name, orderInstances.Current[f]);
        }
        Console.WriteLine();
    }
```

LISTING 11.3   Continued

```
    Console.ReadLine();
}
}
}
```

An identifier is defined within the BDC metadata for the AdventureWorks database that allows customer entities to be located by their ID. In the case of the preceding code, the entity with the ID of 746 is located within the AdventureWorks instance. The fields belonging to that entity are then retrieved and sent to the console. Finally, all of the orders associated with customer 746 are retrieved using the GetAssociatedInstances method.

The following text is the output produced by the code in Listing 11.3. Remember that you need to have the AdventureWorks SQL server database and the sample BDC application installed for this to work properly.

```
Customer Fields:
IndividualID:740
FirstName:Aaron
LastName:King
        SalesOrderID:37692
        OrderDate:7/17/2003 12:00:00 AM
        IndividualID:740
        SubTotal:2359.9800
        SalesOrderID:40879
        OrderDate:10/11/2003 12:00:00 AM
        IndividualID:740
        SubTotal:2398.0500
```

Using a Filter Finder

Filter Finders are methods used to retrieve *only the data that is necessary to apply a filter*. Assuming you have an entity that can be filtered either by ID or by Name, you might create a filter Finder that returns just the ID and name of each entity in the system so that a filter could be applied.

The code in Listing 11.4 invokes a filter Finder and displays all of the fields returned for each entity in the system.

LISTING 11.4   Retrieving Entities Using a Filter Finder

```
using System;
using System.Collections.Generic;
using System.Text;
using Microsoft.Office.Server.ApplicationRegistry.MetadataModel;
```

LISTING 11.4   Continued

```csharp
using Microsoft.Office.Server.ApplicationRegistry.Runtime;
using Microsoft.Office.Server.ApplicationRegistry.SystemSpecific;
using Microsoft.Office.Server.ApplicationRegistry.Infrastructure;
using Microsoft.SharePoint.Administration;
using Microsoft.Office.Server.Administration;

namespace ExecuteFinder
{
class Program
{
static void Main(string[] args)
{
    SqlSessionProvider.Instance().SetSharedResourceProviderToUse(
      "SharedServices1");
    NamedLobSystemInstanceDictionary sysInstances =
      ApplicationRegistry.GetLobSystemInstances();
    LobSystemInstance advWorksInstance =
      sysInstances["AdventureWorksSampleInstance"];
    Entity custEntity = advWorksInstance.GetEntities()["Customer"];
    FilterCollection fc = custEntity.GetFinderFilters();
    Console.WriteLine("Customer Filters Available:");
    foreach (FilterBase filter in fc)
    {
        Console.WriteLine("\t" + filter.Name);
    }
    custEntity.FindFiltered(fc, advWorksInstance);
    IEntityInstanceEnumerator custEntityInstanceEnumerator =
        custEntity.FindFiltered(fc, advWorksInstance);
    // runs through the entire DB, providing ID and Name
    // (the two potential fields on which to filter
    while (custEntityInstanceEnumerator.MoveNext())
    {
        IEntityInstance entityInstance =
            custEntityInstanceEnumerator.Current;
        foreach (Field f in custEntity.GetFinderView().Fields)
            Console.Write("{0} ", entityInstance[f]);
        Console.WriteLine("");
    }

    Console.ReadLine();
}
}
}
```

Using a Wildcard Finder

Using filter Finders is extremely useful for obtaining the smallest amount of filterable data available for each entity, but if you want to return a subset of entities that have been filtered based on a wildcard search query, you can use a wildcard Finder, such as the code shown in Listing 11.5.

LISTING 11.5   Using a Wildcard Finder

```
using System;
using System.Collections.Generic;
using System.Text;
using Microsoft.Office.Server.ApplicationRegistry.MetadataModel;
using Microsoft.Office.Server.ApplicationRegistry.Runtime;
using Microsoft.Office.Server.ApplicationRegistry.SystemSpecific;
using Microsoft.Office.Server.ApplicationRegistry.Infrastructure;
using Microsoft.SharePoint.Administration;
using Microsoft.Office.Server.Administration;


namespace WildcardFinder
{
class Program
{
static void Main(string[] args)
{
    SqlSessionProvider.Instance().SetSharedResourceProviderToUse(
      "SharedServices1");
    NamedLobSystemInstanceDictionary sysInstances =
        ApplicationRegistry.GetLobSystemInstances();
    LobSystemInstance advWorksInstance =
        sysInstances["AdventureWorksSampleInstance"];
    Entity custEntity = advWorksInstance.GetEntities()["Customer"];
    FilterCollection fc = custEntity.GetFinderFilters();
    FilterBase nameFilter = fc[1]; // ID is 0, Name is 1

    FilterCollection newfc = new FilterCollection();
    newfc.Add(nameFilter);
    ((WildcardFilter)newfc[0]).Value = "Aaron%";

    IEntityInstanceEnumerator custEntityInstanceEnumerator =
        custEntity.FindFiltered(newfc, advWorksInstance);
    while (custEntityInstanceEnumerator.MoveNext())
    {
        IEntityInstance entityInstance =
          custEntityInstanceEnumerator.Current;
        foreach (Field f in custEntity.GetFinderView().Fields)
            Console.Write("{0} ", entityInstance[f]);
```

LISTING 11.5   Continued

```
        Console.WriteLine("");
    }
    Console.ReadLine();
}
}
}
```

Executing Methods Directly

Each BDC application metadata contains a list of method instances. These methods can be invoked directly through the BDC API, as shown in Listing 11.6.

LISTING 11.6   Direct Method Execution—Finding a Single Entity

```
using System;
using System.Collections.Generic;
using System.Text;
using Microsoft.Office.Server.ApplicationRegistry.MetadataModel;
using Microsoft.Office.Server.ApplicationRegistry.Runtime;
using Microsoft.Office.Server.ApplicationRegistry.SystemSpecific;
using Microsoft.Office.Server.ApplicationRegistry.Infrastructure;
using Microsoft.SharePoint.Administration;
using Microsoft.Office.Server.Administration;

namespace ExecuteMethod
{
class Program
{
static void Main(string[] args)
{
    SqlSessionProvider.Instance().SetSharedResourceProviderToUse(
      "SharedServices1");
    NamedLobSystemInstanceDictionary sysInstances =
      ApplicationRegistry.GetLobSystemInstances();
    LobSystemInstance advWorksInstance =
      sysInstances["AdventureWorksSampleInstance"];
    Entity custEntity = advWorksInstance.GetEntities()["Customer"];
    MethodInstance methodInstance = custEntity.GetFinderMethodInstance();
    Object[] methodArgs =
      methodInstance.GetMethod().
      CreateDefaultParameterInstances(methodInstance);
    methodArgs[0] = 1760;
    methodArgs[1] = 1760;
```

LISTING 11.6   Continued

```
IEntityInstanceEnumerator custEntityInstanceEnumerator =
    (IEntityInstanceEnumerator)
    custEntity.Execute(methodInstance, advWorksInstance,
    ref methodArgs);
while (custEntityInstanceEnumerator.MoveNext())
{
    IEntityInstance entityInstance =
        custEntityInstanceEnumerator.Current;
    foreach (Field f in custEntity.GetFinderView().Fields)
        Console.Write("{0} ", entityInstance[f]);
    Console.WriteLine("");
}
Console.Read();
}
}
}
```

Creating BDC-friendly Applications

Now that you've seen how SharePoint and SharePoint developers consume LOB data using the BDC and its associated APIs, you should be able to start creating applications that will integrate seamlessly with SharePoint and the BDC.

Building BDC-compatible Web Services

Working from the list of actions that you can take with the BDC API, you should now have a fairly clear idea of the kinds of operations that a BDC-friendly web service should support. The following is a list of some of the methods that, when implemented in a web service, will make for a considerably more BDC-friendly service:

▶ A method to retrieve each entity by a single piece of uniquely identifying information. For example, for Adventure Works, you need a method that retrieves a customer by ID, a method that retrieves an order by ID, and so on.

▶ A method for each type of filter you might want to support. If you plan to allow filters by name, by ID, or by any other field, you should provide a web service method for each type of filter.

▶ A method for retrieving entities related to another entity. For example, if you have a relationship between customers and orders, you need to provide a method that retrieves all orders for a given customer. If the relationship is two-way, you need to provide two methods: one for each direction.

Exposing Relational Data to SharePoint

Thankfully, exposing normalized relational data is virtually done for you. Any database that is in third normal form or relatively close will be able to be exposed via an abstraction that involves entities, entity associations, entity properties, identifier columns, filter methods, and Finders. During the process of defining the metadata for a business data application, you might find that all of the queries you need to satisfy the BDC requirements have already been written as stored procedures or defined in code elsewhere.

Summary

The BDC is an extremely powerful new addition to the arsenal of tools available to the SharePoint developer. Knowing how much functionality is available through the use of the runtime and administration APIs can be invaluable in making technology decisions, architecture decisions, and in developing your own custom code. This chapter provided code samples and guidance for interacting with the BDC at the object model level.

CHAPTER 12

Working with User Profiles

IN THIS CHAPTER

▶ Accessing User Profiles with the Object Model

▶ Configuring the User Profile Store with the Object Model

User profiles in Microsoft Office SharePoint Server (MOSS) 2007 not only provide a means by which basic information can be stored about individual users, but user profiles also provide features for community building, social networking, and much more.

This chapter shows you how to create, update, and manipulate user profiles and user profile properties using the object model.

Accessing User Profiles with the Object Model

Accessing user profiles with the object model involves a few simple steps. First, your code must have references to the `Microsoft.SharePoint`, `Microsoft.Office.Server`, and `System.Web` Assemblies. With those references available, you can use the `SPSite` class and the `UserProfileManager` class as entry points into the user profile subsystem within MOSS.

The following sections provide samples of the various ways that you can access user profiles.

Retrieving User Profiles

Retrieving user profiles can be done one of two ways. The first way is done simply by enumerating through the entire list of user profiles stored on a given farm. The second way is by retrieving the profile of an individual user. Note that there are two ways to get a user profile into the system. The first is by manually creating the user profile through SharePoint administrative tools. User profiles are created automatically the first time a user navigates to their My Site. In other words, you cannot guarantee that the system will have a stored user profile even if the account in question is a valid Active Directory account.

Listing 12.1 shows how to enumerate profiles as well as retrieve individual profiles.

LISTING 12.1   Retrieving User Profiles

```csharp
using System;
using System.Collections.Generic;
using System.Text;
using Microsoft.Office.Server;
using Microsoft.Office.Server.Administration;
using Microsoft.Office.Server.UserProfiles;
using Microsoft.SharePoint;
using System.Web;

namespace UserProfilesApp
{
class Program
{
static void Main(string[] args)
{

using (SPSite site = new SPSite("http://win2k3r2lab"))
{
    ServerContext context =
        ServerContext.GetContext(site);
    UserProfileManager profileManager = new UserProfileManager(context);

    Console.WriteLine("All Profiles:");
    foreach (UserProfile p in profileManager)
    {
        Console.WriteLine("{0} : {1}", p.ID, p.MultiloginAccounts[0]);
    }
    Console.WriteLine(" — ");
    string userName = @"win2k3r2lab\Administrator";
    if (profileManager.UserExists(userName))
    {
        UserProfile profile = profileManager.GetUserProfile(userName);
        Console.WriteLine("Found User Profile {0}", profile.ID);
        Console.WriteLine("\tPersonal Site: {0} ({1})",
            profile.PersonalSite.RootWeb.Title,
            profile.PersonalSite.Url);
    }
    else
```

LISTING 12.1   Continued

```
    {
        Console.WriteLine("No account found for " + userName);
    }

    Console.ReadLine();
}
}
}
}
```

On the test system, the output of the preceding code produces the following block of text:

```
All Profiles:
efa58ace-c2c9-4e8c-a105-82a487e303ee : WIN2K3R2LAB\Administrator
59646db2-4c20-4b42-b801-01eef1370ad4 : WIN2K3R2LAB\bjohnson
--
Found User Profile efa58ace-c2c9-4e8c-a105-82a487e303ee
        Personal Site:
WIN2K3R2LAB\Administrator
(http://win2k3r2lab:21154/personal/administrator)
```

Retrieving Profile Properties

Each profile has a stock set of properties that are defined by SharePoint and come with every installation of the product such as first name, last name, email address, and so on. In addition to the stock set of properties, you can create custom profile properties that store information relevant to your organization.

Listing 12.2 illustrates code that will retrieve the properties configured in SharePoint for a given user profile.

LISTING 12.2   Retrieving Profile Properties

```
using System;
using System.Collections.Generic;
using System.Text;
using Microsoft.Office.Server;
using Microsoft.Office.Server.Administration;
using Microsoft.Office.Server.UserProfiles;
using Microsoft.SharePoint;
using System.Web;

namespace EnumProfileProperties
{
```

LISTING 12.2   Continued

```
class Program
{
static void Main(string[] args)
{
    using ( SPSite site = new SPSite("http://win2k3r2lab"))
    {
        ServerContext context = ServerContext.GetContext(site);
        UserProfileManager profileManager =
            new UserProfileManager(context);

        UserProfile bob = profileManager.GetUserProfile(@"win2k3r2lab\bjohnson");
        Console.WriteLine("Profile {0}", bob.MultiloginAccounts[0]);
        foreach (Property prop in profileManager.Properties)
        {
            Console.WriteLine("\t{0} : {1}",
                prop.DisplayName,
                RenderProperty(bob, prop));
        }

        Console.ReadLine();
    }
}

static string RenderProperty(UserProfile profile, Property prop)
{
    UserProfileValueCollection values = profile[prop.Name];
    if (values.Value == null)
        return "(NULL)";
    if (prop.IsMultivalued)
    {
        StringBuilder sb = new StringBuilder();
        foreach (object o in values)
        {
            sb.AppendFormat("{0} ", o);
        }
        return sb.ToString();
    }
    else
    {
        return values.ToString();
    }
}
}
}
```

On the test server on which this code was written, the output of the preceding code is as follows:

```
Profile WIN2K3R2LAB\bjohnson
        Id : 59646db2-4c20-4b42-b801-01eef1370ad4
        SID : S-1-5-21-3651063265-1625534247-2901028135-1016
        Active Directory Id : (NULL)
        Account name : WIN2K3R2LAB\bjohnson
        First name : Bob
        Last name : Johnson
        Name : WIN2K3R2LAB\bjohnson
        Work phone : 555-555-1212
        Office : 555-555-1212
        Department : Accounting
        Title : Accountant
        Manager : WIN2K3R2LAB\administrator
        About me : <div></div>
        Personal site : (NULL)
        Picture : (NULL)
        User name : bjohnson
        Quick links : (NULL)
        Web site : (NULL)
        Public site redirect : (NULL)
        Dotted-line Manager : (NULL)
        Peers : (NULL)
        Responsibilities : (NULL)
        Skills : (NULL)
        Past projects : (NULL)
        Interests : (NULL)
        Schools : (NULL)
        SIP Address : (NULL)
        Birthday : 1/1/1970 12:00:00 AM
        My Site Upgrade : False
        Don't Suggest List : (NULL)
        Proxy addresses : (NULL)
        Hire date : (NULL)
        Last Colleague Added : (NULL)
        Outlook Web Access URL : (NULL)
        Resource Forest SID : (NULL)
        Resource Forest Account Name : (NULL)
        Master Account Name : (NULL)
        Assistant : (NULL)
        Work e-mail : bob@bobjohnson.com
        Mobile phone : (NULL)
        Fax : (NULL)
        Home phone : (NULL)
```

12

Modifying a User Profile

Modifying a user profile after you have a reference to it is actually quite easy. Most of the modifications to a user profile involve modifying the user profile properties. You can modify the property using a reference to the predefined property name constants, as shown in this snippet:

```
profile[PropertyConstants.HomePhone].Value = "555-555-1212";
```

Or, you can modify them using the names of your own custom created profile properties:

```
profile["FavoriteColor"] = "Blue";
```

Be careful not to use names of properties that have not been added to the user profile, or SharePoint will throw an exception indicating that the given indexer was out of range.

Make sure that you call the Commit method when you are finished making changes to the profile:

```
profile.Commit();
```

Retrieving Recent Changes

In addition to making changes to user profiles, you can also obtain the change log history for any given user profile. The code for retrieving and enumerating through the change list for a given user profile is shown in Listing 12.3.

You can specify a change log query that can narrow or broaden the search for modifications.

LISTING 12.3   Getting Recent Changes from the Change Log

```
using System;
using System.Collections.Generic;
using System.Text;
using Microsoft.Office.Server;
using Microsoft.Office.Server.Administration;
using Microsoft.Office.Server.UserProfiles;
using Microsoft.SharePoint;
using System.Web;

namespace UserProfilesOMApp
{
class Program
{
static void Main(string[] args)
{

    using (SPSite site = new SPSite("http://win2k3r2lab"))
```

LISTING 12.3   Continued

```
{
    ServerContext context = ServerContext.GetContext(site);
    UserProfileManager profileManager =
        new UserProfileManager(context);

    // Get all changes to profile made in the last 5 days
    DateTime startDate =
        DateTime.UtcNow.Subtract(TimeSpan.FromDays(5));
    UserProfileChangeQuery changeQuery =
        new UserProfileChangeQuery(false, true);
    UserProfileChangeToken changeToken =
        new UserProfileChangeToken(startDate);
    changeQuery.ChangeTokenStart = changeToken;
    changeQuery.Anniversary = true;
    changeQuery.SingleValueProperty = true;
    changeQuery.MultiValueProperty = true;
    changeQuery.DistributionListMembership = true;
    changeQuery.SiteMembership = true;

    UserProfile bobProfile = profileManager.GetUserProfile(
        @"win2k3r2lab\bjohnson");

    UserProfileChangeCollection changes =
        bobProfile.GetChanges(changeQuery);

    foreach (UserProfileChange change in changes)
    {
        Console.WriteLine(change.EventTime.ToString());
        if (change is UserProfilePropertyValueChange)
        {
            UserProfilePropertyValueChange propertyChange =
                (UserProfilePropertyValueChange)change;
            Console.WriteLine("Property {0} - {1}",
                propertyChange.ProfileProperty.Name,
                propertyChange.ChangeType.ToString());
        }
        else if (change is UserProfileMembershipChange)
        {
            UserProfileMembershipChange membershipChange =
                (UserProfileMembershipChange)change;
            Console.WriteLine("Membership {0} - {1}",
                membershipChange.MemberGroup.DisplayName,
                membershipChange.ChangeType.ToString());
        }
```

LISTING 12.3   Continued

```
        }
        Console.ReadLine();
    }
}
}
}
```

When the preceding code is executed, it will show output similar to the following (varying, of course, on the user examined and the changes that have occurred on your own system):

```
1/15/2007 10:06:08 PM
Property FirstName - Add
1/15/2007 10:06:08 PM
Property LastName - Add
1/15/2007 10:06:08 PM
Property WorkPhone - Add
1/15/2007 10:06:08 PM
Property Office - Add
1/15/2007 10:06:08 PM
Property Department - Add
1/15/2007 10:06:08 PM
Property Title - Add
1/15/2007 10:06:08 PM
Property Manager - Add
1/15/2007 10:06:08 PM
Property AboutMe - Add
1/15/2007 10:06:08 PM
Property SPS-Birthday - Add
1/15/2007 10:06:08 PM
Property WorkEmail - Add
```

Configuring the User Profile Store with the Object Model

Although many programming tasks related to user profiles can be accomplished by accessing user profiles and reading and writing profile properties, you can also programmatically manipulate the user profile store by creating new profiles and profile properties.

This section of the chapter contains code samples illustrating creating user profiles, simple profile properties, and complex profile properties such as multivalued properties and choice list properties.

Creating a User Profile

To create a user profile, you just need to supply the account name on which the profile will be based to the CreateUserProfile method on the UserProfileManager class, as shown in the following code block:

```
UserProfileManager profileManager = new
    UserProfileManager(context);
string accountId = @"win2k3r2lab\johndoe";


if (!profileManager.UserExists(accountId))
{
   UserProfile profile = profileManager.CreateUserProfile(accountId);

   if (profile == null)
     Console.WriteLine("Could not create profile, an error occurred.");
   else
     Console.WriteLine("User profile created.");
}
else
   Console.WriteLine("User profile for account " + accountId + " already exists.");
```

Creating a User Profile Property

To create a new user profile property, you will need to call the Create method on the ProfilePropertyCollection class, as shown in the following code snippet that creates a new profile property for storing the user's favorite color:

```
using (SPSite site = new SPSite("http://win2k3r2lab"))
{
    ServerContext context =
        ServerContext.GetContext(site);
    UserProfileManager profileManager = new UserProfileManager(context);

    PropertyCollection pc = profileManager.Properties;
    Property p = pc.Create(false);
    p.Name = "FavoriteColor";
    p.DisplayName = "Favorite Color";
    p.Type = "String";
    p.Length = 50;
    p.PrivacyPolicy = PrivacyPolicy.OptIn;
    p.DefaultPrivacy = Privacy.Organization;
    pc.Add(p);
}
```

12

Keep in mind that profile properties created like this can be accessed, read, and updated using the code shown earlier in the chapter. There is no difference between the code to manipulate built-in properties and custom created profile properties.

Creating Advanced User Profile Properties

Two additional types of user profile properties store values slightly more complex than the scalar values (string, integer, Boolean) shown previously: multivalued properties and choice list properties.

The multivalued property is extremely easy to create. You simply need to set the IsMultiValued property of a profile property to true, as follows:

```
p.IsMultiValued = true;
```

To create a user profile property that allows selections from a choice list, you just add values to the ChoiceList property of the user profile property object:

```
Property property = profileManager.Properties.Create(false);
property.Type = PropertyDataType.String;
property.Name = "ProgrammingLanguages";
property.DisplayName = "Programming Languages";
property.Length = 250;
property.DefaultPrivacy = Privacy.Organization;
property.PrivacyPolicy = PrivacyPolicy.OptIn;
property.IsUserEditable = true;
property.ChoiceType = ChoiceTypes.Closed;
string[] choices =
  new string[] { "C#", "VB.NET", "Java", "Python", "Perl", "Ruby", "PHP" };
foreach (string choice in choices)
{
  property.ChoiceList.Add(choice);
}
property.Commit();
```

Changing the Separator Value for Multi-valued Properties

Depending on what you're using a given user profile property for, you might want to create new properties with alternate value delimiters, or you might want to modify the value separator for an existing property. You can do this by modifying the Separator property of a user profile property object:

```
property.Separator = MultiValueSeparator.Comma;
```

The MultiValueSeparator enumeration has the following values: Comma, Newline, Semicolon, Unknown.

Manipulating Memberships

User profiles are far more than just repositories for information about individual people. They also provide community-building and social networking features through group memberships. You can create custom groups dynamically using code and you can add individual user profiles to those groups, as shown in the following code snippet:

```
using (SPSite site = new SPSite("http://win2k3r2lab"))
{
  ServerContext context = ServerContext.GetContext(site);
  UserProfileManager profileManager =
   new UserProfileManager(context);

  MemberGroup newGroup =
   profileManager.GetMemberGroups().
   CreateMemberGroup(PrivacyPolicyIdConstants.MembershipsFromDistributionLists,
   "Research Department",
   "Research Department",
   "The members of the Research Department",
   "http://win2k3r2lab/sites/research",
   "research");

// Add Bob Johnson to the Research Department
  string account = @"win2k3r2lab\bjohnson";
  UserProfile u = profileManager.GetUserProfile(account);
  u.Memberships.Create(newGroup,
     MembershipGroupType.UserSpecified,
     "Customer Connection Team", Privacy.Organization);
}
```

The final argument to the CreateMemberGroup method is called sourceEntry. The source entry argument indicates the directory entry of the distribution list from Active Directory, or the SPWeb or SPSite object depending on the MemberGroup and the configuration of shared services.

Viewing Commonalities Among Profiles

In an effort to provide enhanced social networking features for user profiles in MOSS, you can now programmatically obtain a list of commonalities among user profiles by using several methods for retrieving common data:

▶ GetCommonMemberships—Method called on the MembershipManager class for retrieving common memberships among profiles

▶ GetCommonManager—Method called on the UserProfile class for retrieving a common manager

The following code snippet shows how to obtain and enumerate commonalities among user profiles. (Note that this code will only work if there is a common manager found.)

```
using (SPSite site = new SPSite("http://win2k3r2lab"))
{
   ServerContext context = ServerContext.GetContext(site);
   UserProfileManager profileManager =
      new UserProfileManager(context);
   string accountId = @"win2k3r2lab\Administrator";
   UserProfile adminProfile = profileManager.GetUserProfile(accountId);

   MemberGroup[] memberGroups = adminProfile.Memberships.GetCommonMemberships();
   foreach (MemberGroup memGroup in memberGroups)
   {
      Console.WriteLine(memGroup.DisplayName);
   }
   UserProfile manager = adminProfile.GetCommonManager();
   Console.WriteLine(manager["DisplayName"]);
}
```

Summary

This chapter provided an overview and many code samples illustrating how you can write code to interact with the powerful user profile store in MOSS 2007. Using custom profile properties, advanced profile properties, social networking features, and much more, you can write code for the SharePoint object model that does extremely powerful and useful things with the user profile store.

CHAPTER 13

Building Workflows

IN THIS CHAPTER

▶ Workflow as a Solution

▶ Building the Workflow

Workflows in Microsoft Office SharePoint Server (MOSS) 2007 are built on top of the Windows Workflow Foundation (WF) and extend the base functionality to integrate seamlessly into the SharePoint 2007 infrastructure. Though you can build workflows with WF that extend into multiple systems, most workflows in MOSS are document- or list-centric. This chapter discusses the concepts of building workflows by stepping through an example provided by the SharePoint 2007 Software Development Kit (SDK).

Workflow as a Solution

Before you can begin building workflow solutions for SharePoint 2007, you must do several things to your development environment to ease the complexity of the Windows Workflow Foundation. This largely relates to installing a series of templates provided by the MOSS SDK.

When you install the .NET Framework 3.0 SDK on your development machine, only the Assemblies and supporting tools get installed. This doesn't install any templates in Visual Studio 2005 that will help you develop workflows. There are, however, templates available for download that will make it much easier to design and develop workflows for both SharePoint 2007 and WF.

> **NOTE**
>
> It is important to note that you can create workflows with WF that do not utilize SharePoint 2007. It is a common misconception that workflows *must* be installed on your SharePoint 2007 server. This is not true because you can have workflows that integrate into any type of managed application—all without using SharePoint 2007.

The two templates that you should install are the "Visual Studio 2005 Extensions for Windows Workflow Foundation" and the SharePoint 2007 SDK. The following list provides links to these templates:

▶ Visual Studio 2005 Extensions for Windows Workflow Foundation: http://www.microsoft.com/downloads/details.aspx?familyid=5D61409E-1FA3-48CF-8023-E8F38E709BA6&displaylang=en

▶ SharePoint 2007 SDK: http://www.microsoft.com/downloads/details.aspx?familyid=6d94e307-67d9-41ac-b2d6-0074d6286fa9&displaylang=en

After these two building blocks are installed, you can begin to build custom workflows.

Figure 13.1 illustrates the templates that are installed with the Visual Studio 2005 Extensions for WF, and Figure 13.2 shows the templates that are installed with the SharePoint 2007 SDK (which extend the Visual Studio 2005 Extensions for WF).

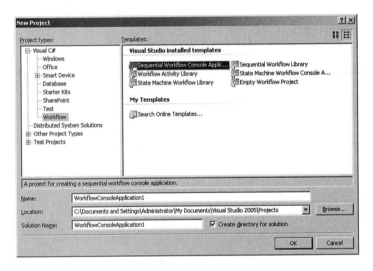

FIGURE 13.1   Visual Studio 2005 Extensions for WF templates.

SharePoint Workflows

Workflow solutions that run within the context of SharePoint are typically document- or list-centric, which means that they are associated with some sort of document library or list and facilitate a process around items in the list. When a SharePoint workflow is processed, tasks are typically assigned to a user in response to something that has happened to an item in the list.

A sample workflow is a simple approval workflow. When an item is saved to a SharePoint list with an approval workflow association, the item is routed to an "approver," where he can then either approve or reject the new item.

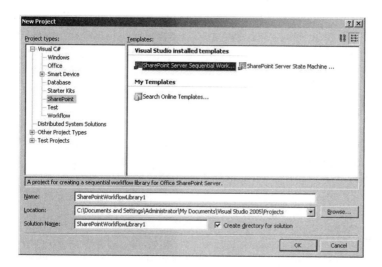

FIGURE 13.2   SharePoint 2007 SDK Visual Studio 2005 templates.

As you are thinking about workflows and their design, it is important to remove your coding hat for a moment. Workflows are typically human-based, so at the very high level, try to think about how the workflow will work as a process level and not as a code level. In the approval workflow sample, as items flow through the workflow, tasks are created for both the approver and possibly again for the submitter as list items flow through the process.

> **NOTE**
>
> As you will see later in this chapter, the workflow designer in Visual Studio 2005 is very good at first letting you design your workflow as a process diagram and then filling in the code later.

Workflow Objects

Before you learn how to design and develop workflows, it is important to understand the three objects that you will be creating: templates, associations, and instances.

Workflow Templates

Workflow templates are actually called Features and are what you will develop in Visual Studio 2005. Note that the term Feature will mean more to you later on in this chapter when the workflow template is deployed. Templates (or Features) define the workflow itself, how information is processed through the workflow, and any forms (.aspx or InfoPath forms) that are required by the workflow. Workflow templates are then installed on the server and associated with a site collection.

Workflow Associations

After a workflow template has been installed on your SharePoint server, it must be associated with a document library or a list. This means that items that are added to the list are assigned the workflow process defined by the template, assuming that the specified criteria have been met.

Workflow Instances

Workflow instances are the physical running instances of the workflow processes that have been associated with a list. They are different from associations because associations define the process that is to be assigned to list items, whereas a workflow instance is similar to an objected instance of an association that is dehydrated and rehydrated as the workflow process advances.

Building the Workflow

Building workflows is quite complex, so instead of introducing a new workflow template, this section explains the concepts of building a workflow using the `HelloWorldSequential` sample that is available in the MOSS SDK.

When learning how to code workflows in SharePoint 2007 and WF, you are typically consumed with the details of *how* to get the workflow up and running. It is important to remember that the workflows that you are building are used for human interaction—meaning that your users initiate the workflow and respond to tasks that are assigned to them during a workflow's lifespan. You can take several paths to design and build your workflow; however, the road map that typically works best (for most people) looks like the following:

1. Design the forms (InfoPath or ASPX) that your users will use to move data through a workflow.

2. Model the workflow with Visual Studio 2005.

3. Code the workflow.

4. Deploy the workflow.

5. Debug the workflow (locally).

> **NOTE**
>
> These steps are meant for you to use as a guideline. They are not set in stone and can be done in more than one way. Find a path that you are comfortable with and stick with it.

The next few sections describe each step that is required to get a workflow deployed to your SharePoint 2007 server. This chapter's example is the `HelloWorldSequential` workflow example from the SharePoint 2007 SDK.

Designing the Forms

The first step in designing the workflow involves getting the data to SharePoint so that your workflow instance can be started. In this example, this is by way of an InfoPath form, but can also be from an ASPX file that is created in Visual Studio.

Figure 13.3 illustrates the InfoPath 2007 designer. Notice that each text box in the designer (Assignee, Instructions, and Comments) has been named appropriately. This is very important because when you receive the data from the text boxes into the workflow, you need a way to identify what data is being received.

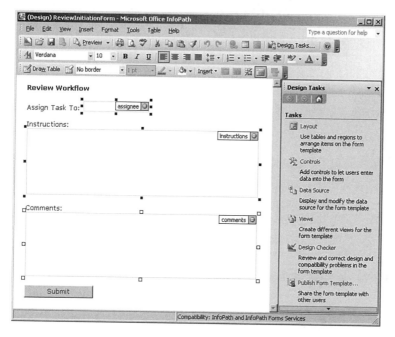

FIGURE 13.3   Designing the `ReviewInitiation` InfoPath form.

In this example, there is one Submit button on the page. In the Submit buttons on your forms, you can choose to do any number of custom actions from the very simple to the extremely complex; however, in this example only two rules are applied: Submit the data using a data connection and close the form. This allows the user to fill out the form and when they click Submit, the data is sent to SharePoint and the form is closed (assuming that validation has been placed on the text boxes). Figure 13.4 illustrates the rules that are applied behind the form's Submit button.

Next, you must give the form domain-level trust for it to access resources on the SharePoint server. Note that if you do not perform this task, your form will not work when you deploy your workflow. You can access the form's security properties by clicking Tools, Form Options and then clicking on the Security and Trust subtab. Figure 13.5 illustrates setting domain-level trust on your InfoPath 2007 form.

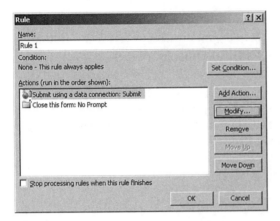

FIGURE 13.4   Rules behind the Submit button.

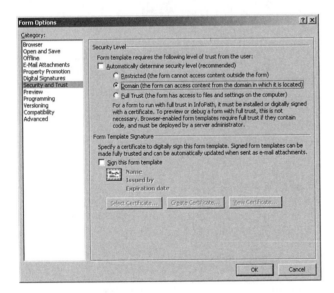

FIGURE 13.5   Configuring domain-level trust.

After your form is set up and configured, you should publish the form to the same directory in which you plan to develop your Visual Studio 2005 solution.

TIP

When developing the workflow data collection forms in InfoPath, it is important to note that because your SharePoint 2007 workflows are document-centric, InfoPath 2007 actually integrates the forms into your Office 2007 documents or SharePoint 2007 lists without opening InfoPath separately. You can write your own forms; however, InfoPath is the simplest approach as a lot of the "plumbing" code is baked into the Office 2007 system.

The next section describes modeling the workflow in Visual Studio 2005.

Modeling the Workflow in Visual Studio 2005

Workflows are modeled by using the Visual Studio 2005 Extensions for Windows Workflow Foundation (link provided earlier in this chapter). After these extensions are installed, you will notice several new project templates when you create a new project. Figure 13.6 illustrates the new project templates.

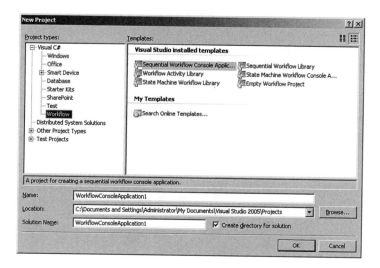

FIGURE 13.6   Workflow project templates.

When you install the Office 2007 SDK, the SharePoint workflow project templates get installed. These templates are different than the traditional workflow project templates in that there are only two (SharePoint Server Sequential Workflow and SharePoint Server State Machine Workflow) and they include all of the references and setup/configuration that you need to develop workflows for SharePoint.

> **NOTE**
>
> A common misconception is that workflows must run in SharePoint. This is not true in that you can develop workflows with WF that run in any .NET 3.0 managed application. SharePoint 2007 just extends this functionality and makes it easy to apply workflows to a document or a list.

Figures 13.7 and 13.8 show the new controls that are available to create both SharePoint 2007 and Windows workflows.

FIGURE 13.7   SharePoint 2007 workflow.

FIGURE 13.8   Windows workflows.

As you take a look at the `HelloWorldSequential` workflow project in the Office 2007 SDK, take a few minutes to look at the workflow designer in Visual Studio (Figure 13.9).

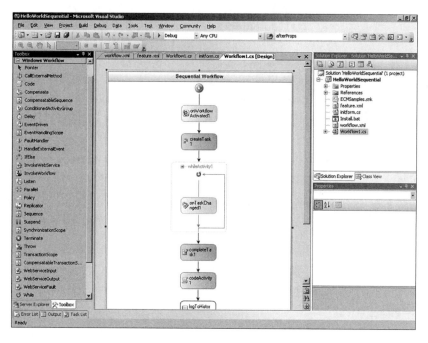

FIGURE 13.9   `HelloWorldSequential` workflow Project Workflow Designer.

As you can see, workflows are designed by using a flowchart-based designer. As you are designing the workflow, you need to think more about the business processes that are happening rather than the code that needs to be written behind the scenes to actually get the workflow to work.

Correlation Tokens

As you are stepping through the workflow and looking at the properties of each item in the workflow, notice one common property: `CorrelationToken`. This property is very important because it is used to specify the "context" for which each process of the workflow executes. It is used to identify each activity to determine the scope for which task is executed. It is possible for a workflow to use the same correlation token; however, it is not recommended because most workflows have multiple activities that need to commit as an individual unit or as a group.

Coding the Workflow

The code behind the workflow contains event handlers for each step in the workflow. In the `HelloWorldSequential` workflow example, each activity contains an event handler of the same name. If you follow through the flowchart, you can see the order in which each event handler will fire. The following set of steps is a description of what is happening in each event:

1. The workflow first receives Extensible Markup Language (XML) data from the InfoPath in the onWorkflowActivated method and stores that data in local properties.

2. The task is assigned to someone in the createTask method and enters the While activity. This loops until the user selects the isFinished check box to complete the workflow. Note that this begins a new correlationToken.

3. As the data in the InfoPath forms are changed, the While loop checks the isFinished property.

4. When the user selects isFinished, the task exits the While activity and marks the task as complete. The correlationToken that was created in step 2 ends here.

5. The custom code activity sets some history information on the workflow.

6. The logToHistoryListActivity activity logs the history information to the list's history.

7. Finally, an email is sent to inform the user of the status of the workflow.

Deploying the Workflow

When you are ready to deploy your workflow, several requirements must be met before you can start. First, you need to configure two XML files that describe your workflow: feature.xml and workflow.xml.

The following feature.xml and workflow.xml files describe the HelloWorldSequentialWorkflow Assembly:

LISTING 13.1   Feature.xml File

```
<Feature  Id="1E6D3BDD-9877-41ec-826C-EDE276EB560B"
          Title="Hello World Sequential Workflow"
          Description="Simple workflow that creates a review task
➥and waits for the user to complete it."
          Version="12.0.0.0"
          Scope="Site"
          ReceiverAssembly="Microsoft.Office.Workflow.Feature, Version=12.0.0.0,
➥Culture=neutral, PublicKeyToken=71e9bce111e9429c"
          ReceiverClass="Microsoft.Office.Workflow.Feature.WorkflowFeatureReceiver"
          xmlns="http://schemas.microsoft.com/sharepoint/">
  <ElementManifests>
    <ElementManifest Location="workflow.xml" />
  </ElementManifests>
  <Properties>
```

LISTING 13.1   Continued

```
    <Property Key="GloballyAvailable" Value="true" />

    <!-- Value for RegisterForms key indicates the path to the forms relative to
➥feature file location -->
    <!-- if you don't have forms, use *.xsn -->
    <Property Key="RegisterForms" Value="*.xsn" />
  </Properties>
</Feature>
```

LISTING 13.2   Workflow.xml File

```
<Elements xmlns="http://schemas.microsoft.com/sharepoint/">
  <Workflow
      Name="Sample: Hello World Sequential"
      Description="Simple workflow that creates a review task
➥and waits for the user to complete it."
      Id="48500BEB-D1BE-4ec4-8D21-5DEF76BEEDA8"
      CodeBesideClass="Microsoft.Office.Samples.ECM.Workflow.
➥HelloWorldSequential"
      CodeBesideAssembly="Microsoft.Office.Samples.ECM.Workflow.
➥HelloWorldSequential, Version=3.0.0.0, Culture=neutral,
➥PublicKeyToken=ec457ebe7d96977c"
            TaskListContentTypeId="0x01080100C9C9515DE4E24001905074F980F93160"
      AssociationUrl="_layouts/CstWrkflIP.aspx"
      InstantiationUrl="_layouts/IniWrkflIP.aspx"
      ModificationUrl="_layouts/ModWrkflIP.aspx">

    <Categories/>
    <!-- Tags to specify InfoPath forms for the workflow;
➥delete tags for forms that you do not have -->
    <MetaData>
      <Instantiation_FormURN>urn:schemas-microsoft-com:
➥office:infopath:ReviewInitiationForm2:-myXSD-2005-11-22T23-49-53</
➥Instantiation_FormURN>
      <Association_FormURN>urn:schemas-microsoft-com:
➥office:infopath:ReviewInitiationForm2:-myXSD-2005-11-22T23-49-53</
➥Association_FormURN>
      <Task0_FormURN>urn:schemas-microsoft-com:office:infopath:ReviewTaskForm:
➥-myXSD-2005-11-22T23-52-35</Task0_FormURN>

      <StatusPageUrl>_layouts/WrkStat.aspx</StatusPageUrl>
    </MetaData>
  </Workflow>
</Elements>
```

The `feature.xml` file describes the Assembly's properties that will get installed as a work-flow on your SharePoint server, whereas the `workflow.xml` file describes how your work-flow will get processed (that is, the processing pages and a few basic Assembly properties).

Finally, you must deploy your workflow. It is easiest to create a batch file for installation because several steps are required:

1. Copy the Assemblies to a common location.

2. Copy the `feature.xml` and `workflow.xml` files to the common location.

3. Copy the `InfoPathForms` to the common location.

4. GAC your Assemblies.

5. Install and activate the workflow by using the `stsadm.exe` command-line utility.

The following is an excerpt of the `install.bat` file included with the SDK sample. You should note that steps 1 through 4 can be accomplished by copying and pasting using Windows Explorer. However, it is recommended that you include these steps in the batch file because it is easy to replicate installation either by deploying an update to the SharePoint server or deploying to a QA/Production server.

LISTING 13.3   Excerpt from `Install.bat`

```
echo Copying the feature...
rd /s /q "%CommonProgramFiles%\Microsoft Shared\web server
➥extensions\12\TEMPLATE\FEATURES\HelloWorldSequential"
mkdir "%CommonProgramFiles%\Microsoft Shared\web server
➥extensions\12\TEMPLATE\FEATURES\HelloWorldSequential"

copy /Y feature.xml  "%CommonProgramFiles%\Microsoft Shared\web server
➥extensions\12\TEMPLATE\FEATURES\HelloWorldSequential\"
copy /Y workflow.xml "%CommonProgramFiles%\Microsoft Shared\web server
➥extensions\12\TEMPLATE\FEATURES\HelloWorldSequential\"
xcopy /s /Y *.xsn "%programfiles%\Common Files\Microsoft Shared\web server
➥extensions\12\TEMPLATE\FEATURES\HelloWorldSequential\"

echo Adding assemblies to the GAC...
"%programfiles%\Microsoft Visual Studio 8\SDK\v2.0\Bin\gacutil.exe"
➥-uf Microsoft.Office.Samples.ECM.Workflow.HelloWorldSequential
"%programfiles%\Microsoft Visual Studio 8\SDK\v2.0\Bin\gacutil.exe"
➥-if bin\Debug\Microsoft.Office.Samples.ECM.Workflow.HelloWorldSequential.dll

echo Activating the feature...
pushd %programfiles%\common files\microsoft shared\web server extensions\12\bin
stsadm -o deactivatefeature -filename HelloWorldSequential\feature.xml
➥-url http://localhost
```

LISTING 13.3   Continued

```
stsadm -o uninstallfeature -filename HelloWorldSequential\feature.xml

stsadm -o installfeature -filename HelloWorldSequential\feature.xml -force
stsadm -o activatefeature -filename HelloWorldSequential\feature.xml
➥-url http://localhost

echo Doing an iisreset...
popd
iisreset
```

Summary

Workflow is one of the most important facets of SharePoint 2007 because it allows you to create and customize workflows around your documents and lists. This chapter showed you how to create workflow solutions by discussing different scenarios for using them as well as the concepts of a working workflow solution.

PART III

Programming SharePoint Web Parts

IN THIS PART

CHAPTER 14 ASP.NET Server Control Primer   163

CHAPTER 15 Introduction to Web Parts   173

CHAPTER 16 Developing Full-Featured Web Parts 191

CHAPTER 17 Building Web Parts for Maintaining
            SharePoint 2007 Lists   205

CHAPTER 18 Building Connected Web Parts   217

CHAPTER 19 Debugging and Deploying Web
            Parts   229

ASP.NET Server Control Primer

IN THIS CHAPTER

▸ Contrasting Server Controls and User Controls

▸ Building Your First Server Control

Before discussing creating Web Parts that integrate into Microsoft Office SharePoint Server (MOSS), you must first look at creating ASP.NET server controls because a Web Part is actually a special type of server control.

Contrasting Server Controls and User Controls

Learning the art of creating a server control is necessary knowledge that you must have as a SharePoint developer. Server controls are at the very core of Web Part development, so it is important to understand the basics of server control development before you learn how to build your first Web Part. Before discussing ASP.NET server controls, it is important to understand how they differ from ASP.NET user controls, as they are often confused with each other.

Figure 14.1 illustrates a few subtle differences between server controls and user controls. This section breaks down the differences in the two, beginning with user controls.

User controls are very similar to ASP.NET web pages in that they can contain both a Hypertext Markup Language (HTML) and a code-behind (or code-beside) programmable interface. You can easily create a user control with the Visual Studio .NET Integrated Development Environment (IDE). The following listing creates a user control that simply collects information about a user on your website and displays that information in a ListBox control. To keep it simple, the example only collects a user's first name, last name, and phone number. Note that the server-side code is coded inline with the user control's HTML.

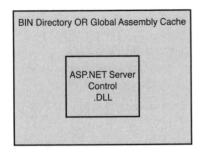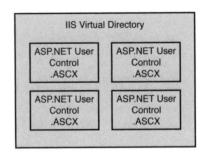

FIGURE 14.1   Server controls versus user controls.

LISTING 14.1   Information Collection User Control

```
<%@ Control Language="C#" ClassName="CollectUserInfo" %>

<script runat="server">

    protected void btnAdd_Click(object sender, EventArgs e)
    {
        lstUserInfo.Items.Add(txtFirstName.Text + " " + txtLastName.Text + " "
➥+ txtPhoneNumber.Text);
        txtFirstName.Text = string.Empty;
        txtLastName.Text = string.Empty;
        txtPhoneNumber.Text = string.Empty;
    }
</script>

<table>
    <tr>
        <td>First Name:</td>
        <td><asp:TextBox runat="server" ID="txtFirstName"></asp:TextBox></td>
    </tr>
    <tr>
        <td>Last Name:</td>
        <td><asp:TextBox runat="server" ID="txtLastName"></asp:TextBox></td>
    </tr>
    <tr>
        <td>Phone Number:</td>
        <td><asp:TextBox runat="server" ID="txtPhoneNumber"></asp:TextBox>
            <asp:RegularExpressionValidator ID="valPhone" runat=server
➥ControlToValidate="txtPhoneNumber"
            Display="Dynamic" SetFocusOnError="True"
            ValidationExpression="((\(\d{3}\) ?)¦(\d{3}-))?\d{3}-\d{4}"
➥>Invalid Phone Number</asp:RegularExpressionValidator>
```

LISTING 14.1   Continued

```
        </td>
    </tr>
    <tr>
        <td></td>
        <td><asp:Button runat="Server" ID="btnAdd" Text="Add User Info"
➥OnClick="btnAdd_Click" /></td>
    </tr>
    <tr>
        <td colspan="2"><asp:ListBox ID="lstUserInfo" runat="server"
➥Width="100%"></asp:ListBox></td>
    </tr>
</table>
```

As you can see by looking at the code, our user control looks very similar to a standard
.aspx web page in that it contains both server-side logic as well as HTML code to display
information to the user. However, instead of a complete HTML page, all that is required is
the piece that will be "snapped" into your page. When your web application is compiled,
all of the server-side logic gets compiled into the web application's Assembly, which
means that when you compile and deploy your web application (including Assemblies
and all dependent files), your user controls get wrapped up as distinct units of your application.

It is typically a best practice to utilize user controls to break out functionality of a page
into modular pieces. For example, in a large, team environment, you can easily break up
the functionality of complex pages into user controls and distribute the work among the
team.

Server controls, on the other hand, are a little more difficult to develop. Unlike user
controls, server controls don't have a "user interface," so to speak. When you create a
server control, it must be compiled into a class library (or .dll file) and deployed separately from your application.

Server controls are meant to be shared by multiple web applications, whereas user
controls are meant to be used by a single web application. You should consider a few
things when you are creating server control libraries for your applications.

NOTE

If you are creating a server control library that will be common to multiple web applications, you might consider strong-naming the Assembly and deploying to the Global
Assembly Cache. This ensures that the Assembly will be deployed once as well as
provides the ability for versioning your controls.

If you separate your pages into distinct, reusable web controls, you can take advantage of
using fragment caching, which is where you cache data-bound controls to reduce the

number of trips to the database that are required to reload controls that are rendered on the page. The ASP.NET runtime keeps these controls prerendered in memory, thus significantly increasing performance. The following example demonstrates the processing instruction that is required to enable caching on a control.

```
<%@ OutputCache VaryByParam="true" Duration="60" %>
```

This tells the runtime to cache the control by using an algorithm created by a query string or form parameters that are posted back to the server, for a duration of 60 seconds. Fragment caching is outside of the scope of this chapter, but if used properly, it can considerably increase the performance and scalability of your application.

Now that you have reviewed ASP.NET user controls, the following section takes a look at building a server control.

Building Your First Server Control

Building server controls is quite a bit different than building web controls because there is not a user interface that you can "drag and drop" controls to. This makes a lot of developers shy away from the topic, but given the proper knowledge, you can create some very powerful controls that encapsulate logic that can be reused in your enterprise applications.

Two methodologies are considered generally accepted practices when creating custom server controls:

▶ A class that inherits from an existing control class in ASP.NET

▶ A custom class that inherits from the Control or WebControl class

The good news is that a lot of the base functionality has already been written for you, no matter what type of control you need to create. All custom server controls must be compiled into a Class Library project, the result of which is a .dll Assembly.

Let's take a look at the first methodology: creating a class that inherits from an existing control class. Before writing any code, you need to add a special class to your Class (control) Library project that is provided by Visual Studio 2005, which will help you to easily create custom server controls. You can use the Web Custom Control item template, as illustrated in Figure 14.2.

The Web Custom Control template adds a new class that inherits from the System.Web.UI.WebControls.WebControl class. Because you are creating a customized TextBox, you change the class definition to derive from the System.Web.UI.WebControls.TextBox class. The following example of a custom TextBox control only allows numeric input. The TextBox accepts any input, but if anything but a numeric value is entered, the background color changes to red and "0" is displayed in the TextBox control; otherwise, the TextBox displays the numeric value normally.

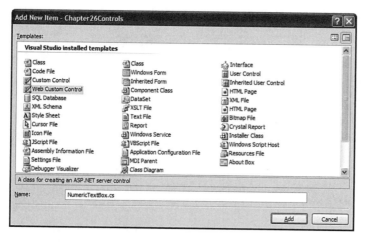

FIGURE 14.2   Add a Web Custom Control to your project.

LISTING 14.2   Numeric Textbox Server Control

```csharp
using System;
using System.Collections.Generic;
using System.ComponentModel;
using System.Text;
using System.Web;
using System.Web.UI;
using System.Web.UI.WebControls;
using System.Drawing;

namespace Chapter14Controls
{
    [DefaultProperty("Text")]
    [ToolboxData("<{0}:NumericTextBox runat=server></{0}:NumericTextbox>")]
    public class NumericTextbox : TextBox
    {
        [Bindable(true)]
        [Category("Appearance")]
        [DefaultValue("")]
        [Localizable(true)]
        public override string Text
        {
            get
            {
                String s = (String)ViewState["Text"];
                return ((s == null) ? String.Empty : s);
            }
```

LISTING 14.2   Continued

```
        set
        {
            int i = 0;
            if (int.TryParse(base.Text, out i))
            {
                base.BackColor = Color.White;
                ViewState["Text"] = value;
            }
            else
            {
                base.Text = "0";
                base.BackColor = Color.Red;
            }
        }
    }

    protected override void RenderContents(HtmlTextWriter output)
    {
        output.Write(Text);
    }
  }
}
```

The logic that is defined in the control class is very simple; you quite simply need to override the base functionality of the Text property of the TextBox, most specifically the set statement. In the set statement, the value that is being set is attempted to be parsed into an Integer. If it parses (or if it is numeric), change the BackColor of the TextBox to the default color of white. Else, if the value doesn't parse, change the BackColor property to red and reset the Text property to "0".

At its root, the previous example is very simplistic in that all that is required to create the server control is to derive a class that is already implemented by the .NET Framework application programming interface (API). The following section takes a look at a more advanced example of a server control that derives from System.Web.UI.WebControls.WebControl.

Extending Server Controls

Deriving a class from System.Web.UI.WebControls.WebControl allows you to emit HTML that will function as a server control at runtime. This might be the scenario when you need functionality that isn't provided by the default web controls (TextBox, Label, DropDownList, and so on), but can be done with HTML. For simplicity (these types of controls can get very complex), the following example creates a custom, multiline TextBox control that resizes itself vertically based on the content that is contained within the control. This functionality isn't native to any of the controls in the .NET Framework, so you need to emit custom HTML that renders a `TextArea` control.

LISTING 14.3   Resizing TextBox Control

```
using System;
using System.Collections.Generic;
using System.ComponentModel;
using System.Text;
using System.Web;
using System.Web.UI;
using System.Web.UI.WebControls;

namespace Chapter14Controls
{
    [ToolboxData("<{0}:ExpandingTextBox runat=server></{0}:ExpandingTextBox>")]
    public class ExpandingTextBox : WebControl, IPostBackDataHandler,
➥INamingContainer
    {
        [Bindable(true)]
        [Category("Appearance")]
        [DefaultValue("")]
        [Localizable(true)]
        public string Value
        {
            get
            {
                String s = (String)ViewState["Value"];
                return ((s == null) ? String.Empty : s);
            }

            set
            {
                ViewState["Value"] = value;
            }
        }

        protected override void Render(HtmlTextWriter writer)
        {
            if (!this.Page.ClientScript.IsStartupScriptRegistered(
➥this.GetType(), "ExpandingTextBoxJS"))
            {
                this.Page.ClientScript.RegisterStartupScript(
➥this.GetType(), "ExpandingTextBoxJS", "function expand(obj)
➥{if (obj.value && obj.value.length > 0)
➥{obj.rows = obj.value.split('\\n').length + 1;}
```

LISTING 14.3   Continued

```
else {obj.rows = 2;}}", true);
            }
            writer.AddAttribute("id", this.ClientID);
            writer.AddAttribute("name", this.UniqueID);
            writer.AddAttribute("value", this.Value);
            writer.AddAttribute("style",
"overflow-y:hidden;overflow-x:auto;width:80%;");
            writer.AddAttribute("onkeyup", "javascript:expand(this);", false);
            writer.RenderBeginTag(HtmlTextWriterTag.Textarea);
            writer.RenderEndTag(); //input

            this.EnsureChildControls();
            this.RenderContents(writer);
            base.Render(writer);
        }
    }
}
```

Note that this code snippet is incomplete, but the discussion continues in the next few sections to complete the code for the Server Control. Take a look at the Render method in the ExpandingTextBox class. This method is fired when the control gets rendered to the page, so this is where you need to create the HTML that is required to render your control. As you can see, you use the HtmlTextWriter object to pump HTML to the output stream of the response object, as well as register a client-side script block that provides the resizing functionality of the TextArea.

When the control gets rendered, it resizes itself, as illustrated in Figure 14.3.

Managing ViewState

If you compile the preceding code sample into a custom control and add it to your page, the control is rendered and functions as expected (that is, it resizes itself). But alas, you are not without problems yet. Although the control functions, it loses its state when you post back to the server. Because you emitted a custom HTML control, the System.Web.UI.WebControls.WebControl class doesn't provide the logic to save the control's state to ViewState.

You must follow a few steps to have your control save to ViewState. Your class must implement the IPostBackDataHandler interface to be able to save back down to ViewState. This allows you to code against two events that are required for PostBacks: LoadPostBackData and RaisePostDataChangedEvent. The following code implements these methods:

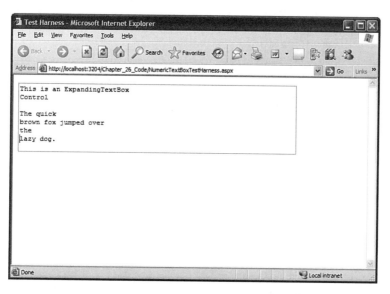

FIGURE 14.3   Expanding TextBox control.

LISTING 14.4   Saving ViewState

```
public event EventHandler Changed;

protected override void OnPreRender(EventArgs e)
{
    this.Page.RegisterRequiresPostBack(this);
    base.OnPreRender(e);
}


protected virtual void OnChange(EventArgs e)
{
    if (Changed != null)
        Changed(this, e);
}


#region IPostBackDataHandler Members
void IPostBackDataHandler.RaisePostDataChangedEvent()
{
    OnChange(EventArgs.Empty);
}
```

LISTING 14.4   Continued

```
bool IPostBackDataHandler.LoadPostData(string postDataKey,
➥System.Collections.Specialized.NameValueCollection postCollection)
{
    string currentText = this.Value;
    string postedText = postCollection[postDataKey];
    if (!currentText.Equals(postedText, StringComparison.Ordinal))
    {
        this.Value = postedText;
        return true;
    }
    return false;
}
#endregion
```

The code that is contained in the LoadPostData method checks the data that has been posted back to the server. If it has changed, the Value property is set and the method returns true (that is, the data has changed in the control). This is what actually commits the changed data to ViewState, so the functionality of this method is essential for your control to post back properly.

The LoadPostData method does not get fired automatically, however. You must first register the control with the page by calling the RegisterRequiresPostBack method inside of the PreRender event of the control. This registers the control to ViewState and causes the LoadPostData method to fire when the page posts back.

Summary

This chapter showed you how to create a custom server control that emits JavaScript to provide functionality that is not covered in the .NET Framework API, as well as how to handle posting data back to the server.

CHAPTER 15

Introduction to Web Parts

IN THIS CHAPTER

▶ Introduction to the ASP.NET 2.0 Web Part Infrastructure

▶ Primer on Creating ASP.NET 2.0 Web Parts

▶ Integrating Server Controls and Web User Controls

▶ Using the HelloWorld WebPart Control with SharePoint

Introduction to the ASP.NET 2.0 Web Part Infrastructure

ASP.NET 2.0 provides an infrastructure (external to Microsoft Office SharePoint Server [MOSS]) for creating and hosting Web Parts. It offers the basic portal framework, so that you can have the benefits of UI and personalization in your web pages that SharePoint provides. As your SharePoint development experience and knowledge increases, you will find that learning how these controls work are essential skills that can be used in both SharePoint development and in ASP.NET 2.0 development. This section discusses the controls that are available in ASP.NET and how you can interact with them in your pages.

ASP.NET 2.0 has a number of controls that are available for the portal framework that make it very easy to provide SharePoint-like functionality in your applications. Table 15.1 lists and describes each of these controls. You will learn how to use these controls in an application later in this chapter.

TABLE 15.1 ASP.NET Web Part Controls

Class	Description
WebPartManager	Central controller class for any ASP.NET 2.0 page that contains Web Parts
ProxyWebPartManager	Proxy to a WebPartManager control declared in a master page
WebPartZone	Container for Web Parts
CatalogZone	Container for catalog Web Parts

TABLE 15.1   Continued

Class	Description
DeclarativeCatalogPart	Web Part that allows you to configure a library of Web Parts that users can use to personalize their page
PageCatalogPart	Web Part that keeps track of all Web Parts that have been marked as "Closed" on the page; this allows for users to gain a reference back to controls that have been closed
ImportCatalogPart	Web Part control that allows users to import a Web Part to the page using a Web Part description file
EditorZone	Container for editor Web Parts
AppearanceEditorPart	Web Part that allows users to change appearance user interface properties on an associated Web Part
BehaviorEditorPart	Web Part that allows users to change behavior user interface properties on an associated Web Part
LayoutEditorPart	Web Part that allows users to change the zone in which an associated Web Part belongs
PropertyGridEditorPart	Editor Web Part that allows users to change custom properties on associated Web Parts

These controls are very easy to use and provide a lot of "out-of-the-box" functionality in ASP.NET 2.0. These controls can be broken into three distinct categories: Managers, Zones, and Web Parts. Figure 15.1 illustrates how these controls interact with ASP.NET 2.0 pages.

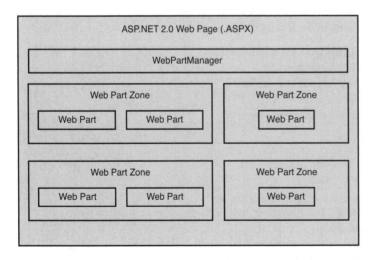

FIGURE 15.1   ASP.NET Web Part integration.

Starting at the top of Figure 15.1 and working downward, the first thing that is required of any ASP.NET 2.0 page that uses Web Parts is a WebPartManager control. This control acts as the controller for the portal page and provides functionality for users to interact with and customize their portal pages. You are only allowed to have one WebPartManager control per page.

From a coding perspective, the WebPartManager control is used to manage the Web Parts and zones that are on your page. For example, the code in the following example uses the WebPartManager (named "wpm") to change a page's mode to provide the user with the ability to edit their page layout.

LISTING 15.1   Web Part Manager

```
<%@ Page Language="C#" %>

<!DOCTYPE html PUBLIC "-//W3C//DTD XHTML 1.0 Transitional//EN"
➥ "http://www.w3.org/TR/xhtml1/DTD/xhtml1-transitional.dtd">

<script runat="server">

    protected void lnkEditPage_Click(object sender, EventArgs e)
    {
        if (wpm.DisplayMode == WebPartManager.BrowseDisplayMode)
        {
            wpm.DisplayMode = WebPartManager.DesignDisplayMode;
            lnkEditPage.Text = "View Page";
        }
        else
        {
            wpm.DisplayMode = WebPartManager.BrowseDisplayMode;
            lnkEditPage.Text = "Edit Page";
        }
    }
</script>

<html xmlns="http://www.w3.org/1999/xhtml" >
<head runat="server">
    <title>Untitled Page</title>
</head>
<body>
    <form id="form1" runat="server">
        <asp:WebPartManager ID="wpm" runat="server">
```

LISTING 15.1   Continued

```
            <Personalization InitialScope="User" />
        </asp:WebPartManager>
        <table width="100%">
            <tr>
                <td colspan="2" align="right">
                    <asp:LinkButton ID="lnkEditPage" runat="server"
➥OnClick="lnkEditPage_Click">Edit Page</asp:LinkButton></td>
            </tr>
            <tr>
                <td width="80%">
                    <asp:WebPartZone ID="WebPartZone1" runat="server" Width="100%">
                    </asp:WebPartZone>
                </td>
                <td width="20%"><asp:WebPartZone ID="WebPartZone2" runat="server"
Width="100%">
                    </asp:WebPartZone></td>
            </tr>
            <tr>
                <td><asp:WebPartZone ID="WebPartZone3" runat="server" Width="100%">
                    </asp:WebPartZone></td>
                <td><asp:WebPartZone ID="WebPartZone4" runat="server" Width="100%">
                    </asp:WebPartZone></td>
            </tr>
            <tr>
                <td><asp:WebPartZone ID="WebPartZone5" runat="server" Width="100%">
                    </asp:WebPartZone></td>
                <td><asp:WebPartZone ID="WebPartZone6" runat="server" Width="100%">
                    </asp:WebPartZone></td>
            </tr>
            <tr>
                <td colspan="2"><asp:WebPartZone ID="WebPartZone7" runat="server"
➥Width="100%">
                    </asp:WebPartZone></td>
            </tr>
        </table>
    </form>
</body>
</html>
```

This page is simple; it contains a WebPartManager control and seven WebPartZone controls (which are used in an example later in the chapter), and a LinkButton control. When the user clicks on the LinkButton control, the WebPartManager is used to put the page into a Design mode, which allows the user to configure which Web Parts belong to which zones and persist that data to the database. While in Design mode, each WebPartZone becomes visible so that users can drag and drop controls into and between zones, as illustrated in Figure 15.2.

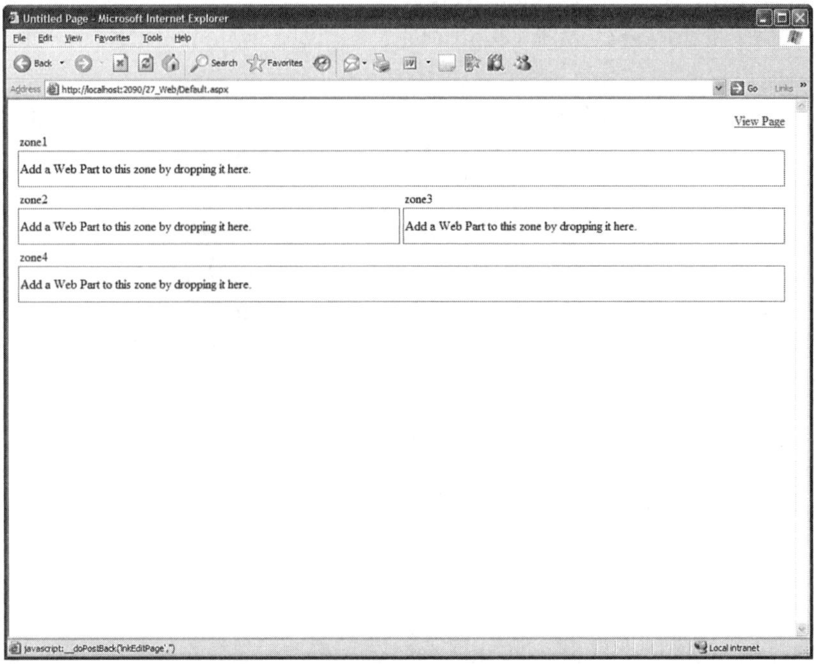

FIGURE 15.2   ASP.NET Web Part page in Design mode.

Another functionality that the WebPartManager control provides is how design changes to a portal page affect other users. By default, each change is scoped to the user level, which means that if one user makes a change to a page, it doesn't affect the other users' views of the page. However, you can easily change that scope so that changes made to the page are global to all users by setting the Initial Scope property of the WebPartManager control to Shared, instead of User, which is the default.

TIP

In ASP.NET 2.0, the default location for persisting personalization settings is a SQL Server 2005 Express database named ASPNETDB.MDF, which is created inside of the App_Data directory of your website. If you are deploying your site to a web farm environment, you need to configure this database to run on a centralized database server. This can easily be done by running the aspnet_regsql.exe file, which is found in the C:\WINDOWS\Microsoft.NET\Framework\v2.0.XXXXX directory. When you run this executable, you are guided through a wizard that helps you configure a blank SQL Server database instance for hosting personalization settings for your ASP.NET 2.0 websites.

The next sets of controls in Figure 15.1 are `WebPartZones`. `WebPartZones` (or "zones") are containers for Web Parts. You can add several types of zones to your page that provide selective functionality to your sites. For example, you can use the `WebPartZone` control to host most of the custom Web Parts that you develop, whereas you can use a `CatalogZone` control to host a library (or catalog) of Web Parts that can be used on your portal page. Both the `WebPartZone` and the `CatalogZone` controls are discussed in more detail later in this chapter.

Now that you have reviewed the ASP.NET Web Part infrastructure, you can begin by building a few simple Web Parts for both the ASP.NET 2.0 Portal Framework and SharePoint.

Primer on Creating ASP.NET 2.0 Web Parts

Creating Web Parts with the ASP.NET 2.0 object model is very similar to creating server controls like you did in Chapter 14, "ASP.NET Server Control Primer." In Chapter 14, you created a Class Library project with a class that derives from the `System.Web.UI.WebControls.WebControl` class. Web Parts are very similar, but to create a Web Part, you must create a new class that derives from the `System.Web.UI.WebControls.WebParts.WebPart` class. This class provides all of the necessary logic to integrate into both the ASP.NET Portal Framework, as well as SharePoint. The following section shows you how to create a simple Web Part. Later in this chapter, you learn how to extend the functionality of that Web Part.

Creating an ASP.NET 2.0 Web Part

Creating a Web Part in ASP.NET 2.0 is easier than you might think.

You can use the following steps as a guide to create your Web Parts:

1. Create a new Class Library project.

2. Set a reference to `System.Web.dll`.

3. Create a class that derives from `System.Web.UI.WebControls.WebParts.WebPart`.

4. Override the `Render` method.

5. (Optional) Strong name your Assembly.

It is best to create a new class library for your Web Parts and set a reference to the `System.Web.dll` file, as illustrated in Figure 15.3.

Although it is not required, packaging your Web Parts in a Class Library project provides you with several advantages. The first advantage is that it allows you to encapsulate your Web Part logic into a reusable, distributable library. This allows you to reuse your Web Parts in multiple websites, and when you are developing for SharePoint, you can reuse your Web Parts in multiple sites. Another advantage is that you can easily create a strong name for your Web Parts Assembly and place that Assembly in the Global Assembly Cache (GAC) on your server. This prevents you from having to deploy an instance of your library every time that it is used in a website or SharePoint portal, as well as allows you to deploy multiple versions of your Web Parts.

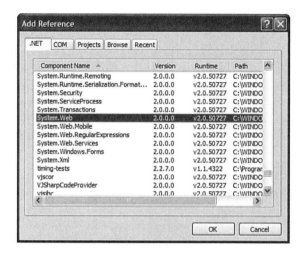

FIGURE 15.3   Adding a reference to System.Web.dll.

After a reference has been set to the System.Web.dll file in your Class Library project, you are ready to start building Web Parts for the ASP.NET 2.0 Portal Framework.

NOTE

Note that you also have to set a reference to the SharePoint.dll file to code against the SharePoint object model. This topic is covered in more detail in Chapter 2, "Introduction to the SharePoint Object Model."

You can now create a class that derives from the System.Web.UI.WebControls.WebParts. WebPart class and override the Render method, as in Listing 15.2.

LISTING 15.2   HelloWorld Web Part

```
using System;
using System.Collections.Generic;
using System.Text;
using System.Web;
using System.Web.UI;
using System.Web.UI.WebControls;
using System.Web.UI.WebControls.WebParts;

namespace WebParts
{
    public class HelloWorld : WebPart, INamingContainer
    {
        /// <summary>
```

LISTING 15.2   Continued

```
        /// Default constructor
        /// </summary>
        public HelloWorld() { }

        /// <summary>
        /// Renders HTML to the web part page
        /// </summary>
        /// <param name="writer"></param>
        protected override void Render(HtmlTextWriter writer)
        {
            writer.Write("Hello world!");
        }
    }
}
```

Just as when creating a server control, you can override the Render method to emit Hypertext Markup Language (HTML) to the browser window by using the HtmlTextWriter object; Chapter 16, "Developing Full-Featured Web Parts," digs deeper into this topic.

To finish out the loop on creating a Web Part, you should strong name your Assembly and register it in the GAC. In Visual Studio 2005, it is easy to strong name your Assembly. This can be done from your project Properties page (right-click your project and then click Properties), as displayed in Figure 15.4.

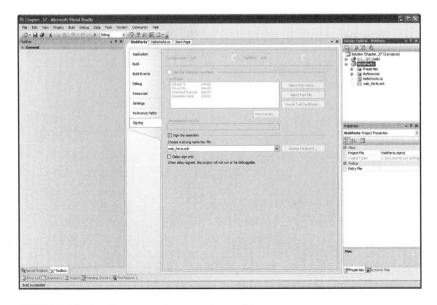

FIGURE 15.4   Strong naming your Assembly.

After your Assembly has been assigned a strong name, you can now compile it and register it in the GAC. You can do this either by using the command-line utility GacUtil.exe, by using the .NET Framework 2.0 Configuration Utility, or by opening Windows Explorer and dropping the strong-named assembly into the C:\WINDOWS\Assembly directory, as shown in Figure 15.5.

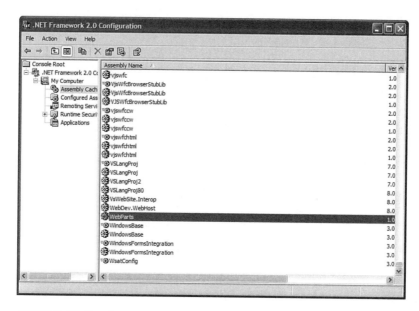

FIGURE 15.5   Adding the Assembly to the GAC.

Testing the Web Part

Testing the Web Part is very simple if you refer to the diagram in Figure 15.1 and remember that you need three things:

▶ A Web Part to test

▶ A Web Part zone

▶ A WebPartManager control

This section covers testing the Web Part. Because you registered your Web Part in the GAC, it is easy to find and add a reference to. Also, a Web Part is similar to a server control in that you can add it to your Toolbox in Visual Studio 2005, as shown in Figures 15.6 and 15.7.

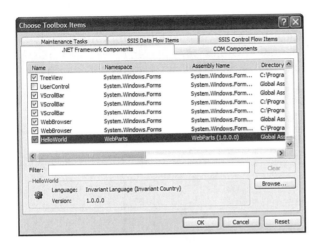

FIGURE 15.6   Adding the HelloWorld Web Part to the Visual Studio 2005 Toolbox.

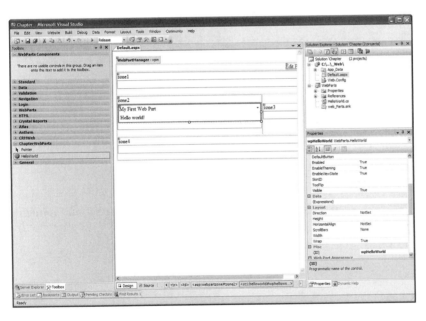

FIGURE 15.7   Adding the HelloWorld Web Part to the page.

By using the code discussed earlier in this chapter, you can drag and drop the HelloWorld control into one of the four WebPartZones that are on the page. You can test your control by either looking in the Visual Studio Page Designer (Figure 15.7), or by running the application and verifying that it works in the browser (if your Web Part provides any custom functionality), which is shown in Figure 15.8.

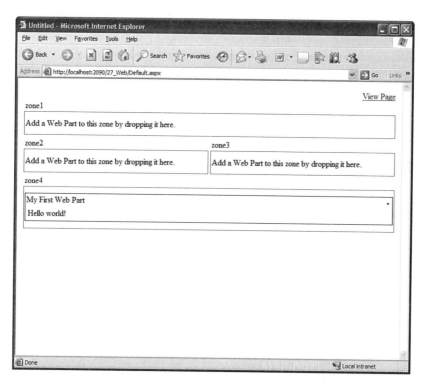

FIGURE 15.8   Testing the HelloWorld Web Part in the browser.

Note that in Figure 15.8, the HelloWorld Web Part renders in the browser and also that the WebPartManager control has been set to display in DesignDisplayMode (which allows the user to drag and drop controls between zones on the page). In addition, the control has been dragged to another zone than the one displayed in Figure 15.7. If your control needs to "live" inside of a SharePoint site, but doesn't utilize any of the SharePoint application programming interface (API), the ASP.NET Portal Framework makes for a great testing ground for your Web Parts because you have everything that you need to debug and test your Web Parts built right in to the ASP.NET Portal Framework.

Web Part development can get quite complex—depending on what you are trying to accomplish. However, if you follow the basic steps covered in this section, it is much easier than you might think. The next section explores using the HelloWorld control inside of a SharePoint portal.

Integrating Server Controls and Web User Controls

One problem with previous versions of SharePoint was that Web Parts were not only difficult to develop and maintain, but they were also the only way to develop custom pieces that integrated into SharePoint. A few third-party tools are available such as SmartPart (http://www.gotdotnet.com/workspaces/workspace.aspx?id=6cfaabc8-db4d-41c3-8a88-3f974a7d0abe) that allow you to snap web user controls into your SharePoint site, which is a Band-Aid fix for a bigger issue; you can only truly customize SharePoint using Web Parts.

In the ASP.NET 2.0 Portal Framework and SharePoint 2007, you can now drop web user controls and custom (or standard) server controls into the zones on your pages. This is illustrated in Figure 15.9.

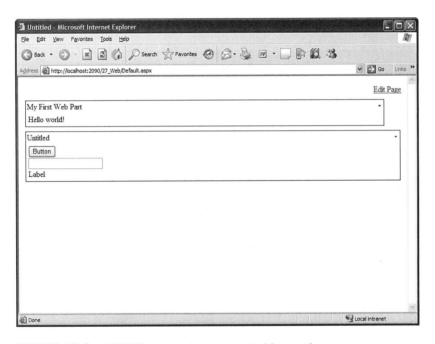

FIGURE 15.9   ASP.NET user and server control integration.

Behind the scenes when you drop a web user control or server control into a zone, an instance of the `GenericWebPart` class is created and it is used as a wrapper to host your control. The `GenericWebPart` class inherits from `WebPart`, but you are limited in what you can actually do inside of the zone. For example, notice in Figure 15.9 that the title of the new Web Part defaults to "Untitled." This cannot be easily changed because controls that inherit from the `Control` base class (which also includes `WebControl`) cannot support the use of the built-in Web Part properties, such as `Title` and `Description`.

Although it is easy to drag and drop server and user controls into your zones, the preferred method is still to use Web Parts to provide the maximum flexibility within your portals.

Using the HelloWorld WebPart Control with SharePoint

It is very easy to integrate your ASP.NET 2.0 Web Parts right into SharePoint, as the SharePoint Web Part infrastructure is built on top of the ASP.NET 2.0 Portal Framework. This section illustrates the key differences in Web Parts developed for ASP.NET and those developed for SharePoint.

ASP.NET Web Parts Versus SharePoint Web Parts

There is a fundamental difference in developing Web Parts for SharePoint 2007 versus creating Web Parts for SharePoint 2003. Web Parts developed for SharePoint 2007 are based on the ASP.NET Portal Framework. SharePoint 2007's portal infrastructure uses the ASP.NET Portal Framework classes as base classes, so just like ASP.NET, SharePoint also has WebPartManager, WebPartZone, and WebPart that function almost identically to each other.

SharePoint's WebPartManager class (called SPWebPartManager) inherits from the System.Web.UI.WebControls.WebParts.WebPartManager class and its functionality is implemented by SharePoint when you get to the point of adding custom web controls. For example, SharePoint generates all of the "plumbing" code for you when you create a new portal site, which you are required to write for yourself with the ASP.NET Portal Framework. The same is true for SharePoint's WebPartZone class in that it inherits from the System.Web.UI.WebControls.WebParts.WebPartZone class and is used to host Web Parts inside of SharePoint.

The heart of SharePoint development is in the WebPart class. In ASP.NET 2.0, the System.Web.UI.WebControls.WebParts.WebPart class is what you must derive from to create a custom Web Part. SharePoint's WebPart class (Microsoft.SharePoint. WebPartPages.WebPart) inherits from ASP.NET's WebPart class, which makes the learning curve to develop Web Parts for SharePoint very small. This also means that you can develop and test your SharePoint Web Parts by using the ASP.NET Portal Framework. So, why would you use one Web Part over the other (SharePoint versus ASP.NET)? You can use the ASP.NET WebPart class for most custom Web Parts that you will be creating because it provides the basic functionality that is needed to integrate with SharePoint. SharePoint's WebPart class provides additional functionality for connected Web Parts, client-side functionality, and a data-caching infrastructure, which is covered in Chapter 18, "Building Connected Web Parts."

SharePoint Integration

This section looks at how easy it is to integrate a Web Part with SharePoint 2007. Probably the single biggest complaint that developers had with SharePoint 2003 was that there wasn't a way to actually test Web Parts outside of SharePoint. Because, as you have learned in this chapter, SharePoint's portal infrastructure is an extension of the ASP.NET 2.0 Portal Framework, and Web Parts operate seamlessly between the two.

You must follow several steps before you can use your Web Part inside of the SharePoint infrastructure, which makes the deployment of your SharePoint-based Web Parts significantly different than those of ASP.NET 2.0. The following is a guide for you to follow when deploying Web Parts to SharePoint:

1. Do *at least* one of the following when you are compiling the Assembly that contains your Web Parts:

    a. Assign a strong name.

    b. Mark the Assembly with the `AllowPartiallyTrustedCallers` attribute.

    c. Configure the `<trust level="">` attribute inside your SharePoint site's `Web.Config` file.

2. Mark your Assembly as a `SafeControl` inside of your SharePoint site's `Web.Config` file.

3. Add your Web Part Library to the site's Web Part Gallery.

4. Add Web Parts from your Assembly to pages in your site.

It sounds much more complicated than it actually is. The hardest part is already finished; you already have a Web Part that works and has been tested inside of the ASP.NET 2.0 Portal Framework! In addition, you have already marked the Assembly with a strong name and registered it in the GAC, so you can skip step 1.

Next, you need to modify the portal site's `Web.Config` file to "register" the control with the site. This can easily be done by adding the following line of code to the `<SafeControls>` section of the `Web.Config` file:

```
<SafeControl Assembly="WebParts,
       Version=1.0.0.0, Culture=neutral,
       PublicKeyToken=2e097026f9c7d6df"
       Namespace="WebParts" TypeName="*" />
```

This is a very important step because your Assembly does not become available to SharePoint until you mark it as `Safe`. In addition, your Assembly has a unique `PublicKeyToken`, which is different from the one listed previously. You can discover the `PublicKeyToken` in several ways. If your Assembly is registered in the GAC, you can retrieve the `PublicKeyToken` from the Assembly's Properties window in the .NET 2.0 Framework Configuration Tool, as illustrated in Figure 15.10.

At this point, you are ready to add the `WebParts` Assembly to your site's Web Part Gallery. This can be done by going to the Site Actions, Site Settings, Modify All Site Settings link, as shown in Figure 15.11.

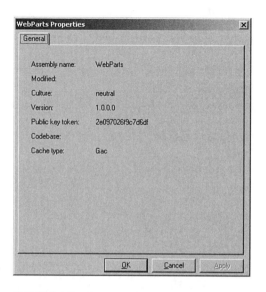

FIGURE 15.10   Retrieving the `PublicKeyToken` from an Assembly.

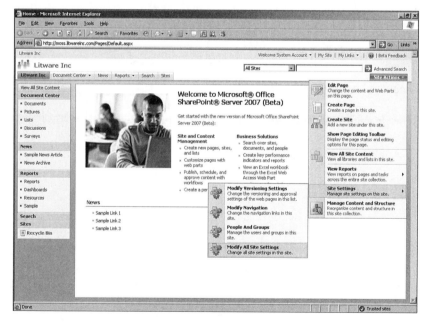

FIGURE 15.11   Modify All Site Settings.

This takes you to the Site Settings page. You should click on the Galleries, Web Parts link
to modify the Web Part Gallery of your site.

This displays a list of Web Parts that are already in your Web Part Gallery. Click the New link to go to the Import Web Part page and select your Web Part, as shown in Figure 15.12.

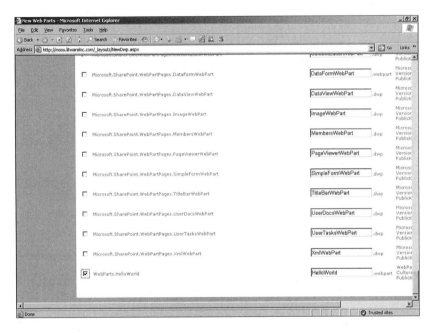

FIGURE 15.12   Import a new Web Part.

When you have selected your new Web Parts, click the Populate Gallery button. This imports your new Web Parts into your site's Web Part Gallery. Once in the gallery, the Web Part can now be added to your page, as shown in Figure 15.13.

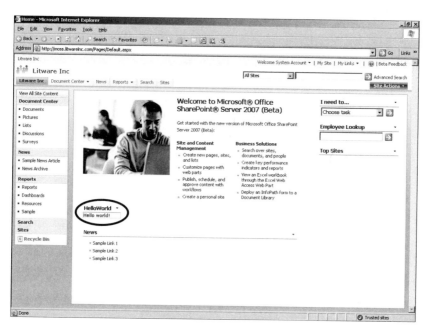

FIGURE 15.13   New Web Part displayed in SharePoint.

Summary

This chapter discussed creating Web Parts by first looking at the ASP.NET Portal Framework and how it relates to SharePoint 2007. This chapter examined all of the controls that are available in ASP.NET 2.0 for creating and debugging Web Parts, specifically `WebPartManager`, `WebPartZone`, and `WebPart` controls. This chapter then showed you how to create a Web Part and test it in the ASP.NET Portal Framework and then in SharePoint 2007.

CHAPTER 16

Developing Full-Featured Web Parts

IN THIS CHAPTER

▶ Web Part Properties

▶ Picking Property Values from a List

▶ Interactive Web Parts

The ASP.NET 2.0 Portal Framework and the SharePoint 2007 object model make it easier to develop full-featured Web Parts. This chapter shows you how to extend your Web Parts so that they are more interactive to the user and better integrate into your enterprise.

Web Part Properties

Out of the box, the WebPart class provides you with a lot of the functionality needed to integrate with the ASP.NET 2.0 Portal Framework and SharePoint 2007. There are too many properties to list in this book (and why reiterate the documentation), so this section shows you how to write custom properties for Web Parts.

Customizing Web Parts with Properties

The first thing that you can do to enhance your Web Parts is add properties to your Web Part classes. This allows you to provide either Web Part administrators or users of the Web Part the ability to very easily apply custom settings to Web Parts on the page. The syntax for creating a Web Part property is exactly the same as creating a property on any other class, with the addition of one or more Web Part–specific attributes. Listing 16.1 illustrates a Web Part that calculates a simple estimated payment for a loan. It uses properties to allow the user to configure values for Loan Value, Number of Months, and Interest Rate. When the Web Part renders, it calculates the values that the user provides and renders the estimated monthly payment.

LISTING 16.1   SimpleLoanCalculator Web Part

```csharp
using System;
using System.Collections.Generic;
using System.Text;
using System.Web.UI.WebControls.WebParts;

namespace WebParts
{
    public class SimpleLoanCalculator : Microsoft.SharePoint.WebPartPages.WebPart
    {
        public SimpleLoanCalculator() { }

        private string _textToRender = string.Empty;
        private double _pv = 0;
        private double _n = 0;
        private double _rate = 0;

        [WebBrowsable(true),
        WebDisplayName("Loan Value"),
        WebDescription("Enter a loan amount"),
        Personalizable(PersonalizationScope.User)]
        public double PV
        {
            get { return this._pv; }
            set
            {
                if (value < 0)
                {
                    this._pv = 0;
                }
                else
                {
                    this._pv = value;
                }
            }
        }

        [WebBrowsable(true),
        WebDisplayName("Time in Months"),
        WebDescription("Enter time in months"),
        Personalizable(PersonalizationScope.User)]
        public double N
        {
            get { return this._n; }
```

LISTING 16.1   Continued

```
            set
            {
                if (value < 0)
                {
                    this._n = 0;
                }
                else
                {
                    this._n = value;
                }
            }
        }

        [WebBrowsable(true),
         WebDisplayName("Interest Rate"),
        WebDescription("Enter a valid interest rate"),
        Personalizable(PersonalizationScope.User)]
        public double Rate
        {
            get { return this._rate; }
            set
            {
                if (value < 0)
                {
                    this._rate = 0;
                }
                else
                {
                    this._rate = value;
                }
            }
        }

        protected override void Render(System.Web.UI.HtmlTextWriter writer)
        {
            writer.Write(string.Format("Your estimated loan payment " +
➥will be {0:$#,##0.00;($#,##0.00);Zero}", this.calcPayment(
➥this._pv, this._n, this._rate)));
        }

        private double calcPayment(double PV, double N, double Rate)
        {
            return (PV) * (Rate / 1200) / (1 - (1 / Math.Pow(
➥(1 + Rate / 1200), N)));
```

LISTING 16.1   Continued

```
        }

    }

}
```

> **NOTE**
>
> Note that, as in the previous chapters, the Assembly that contains this code has been signed and will be installed into the Global Assembly Cache (GAC) on the SharePoint server.

The code in Listing 16.1 is very similar to the code that you have already seen in previous examples in Chapter 14, "ASP.NET Server Control Primer," and Chapter 15, "Introduction to Web Parts," with the following attributes that have been used to describe each of the public properties: WebBrowsable, WebDisplayName, WebDescription, and Personalizable.

Attributes

The WebBrowsable attribute allows your property to be exposed to the ASP.NET 2.0 Portal Framework (in an Editor Zone) and SharePoint 2007. In addition, you might have other properties that can be set dynamically in code that you don't want exposed to your SharePoint users, so configuring a property as WebBrowsable is not required for every property in your Web Part, just the ones that you want to provide to the user.

Whereas the WebBrowsable attribute allows you to determine whether a user sees a property, the WebDisplayName and WebDescription attributes allow you to customize "what" the user sees. A lot of times, we, as developers, come up with brilliant names for objects in our classes, which might not mean anything to the users of our systems. For example, in Listing 16.1, notice the property called "PV", which has a WebDisplayName of "Loan Value" and a WebDescription of "Enter a loan amount". Although "PV" might or might not have a meaning with your users, the WebDisplayName "Loan Value" is much more obvious to the user what value you are actually looking for. By using the WebDescription attribute, you can provide a more detailed description to the user that will be displayed in a ToolTip when the user hovers over the property in the Modify Shared Web Part frame.

The Personalization attribute allows you to specify how your data is scoped. You can scope your data so that changes affect either a single user or all users of your control. This is accomplished via the PersonalizationScope enumeration. In Listing 16.1, all three properties are scoped to the user. Figure 16.1 illustrates the SimpleLoanCalculator Web Part as it is rendered by SharePoint. Also notice the Modify Shared Web Part frame and how the control's properties can be configured.

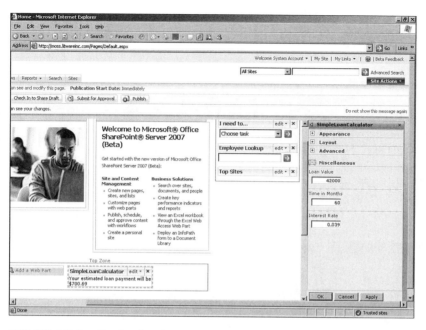

FIGURE 16.1   Configuring the `SimpleLoanCalculator` control.

Your Web Part properties will render differently, depending on how they are declared. Primarily, your properties will render a `TextBox` so that you can type in a text value for your property and it will get saved, if it is a valid value for the property (for example, string data can't be saved to a numeric data type). The two exceptions that will not render as a `TextBox` in the page designer are `bool` and `enum` data types. `Bool` renders as a `CheckBox` and enum renders as a `DropDownList`. This is something that you want to keep in mind, especially if you are looking for specific data from the user, instead of having them type in a free-form `TextBox`. The next example looks at adding an enum property to the `SimpleLoanCalculator` Web Part.

Picking Property Values from a List

Often, you are looking for specific information from your users who are personalizing Web Parts and can't accurately capture that data with a property that gets rendered as a free-form `TextBox`. Any property that you declare that returns an enum data type automatically gets rendered as a `DropDownList` control. Taking the `SimpleLoanCalculator`, for example, you might want to store information about what time of month the user intends to pay his loan payment. All that is required is to declare an enum called `PayDate` and set up a property to get and set the `PayDate` value, as illustrated in the following code example:

```
public enum PayDate
{
    FirstOfMonth
```

```
    ,MiddleOfMonth
    ,LastOfMonth
}


[WebBrowsable(true),
        WebDisplayName("When would you like to pay?"),
        WebDescription("The sooner, the better!"),
        Personalizable(PersonalizationScope.User)]
public PayDate payDate
{
    get { return this._pd; }
    set { this._pd = value; }
}
```

Figure 16.2 illustrates the drop-down list that gets rendered in the Modify Shared Web
Part frame.

FIGURE 16.2   Selecting a property as a DropDownList.

Interactive Web Parts

Most of the custom Web Parts that you will write will need to do more than just output
text and maintain state for property values. Although this is important knowledge for
creating Web Parts, it isn't enough when you need to create a Web Part that integrates

with your current systems. The ASP.NET 2.0 Portal Framework and SharePoint 2007 object model provide a lot of functionality that you can use to integrate your systems into SharePoint. This section shows you how to build a Web Part that integrates with an existing system: the AdventureWorks sample database. Although the following example is very simple, it provides the knowledge required to extend the functionality into your own systems.

Because there is currently not a formal designer-based tool available for creating custom Web Parts, you must consider a lot of things before you begin. First, what functionality does your Web Part need to provide your users? This is an important and seemingly obvious question, but the functionality that is required affects what controls, methods, and properties you will implement to deliver a working solution to your users. In addition, you need to consider how your page will be laid out because depending on the complexity of the Web Part's layout, a considerable amount of code must be written and maintained to provide a clean look and feel to your Web Parts.

Because of these complexities, the example that is used in this section is simple: Provide users with the ability to execute a Structured Query Language (SQL) statement against any specified database and display the results in a grid. Although it might not be something that is immediately usable in your environment, you will learn how to add standard .NET controls to your Web Part, provide a layout in which to display the controls, and handle postbacks from within your Web Parts. Figure 16.3 illustrates the final Web Part (called the SQLExecute Web Part) that will be built during this section of the chapter.

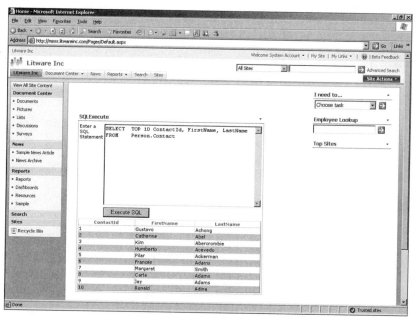

FIGURE 16.3   SQLExecute Web Part in SharePoint 2007.

Although the layout is simple, a considerable amount of code is required by the requirements that have been defined.

CAUTION

As with any control, it is best to render the contents inside of a table so that its contents will line up properly when rendered. The code that is required to properly output a table can get quite cumbersome, so it is best to comment your code very carefully during this process so that it will be easily maintained in the future.

Before looking at an actual Web Part, take a quick look at a simple Web Part template (Listing 16.2) that can be used as a base for creating custom Web Parts.

LISTING 16.2　Web Part Template

```
using System;
using System.Collections.Generic;
using System.Text;
using System.Web.UI;
using System.Web.UI.WebControls;
using System.Web.UI.WebControls.WebParts;
using System.Data;
using System.Data.SqlClient;
using System.Drawing;

namespace WebParts
{
    public class WebPartTemplate : WebPart
    {
        public WebPartTemplate() { }

        //control definitions HERE

        //overrides
        protected override void CreateChildControls()
        {
            //setup controls that will be placed on your web part
        }

        protected override void Render(System.Web.UI.HtmlTextWriter writer)
        {
            //render controls to the writer object
        }

        //control events HERE
    }
}
```

The Web Part template can be used to get started creating custom Web Parts because it defines a common framework that you can use to build a Web Part. You must override two events if you plan to add any web controls (for example, Button, TextBox, GridView) to your Web Part: CreateChildControls and Render.

Because there is not a designer available that will create this code for you, when you are developing Web Parts, it is best to think like you would if you were designing a web page—you just have to create the code manually instead of having Visual Studio do it for you. With that in mind, you will use the CreateChildControls method exactly like a web page (.aspx) uses the Init event; you need to instantiate any custom web controls that you want to place in your Web Part, configure their properties, and add them to the Web Part's control collection.

The Render event is used to render your Web Part in the user's browser. Because Render controls everything that gets pushed down to the user, you will quickly see code stack up in this event. As you will see in Listing 16.3, the Render method outputs a table with two columns and four rows, but requires about 30 lines of code to make this possible.

Listing 16.3 illustrates the SQLExecute Web Part class file.

LISTING 16.3   SQLExecute Web Part

```csharp
using System;
using System.Collections.Generic;
using System.Text;
using System.Web.UI;
using System.Web.UI.WebControls;
using System.Web.UI.WebControls.WebParts;
using System.Data;
using System.Data.SqlClient;
using System.Drawing;

namespace WebParts
{
    public class SQLExecute : WebPart
    {
        public SQLExecute() { }
        private string _cnString = string.Empty;

        //control definitions
        protected Label lblError;
        protected Button btnExecuteSQL;
        protected TextBox txtSQL;
        protected GridView gvResults;

        [WebBrowsable(true),
        WebDisplayName("Connection String"),
```

16

LISTING 16.3   Continued

```
        WebDescription("Enter connection string"),
        Personalizable(PersonalizationScope.User)]
        public string CNString
        {
            get { return this._cnString; }
            set { this._cnString = value; }
        }

        //overrides
        protected override void CreateChildControls()
        {
            //label
            lblError = new Label();
            this.Controls.Add(lblError);
            //textbox
            txtSQL = new TextBox();
            txtSQL.Width = Unit.Pixel(400);
            txtSQL.Height = Unit.Pixel(200);
            txtSQL.TextMode = TextBoxMode.MultiLine;
            this.Controls.Add(txtSQL);

            //button
            btnExecuteSQL = new Button();
            btnExecuteSQL.Text = "Execute SQL";
            btnExecuteSQL.Click += new EventHandler(btnExecuteSQL_Click);
            this.Controls.Add(btnExecuteSQL);

            //gridview
            gvResults = new GridView();
            gvResults.Width = Unit.Percentage(100) ;
            gvResults.AlternatingRowStyle.BackColor = Color.LightBlue;
            this.Controls.Add(gvResults);
        }

        protected override void Render(System.Web.UI.HtmlTextWriter writer)
        {
            writer.RenderBeginTag(HtmlTextWriterTag.Table);
                writer.RenderBeginTag(HtmlTextWriterTag.Tr);
                    writer.AddAttribute(HtmlTextWriterAttribute.Colspan, "2");
                    writer.RenderBeginTag(HtmlTextWriterTag.Td);
                    lblError.RenderControl(writer);
                    writer.RenderEndTag(); //td
                writer.RenderEndTag();//tr
                writer.AddAttribute(HtmlTextWriterAttribute.Valign, "top");
```

LISTING 16.3   Continued

```
            writer.RenderBeginTag(HtmlTextWriterTag.Tr);
                writer.RenderBeginTag(HtmlTextWriterTag.Td);
                writer.Write("Enter a SQL Statement");
                writer.RenderEndTag(); //td
                writer.RenderBeginTag(HtmlTextWriterTag.Td);
                txtSQL.RenderControl(writer);
                writer.RenderEndTag(); //td
            writer.RenderEndTag();//tr
            writer.RenderBeginTag(HtmlTextWriterTag.Tr);
                writer.RenderBeginTag(HtmlTextWriterTag.Td);
                writer.RenderEndTag(); //td
                writer.RenderBeginTag(HtmlTextWriterTag.Td);
                btnExecuteSQL.RenderControl(writer);
                writer.RenderEndTag(); //td
            writer.RenderEndTag();//tr
            writer.RenderBeginTag(HtmlTextWriterTag.Tr);
                writer.AddAttribute(HtmlTextWriterAttribute.Colspan, "2");
                writer.RenderBeginTag(HtmlTextWriterTag.Td);
                gvResults.RenderControl(writer);
                writer.RenderEndTag(); //td
            writer.RenderEndTag();//tr
        writer.RenderEndTag(); //table
    }


    //events
    protected void btnExecuteSQL_Click(object sender, EventArgs e)
    {
        if (this._cnString.Trim() != string.Empty)
        {
            try
            {
                SqlConnection cn = new SqlConnection(this._cnString);
                SqlCommand cmd = new SqlCommand(this.txtSQL.Text, cn);
                SqlDataAdapter adp = new SqlDataAdapter(cmd);
                DataSet ds = new DataSet();
                adp.Fill(ds);
                this.gvResults.DataSource = ds.Tables[0].DefaultView;
                this.gvResults.DataBind();
            }
            catch (Exception ex)
            {
                this.gvResults.DataSource = null;
                this.gvResults.DataBind();
                lblError.Visible = true;
```

16

LISTING 16.3   Continued

```
                lblError.Text = ex.Message;
            }
        }
        else
        {
            this.gvResults.DataSource = null;
            this.gvResults.DataBind();
            lblError.Visible = true;
            lblError.Text = "Please enter a connection string!";
        }


    }
  }
}
```

The code in Listing 16.3 defines one property named CNString and four controls, which are listed in Table 16.1.

TABLE 16.1   SQLExecute Web Part Controls

Control Name	Type
lblError	System.Web.UI.WebControls.Label
btnExecuteSQL	System.Web.UI.WebControls.Button
txtSQL	System.Web.UI.WebControls.TextBox
gvResults	System.Web.UI.WebControls.GridView

Notice that the controls are defined as protected member variables so that if any class is derived from the SQLExecute Web Part class, these controls will be made available in the derived class. In addition, it is a best practice to instantiate these controls in the CreateChildControls event, instead of in their declaration.

The CreateChildControls event is used to initialize all of the web controls that will be used by your Web Part and add them to the Web Part's controls collection. Take a look at the following code excerpt, which is taken from the CreateChildControls event of the SQLExecute Web Part:

```
//textbox
1: txtSQL = new TextBox();
2: txtSQL.Width = Unit.Pixel(400);
3: txtSQL.Height = Unit.Pixel(200);
4: txtSQL.TextMode = TextBoxMode.MultiLine;
5: this.Controls.Add(txtSQL);
```

Note that the line numbers are for reference only. The first thing you must do is instantiate your control, which is demonstrated in line 1 of the code, where a new instance of a TextBox control is created. Lines 2–4 are examples of setting the TextBox's properties, which control what type of TextBox will be used by your Web Part. Finally, and most important, you need to add each web control to your Web Part's Controls collection, as in line 5 of the code excerpt. This registers your control object with your Web Part and allows it to properly render the control, as well as maintain the registered control's ViewState and associated events (for example, a button's click event), which is very important when your control does a postback.

Handling Postback

Chances are likely that at some point, your Web Part will need to perform a postback to provide the user with feedback when they interact with your Web Part. You can use the following checklist to ensure that your controls handle postbacks elegantly.

1. Define your web control with the public or protected access modifier.

2. Override your Web Part's CreateChildControls event.

   a. Instantiate your web control.

   b. Configure your web control's properties.

   c. Add any event handlers to your web control.

   d. Add your web control to the Controls collection of your Web Part.

A good example of a control in the SQLExecute Web Part that follows all of these rules is the button control that is used to execute the given SQL statement. The following code provides an example of all five of the rules:

```
//button
btnExecuteSQL = new Button();
btnExecuteSQL.Text = "Execute SQL";
btnExecuteSQL.Click += new EventHandler(btnExecuteSQL_Click);
this.Controls.Add(btnExecuteSQL);
```

The code is again taken from the CreateChildControls event of the SQLExecute Web Part from Listing 16.3. Notice that an event handler is attached to the Click event of the button just before the button control is added to Web Part's Controls collection. If you forget to add the button control to the Web Part's Controls collection, the Click event handler (btnExecuteSQL_Click) never gets fired. This is a common mistake made by Web Part developers, so this is one of the first things you should look at if your web control's event handlers are not getting fired.

Including JavaScript

Often, you might want to include some JavaScript with your Web Part to provide client-side validation before a postback happens in your control. You can easily add client script by either using the `Page.ClientScript` class or adding client-side event handlers to your controls. The following code excerpt is an example of attaching a client-side `onclick` event to the `btnExecuteSQL` button that will evaluate whether the user has entered text into the `txtSQL` TextBox:

```
//add JavaScript
1: StringBuilder sbJS = new StringBuilder();
2: sbJS.Append("if(document.getElementById('");
3: sbJS.Append(txtSQL.ClientID);
4: sbJS.Append("').value == ''){
➥alert('You must specify a SQL statement');return false;}");
5: btnExecuteSQL.Attributes.Add("onclick", sbJS.ToString());
```

Note that the line numbers are for reference only. When you are writing JavaScript that is being emitted by your Web Part (or page, or user control), it is important to keep in mind that you are creating this JavaScript on the server and it is being pushed to the client. This means that if you plan to reference any controls that are rendered on the client, you need to reference them by their `ClientID` property, as illustrated in line 3 of the preceding code example. This is because you can't guarantee what the ASP.NET runtime will name your object when it gets pushed to the client. In this script, if the user hasn't entered anything in the `txtSQL` TextBox and he clicks the Execute SQL Button, he receives a message telling him to specify a SQL statement. In addition, notice that if the user receives the alert box, the script returns a value of `false`, which cancels the postback to the server, thus handling this validation completely client-side.

Summary

This chapter showed you how to extend Web Parts using properties that are configurable at runtime from within the ASP.NET 2.0 Portal Framework and SharePoint 2007. In addition, this chapter showed you how to use an external data source with your Web Parts so that you can write Web Parts that integrate into your enterprise systems.

CHAPTER 17

Building Web Parts for Maintaining SharePoint 2007 Lists

IN THIS CHAPTER

▸ Web Parts and SharePoint Lists

▸ The SharePoint List Example

▸ Accessing a List

▸ Updating List Data

Extending the concept of building Web Parts, this chapter discusses creating Web Parts that interact with Microsoft Office SharePoint Server (MOSS) lists. This chapter shows you how to easily manipulate data that is contained in lists.

Web Parts and SharePoint Lists

Out of the box, a lot of power is built in to SharePoint 2007 lists. You can easily create custom lists that fit the needs for whatever kind of data you are trying to collect; however, there are some drawbacks. For example, it is difficult to customize the way that you collect data in a list without a little bit of custom code. This chapter's example shows you how to interact with data in a list by using a Web Part, as well as some of the reasons why you would need to use a Web Part to customize your list interaction.

The SharePoint List Example

The example that is used in this chapter is a simple list that contains time sheet information from users. This is a common scenario as many enterprises are using SharePoint to collect data such as this from users; the common problems that you encounter in this chapter map to the real world.

The list contains five columns: Employee Name, Week End Date, Total Hours Worked, Client, and Project. Each user submits a time sheet at the end of each week that states how many hours he worked in a given week. Out of the

box, this is quite a simple list; however, when a user enters their time sheet, more validation is needed to require the user to submit time where Week End Date is a Friday.

> **NOTE**
>
> Note that although you could accomplish this goal in many other ways, this scenario is
> being used to illustrate how to write a custom Web Part to manipulate data in a
> SharePoint list.

Figure 17.1 illustrates the list that contains time sheet entries for two people.

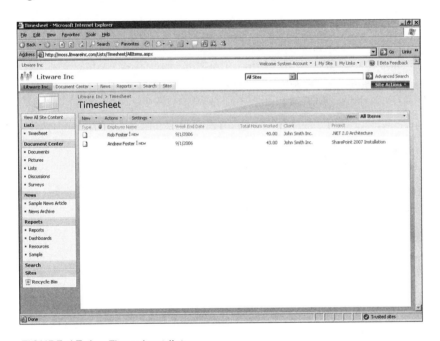

FIGURE 17.1   Time sheet list.

The next section shows you how to configure a Visual Studio 2005 Class Library project
to access a SharePoint list.

Accessing a List

The example used in this chapter starts out as a very simple Web Part class that displays
data in a list and expands into a library of Web Parts that will be used to maintain the
list's data.

There is a hierarchy that must be followed to "walk down" to lists in SharePoint. Figure
17.2 illustrates this hierarchy.

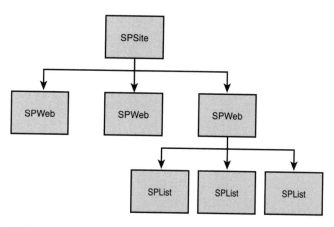

FIGURE 17.2   SharePoint hierarchy.

At its core, SharePoint is a collection of related Site, Web, and List objects. A single site (SPSite) can contain multiple webs (SPWeb). Each web can contain multiple lists (SPList). You can easily walk down this chain of objects to get to the object with which you want to interact.

Luckily for the developer community, the SharePoint object model provides a lot of functionality to make this process easy. The Microsoft.SharePoint namespace contains an object called SPContext that you can use to get a handle to a SharePoint site. You can think of using the SPContext object with SharePoint as you would use the HTTPContext object with your web applications. From the Web Part perspective, SPContext allows you to "hook" into the instance of SharePoint in which your Web Part is running. This is important because you can get a reference to whatever object (list, workflow, and so forth) that you would like to access and utilize the SharePoint application programming interface (API) to manipulate that object.

By using the Current property of SPContext, you can gain access to practically every object in your site. Table 17.1 describes the three core objects that you will utilize in your custom code libraries.

TABLE 17.1   Core SharePoint Objects

Object	Description
.Site	Returns an instance of SPSite and is used mainly for configuring global settings for all of your webs. For example, you can configure SharePoint's search, as well as the Recycle Bin.
.Web	Returns an instance of SPWeb and is the SharePoint web in which your code is executing. Here, you can gain access to every object in your web. Examples are Alerts, Users, Lists, Documents, and so on.
.List	Returns an instance of SPList and represents a list inside of your SharePoint web.

17

Listing 17.1 illustrates a very simple example of a Web Part that utilizes `SPContext` to gain access to the `Timesheet` list described earlier in this chapter and output the total number of hours entered by the users.

LISTING 17.1   Using `SPContext` to Reference Timesheet List

```
using System;
using System.Web;
using System.Collections.Generic;
using System.Text;
using Microsoft.SharePoint;
using Microsoft.SharePoint.Utilities;
using Microsoft.SharePoint.WebControls;
using Microsoft.SharePoint.WebPartPages;

namespace WebParts29
{
    public class Timesheet : System.Web.UI.WebControls.WebParts.WebPart
    {
        private Microsoft.SharePoint.SPWeb _web = null;
        private Microsoft.SharePoint.SPList _timesheetList = null;

        public Timesheet()
        {

        }

        protected override void Render(System.Web.UI.HtmlTextWriter writer)
        {

            try
            {
                //get the web
                this._web = Microsoft.SharePoint.SPContext.Current.Web;

                //get the timesheet list
                this._timesheetList = this._web.Lists["Timesheet"];

                double totalHoursWorked = 0;
                foreach (SPListItem i in this._timesheetList.Items)
                {
                    totalHoursWorked += Convert.ToDouble(i["Total Hours Worked"]);
                }
```

LISTING 17.1   Continued

```
            writer.Write("The total number of hours worked are {0}",
➥totalHoursWorked.ToString());
        }
        catch (Exception)
        {
            //show the user something pretty here
            writer.Write("Error loading Timesheet list.
➥Please contact an administrator.");
        }
    }
}
}
```

In the `Render` method of this Web Part, an instance of the `SPWeb` object is created and references a handle to the current web in which the Web Part is running. Next, an instance of the Timesheet list is created by accessing the current web's `Lists` collection. You can reference list items by either string name, unique ID (as a globally unique identifier [GUID]), or index. Because the list is named "Timesheet," it is easiest to reference it by name.

> **NOTE**
>
> Note that accessing lists by name performs a bit slower than accessing lists by index or unique ID; however, if you ever restore or redeploy your site to another server, these values could change, so it is best to access lists by string name, even though it performs slower.

After the list object is created, you can then iterate the list in a loop and total up the Total Hours Worked column of the list. Notice that the column in the list is referenced exactly as it is named. Like the list, you can also access columns by name, by unique ID (GUID), or by index.

What's common about the SharePoint object model and what you are probably familiar with already is that a list object is simply a collection of list items, which can be iterated just like any other collection. If you bypass the learning curve and think of a list as you would a `DataTable`, it makes learning the object model a lot easier. As you progress into the next section, "Updating List Data," this becomes even more evident.

Updating List Data

More than likely, if you are interacting with a list, you are probably providing some sort of customized data entry Web Part for the user. In the previous section, you learned how to create a Web Part that accessed list data, iterated all of the list data, and displayed a sum of the Total Hours Worked column. This is a good example to provide a setup to this section, but its functionality can easily be replicated in a customized view without writing any code.

An example of when you might want to provide some custom functionality to a list is a Web Part that allows a user to enter information that will be saved to a list. For example, out of the box, SharePoint provides a couple of default interfaces for entering data into a list. You can either use the Create New Item interface, which provides labels and data entry controls (TextBoxes, DropDowns, Calendars, and so forth) for entering data, or you can use the Edit in DataSheet interface to edit the records in a spreadsheet-style interface.

Although very powerful, these interfaces don't always provide the functionality or validation required to accurately collect data from the users. For example, in the Timesheet list, what if you only want users to enter time where the "Week End Date" occurs on a Friday? This is difficult to do out of the box, but can be easily achieved by using a Web Part to validate the data and then add the new record to the list.

Listing 17.2 illustrates the Timesheet Entry Web Part class.

LISTING 17.2   Timesheet Entry Web Part

```
using System;
using System.Web;
using System.Web.UI.WebControls;
using System.Collections.Generic;
using System.Text;
using Microsoft.SharePoint;
using Microsoft.SharePoint.Utilities;
using Microsoft.SharePoint.WebControls;
using Microsoft.SharePoint.WebPartPages;


namespace WebParts17
{
    public class TimesheetEntry : System.Web.UI.WebControls.WebParts.WebPart
    {
        public TimesheetEntry() { }

        protected TextBox txtEmployeeName;
        protected TextBox txtWeekEndDate;
        protected TextBox txtClient;
        protected TextBox txtProject;
        protected TextBox txtTotalHoursWorked;
        protected Label lblValidationError;
        protected Button btnSave;

        protected override void CreateChildControls()
        {
```

LISTING 17.2   Continued

```
            //initialize textboxes
            txtEmployeeName = new TextBox();
            txtWeekEndDate = new TextBox();
            txtClient = new TextBox();
            txtProject = new TextBox();
            txtTotalHoursWorked = new TextBox();

            //initialize label
            lblValidationError = new Label();
            lblValidationError.CssClass = "ms-formvalidation";
            lblValidationError.Visible = false;

            //initialize button
            btnSave = new Button();
            btnSave.Text = "Save";
            btnSave.Click += new EventHandler(btnSave_Click);
        }

    protected override void Render(System.Web.UI.HtmlTextWriter writer)
    {
        writer.Write("<table width=100%>");
            writer.Write("<tr>");
                writer.Write("<td colspan=2>");
                lblValidationError.RenderControl(writer);
                writer.Write("</td>");
            writer.Write("</tr>");
            writer.Write("<tr>");
                writer.Write("<td>Employee Name:
➥<span class='ms-formvalidation'>*</span></td>");
                writer.Write("<td>");
                txtEmployeeName.RenderControl(writer);
                writer.Write("</td>");
            writer.Write("</tr>");
            writer.Write("<tr>");
                writer.Write("<td>Week End Date:
➥<span class='ms-formvalidation'>*</span></td>");
                writer.Write("<td>");
                txtWeekEndDate.RenderControl(writer);
                writer.Write("</td>");
            writer.Write("</tr>");
            writer.Write("<tr>");
                writer.Write("<td>Client: <span
➥class='ms-formvalidation'>*</span></td>");
```

17

LISTING 17.2   Continued

```
                writer.Write("<td>");
                txtClient.RenderControl(writer);
                writer.Write("</td>");
            writer.Write("</tr>");
            writer.Write("<tr>");
                writer.Write("<td>Project: <span
➥class='ms-formvalidation'>*</span></td>");
                writer.Write("<td>");
                txtProject.RenderControl(writer);
                writer.Write("</td>");
            writer.Write("</tr>");
            writer.Write("<tr>");
                writer.Write("<td>Total Hours Worked: <span
➥class='ms-formvalidation'>*</span></td>");
                writer.Write("<td>");
                txtTotalHoursWorked.RenderControl(writer);
                writer.Write("</td>");
            writer.Write("</tr>");
            writer.Write("<tr>");
                writer.Write("<td>");
                writer.Write("</td>");
                writer.Write("<td>");
                btnSave.RenderControl(writer);
                writer.Write("</td>");
            writer.Write("</tr>");
        writer.Write("</table>");
    }


    void btnSave_Click(object sender, EventArgs e)
    {
        //if data is valid
        if (DateTime.Parse(txtWeekEndDate.Text).DayOfWeek != DayOfWeek.Friday)
        {
            lblValidationError.Visible = true;
            lblValidationError.Text = "Week End Date must be a Friday";
        }
        else
        {
            //save to list
            lblValidationError.Visible = false;
            lblValidationError.Text = string.Empty;
```

LISTING 17.2   Continued

```
                    SPWeb web = SPContext.Current.Web;
                    SPList timesheetList = web.Lists["Timesheet"];

                    SPListItem newTimesheetEntry = timesheetList.Items.Add();
                    newTimesheetEntry["Employee Name"] = txtEmployeeName.Text;
                    newTimesheetEntry["Week End Date"] = txtWeekEndDate.Text;
                    newTimesheetEntry["Client"] = txtClient.Text;
                    newTimesheetEntry["Project"] = txtProject.Text;
                    newTimesheetEntry["Total Hours Worked"] = txtTotalHoursWorked.Text;
                    newTimesheetEntry.Update();
                    timesheetList.Update();
                }
            }
        }
}
```

Most of the functionality of the Web Part has been covered in previous chapters, but just in case, here's a quick review of how the control is laid out; you will learn about inserting the data in the next few paragraphs.

The Web Part itself generates a table with controls that collect time sheet data from the user. The controls are defined as member variables of the Web Part class and initialized in the CreateChildControls event. Each control contains the data that needs to be validated either by using client-side JavaScript and/or server-side code.

Extending This Web Part

To provide brevity in this example, not all of the validation functionality has been implemented. In addition, the control only provides basic functionality to collect information from the user. In the real world, you might consider adding more custom functionality such as a DropDown calendar picker control or a DropDown list of current clients to the Web Part to make it a little richer experience for the user.

The Render event is used to output the actual table that the user will see. Notice that every label (left column on each row of the table) has an asterisk that is surrounded by a span tag, which has a class called ms-formvalidation associated with it. This is a class that is built in to SharePoint's style sheets. You can view the style sheets that are built in to SharePoint by opening the /_layouts/1033/styles/core.css file, which is associated with your site. If you don't feel like digging through all those lines of code, you have another option. When you see a style that you like inside your SharePoint site, the easiest approach is to view the Hypertext Markup Language (HTML) source and find the particular style in the HTML code. Figure 17.2 illustrates the Web Part as it is rendered in SharePoint.

17

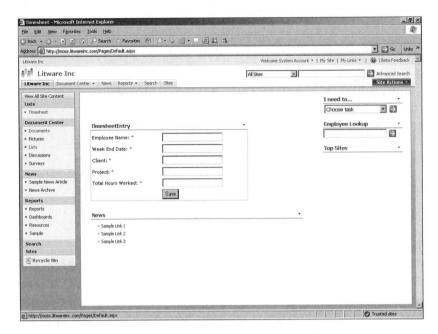

FIGURE 17.3   Time sheet entry Web Part.

The functionality to insert data into the list is contained in the btnSave_Click event. Due to brevity and to give the Web Part some validation functionality, the first couple lines of code ensure that the date entered is a Friday. If the date is a Friday, the record is inserted; otherwise, an error message is displayed to the user.

Inserting the data is quite simple. After you have a reference to your web and your list, you can call the list's Items.Add method. This returns an instance of a new row in your list. In this example, a new row in the Timesheet list is returned, where each column is set to the corresponding TextBox value. To add the row to the list, you must call the Update method of the SPListItem, or in this example, newTimesheetEntry.

There are a lot of different solutions to this problem; however, you have a lot of flexibility when you write your own Web Part to update data in a list. In addition, in a lot of scenarios, your Web Part must interact with external enterprise systems (that is, outside of SharePoint), so a Web Part-based solution makes integration and maintenance a lot easier on you as a developer. The following is a small list of things to watch out for when interacting with data in a list:

▶ If you are getting an exception thrown when you try to access a column in a list, make sure that the column's name wasn't initially "Title." When you set up a list, it has a text-only field called Title associated with it, which can't be deleted. If you change the column name to something different, its root name is still Title, so you must reference it as such.

▸ Make sure that you call the Update method when you are ready to commit your changes to the list. Failure to call Update rolls back any changes that you have made to the data.

▸ Know that when you utilize SPContext.Current from within a Web Part, you are getting instances to objects in the site/web where the Web Part is running. If you create a generic Web Part that will be used in multiple sites/webs, ensure that you have access to the appropriate objects that you will be accessing.

Summary

The examples in this chapter are not complete solutions in their entirety, but are meant to give you a base skill set that you can build upon to provide better solutions to your users. This chapter showed you how to manipulate data in a SharePoint list by first learning how to use the SharePoint API to iterate a list and output a calculation of one column. Then, this chapter showed you how to customize a data entry Web Part that allows you to provide custom validation of data that the user enters.

17

CHAPTER 18

Building Connected Web Parts

IN THIS CHAPTER

▶ Building the Provider

▶ Building the Consumer

▶ Connecting Web Parts

Connected Web Parts make it easy to share data across Web Parts that are running on your page or, more formally, allow your interactions with one Web Part to "trickle down" to other Web Parts. This chapter discusses two Web Parts that provide Master—Detail functionality on the page. This is a typical scenario of two Web Parts that are connected in which selecting a record in the master (or provider) Web Part changes the values of the details (or consumer) Web Part.

You need four things to create connected Web Parts:

- ▶ An agreed-upon interface for the data that will be provided

- ▶ A provider Web Part

- ▶ A consumer Web Part

- ▶ A connection between the two Web Parts

This chapter shows you how to complete these four steps to creating connected Web Parts.

Building the Provider

This chapter's example is based on the Customers—Orders Master-Detail relationship in the Northwind database. It contains two connected Web Parts, a provider and a consumer, as well as an interface that defines the type of data that will be consumed. Figure 18.1 illustrates the conceptual design of the two Web Parts on the page.

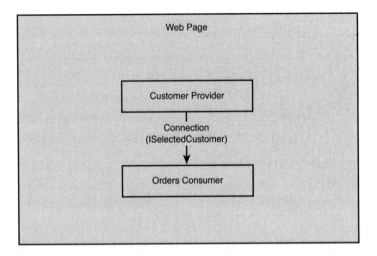

FIGURE 18.1   Connected Web Parts example.

Creating the Data Interface

You define what data will be served up by your provider Web Part by creating a contract, which is actually an interface that is defined in your code. This interface is implemented by the provider Web Part so that consumers will know what data will be sent to them by the provider. The following code excerpt defines the interface for the chapter example:

```
public interface ISelectedCustomer
{
    string CustomerID { get;}
}
```

The ISelectedCustomer interface defines one read-only property, CustomerID. The CustomerID property is the actual data point that will be passed to the consumer Web Part and will be used to retrieve all orders for a selected customer.

> **NOTE**
>
> Note that in this example, only one property is sent to consumers; however, you aren't limited by the number of properties in which your provider can send.

Creating the Provider Web Part

After you have decided on what data your provider Web Part will be sending out, you can now create the Web Part. As with all other Web Parts, this inherits from the WebPart class and also implements the ISelectedCustomer interface, which physically defines the read-only CustomerID property. Listing 18.1 defines a provider Web Part that renders a DropDownList of customers from the Northwind database.

LISTING 18.1   Provider Web Part

```
using System;
using System.Collections.Generic;
using System.Text;
using System.Web.UI.WebControls;
using System.Web.UI.WebControls.WebParts;
using System.Data;
using System.Data.SqlClient;

namespace WebParts30
{
    public class CustomersProvider : WebPart, ISelectedCustomer
    {
        public CustomersProvider() { }

        protected DropDownList ddlCustomers;

        protected override void CreateChildControls()
        {
            ddlCustomers = new DropDownList();
            ddlCustomers.AutoPostBack = true;
            ddlCustomers.SelectedIndexChanged += new
➥EventHandler(ddlCustomers_SelectedIndexChanged);
            this.loadCustomers();
        }

        protected override void Render(System.Web.UI.HtmlTextWriter writer)
        {
            ddlCustomers.RenderControl(writer);
        }

        private void loadCustomers()
        {
            try
            {
                //omitted for brevity
            }
            catch (Exception)
            {
                //error handler here
            }
        }

        [ConnectionProvider("CustomerID", "CustomerID")]
        public ISelectedCustomer GetCustomerID()
```

LISTING 18.1   Continued

```
        {
            return this as ISelectedCustomer;
        }

        void ddlCustomers_SelectedIndexChanged(object sender, EventArgs e)
        {
            //omitted for brevity
        }
        #region ISelectedCustomer Members
        public string CustomerID
        {
            get { return this.ddlCustomers.SelectedValue; }
        }
        #endregion
    }
}
```

You should pay particular attention to the three pieces of this class definition that relate to a provider Web Part. First, as has already been discussed, the class must inherit the interface that defines the data that will be provided to any consuming Web Parts. Second (and obviously), any properties and methods that are defined by the interface must be implemented. In this example, the class must have a `CustomerID` property. Third, you must define a method that will return an instance of the implemented interface, as illustrated in the following code:

```
[ConnectionProvider("CustomerID", "CustomerID")]
public ISelectedCustomer GetCustomerID()
{
    return this as ISelectedCustomer;
}
```

Notice that the method is decorated with the `ConnectionProvider` attribute. The parameters that are passed into this attribute (in this example) define the `DisplayName` and `UniqueID` of the data that is being provided. Though it isn't a required parameter, the `UniqueID` parameter will be used when connecting your provider and consumer Web Parts, so it is a good idea to always specify a Unique ID for your provider's data. Note that there are many overloads of this attribute, so choose the one that best fits your scenario. The `ConnectionProvider` attribute tells the ASP.NET runtime that *this* is the data that is being served up by your Web Part. The method returns an instance of the `ISelectedCustomer` interface. Because your class implements this interface, you can simply return the active instance of the class (or `this`), which exposes the `CustomerID` property to any consumers.

Building the Consumer

Building a Web Part consumer is quite easy, compared to building a provider. All that is required is to account for receiving the data that is being served up by a provider Web Part!

Coding a consumer is the same as coding a standard Web Part with a few minor additions. First, you need to define a variable in your class to hold the data that is being consumed (continuing with this example, it will be an instance of ISelectedEmployee). Next, you need to define a way to receive the data that is being sent to the consumer. Listing 18.2 is an example of a Web Part consumer that receives an instance of ISelectedEmployee and displays a customer's orders in a GridView control.

LISTING 18.2   Consumer Web Part

```
using System;
using System.Collections.Generic;
using System.Text;
using System.Web.UI.WebControls;
using System.Web.UI.WebControls.WebParts;
using System.Data;
using System.Data.SqlClient;

namespace WebParts30
{
    public class OrdersConsumer : WebPart
    {
        public OrdersConsumer() { }

        private ISelectedCustomer _customer = null;
        protected GridView gvOrders = null;

        [ConnectionConsumer("CustomerID", "CustomerID")]
        public void SetCustomer(ISelectedCustomer c)
        {
            this._customer = c;
        }

        protected override void CreateChildControls()
        {
            gvOrders = new GridView();
            loadGrid();
        }

        protected override void Render(System.Web.UI.HtmlTextWriter writer)
        {
            try
```

LISTING 18.2   Continued

```
            {
                gvOrders.RenderControl(writer);
            }
            catch (Exception)
            {
                //throw;
            }
        }

        private void loadGrid()
        {
            try
            {
                string cnString = "Data Source=localhost;initial " +
➥"catalog=northwind;user id=sa;password=bandit;";
                SqlConnection cn = new SqlConnection(cnString);
                SqlCommand cmd = new SqlCommand(string.Format("SELECT " +
➥ "OrderID, ShippedDate, ShipName FROM Orders where customerid='{0}'",
➥ this._customer.CustomerID), cn);
                cmd.CommandType = CommandType.Text;
                SqlDataAdapter adp = new SqlDataAdapter(cmd);
                DataSet ds = new DataSet();
                adp.Fill(ds);
                gvOrders.DataSource = ds.Tables[0].DefaultView;
                gvOrders.DataBind();
            }
            catch (Exception ex)
            {
                //error handler here
            }
        }
    }
}
```

If you look carefully at the preceding code example, you'll notice an instance of
ISelectedCustomer called _customer is defined. This is where the data that you are
consuming from the provider will be stored. The following is an excerpt of the method
definition that populates the _customer object with the data that is being provided.

```
[ConnectionConsumer("CustomerID", "CustomerID")]
public void SetCustomer(ISelectedCustomer c)
{
    this._customer = c;
}
```

The `SetCustomer` method is decorated with the `ConnectionConsumer` attribute, which defines the data that is being provided to the Web Part. Like the `ConnectionProvider` attribute that was set up in the provider Web Part, the `ConnectionConsumer` attribute also specifies a Display Name and Unique ID parameter, which again will be used to identify the data when you connect the two Web Parts.

The `SetCustomer` method acts very similarly to a "loader" event handler, as it gets executed when your control loads and is connected to a provider. Although you can (and probably will) use a different name for your consumer method, this method is required of all Web Part consumers. It must be defined as a `public` `void` method and must contain one parameter, which is the instance of your interface that will be coming into the Web Part from the provider.

> **NOTE**
>
> Note that if you forget these rules on how to define your method, Visual Studio 2005 does a good job of letting you know the requirements when you compile your code.

Connecting Web Parts

After you have finished developing your provider and consumer Web Parts, the hard part is over. To complete the cycle of developing connected Web Parts, you must "connect" your provider and consumer Web Parts. This allows the provider to send out data to any consumers. The three approaches to connecting Web Parts are as follows:

- ▶ In code, using the `ProviderConnectionPoint`, `ConsumerConnectionPoint`, and `ConnectionPoint` classes
- ▶ Configuring each Web Part inside of the SharePoint user interface
- ▶ Configuring a static connection with the `WebPartManager` on the page

All three of these approaches accomplish the same goal—they allow your connected Web Parts to talk. This section shows you how to connect Web Parts by using the third approach, using a static connection with the `WebPartManager` on the page.

In the ASP.NET 2.0 Portal Framework, the `WebPartManager` class is required to manage the interaction and functionality of Web Parts on the page. So far in this book, you have learned that this includes the personalization aspects of the Web Parts that are viewable on the page. In addition, the `WebPartManager` class functionality includes managing connections between provider and consumer Web Parts. Figure 18.2 illustrates the Properties window of the `WebPartManager` class in Visual Studio 2005.

To add a static connection to your Web Part manager, click the Build (ellipsis) button. This opens up the `WebPartConnection` Collection Editor, which is shown in Figure 18.3.

FIGURE 18.2   `WebPartManager` Properties window.

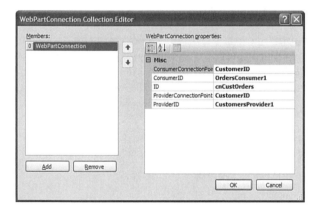

FIGURE 18.3   `WebPartConnection` Collection Editor.

To set up the static connection, you must first configure five properties, which are described in Table 18.1.

TABLE 18.1   Properties Required to Set Up a Static Connection

Property	Description
ID	The name of the connection itself
ProviderID	The name of the provider Web Part
ConsumerID	The name of the consumer Web Part
ProviderConnectionPoint	The Unique ID that is specified by the `ConnectionProvider` attribute in the provider Web Part
ConsumerConnectionPoint	The Unique ID that is specified by the `ConnectionConsumer` attribute in the consumer Web Part

After you configure the static connection, a new section will appear in the Hypertext Markup Language (HTML) markup area of the ASP.NET web page that contains the `WebPartManager` control. Listing 18.3 is an example of an ASP.NET web page that has been configured with the provider and consumer Web Parts that you learned how to build in this chapter.

LISTING 18.3   Connecting Provider and Consumer Web Parts

```
<%@ Page Language="C#" %>
<%@ Register Assembly="WebParts30" Namespace="WebParts30" TagPrefix="cc1" %>

<!DOCTYPE html PUBLIC "-//W3C//DTD XHTML 1.0 Transitional//EN"
➥ "http://www.w3.org/TR/xhtml1/DTD/xhtml1-transitional.dtd">

<script runat="server">

</script>

<html xmlns="http://www.w3.org/1999/xhtml" >
<head runat="server">
    <title>Untitled Page</title>
</head>
<body>
    <form id="form1" runat="server">
    <div>
        <asp:WebPartManager ID="wpm" runat="server">
            <StaticConnections>
                <asp:WebPartConnection ID="cnCustOrders"
➥ ConsumerConnectionPointID="CustomerID" ConsumerID="OrdersConsumer1"
➥                    ProviderID="CustomersProvider1"
➥ProviderConnectionPointID="CustomerID">
                </asp:WebPartConnection>
            </StaticConnections>
        </asp:WebPartManager>
        <table width="100%">
            <tr>
                <td colspan="2">
                    <asp:WebPartZone ID="topZone" runat="server" Width="100%">
                        <ZoneTemplate>
                            <cc1:CustomersProvider ID="CustomersProvider1"
➥runat="server" />
                        </ZoneTemplate>
                    </asp:WebPartZone>
                </td>
            </tr>
            <tr>
```

18

LISTING 18.3   Continued

```
                <td>
                    <asp:WebPartZone ID="leftZone" runat="server" Width="100%">
                        <ZoneTemplate>
                            <cc1:OrdersConsumer ID="OrdersConsumer1"
➥runat="server" />
                        </ZoneTemplate>
                    </asp:WebPartZone>
                </td>
                <td>
                    <asp:WebPartZone ID="rightZone" runat="server" Width="100%">
                    </asp:WebPartZone>
                </td>
            </tr>
            <tr>
                <td colspan="2">
                    <asp:WebPartZone ID="bottomZone" runat="server" Width="100%">
                    </asp:WebPartZone>
                </td>
            </tr>
        </table>

    </div>
    </form>
</body>
</html>
```

If you first take note of the markup that has been generated for the static connection, you can see the results of configuring the static connection property of the WebPartManager class. Figure 18.4 illustrates the rendered page where the user selects a customer from the DropDownList control and that customer's order information is displayed in the grid.

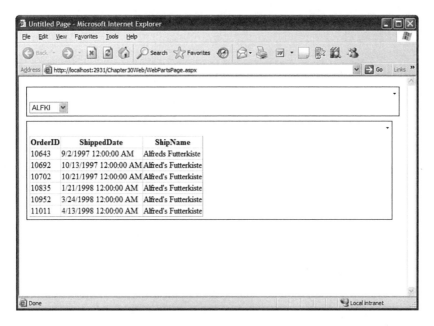

FIGURE 18.4   Provider and consumer Web Parts on a page.

Summary

In this chapter, you learned how to create a Web Part that provides data, a Web Part that consumes data, and a Web Part that connects the two. You can use these skills to create a robust suite of reusable Web Parts that can provide data to and consume data from other Web Parts in your site infrastructure.

18

CHAPTER 19

Debugging and Deploying Web Parts

IN THIS CHAPTER

▶ Debugging Web Parts

▶ Deploying Web Parts

In most development scenarios, debugging and deploying your Assemblies is an integral part of the software development life cycle. This chapter shows you how to debug a Web Part using Visual Studio 2005 and how to compile an .msi installer file that can be deployed to your SharePoint servers.

Debugging Web Parts

Because the majority of your Web Parts will be developed and tested from within Visual Studio 2005, a lot of the headaches of debugging your Web Parts are solved. However, in some instances, you need to utilize the debugger to determine what's going on inside the code of your Web Part as it executes. This section covers how to debug a Web Part that is executing inside of Microsoft Office SharePoint Server (MOSS) with Visual Studio.

The Developer's Machine Configuration

To effectively debug your Web Parts that are running inside of SharePoint, you need to install SharePoint on your development workstation because it isn't realistic to install and run Visual Studio on your SharePoint server. A SharePoint development workstation typically has the following items installed:

▶ Windows Server 2003

▶ Internet Information Services 6

▶ SQL Server 2005/2000

▶ Windows SharePoint Services 3.0

- SharePoint 2007

- Office 2007

- Visual Studio 2005

The aforementioned software should be installed so that you are able to debug code with the Visual Studio that's physically running inside of the SharePoint server. The next section discusses how to debug a Web Part that is running inside of SharePoint 2007.

Debugging

If you are in a situation where you must debug a Web Part that is running in an instance of SharePoint 2007, you should note two things: First, you are going to need A LOT of random access memory (RAM) and second, debugging Web Parts that run in SharePoint is a slow process. Because of the amount of resources that SharePoint, SQL Server, and Visual Studio require, your machine will be very busy trying to keep up with the debugging process.

With that said, the debugging process is very straightforward. The method that you use to debug your Web Parts in SharePoint is very similar to debugging a standard server control. You can use the following steps as a guide:

1. Develop the Web Part.

2. Deploy the Web Part to your "debugging" SharePoint workstation.

3. Set breakpoints in your Web Part.

4. Attach to the SharePoint process.

5. Step through the code.

The following examples show you how to use Visual Studio 2005 to debug a Web Part. For the sake of demonstrating the functionality of debugging a Web Part, the simple Web Part in Listing 19.1 is used.

LISTING 19.1   Simple Web Part to Debug

```
using System;
using System.Collections.Generic;
using System.Text;
using System.Web.UI.WebControls.WebParts;
using Microsoft.SharePoint;
```

LISTING 19.1   Continued

```
namespace DebugDeploy19
{
    public class TimesheetList : WebPart
    {
        protected override void Render(System.Web.UI.HtmlTextWriter writer)
        {
            SPWeb web = SPContext.Current.Web;
            SPList timesheet = web.Lists["Timesheet"];
            foreach (SPListItem i in timesheet.Items)
            {
                writer.Write("<H2>");
                writer.Write(i["Employee Name"].ToString() + " -- " +
➥i["Total Hours Worked"].ToString());
                writer.Write("<HR><BR>");
                writer.Write("</H2>");
            }
        }
    }
}
```

In this example, the Web Part simply iterates a list and outputs items in the list in a string format. The line of code that will bomb if this Web Part isn't running in SharePoint (or Windows SharePoint Services [WSS]) is where the SPWeb object is created from an instance of the current SharePoint web's context object, as follows:

```
SPWeb web = SPContext.Current.Web;
```

To properly step through this code, you must do so while the Web Part is running inside of the context of SharePoint. Figure 19.1 illustrates the sample Web Part as it is rendered inside of SharePoint 2007.

To begin the debugging process, you need to compile and deploy your Web Part library with the debug symbols (including the .pdb files). If you don't compile with the debug symbols, your Web Part library will execute in SharePoint, but you will not be able to debug it because there is nothing for Visual Studio to map to. This process is very important, but often overlooked. Deploying Web Parts is covered later in this chapter.

To begin the debugging process after you deploy your Web Part, you need to first set a breakpoint in your code in Visual Studio and then manually attach to the process in which your portal is running. Figures 19.2 and 19.3 illustrate attaching to the w3wp.exe process. Note that this functionality is not available in the Visual Studio Express editions.

19

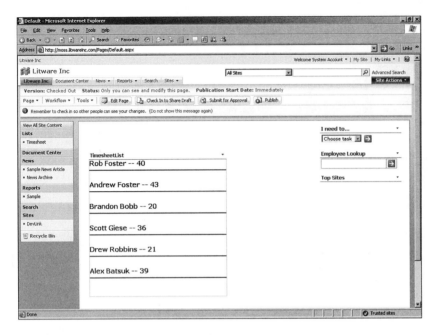

FIGURE 19.1   Timesheet list Web Part.

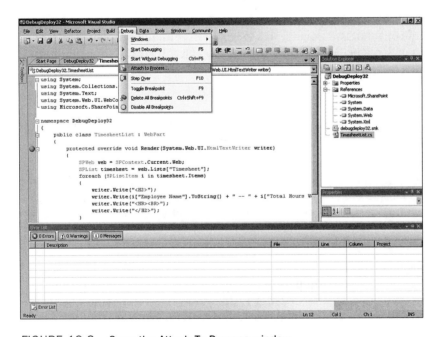

FIGURE 19.2   Open the Attach To Process window.

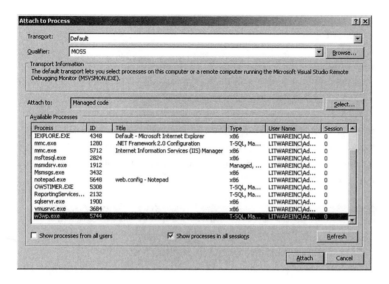

FIGURE 19.3   Attach to `w3wp.exe`.

When you click the Attach button, Visual Studio enters a Running state and appears as if it is running an application in Debug mode, but your breakpoint does NOT occur until you navigate to a page in the portal that executes the code where your breakpoint is located.

After you start hitting your breakpoints, you will notice that most of the functionality of the Visual Studio debugger is available; however, making changes is a bit more involved than traditional ASP.NET development. When you need to make a change, you must uninstall your Web Part classes from the Global Assembly Cache (GAC), redeploy your changes, and reattach to the `w3wp.exe` process. After doing this once or twice, you will discover that this isn't the most efficient process.

So, what if you don't want to go through the hassle of configuring SharePoint or WSS on your local development machine but still want the ability to debug Web Parts? Remember that Web Parts are really developed on top of the ASP.NET 2.0 Portal Framework, so you can actually debug them *without* SharePoint or WSS! Take the following modified code excerpt:

```
protected override void Render(System.Web.UI.HtmlTextWriter writer)
{
    SPSite site = new SPSite("http://moss.litwareinc.com");
    SPWeb web = site.AllWebs[0];

    SPList timesheet = web.Lists["Timesheet"];
    foreach (SPListItem i in timesheet.Items)
    {
        writer.Write("<H2>");
```

19

```
            writer.Write(i["Employee Name"].ToString() + " -- " +
➡i["Total Hours Worked"].ToString());
            writer.Write("<HR><BR>");
            writer.Write("</H2>");
        }
    }
```

Notice now the web's context is gained by first connecting to a SharePoint site (SPSite object) by uniform resource identifier (URI) and then gaining access to the web. If you use this method to connect to your SharePoint webs, you can easily debug your Web Parts by using the ASP.NET 2.0 Portal Framework as a host.

> **NOTE**
>
> Note that even though you can deploy this solution to production as is and it will run, you still need to change the code to get access to the web's context by using the SPContext object because it is easier to manage and performs much better in a server environment.

Debugging Web Parts is a fundamental part of your Web Part development. Whether you choose to install a full-blown version of SharePoint 2007 on your development workstation, set up a Virtual PC image with SharePoint installed, or test your Web Parts against a common instance of SharePoint is up to you. Tables 19.1 and 19.2 list the pros and cons of each method.

TABLE 19.1   Install SharePoint Locally

Pros	Cons
Maximum control of hooking into the running SharePoint processes	Difficult to set up and maintain
Full control of the local environment	Version skew with what might be running in another environment (for example, dev/qa/production)
Easy to deploy updates	Resource intensive

TABLE 19.2   Debug Against a Common SharePoint Server

Pros	Cons
Easy to test your components against common data in a large environment	You might or might not have full control over this environment
Reduced setup time in a large, team environment	More difficult to deploy changes
Easy to unit test	

Deploying Web Parts

You can deploy Web Parts to your SharePoint servers in several ways. This section shows you how to deploy Web Parts by creating an `.msi` file from within Visual Studio 2005.

Like with any .NET application or component, the two most popular ways to deploy Web Parts are 1) creating an `.msi` installer file and 2) manually deploying the files to the appropriate directories. There are numerous advantages of using an MSI-based deployment model. One such advantage is being able to query your servers to determine not only which components are installed, but also which versions of which components are currently installed in an environment. This can be easily done with a custom Windows Management and Instrumentation (WMI) query or via Systems Management Server (SMS) (as well as many other tools). In addition, MSI files make for a very clean deployment in that you simply run an installer and your component can immediately be used on the server to which it was deployed.

To create an installer file for your Web Parts, complete the following steps:

1. Add a setup project to your solution.
2. Configure setup application.
3. Compile setup application (creates an MSI file).
4. Deploy the components.

Adding a Setup Project to Your Solution

To add a setup project to your solution, click the File menu, click New, and then click Project. The Add New Project window opens. In the Project Types section, select Other Project Types, select Setup and Deployment, and then select Setup Project, as illustrated in Figure 19.4.

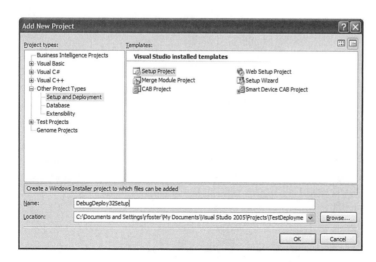

FIGURE 19.4   Create a new setup project.

Configuring Setup Application

After creating the setup project, you need to configure your project to include the primary output from the DebugDeploy32 project. Because the components need to be deployed to the GAC, you need to add a Special Folder to the project by opening the File System Editor, right-clicking the File System item, and selecting Add New Special Folder. You need to add a Global Assembly Cache Folder to the list so that your component can be deployed to the GAC.

> **NOTE**
>
> Note that this process assumes that your project will be deployed to the Global Assembly Cache, so it must have a strong name associated with it.

Figure 19.5 displays the option to add a Global Assembly Cache Folder to the File System Editor.

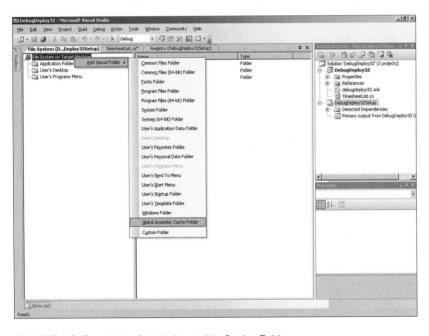

FIGURE 19.5   Add a Global Assembly Cache Folder.

After the Global Assembly Cache Folder has been added, you will need to add the primary output of the DebugDeploy32 project to the Global Assembly Cache Folder. You can do this by right-clicking the Global Assembly Cache Folder and then clicking Add, Project Output, as shown in Figure 19.6.

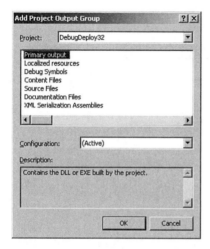

FIGURE 19.6   Add a Project Output.

Compile Setup Application (Creates an `.msi` File) and Deploy the Components

Next, you need to compile your setup project. This builds an `.msi` file that can be installed on your SharePoint server. When you run the installer, your components are registered in the GAC on that server and can then be shared by multiple sites and webs.

> **CAUTION**
>
> If your Visual Studio 2005 settings are configured to automatically increment the version number of your assembly when you compile, then you will need to update this setting in the safeControls section of your web's `Web.Config` file.

After your components have been deployed, you can verify that they got deployed to the GAC by opening the .NET Framework 2.0 Configuration Utility from the Administrative Tools menu. This is illustrated in Figure 19.7.

19

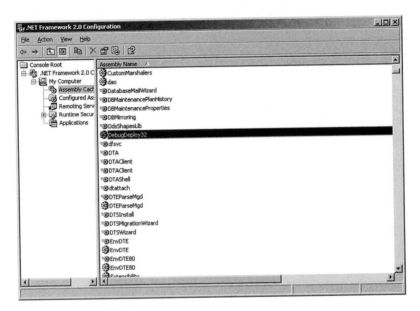

FIGURE 19.7   Verifying the Global Assembly Cache.

Summary

Debugging and deploying Web Parts is an essential part of your SharePoint development experience. This chapter showed you how to successfully debug a Web Part using Visual Studio 2005 and how to deploy this Web Part to the Global Assembly Cache on your SharePoint servers.

PART IV

Programming the SharePoint 2007 Web Services

IN THIS PART

CHAPTER 20	Using the Document Workspace Web Service	241
CHAPTER 21	Using the Imaging Web Service	255
CHAPTER 22	Using the Lists Web Service	273
CHAPTER 23	Using the Meeting Workspace Web Service	291
CHAPTER 24	Working with User Profiles and Security	307
CHAPTER 25	Using Excel Services	321
CHAPTER 26	Working with the Web Part Pages Web Service	337
CHAPTER 27	Using the Business Data Catalog Web Services	347
CHAPTER 28	Using the Workflow Web Service	359
CHAPTER 29	Working with Records Repositories	369
CHAPTER 30	Additional Web Services	377

CHAPTER 20

Using the Document Workspace Web Service

IN THIS CHAPTER

▶ Overview of Document Workspaces

▶ Managing Document Workspace Sites

▶ Managing Document Workspace Data

▶ Working with Folders

▶ Locating Documents in a Workspace

▶ Managing Workspace Users

Document Workspace sites are Windows SharePoint sites that facilitate team collaboration around one or more documents. This chapter provides you with an overview of Document Workspace sites and how to query and manipulate them using the Document Workspace Web Service. This chapter provides coverage of how to manage the Document Workspace (DWS) sites themselves, as well as how to manipulate DWS data, work with folders, find documents, and even manage DWS users.

Overview of Document Workspaces

Document Workspace sites (often just called Document Workspaces) are collaborative Windows SharePoint Services (WSS) sites that revolve around one or more documents. The purpose of these sites is to facilitate collaboration in the creation and revision of the document or documents. For example, you might have a team that has been tasked with creating a project plan for a project, or a team that must create a budget document for FY 2007. Document Workspaces provide document libraries and other relevant SharePoint lists that teams might need to collaborate on these documents. After the collaboration is complete and an artifact has been produced, teams often publish the artifacts to other SharePoint sites or to the central portal.

Document Workspaces are also used heavily within Microsoft Office Outlook when users exchange shared attachments. For more information on Document Workspaces from a user and administrator perspective, the Microsoft Office SharePoint Server (MOSS) 2007 online help is a great place to start.

Managing Document Workspace Sites

There are three main management tasks when dealing with Document Workspaces. The first task is to validate a potential DWS uniform resource locator (URL) to ensure that it doesn't contain any invalid characters, and the second and third tasks are to create and delete a Document Workspace. This section shows you how to perform these tasks using the DWS Web Service that can be found at the URL [server]/_vti_bin/dws.asmx.

Validating Document Workspace Site URLs

Before you create a new Document Workspace, you should first check to see if the URL you intend to use is valid. The CanCreateDwsUrl method performs several operations. First, it checks to see if the calling user has permissions to create the site. Next, it validates the URL and trims it to the appropriate size and replaces any special characters with URL-safe equivalents. This method returns the modified and validated URL in a simple Extensible Markup Language (XML) string that can then be used to create a Document Workspace site.

The format of the return value for this method is

```
<Result>(altered and validated URL)</Result>
```

Creating and Deleting Document Workspace Sites

After you know the name of the DWS you plan to create, and you have validated that name using the CanCreateDwsUrl method, you can create the new site. To create a new DWS, use the CreateDws method with the following parameters:

- name—This is the URL of the new DWS. This argument is optional, and calls to this method often work much more reliably without sending this parameter.

- users—This is an XML string containing a list of users to add to the site after it is created. This XML has the following format:

```
<UserInfo>
<Item Name="display name" Email="e-mail address of user"/>
</UserInfo>
```

- title—This is the title of the new DWS site. If the name parameter is left blank, this parameter is validated using the same process as in CanCreateDwsUrl and then used as the new site's URL.

- documents—This is an optional list of documents that will be retained as potential results for calls to the FindDwsDoc (discussed later in this chapter) method. This parameter is primarily used by Outlook.

The following code validates a new URL, displays the validated result, and then proceeds to create and delete a new DWS. The `localhost` reference was created by obtaining a web reference from http://localhost/_vti_bin/dws.asmx. When creating this sample, you should obviously obtain a web reference from your own server.

LISTING 20.1   Creating and Deleting Document Workspace Sites

```
using System;
using System.Collections.Generic;
using System.Text;
using System.Xml;

namespace ConsoleApplication1
{
class Program
{
    static void Main(string[] args)
    {
        localhost.Dws dws = new ConsoleApplication1.localhost.Dws();
        dws.Credentials =
          new System.Net.NetworkCredential("Administrator", "password");

        string modifiedUrl = dws.CanCreateDwsUrl("FY 2006&2007 Budget");
        Console.WriteLine(modifiedUrl);
        string result =
          dws.CreateDws(string.Empty, string.Empty,
          "FY 2006&2007 Budget", string.Empty);
        XmlDocument doc = new XmlDocument();
        doc.LoadXml(result);
        Console.WriteLine("DWS Created. Doclib URL: {0}",
            doc.SelectSingleNode("//DoclibUrl").InnerText);

        // attach to the DWS Web Service of the newly created website
        XmlDocument doc2 = new XmlDocument();
        doc2.LoadXml(modifiedUrl);
        string newUrl = doc2.SelectSingleNode("//Result").InnerText;
        dws.Url = "http://localhost/" + newUrl + "/_vti_bin/dws.asmx";
        dws.DeleteDws();
        Console.WriteLine("DWS @ " + newUrl + " Deleted.");
        Console.ReadLine();
    }
}
}
```

20

One important thing to note about the preceding code is that the DWS was created using the web service at the root of the portal, but the code had to attach to the DWS itself to delete it. This model is used throughout the MOSS 2007 web services. The parent site to which the web reference is made will be the parent site for a new DWS when created.

If all went well when running this application, your console output should be as follows:

```
<Result>FY 2006_2007 Budget</Result>
DWS Created. Doclib URL: Shared Documents
DWS @ FY 2006_2007 Budget Deleted.
```

Note how the ampersand from the original title has been replaced with an underscore because the ampersand is not a URL-safe character.

Managing Document Workspace Data

The Document Workspace Web Service exposes several methods for dealing with data and metadata related to the DWS and to the documents contained within it. This section provides an overview of how to utilize those methods: GetDwsData and GetDwsMetaData.

Getting DWS Data

The GetDwsData method provides detailed information about a given document within the DWS as well as information about the DWS itself such as its title, member list, and list of potential assignees for a document. Listing 20.2 illustrates a console application that executes this method and displays the results. The results of this method call are an XML format string with the following top-level elements: Title, User, LastUpdate, Members, Assignees, and multiple elements called List containing the IDs of all lists in the DWS. You can use these IDs in conjunction with the Lists Web Service (see Chapter 22, "Using the Lists Web Service") to find out more detail about each list.

LISTING 20.2   Using the GetDwsData Method

```
using System;
using System.Xml;
using System.Collections.Generic;
using System.Text;

namespace DwsData
{
class Program
{
static void Main(string[] args)
{
    localhost.Dws docWs = new DwsData.localhost.Dws();
```

LISTING 20.2   Continued

```csharp
    docWs.Url = "http://localhost/Budget/_vti_bin/dws.asmx";
    docWs.Credentials = System.Net.CredentialCache.DefaultCredentials;

    string response = docWs.GetDwsData("budget.docx", string.Empty);
    XmlDocument doc = new XmlDocument();
    doc.LoadXml(response);
    Console.WriteLine("Title: {0}", doc.SelectSingleNode("//Title").InnerText);
    Console.WriteLine("Last Update: {0}",
        doc.SelectSingleNode("//LastUpdate").InnerText);
    Console.WriteLine("User: {0} / E-Mail : {1}",
        doc.SelectSingleNode("//User/Name").InnerText,
        doc.SelectSingleNode("//User/Email").InnerText);
    Console.WriteLine("Assignees:");
    foreach (XmlNode assigneeNode in doc.SelectNodes("//Assignees/Member"))
    {
        Console.WriteLine("\t{0}",
            assigneeNode.SelectSingleNode("Name").InnerText);
    }
    Console.WriteLine("Members:");
    foreach (XmlNode memberNode in doc.SelectNodes("//Members/Member"))
    {
        Console.WriteLine("\t{0}",
            memberNode.SelectSingleNode("Name").InnerText);
    }

    Console.WriteLine("Lists:");
    foreach (XmlNode listNode in doc.SelectNodes("//List"))
    {
        // if the list exists...
        if (listNode.SelectNodes("ID").Count > 0)
        {
            Console.WriteLine("\t{0}",
                listNode.SelectSingleNode("ID").InnerText);
        }
    }

    Console.ReadLine();
}
}
}
```

20

On a file uploaded to a sample Document Workspace (in this case it is "Budget Committee", but you should feel free to create your own) called `Budget.docx`, the output of the console application will be similar to the following text:

```
Title: Budget Committee
Last Update: 632893747029086336
User: WIN2K3R2LAB\administrator / E-Mail : someone@example.com
Assignees:
        NT AUTHORITY\local service
        System Account
        WIN2K3R2LAB\administrator
Members:
        NT AUTHORITY\authenticated users
        Approvers
        Designers
        Hierarchy Managers
        Home Members
        Home Owners
        Home Visitors
        Quick Deploy Users
        Restricted Readers
Lists:
        {B8CC66A7-BBC6-458E-AD86-98204258B0AE}
        {D222FB14-5EC6-4004-9FD3-40CFF14C39D1}
```

Getting DWS MetaData

The `GetDwsMetaData` method returns extended information about a Document Workspace above and beyond what is returned by `GetDwsData`. This method returns an XML string that contains the following top-level elements:

- `SubscribeUrl`—The URL to create a new alert on the DWS.

- `MtgInstance`—If the workspace is a Meeting Workspace, the node that contains the meeting instance ID.

- `SettingUrl`—The node that contains the URL to the Site Settings page for the workspace.

- `PermsUrl`—The URL for site permissions configuration.

- `UserInfoUrl`—The URL for managing user information and security settings for the site.

- `Roles`—A list of site roles.

- `Schema`—If the `GetDwsMetaData` method is invoked with the `Minimal` parameter set to `false`, one or more Schema nodes is returned describing the DWS schemas.

- ListInfo—As with Schema, when the Minimal parameter is set to false, one or more of these nodes is returned containing detailed information on the site lists.

- Permissions—A list of site permissions.

- HasUniquePerm—A true/false node indicating whether the site has unique permissions or if they are inherited from the parent.

- WorkspaceType—A string indicating the type of workspace: DWS (Document Workspace), MWS (Meeting Workspace), SPS, or blank.

- IsADMode—A value indicating whether the site is in Active Directory mode.

- DocUrl—The URL of the document (note that this doesn't include the URL of the server itself, just the relative path of the document).

- Minimal—A value indicating if the method call was requested with Minimal information.

- Results—The entire set of results returned by the GetDwsData method for the same document.

The following code illustrates taking the XML string returned by GetDwsMetaData and populating a List view with the XML nodes and their contents. This can be a helpful tool for examining the data before writing production code against the DWS service.

```
localhost.Dws docService = new localhost.Dws();
docService.Url = "http://localhost/budget/_vti_bin/dws.asmx";
docService.Credentials = System.Net.CredentialCache.DefaultCredentials;

string metaData = docService.GetDwsMetaData(
    @"Shared Documents\Budget.docx", "", false);

XmlDocument doc = new XmlDocument();
doc.LoadXml(metaData);
foreach (XmlNode node in doc.DocumentElement.ChildNodes)
{
    ListViewItem lvi = new ListViewItem();
    lvi.Text = node.Name;
    lvi.SubItems.Add(node.InnerXml);
    listView1.Items.Add(lvi);
}
```

The output of the preceding code is shown in Figure 20.1.

20

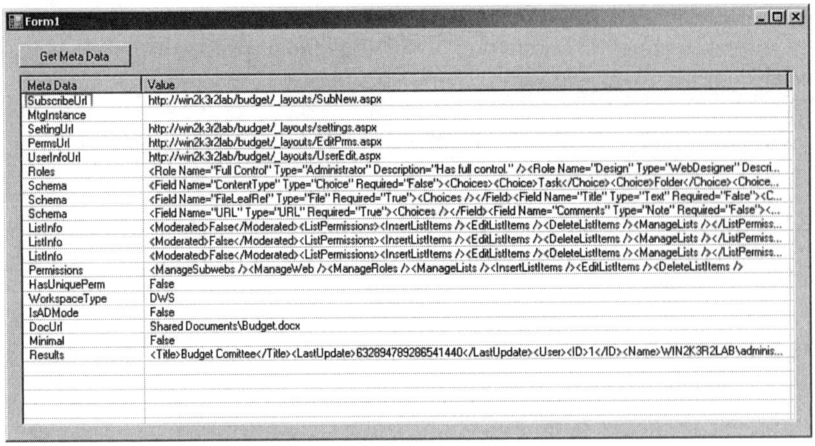

FIGURE 20.1   Results of a call to GetDwsMetaData.

Working with Folders

The Document Workspace Web Service allows developers to add and remove folders from document libraries contained within a Document Workspace through the CreateFolder and DeleteFolder methods. This can be an extremely powerful feature that adds a lot of flexibility for the code developers who write against this web service. If you need to work with content types in regard to the folders, you need to use the Lists Web Service (discussed in Chapter 22).

The following code creates a folder and then pauses—allowing you to see that the change has taken place. Pressing Enter again deletes the folder.

```
localhost.Dws docService = new localhost.Dws();
docService.Credentials = System.Net.CredentialCache.DefaultCredentials;
docService.Url = "http://localhost/budget/_vti_bin/dws.asmx";

string result = docService.CreateFolder("Shared Documents/Rough Drafts");
Console.WriteLine(result);
Console.WriteLine("Folder created. Press enter to delete.");
Console.ReadLine();
result = docService.DeleteFolder("Shared Documents/Rough Drafts");
Console.WriteLine(result);
Console.WriteLine("Folder deleted. Press enter to quit.");
Console.ReadLine();
```

As with most of the DWS Service data manipulation methods, if no errors occurred, the string result contains the <Result/> element. If an error occurred, an <Error> node is returned. The code in Listing 20.3 contains some helper methods for parsing the output of many of the DWS methods, including detecting error conditions and parsing the actual error details. You can also find this code in some of the Software Development Kit (SDK) samples provided by Microsoft.

LISTING 20.3   SDK Sample DWS Utility Methods

```
using System;
using System.Collections.Generic;
using System.Text;

namespace DwsToolsLib
{
/// <summary>
/// Utility functions taken from the SharePoint 2007 SDK
/// </summary>
public class DwsTools
{
public static bool IsDwsErrorResult(string ResultFragment)
{
    System.IO.StringReader srResult =
        new System.IO.StringReader(ResultFragment);
    System.Xml.XmlTextReader xtr =
        new System.Xml.XmlTextReader(srResult);
    xtr.Read();
    if (xtr.Name == "Error")
    {
        return true;
    }
    else
    {
        return false;
    }
}

public static void ParseDwsErrorResult(string ErrorFragment,
    out int ErrorID,
    out string ErrorMsg)
{
    System.IO.StringReader srError =
        new System.IO.StringReader(ErrorFragment);
    System.Xml.XmlTextReader xtr =
        new System.Xml.XmlTextReader(srError);
    xtr.Read();
    xtr.MoveToAttribute("ID");
    xtr.ReadAttributeValue();
    ErrorID = System.Convert.ToInt32(xtr.Value);
    ErrorMsg = xtr.ReadString();
```

20

LISTING 20.3   Continued

```
}

public static string ParseDwsSingleResult(string ResultFragment)
{
    System.IO.StringReader srResult =
        new System.IO.StringReader(ResultFragment);
    System.Xml.XmlTextReader xtr =
        new System.Xml.XmlTextReader(srResult);
    xtr.Read();
    return xtr.ReadString();
}


}
}
```

Figure 20.2 shows the newly created folder in the Shared Documents folder of the Budget
Committee DWS.

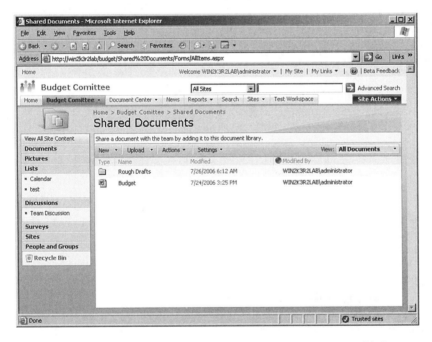

FIGURE 20.2   A programmatically created folder on a Document Workspace.

Locating Documents in a Workspace

Document Workspaces provide a special feature where you can associate a unique identifier with a document so that the URL of the document can be easily retrieved later. Outlook makes extensive use of this feature when creating Document Workspaces around shared attachments.

Using this feature requires two steps. First, when creating the DWS site, you need to supply a list of documents and their associated identifiers. Second, you then need to query the DWS for the URL of a stored document based on the document's unique ID using the FindDwsDoc method.

The code in Listing 20.4 creates a new Document Workspace site and stores a document ID on the new site, and then retrieves the absolute URL of the document using the ID and the FindDwsDoc method.

LISTING 20.4   Creating a Site with Document ID Storage

```
using System;
using System.Xml;
using System.Net;
using System.Collections.Generic;
using System.Text;

namespace DocFind
{
class Program
{
static void Main(string[] args)
{
    localhost.Dws dws = new localhost.Dws();
    dws.Credentials = System.Net.CredentialCache.DefaultCredentials;

    string modifiedUrl = dws.CanCreateDwsUrl("Budget Test Site");
    Console.WriteLine(modifiedUrl);
    Guid newDocGuid = Guid.NewGuid();

    string documents = "<Documents><item ID=\"" +
            newDocGuid.ToString() + "\" Name=\"" +
        "BudgetDocument.docx\"/></Documents>";
    string result = dws.CreateDws(string.Empty,
            string.Empty, "Budget Test Site", documents);
    XmlDocument doc = new XmlDocument();
    doc.LoadXml(result);

    string docLibUrl = doc.SelectSingleNode("//DoclibUrl").InnerText;
    Console.WriteLine("DWS Created. Doclib URL: {0}",
```

20

LISTING 20.4   Continued

```
        docLibUrl);

    // attach to the DWS Web Service of the newly created website
    XmlDocument doc2 = new XmlDocument();
    doc2.LoadXml(modifiedUrl);
    string newUrl = doc2.SelectSingleNode("//Result").InnerText;
    dws.Url = "http://localhost/" + newUrl + "/_vti_bin/dws.asmx";
    string docLocation = dws.FindDwsDoc(newDocGuid.ToString());

    XmlDocument doc3 = new XmlDocument();
    doc3.LoadXml(docLocation);
    Console.WriteLine("Document with ID " +
        newDocGuid.ToString() + " can be found at " +
            doc3.SelectSingleNode("//Result").InnerText);

    Console.ReadLine();
}
}
}
```

The preceding code creates a new DWS site with the CreateDws method and supplies the following string for the documents parameter:

```
<Documents>
    <item ID="{guid}" Name="BudgetDocument.docx"/>
</Documents>
```

This associates a unique identifier with the filename BudgetDocument.docx. When the console application is executed, it produces the following output:

```
<Result>Budget Test Site</Result>
DWS Created. Doclib URL: Shared Documents
Document with ID 68b02155-c9b2-44cc-82fc-50feeb871310 can be found at
http://win2k3r2lab/Budget Test Site/Shared Documents/BudgetDocument.docx
```

If you look closely at the preceding code sample, you might notice something missing. The code never actually uploaded a file into the document library! You can think of this document storage and location feature as a persistent dictionary designed specifically for storing and retrieving a fixed set of documents. It is not designed to be used when you don't know what you're looking for. However, if the code knows ahead of time the unique ID of a document it needs, this feature can be extremely useful, such as in the case of Outlook and shared attachment Document Workspaces.

Managing Workspace Users

You saw earlier in this chapter that when you create a DWS site you can use an XML fragment to specify a list of users that you want to add to the site upon creation.

There is also a function that you can use to remove users from the site: `RemoveDwsUser`. This method takes the ID of the user and removes that user from the DWS. Unfortunately, there are no methods within the Document Workspace Web Service that provide access to a list of user IDs. To gain access to user information such as profile data, security information, group membership, and IDs, you need to use the Users and Groups Web Service, which is covered in Chapter 24, "Working with User Profiles and Security."

To remove a user from a DWS site, simply invoke the `RemoveDwsUser` method, as shown here with an ID retrieved from the Users and Groups Web Service:

```
dwsService.RemoveDwsUser(userIdString);
```

Summary

Document Workspaces are one of Microsoft Office SharePoint Server's most powerful collaboration tools. Tightly integrated into Microsoft Office, they enable users to collaborate on one or more related documents quickly, easily, and with tons of additional features and tools. This chapter introduced you to the Document Workspace Web Service, which can be used to create and delete workspaces, retrieve metadata and detailed information about workspaces, remove users, and even retrieve URLs for documents quickly based on unique identifiers. The DWS Web Service is yet another extremely powerful web service that you can now add to your list of available tools for programming with MOSS.

CHAPTER **21**

Using the Imaging Web Service

IN THIS CHAPTER

▶ Overview of Picture Libraries

▶ Introducing the Imaging Web Service

▶ Locating Picture Libraries and Images

▶ Managing Photos

▶ Building a Practical Sample: Photo Browser

The bane of most programmers who write code that works in a back-end environment or performs "under the hood" functionality is that there is typically very little in the way of visible results. Everyone likes having the satisfaction of being able to sit back and look at their work, but developers rarely get that chance when working with "code plumbing" and web services. Fortunately, working with the Microsoft Office SharePoint Server (MOSS) picture libraries is a much more visible exercise. This chapter contains an overview of the concept behind picture libraries and a complete, in-depth coverage of how to consume the Imaging Web Service for programmable control of picture libraries.

Overview of Picture Libraries

A SharePoint picture library is really just a custom document library where the documents stored are images. Picture libraries can contain subfolders and maintain metadata on the image, such as the image height, width, title, description, keywords, and more.

As you would expect any decent photo album software to do, MOSS picture libraries can be browsed using thumbnail representations of the images, allowing users to click through and view the original, full-sized image if they want.

Picture libraries can be created within any SharePoint site regardless of the site template. This allows for a wide range of uses. Picture libraries can be used "out of the box" to provide convenient, secured, and shared image storage or they can be used as back-end image stores that support custom front-end applications, as you will see throughout this chapter. Figure 21.1 illustrates browsing a picture library called "New York City" on a team site.

FIGURE 21.1   Browsing a MOSS picture library.

Introducing the Imaging Web Service

The Imaging Web Service is the programmable interface to all things related to picture libraries. Although picture libraries are, at their core, document libraries and can be manipulated by document library code, none of the image-specific information or features is available unless you use the Imaging Web Service.

The Imaging Web Service can be found at the following uniform resource locator (URL): http://[server]/[site]/_vti_bin/imaging.asmx.

As with all other MOSS web services, access to the service is secured and the web service client must provide valid credentials to gain access to the service. The user account supplied to the web service client proxy must have at least read access to the site *and* to the picture library to perform any imaging functions.

Table 21.1 contains a summary of the methods available on the Imaging Web Service.

TABLE 21.1   `Imaging.asmx` Methods

Method	Description
CheckSubWebAndList	Analyzes the full URL to a subweb and list such as http://server/site/customlist/allitems.aspx and returns a response element that identifies the unique pieces, such as the server URL, the subweb URL, the list name, and the remaining portion
CreateNewFolder	Creates a new folder within a picture library called "New Folder" optionally containing a numerical postfix if multiple new folders have been created
Delete	Deletes images from a picture library
Download	Downloads images from a picture library
GetItemsByIds	Retrieves list items corresponding to the images with the supplied list of unique IDs
GetItemsXMLData	Gets Extensible Markup Language (XML) metadata corresponding to a given list of items
GetListItems	Gets the list items in a given (optional) folder in a list on the site hosting the service
ListPictureLibrary	Lists all picture libraries on the site
Rename	Renames images in a picture library
Upload	Uploads images to a given picture library

Methods on the Imaging Web Service fall into two basic categories:

▶ **Browse**—These methods provide the ability to iterate through the list of picture libraries on a site, list all images contained in a given picture library, obtain image metadata, and retrieve image detail results based on a list of IDs.

▶ **Manipulate**—These methods provide the ability to manipulate images and the picture libraries in which they are contained. Using manipulation methods, client code can upload, download, rename, and delete images and create folders.

The next two sections provide an in-depth look at the code involved in browsing and manipulating images and picture libraries.

Locating Picture Libraries and Images

Before you can manipulate images or the image libraries, you need to be able to locate them. This section shows you the various techniques for enumerating picture libraries, getting a list of images contained in a library, selecting image items by ID, and obtaining image item metadata.

Enumerating Picture Libraries

Enumerating picture libraries is done with the `ListPictureLibrary` method on the Imaging Web Service. It returns a list of all picture libraries on the site that hosts `Imaging.asmx`. For instance, if you want to retrieve a list of all picture libraries contained in the site "Our Hawaiian Vacation," you might first connect to the web service at http://theserver/hawaiianvacation/_vti_bin/Imaging.asmx.

After you had a proper web reference, you would then invoke the `ListPictureLibrary` method as follows:

```
XmlNode libraryListNode = serviceProxy.ListPictureLibrary();
```

This method returns an XML node with the following structure:

```
<PictLib xmlns="http://schemas.microsoft.com/sharepoint/soap/ois/">
  <Library name="[library list name]"
      title="[library title]"
      guid="[guid]"
    url="[url to the root folder]" />
  <Library . . . />
</PictLib>
```

When run against the sample team site used later in the chapter, this method returns the following XML:

```
<Library name="{6FB03ECB-A08D-4E51-84CB-385DE5CAABD9}"
    title="Boston"
    guid="6fb03ecb-a08d-4e51-84cb-385de5caabd9" url="Boston"
    xmlns="http://schemas.microsoft.com/sharepoint/soap/ois/"/>
<Library name="{F27AA1DA-1D99-4005-946E-DBF30573BF0C}"
    title="New York City"
    guid="f27aa1da-1d99-4005-946e-dbf30573bf0c"
    url="New York City"
    xmlns="http://schemas.microsoft.com/sharepoint/soap/ois/" />
```

As you work more with the Imaging Web Service, you will see that the outputs from certain methods are reused over and over again in other method calls. If you know this up front, you can make sure your code takes that into account. For example, you will make extensive use of the `url` attribute returned by `ListPictureLibrary` for virtually every other method call on the web service. The `url` attribute is in the XML and is required for subsequent method calls to drill down into individual libraries.

Obtaining Picture Library List Items

After you have the list of picture libraries on the site, the next thing you might want to do is obtain a list of all items in each picture library. The `GetListItems` method returns XML data in the "row" format. This is the same format used by the Lists Web Service

(Chapter 22, "Using the Lists Web Service"). That chapter provides you with more details on this XML format. This chapter takes advantage of the fact that the XML "row" format can be read by an ADO.NET `DataSet` and converted into the tables and rows paradigm.

The following code illustrates how to obtain a list of items and immediately turn that list into a `DataSet` that can then be used in data binding or whatever other operations are required:

```
XmlNode listItemsNode =
  imageService.GetListItems(url, "");
DataSet imageSet = new DataSet();

string sourceXml = "<images>" + listItemsNode.InnerXml + "</images>";
imageSet.ReadXml(new System.IO.StringReader(sourceXml));

foreach (DataRow row in imageset.Tables[0].Rows)
{
  // work with each image
}
```

In the preceding code, the `url` variable contains the data from the `url` XML attribute returned by the `ListPictureLibrary` method. The XML returned by `GetListItems` is not a complete, well-formed document. It contains a list of `<z:row>` elements but no root element. As a result, the code to create a `DataSet` from this XML needs to wrap the method output in its own root element.

When converted from XML, the row attributes become columns. Table 21.2 shows a list of the most commonly used column names and their descriptions.

TABLE 21.2   GetListItems Columns

Column	Description
ows_ID	ID of the list item.
ows_Author	User lookup (lookup format of id;#name applies) of the user who uploaded the image.
ows_Created	Date and time when the list item was created.
ows_Modified	Date and time when the list item was modified.
ows_File_x0020_Size	Size of the file. This column is also in lookup format and needs to be parsed to obtain the file size (in bytes).
ows_EncodedAbsUrl	Absolute path to the list item, including the protocol (for example, http://) moniker.
ows_ImageWidth	The image width in pixels.
ows_ImageHeight	The image height in pixels.
ows_Title	Title/name of the image.
ows_ImageCreateDate	Date and time the picture was taken. This is not the same as the date/time when the image was uploaded.

TABLE 21.2   Continued

Column	Description
ows_UniqueId	Lookup format with the right-side of the string containing the globally unique identifier (GUID), for example: 1;#{CA01EDAF-83B5-4411-9CF2-22DC68DBC7CE}
ows_FileRef	Lookup format containing the relative path to the image file. This is used to extract the filename for web service method calls that require a filename.
ows_DocIcon	Type of file extension-based icon that relates to this image (for example, "jpg").
ows_Last_x0020_Modified	Date and time the image was last modified.

Getting Items by ID

If you aren't interested in obtaining the entire list of images, but instead want to retrieve only a subset based on a list of IDs, the GetItemsByIds method is exactly what you need. This method comes in extremely handy when you are creating an application that might be maintaining a list of IDs with which the user wants to work. The syntax of this method call is fairly simple:

```
XmlNode itemsNode = imageService.GetItemsByIds("[list]", array-of-uint-ids);
```

After you have a valid web reference for the Imaging Web Service, you can then call this method with the name of the list in question and an array of uints representing the list of IDs. These are the same IDs that are stored in the ows_ID column from other list item retrieval methods. The format of the XML returned by this method is the same row-style format used by GetListItems and the Lists Web Service discussed in Chapter 22.

Obtaining Item XML Data

The GetItemsXMLData method provides a trimmed-down alternative to retrieving the row-format XML returned by the GetListItems and GetItemsByIds methods. Where the GetItemsByIds method relies on an array of uint identifiers to select items from the library, the GetItemsXMLData method relies on an array of filenames as well as a folder name, as follows:

```
XmlNode metaNode = imageService.GetItemsXMLData(
    url, "", new string[] { fileName });
```

The method returns an XML fragment that looks like the following:

```
<item name="155495642_ce358d3e35.jpg"
  ID="5"
  Author="1;#WIN2K3R2LAB\\administrator"
  Editor="1;#WIN2K3R2LAB\\administrator"
```

```
    File_x0020_Size="140272"
    ImageWidth="500"
    ImageHeight="375"
    Description=
       "An interesting angle shot of the Mac logo in the glass cube
 ↪above the 5th avenue store"
    Title="The 'floating' Mac logo"
    Keywords="mac"
    ImageCreateDate="5/30/2006 6:00:00 AM"
    Created="2006-08-10T02:35:10Z"
    Modified="2006-08-10T02:36:02Z"
    xmlns="http://schemas.microsoft.com/sharepoint/soap/ois/" />
```

The format of the XML returned by this method does not contain the ows_ attribute prefix of some of the other methods. In addition, the values that appear in lookup format (two values separated by the character pair ;#) in other methods do not appear in lookup format in this method.

This is because the picture library is simultaneously a custom list, a document library, and an image library. As such, there are many different perspectives from which you might want to examine its items. If you are purely interested in seeing the image-specific data and don't care about the internal SharePoint identifiers for various elements, this method provides the easiest data to consume. However, if you are relating images to other data contained within SharePoint, you need the internal identifiers and lookup information supplied by the other methods.

Managing Photos

Picture libraries provide a tremendous amount of functionality above and beyond simple browsing and locating. Using the Imaging Web Service, you can upload and download photos, rename photos, delete photos, and create subfolders within existing libraries. This section covers how to perform all of those tasks.

Uploading Photos

Uploading a photo is actually quite easy. The Upload method takes the list name, the folder name, the filename, and an array of bytes containing the raw data of the image to upload. The following few lines of code read a file from disk and upload them to a SharePoint picture library:

```
FileStream fs = new FileStream(@"C:\mypicture.jpg", FileMode.Open);
byte[] fileBytes = new byte[fs.Length];
fs.Read(fileBytes, 0, (int)fs.Length);
string url = "My Library"
XmlNode result = imageService.Upload(url, "", fileBytes,
  "mypicture.jpg", true);
```

The Upload method takes the following parameters:

▶ strListName—The name of the picture library into which the code will be uploading an image.

▶ strFolder—The name of a folder within the picture library. If the image is being uploaded to the root of the picture library, leave this parameter as the empty string.

▶ bytes—The array of bytes containing the raw image data.

▶ fileName—The name of the file for the uploaded image. This is only the filename and should not include any path information.

▶ fOverWriteIfExist—A Boolean indicating whether the uploaded file should overwrite any existing file with the same filename in the same location. If false, and a file exists, an exception will be thrown.

Downloading Photos

Downloading is a little trickier than uploading, but is still pretty easy. You might think that the Download method would return an array of bytes. However, it actually returns an XML node that contains a base-64 encoded array of raw bytes. Thankfully, the .NET Framework comes with the Convert.FromBase64String method that comes in extremely handy in situations like this. The following code downloads a file from a picture library and sets the Image property of a Windows Forms PictureBox to the bytes retrieved from the web service:

```
XmlNode imageNode = imageService.Download("My List", "",
    new string[] { "thepic.jpg" }, 0, false);
string fileByteString = imageNode.InnerText;
byte[] fileBytes = Convert.FromBase64String(fileByteString);
pictureBox.Image = Image.FromStream( new MemoryStream(fileBytes));
```

The Download method takes the following parameters:

▶ strListName—The name of the list

▶ strFolder—The name of the folder in which the image resides, can be string.Empty if the image is in the root folder of the library

▶ itemFileNames—An array of strings representing the list of files to download

▶ type—The type of file to download: 0 = Original, 1 = Thumbnail, 2 = Web Image

▶ fFetchOriginalIfNotAvailable—A Boolean value indicating whether to retrieve the original image if a desired alternate image is not available

Renaming Photos

Renaming pictures is a simple matter of supplying a list of old filenames and a list of new filenames in an XML fragment sent to the Imaging Web Service, as shown in the following example:

```
XmlDocument doc = new XmlDocument();
string fileName = "oldpic.jpg";
string newName = "newpic.jpg";
doc.InnerXml = string.Format(
    "<Request><files><file filename=\"{0}\""+
    " newbasename=\"{1}\" /></files></Request>",
    fileName, newName);
XmlElement requestElement = doc.DocumentElement;
imageService.Rename("My Library", "", requestElement);
```

As with the rest of the image and library manipulation methods, Rename takes the name of the list and the optional name of a folder. Finally, it takes an XML element that contains a list of files to rename.

Deleting Photos

Deleting pictures is another straightforward process using the Delete method. It takes the name of the list, the name of the folder (optionally string.Empty), and an array of filenames to delete. The filenames in the array must be pure filenames and cannot contain any path information. The Delete method returns an XML document containing <result> elements indicating whether each file was deleted. The following code provides a simple example of deleting images in a picture library:

```
XmlNode resultNode = imageService.Delete("Boston", "Museum",
    new string[] { "entrance1.jpg" });
```

The preceding code deletes an image named entrance1.jpg from the folder Museum in the picture library Boston on whatever site imageService is associated with. The result of this operation returns an XML document like the following one:

```
<results xmlns="http://schemas.microsoft.com/sharepoint/soap/ois/">
  <result name="entrance1.jpg" deleted="true"/>
</results>
```

Creating Folders

Creating new folders is an interesting task. The CreateNewFolder method allows you to create a new folder, but it will be named "New Folder". You can optionally specify the parent folder name to create nested folders. The following is a line of code that creates a new folder:

```
XmlNode resultNode = imageService.CreateNewFolder("New York City", string.Empty);
```

Picture Library Folder Creation

One can only guess at the reasoning behind not allowing this web service to specify the name of the new folder to be created. The strongest argument for not allowing this functionality is that folder management is already provided in a full implementation using the Lists Web Service. What most developers discover as they work with the MOSS web services is that they can rarely use a single service on its own. More often than not, code requires a main web service and then an additional service to supplement functionality. In the case of folder management in picture libraries, developers should probably be using both an instance of `Imaging.asmx` and `Lists.asmx`. The Lists Web Service is discussed in Chapter 22.

Building a Practical Sample: Photo Browser

As the functionality of the Imaging Web Service has been unfolding throughout this chapter, it has probably become pretty clear that the features exposed by the web service lend themselves perfectly to creating a photo album application either in ASP.NET or in Windows Forms (or Windows Presentation Foundation for those developers working with the .NET Framework 3.0).

This author has always believed strongly in the idea that simple "Hello World" code snippets are only useful when combined with a real-world application showing how the individual snippets can be applied to a real problem. As a result, there is a fully functioning Windows Forms photo album application included in the code downloads for this chapter.

Before illustrating some of the more important pieces of the source code, take a look at the application in action in Figures 21.2 through 21.7.

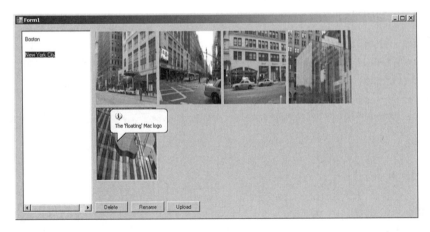

FIGURE 21.2   Downloading thumbnails from a library and using "bubble"-style ToolTips to display picture titles.

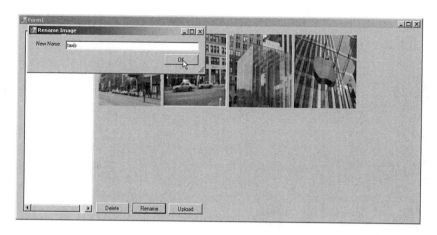

FIGURE 21.3   Renaming an image using the photo album application.

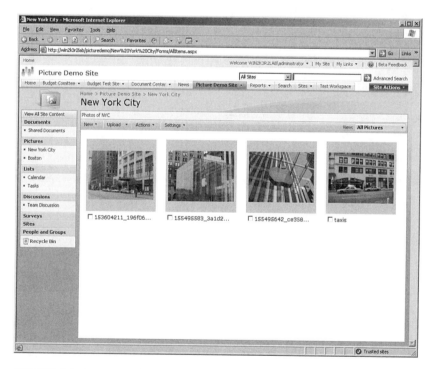

FIGURE 21.4   Image library showing the renamed photo.

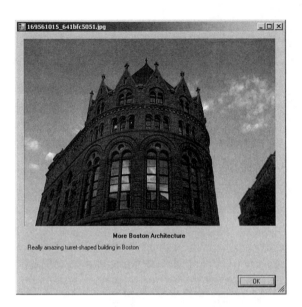

FIGURE 21.5   Downloading and displaying a full-sized picture with accompanying metadata.

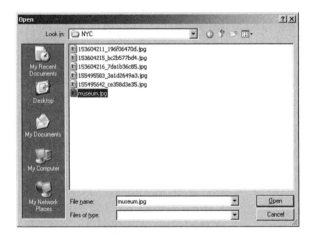

FIGURE 21.6   Open dialog box for uploading files to the picture library.

All of the web service code used in the photo album application has been covered earlier in the chapter, so there are no new methods being used that have not already been explained.

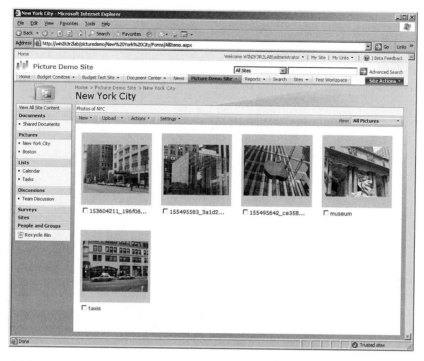

FIGURE 21.7   The picture library after uploading a new image.

The application makes use of the asynchronous method invocation model that is new to the .NET Framework 2.0. This new feature adds event handlers to the auto-generated client proxy to which your application can subscribe. There is an event handler to signal the completion of each asynchronous method call. This makes it extremely easy to set up the asynchronous background downloading of a list of thumbnails.

The main form of the application has a List view on the left that will be populated with the list of all picture libraries on the site. There is also a FlowLayoutPanel that serves as the container for the downloaded image thumbnails. Clicking on an image changes its border to reflect that it has been selected. This enables the buttons at the bottom of the form that allow for uploading, renaming, deleting, and detail viewing. There is also a button that displays the XML metadata for a selected image. Listing 21.1 shows the entire source code for the main form.

LISTING 21.1   Form1.cs (Main Form of the Photo Album Application)

```
using System;
using System.IO;
using System.Collections.Generic;
using System.ComponentModel;
using System.Data;
```

LISTING 21.1   Continued

```csharp
using System.Drawing;
using System.Text;
using System.Xml;
using System.Windows.Forms;

namespace PhotoBrowser
{
public partial class Form1 : Form
{
private win2k3r2lab.Imaging imageService = null;
private DataSet imageSet = null;
private PictureBox lastPictureClicked = null;

public Form1()
{
    InitializeComponent();
    imageService = new PhotoBrowser.win2k3r2lab.Imaging();
    imageService.Url = "http://win2k3r2lab/picturedemo/_vti_bin/imaging.asmx";
    // this only works if your windows ID is acceptable to the site!
    imageService.Credentials = System.Net.CredentialCache.DefaultCredentials;
    imageService.DownloadCompleted +=
        new PhotoBrowser.win2k3r2lab.DownloadCompletedEventHandler(
          imageService_DownloadCompleted);

    XmlNode pictureNode = imageService.ListPictureLibrary();
    foreach (XmlNode library in pictureNode.ChildNodes)
    {
        ListViewItem lvi = new ListViewItem();
        lvi.Text = library.Attributes.GetNamedItem("title").Value;
        lvi.Tag = library.Attributes.GetNamedItem("url").Value;
        libraryList.Items.Add(lvi);
    }
}

void imageService_DownloadCompleted(object sender,
    PhotoBrowser.win2k3r2lab.DownloadCompletedEventArgs e)
{
    XmlNode fileDownload = e.Result;
    int idx = (int)e.UserState;
    string fileByteString = fileDownload.InnerText;
    byte[] fileBytes = Convert.FromBase64String(fileByteString);
    ((PictureBox)imageFlow.Controls[idx]).Image =
        Image.FromStream(new System.IO.MemoryStream(fileBytes));
```

LISTING 21.1   Continued

```csharp
}

private void libraryList_SelectedIndexChanged(object sender, EventArgs e)
{
    if (libraryList.SelectedItems.Count == 0) return;
    imageFlow.Controls.Clear();
    ListViewItem lvi = libraryList.SelectedItems[0];
    string url = (string)lvi.Tag;

    XmlNode listItemsNode = imageService.GetListItems(url, "");
    imageSet = new DataSet();
    string sourceXml = "<images>" + listItemsNode.InnerXml + "</images>";
    imageSet.ReadXml(new System.IO.StringReader(sourceXml));
    int x = 0;
    foreach (DataRow row in imageSet.Tables[0].Rows)
    {
        PictureBox picture = new PictureBox();
        picture.SizeMode = PictureBoxSizeMode.StretchImage;
        picture.Height = 160;
        picture.Width = 140;
        picture.Click += new EventHandler(picture_Click);
        picture.Tag = row;
        pictureToolTip.SetToolTip(picture,
            row["ows_Title"] == DBNull.Value ? "(untitled)" :
            (string)row["ows_Title"]);
        picture.BorderStyle = BorderStyle.None;
        string fileRef = (string)row["ows_FileRef"];
        string[] fileRefs = fileRef.Split(';');
        string fileName = fileRefs[1].Substring(1,
            fileRefs[1].Length - 1); // remove leading #
        fileName = System.IO.Path.GetFileName(fileName);
        // type: 0, original, 1 thumbnail, 2 web image
        System.Diagnostics.Debug.WriteLine("Attempting to download " +
            fileName + " from list " + url);
        imageService.DownloadAsync(url, "",
            new string[] { fileName }, 1, false, x);
        imageFlow.Controls.Add(picture);
        x++;
    }
}

void picture_Click(object sender, EventArgs e)
{
```

LISTING 21.1   Continued

```
    if (lastPictureClicked != null)
        lastPictureClicked.BorderStyle = BorderStyle.None;

    lastPictureClicked = (PictureBox)sender;
    lastPictureClicked.BorderStyle = BorderStyle.Fixed3D;
}

private void deleteButton_Click(object sender, EventArgs e)
{
    string fileName;
    if (lastPictureClicked != null)
    {
        string url = GetListUrl();
        fileName = GetFileName();

        imageService.Delete(url, "", new string[] { fileName });
        imageFlow.Controls.Remove(lastPictureClicked);
        lastPictureClicked = null;
    }
}

private string GetListUrl()
{
    ListViewItem listItem = libraryList.SelectedItems[0];
    return (string)listItem.Tag;
}

private string GetFileName()
{
    DataRow row = (DataRow)lastPictureClicked.Tag;
    ListViewItem listItem = libraryList.SelectedItems[0];
    string url = (string)listItem.Tag;
    string fileRef = (string)row["ows_FileRef"];
    string[] fileRefs = fileRef.Split(';');
    string fileName = fileRefs[1].Substring(1, fileRefs[1].Length - 1);
    fileName = System.IO.Path.GetFileName(fileName);

    return fileName;
}

private void renameButton_Click(object sender, EventArgs e)
{
    using (RenameForm rename = new RenameForm())
```

LISTING 21.1   Continued

```
    {
        rename.ShowDialog();
        string newName = rename.NewName;
        ListViewItem listItem = libraryList.SelectedItems[0];
        string list = (string)listItem.Tag;
        XmlDocument doc = new XmlDocument();
        string fileName = GetFileName();
        doc.InnerXml = string.Format(
            "<Request><files><file filename=\"{0}\" newbasename=\"{1}\""+
              "/></files></Request>",
            fileName, newName);
        XmlElement requestElement = doc.DocumentElement;

        imageService.Rename(list, "", requestElement);
    }
}


private void viewButton_Click(object sender, EventArgs e)
{
    DataRow row = (DataRow)lastPictureClicked.Tag;
    string url = GetListUrl();
    string fileName = GetFileName();
    XmlNode imageNode = imageService.Download(url, "",
            new string[] { fileName }, 0, false);
    string fileByteString = imageNode.InnerText;
    byte[] fileBytes = Convert.FromBase64String(fileByteString);
    using (PhotoDetail detail = new PhotoDetail(row, fileBytes))
    {
        detail.ShowDialog();
    }
}


private void uploadButton_Click(object sender, EventArgs e)
{
    if (uploadDialog.ShowDialog() == DialogResult.OK)
    {
        string fileName = uploadDialog.FileName;
        FileStream fs = new FileStream(fileName, FileMode.Open);
        byte[] fileBytes = new byte[fs.Length];
        fs.Read(fileBytes, 0, (int)fs.Length);
        string url = GetListUrl();
        imageService.Upload(url, "", fileBytes,
            Path.GetFileName(fileName), true);
```

LISTING 21.1   Continued

```
        MessageBox.Show("Image Uploaded.");
    }
}

private void metaButton_Click(object sender, EventArgs e)
{
    string url = GetListUrl();
    string fileName = GetFileName();

    XmlNode metaNode = imageService.GetItemsXMLData(url, "",
      new string[] { fileName });
    MessageBox.Show(metaNode.InnerXml);
}

private void getByIdButton_Click(object sender, EventArgs e)
{
    string url = GetListUrl();
    DataRow row = (DataRow)lastPictureClicked.Tag;
    string id = (string)row["ows_ID"];
    uint itemId = uint.Parse(id);

    XmlNode itemsNode = imageService.GetItemsByIds(url, new uint[] { itemId });
    MessageBox.Show(itemsNode.InnerXml);
}


}
}
```

The full source code of the application is available with the code downloads for this book, available at http://www.samspublishing.com. Make sure you have the ISBN of the book available to download the code.

Summary

This chapter illustrated the flexibility and the power of MOSS picture libraries and the Imaging Web Service. Using the Imaging Web Service, client applications can create subfolders, upload and download thumbnails and full-sized images, delete and rename images, and retrieve image metadata, including the image height and width. At the end of this chapter, the Photo Album application put all of the individual methods of the Imaging Web Service to use in a practical example. Armed with the information in this chapter, you should be ready to start creating powerful, flexible, compelling applications that use MOSS picture libraries as a back-end image and data store.

CHAPTER 22

Using the Lists Web Service

IN THIS CHAPTER

▶ Overview of the SharePoint Lists Web Services

▶ Performing Common List Actions

▶ Working with Revision Control

▶ Querying List Data

▶ Working with Views

Of all of the various things developers do with Microsoft Office SharePoint Server (MOSS), one of the most common programming tasks is exposing SharePoint list data to external applications via web services. This chapter provides a look at the various list-related web services that make this possible. In addition, this chapter covers working with views and even provides some insight into creating a class library that makes programming with SharePoint lists easier and simpler.

Overview of the SharePoint Lists Web Services

You can access SharePoint list data programmatically via web services in two main ways. The following briefly describes each of these web services and what functionality they provide. The rest of the chapter provides you with an in-depth look at how to program against each of these web services.

▶ Lists.asmx—This web service provides methods for retrieving and updating details about the list itself, such as the list title. In addition, you can also use this web service to retrieve and update list items and even retrieve filtered list items based on Collaborative Application Markup Language (CAML) queries.

▶ Views.asmx—Views are a large part of working with SharePoint lists and this web service provides excellent programmability support for views. You can use this web service to create new views, delete views, update views, obtain the list of views available to a list, and so forth.

Performing Common List Actions

When working with relational data sources such as SQL Server or Oracle, developers often refer to an acronym called CRUD. This acronym refers to the minimum required operations that should be supported for any entity: *Create*, *Retrieve*, *Update*, and *Delete*. This section illustrates the various forms of creation, retrieval, deletion, and updating that are available with the Lists Web Service.

Retrieving Lists and List Items

Retrieving lists and list items is done through a few straightforward methods such as `GetList` and `GetListItems`. The columns contained in Table 22.1 are the columns that will be contained in the Extensible Markup Language (XML) resultset from calling `GetList` as attributes. For a list of the attributes of a list that can be modified, see Table 22.2 in the next section.

TABLE 22.1   List Columns

Column/Attribute	Description
Title	Title of the list
DocTemplateUrl	Uniform resource locator (URL) of the document template used for new documents added to the document library
DefaultViewUrl	URL of the default view of the list
Description	Description of the list
ImageUrl	URL of an image associated with the list
Name	Globally unique identifier (GUID) corresponding to the list
BaseType	Base type of the list (for example, Events, Tasks)
FeatureId	GUID of the feature to which the list belongs
Created	Date the list was created
Modified	Date the list was last modified
LastDeleted	Time stamp indicating the last time the list was removed
ServerTemplate	Server template ID number used to create the list
Version	List version number
Direction	Right-to-left (RTL) or left-to-right (LTR) or none
ThumbnailSize	For a picture library list, size of thumbnail images to be displayed
WebImageHeight	Height of web images (picture library only)
WebImageWidth	Width of web images (picture library only)
Flags	Bitmasked flags value
ItemCount	Number of items contained within the list
AnonymousPermMask	Anonymous permission mask
RootFolder	Folder that contains all the files used to work with the list
WriteSecurity	Write security setting for the list
Author	Creator of the list

TABLE 22.1   Continued

Column/Attribute	Description
EventSinkAssembly	Strong identification string corresponding to the Assembly containing the event sink for the list
EventSinkClass	Class name of a class written to respond to events fired by this list
EventSinkData	Arbitrary string value that is passed to event sink listeners
EmailInsertsFolder	Folder for email inserts
EmailAlias	Alias used for emails sent to the list for publication
WebFullUrl	Full URL of the list
WebId	ID of the web to which the list belongs
SendToLocation	Location of the Send To action for items contained within the list
ScopeId	Scope of the list
MajorVersionLimit	Limit for major version of list items
MajorWithMinorVersionLimit	Another version limiter
WorkflowId	ID of the workflow associated with the list
HasUniqueScopes	Value indicating if the list contains unique scopes
AllowDeletion	Value indicating if the list allows items to be deleted
AllowMultiResponses	Value indicating if the list allows multiple survey responses per user (survey list only)
EnableAttachments	Value indicating if attachments are allowed on list items
EnableModeration	Value indicating if list items must be approved before publication
EnableVersioning	Value indicating if changes to list items will create new versions
Hidden	Value indicating if the list is visible in the standard locations
MultipleDataList	For a Meeting Workspace, value indicating if the list contains data for multiple event instances
Ordered	Value indicating if the list is sorted
ShowUser	Value indicating if the user ID is displayed for the list
EnableMinorVersion	Value indicating if minor versions are stored for list item changes
RequireCheckout	Value indicating if a checkout is required to modify list data

To see the Lists.asmx Web Service in action to retrieve lists and list items, create a new Windows application and add a web reference to the Lists.asmx Web Service. You can find this service in the _vti_bin directory beneath any SharePoint site. The Lists Web Service for the root site of a portal can be found at http://[portal-server]/_vti_bin/Lists.asmx and you might find the Lists Web Service for an HR team site at http://[portal-server]/sitedirectory/HR/_vti_bin/Lists.asmx.

After creating the Windows application, add a `TextBox` called `siteUrl`, a button called `retrieveListsButton`, a `ListView` called `siteLists` and, finally, a `ListBox` called `titleLists`. Create event handlers for the button's `Click` event and for `siteLists`' `SelectedIndexChanged` event. The code for this application is shown in Listing 22.1. The application retrieves all of the lists at a given site using the `GetListCollection` method, and then attempts to retrieve the title of each list item using the `GetListItems` method.

LISTING 22.1   The ListRetriever Application

```
using System;
using System.Xml;
using System.Collections.Generic;
using System.ComponentModel;
using System.Data;
using System.Drawing;
using System.Text;
using System.Windows.Forms;

namespace ListRetriever
{
  public partial class Form1 : Form
  {
    private win2k3r2lab.Lists listService = null;

    public Form1()
    {
      InitializeComponent();
    }

    private void retrieveListsButton_Click(object sender, EventArgs e)
    {
      listService = new ListRetriever.win2k3r2lab.Lists();
      listService.Credentials =
        new System.Net.NetworkCredential("Administrator", "password");
      listService.Url = siteUrl.Text;
      XmlNode listCollection = listService.GetListCollection();
      siteLists.Items.Clear();
      MessageBox.Show(listCollection.ChildNodes[0].OuterXml);
      foreach (XmlNode listNode in listCollection.ChildNodes)
      {
        ListViewItem lvi = new ListViewItem();
        lvi.Text = listNode.Attributes.GetNamedItem("Title").Value;
        lvi.Tag = listNode.Attributes.GetNamedItem("ID").Value;
        lvi.SubItems.Add(
          listNode.Attributes.GetNamedItem("ServerTemplate").Value);
```

LISTING 22.1   Continued

```
      siteLists.Items.Add(lvi);
  }
}
private void siteLists_SelectedIndexChanged(object sender, EventArgs e)
{
  titleList.Items.Clear();
  if (siteLists.SelectedItems.Count == 0) return;

  string listGuid = (string)siteLists.SelectedItems[0].Tag;
  XmlNode itemCollection = listService.GetListItems(
    listGuid, string.Empty, null, null, "0", null, string.Empty);

  foreach (XmlNode item in
    itemCollection.SelectNodes("//*[local-name()='row']"))
  {
    titleList.Items.Add(
      item.Attributes.GetNamedItem("ows_Title") == null ? "No title" :
      item.Attributes.GetNamedItem("ows_Title").Value);
  }
}
}
}
}
```

The first thing that you will notice about programming with the Lists Web Service is that *everything* is XML-based. The results of the call to GetListCollection return a set of XML and attributes described in Table 22.1. The call to GetListItems returns XML in a format that is roughly equivalent to the old ADO RecordSet format. Although the XML can be read by an ADO.NET DataSet Class, many simple list item tasks don't require the overhead of a full DataSet.

The other thing you might notice is that the XML returned by GetListItems uses a peculiar "ows_" prefix on all attribute names. This is a throwback from the days before SharePoint 2001 when the product was referred to as the "Office Web Server." Every list item in SharePoint has an ows_ID attribute, and most of them have an ows_Title attribute indicating a short description for the item.

SharePoint List Schema Cheat Sheets

Each SharePoint list has its own schema, and you might find that even though the lists might appear similar in the SharePoint graphical user interface (GUI), their schemas can differ greatly. As you encounter lists against which you want to program, you should print out a schema cheat sheet showing the column name in the GUI, the attribute name in XML, and the data type. Wherever prudent, this book provides you with those schemas but you should make a habit of keeping them nearby as you develop against the Lists Web Service.

Updating Lists

Through the `UpdateList` method, you can update list details such as various configuration settings and the list's title and description. In addition, you also have the ability to create new fields, update existing fields, and delete existing fields within the list. This same functionality is available through the SharePoint front end by clicking Settings and then List Settings when viewing the list.

The `UpdateList` method takes the following parameters:

- ▶ `listName`—The name/GUID of the list to be updated.

- ▶ `listProperties`—An XML node containing all of the list properties to be modified.

- ▶ `newFields`—An XML node containing all of the fields that are to be added during the transaction. This XML contains a list of "method" nodes to provide individual item auditing.

- ▶ `updateFields`—An XML node containing all of the existing fields that are to be modified during the transaction.

- ▶ `deleteFields`—An XML node containing the fields to be deleted.

- ▶ `listVersion`—A String indicating the list version.

The data contained in each of the XML nodes is specific to the list being modified. Essentially, this means that your code should be aware of the list schema before adding, deleting, or updating fields. Table 22.2 shows all of the list properties that can be modified by `UpdateList`.

TABLE 22.2   Updatable List Properties

Property	Description
AllowMultiResponses	For a survey-style list, indicates whether multiple responses can be submitted by the same person for the survey.
Description	Indicates the list's description.
Direction	Indicates the reading direction of list contents: LTR for left-to-right (default), or RTL for right-to-left. Can also be None, indicating no change from the system default.
EnableAssignedToEmail	Enables transmission of an email when an issue is assigned to a user. Only applicable to issue lists.
EnableAttachments	Indicates whether list items can have attachments.
EnableModeration	If true, indicates that all list items must be approved before being made available to other users.
EnableVersioning	If true, indicates that all changes to list items will automatically create a new version and track the change in history.
Hidden	Indicates whether the list is hidden. This is set for system/internal lists such as the Master Page Gallery list.

TABLE 22.2   Continued

Property	Description
MultipleDataList	On a list on a Meeting Workspace site, indicates that the list contains data for multiple meeting instances simultaneously. See Chapter 23, "Using the Meeting Workspace Web Service," for more details.
Ordered	Indicates whether users can control the sort order of list items when editing views.
ShowUser	For survey-type lists, indicates whether the name of the user appears in the survey results.
Title	Indicates the title of the list.

22

Use Backup Lists When Testing Schema-Changing Code

The UpdateList method is extremely powerful and can be extremely handy. However, it can often be difficult or impossible to recover from list schema changes made programmatically. Because of this, it is always a good idea to test your code on duplicate lists with production schemas instead of on lists being used in production.

The following code modifies the properties of an existing list as well as creates two new columns: First Name and Last Name:

```
// if you're renaming a list, use the GUID to be consistent.
string listGuid = "{3DE6337E-7E49-4AD6-9936-8440C20F7711}";
win2k3r2lab.Lists listService = new ListUpdater.win2k3r2lab.Lists();
listService.Url =
    "http://win2k3r2lab/sitedirectory/research/_vti_bin/Lists.asmx";
listService.Credentials =
    new System.Net.NetworkCredential("Administrator", "password");
XmlDocument doc = new XmlDocument();
// list properties
XmlElement properties = doc.CreateElement("List");
properties.SetAttribute("Title", "Updated List Title");
properties.SetAttribute("Description", "Updated List Description");

// new fields (first name, last name)
XmlElement newFields = doc.CreateElement("Fields");
XmlElement newMethod = doc.CreateElement("Method");
newFields.AppendChild(newMethod);
newMethod.SetAttribute("ID", "1");
XmlElement newField = doc.CreateElement("Field");
newMethod.AppendChild(newField);
newField.SetAttribute("ReadOnly", "FALSE");
newField.SetAttribute("DisplayName", "First Name");
```

```
newField.SetAttribute("Name", "FirstName");
newField.SetAttribute("Type", "Text");
newField.SetAttribute("FromBaseType", "TRUE");

// last name
newMethod = doc.CreateElement("Method");
newMethod.SetAttribute("ID", "2");
newField = doc.CreateElement("Field");
newField.SetAttribute("ReadOnly", "FALSE");
newField.SetAttribute("DisplayName", "Last Name");
newField.SetAttribute("Name", "LastName");
newField.SetAttribute("Type", "Text");
newField.SetAttribute("FromBaseType", "TRUE");
newMethod.AppendChild(newField);
newFields.AppendChild(newMethod);

listService.UpdateList(listGuid, (XmlNode)properties,
    (XmlNode)newFields, null, null, string.Empty);
```

All of the XML fragments for updating and creating fields follow the same format:

```
<Fields>
<Method Cmd="#">
   <Field>
      < … >
      <Formula>..</Formula>
   </Field>
</Method>
</Fields>
```

The following code makes use of the optional <Formula> subelement and adds a new calculated field that concatenates the first and last names using the common "last, first" format (note that this call doesn't work unless you've already created the First Name and Last Name columns):

```
// full name
newFields = doc.CreateElement("Fields");
newField = doc.CreateElement("Field");
newFields.AppendChild(newField);
newMethod = doc.CreateElement("Method");
newMethod.SetAttribute("ID", "3");
newField.SetAttribute("ReadOnly", "TRUE");
newField.SetAttribute("DisplayName", "Full Name");
newField.SetAttribute("Name", "FullName");
newField.SetAttribute("Type", "Calculated");
```

```
newField.SetAttribute("ResultType", "Text");
newMethod.AppendChild(newField);
XmlElement formula = doc.CreateElement("Formula");
formula.InnerText = "=[Last Name]&\", \"&[First Name]";
XmlElement formulaDisplayNames =
    doc.CreateElement("FormulaDisplayNames");
formulaDisplayNames.InnerText = "=[Last Name]&[First Name]";
newField.AppendChild(formula);
newField.AppendChild(formulaDisplayNames);
XmlElement fieldRefs = doc.CreateElement("FieldRefs");
fieldRefs.InnerXml =
    "<FieldRef Name='First Name'/><FieldRef Name='Last Name'/>";
newField.AppendChild(fieldRefs);
newFields.AppendChild(newMethod);
listService.UpdateList(listGuid, null, (XmlNode)newFields,
    null, null, string.Empty);
```

Updating, Deleting, and Creating List Items

When updating a list, you need to know the GUID of the list to modify it, and you know which columns can be updated at development time because the list schema is a fixed schema. List items, however, can have varying schemas. The data contained in a Task list is going to vary greatly from the data contained in a DefectTracking list or a Contacts list. As such, the code to update list items is *specific* to the type of items being updated. For each collection of list items to be updated, you will send an XML <Batch> element containing the change list. The following code illustrates changing the title of two different list items contained within the same list as well as adding a new item and deleting yet another item. Note that not only is the list GUID required, but the ID of each item is also required to perform the update. The <Batch> element represents a collection of *New*, *Update*, and *Delete* commands corresponding to individual list items.

Listing 22.2 is from a console application that creates a new list item, updates an existing item, and deletes an existing item. The schema is based on the one created in the previous section (a custom list with a First Name and Last Name field as well as a calculated Full Name field).

LISTING 22.2   Console Application to Create a New List Item, Update Form, and Delete Existing Item

```
using System;
using System.Xml;
using System.Collections.Generic;
using System.Text;

namespace ItemUpdater
{
class Program
```

LISTING 22.2   Continued

```
{
static void Main(string[] args)
{
    win2k3r2lab.Lists listService = new ItemUpdater.win2k3r2lab.Lists();
    listService.Credentials =
      new System.Net.NetworkCredential("Administrator", "password");
    listService.Url = "http://win2k3r2lab/sitedirectory/research/
➥_vti_bin/lists.asmx";

    XmlDocument doc = new XmlDocument();
    XmlElement batchelement = doc.CreateElement("Batch");
    batchelement.SetAttribute("OnError", "Continue");
    batchelement.SetAttribute("ListVersion", "1");

    batchelement.InnerXml =
        "<Method ID=\"1\" Cmd=\"New\"> " +
        "<Field Name=\"Title\">This is a new item</Field>" +
         "<Field Name=\"First_x0020_Name\">Bob</Field>" +
         "<Field Name=\"Last_x0020_Name\">Jones</Field>" +
        "</Method>"+
         "<Method ID=\"2\" Cmd=\"Update\">" +
         "<Field Name=\"ID\">4</Field>" +
         "<Field Name=\"Title\">Title Changed!</Field>" +
         "</Method>" +
         "<Method ID=\"3\" Cmd=\"Delete\">" +
         "<Field Name=\"ID\">4</Field>" +
         "</Method>";

    XmlNode results = listService.UpdateListItems
➥("Updated List Title", batchelement);
    Console.WriteLine(results.OuterXml);
    Console.ReadLine();
}
}
}
```

One of the most useful tools when updating list items is the XmlNode that you get back from the UpdateListItems call. If there is an error, it contains a (usually) precise description of what went wrong. If everything was successful, the node actually contains a copy of each modified row. If you inserted a new item, the copy of that item in the resulting XML contains the automatically assigned ID column.

You might notice that the name of the First Name field, when passed to `UpdateListItems` is `First_x0020_Name`. The `x0020` is an XML representation of the space that occurs in the field name.

NOTE

It is often frustrating to the point of madness to deal with the inconsistencies in representations of data with SharePoint lists. You might have noticed that the data you receive from SharePoint looks nothing like the data you *send* to SharePoint using the Lists Web Service. When working with any SharePoint list, you might want to keep a copy of the output XML (the row/column metaphor) and a copy of a decent input XML (the batch metaphor) handy for reference to keep the confusion as small as possible. Sadly, this is one of the pain points for programmers that did not get fixed in the 2007 version.

Retrieving Parent/Child List Data

In previous versions of SharePoint, the model for dealing with hierarchical data was either extremely immature or simply didn't exist. You had the ability to have one column's value be chosen from a list of items contained in another list, which was well suited to the task of selecting a defect status stored in a Defect Statuses list. However, trying to force that model to support the notion of things like Orders and Order Items or Customers and Customer Phone Numbers didn't work well at all.

Using a new concept in MOSS 2007 called content types, you can create arbitrarily deep hierarchies for storing data in SharePoint lists. For example, you could create a content type called `Order` that inherits from the `Folder` type. This would allow orders to contain items, possibly even items of the content type `Order Item`. This use of content types allows a parent folder to have *separate metadata* from the items contained within it: the ideal scenario for modeling parent/child data in a single SharePoint list. Coupled with the notion that SharePoint list item storage is more efficient than in previous versions and is now highly indexed, this provides a viable alternative for storing data in a relational database if storage within SharePoint is more convenient. Obviously, large database scenarios aren't appropriate for SharePoint, but the ability to store hierarchical data presents new options to developers that might not have been available in SharePoint 2003.

To see how this all works, start with a new team site. On that team site, add a new content type called `Order` and add a column called `Order Number` to that content type. Next, add a site content type called `Order Item` and add the following columns to it: `SKU` and `Item Number`. Now go and create a list and associate the `Order` and `Order Item` content types with that list. If everything has worked, you should see two new drop-down menu items under the `New` button on the list's default view: `New Order` and `New Order Item`.

Before taking a look at the code, you should notice one important thing about how the Lists Web Service provides list items that are associated with a content type. By default, if you request a list of items, you do not get all of the columns like you would if you were dealing with standard list items. Instead, you must use the ViewFields XML element to manually specify the fields you want to retrieve. When you consider that content types allow individual items contained within a list to have completely different schemas, requiring the developer to manually request fields makes a lot of sense. The code in Listing 22.3 shows a complete console application that requests orders (parent folders) and then subsequently requests all items contained within each order. To request list items contained within a folder, you must specify the <Folder> option in the <QueryOptions> XML parameter to GetListItems.

LISTING 22.3   Querying Hierarchical List Item Data Using Content Types

```
using System;
using System.Xml;
using System.Collections.Generic;
using System.Text;

namespace HierarchyDemo
{
class Program
{
static void Main(string[] args)
{
    win2k3r2lab.Lists listService = new HierarchyDemo.win2k3r2lab.Lists();
    listService.Credentials =
        new System.Net.NetworkCredential("Administrator", "password");
    XmlDocument doc = new XmlDocument();

    XmlNode viewFieldsParent = doc.CreateElement("ViewFields");
    viewFieldsParent.InnerXml =
        "<FieldRef Name=\"ID\"/>" +
        "<FieldRef Name=\"Order_x0020_Number\"/>";

    XmlNode listItems = listService.GetListItems(
      "Hierarchy Demo", "", null, viewFieldsParent, "0", null, "");

    foreach (XmlNode item in listItems.SelectNodes("//*[local-name()='row']"))
    {
        Console.WriteLine("Order: " +
          item.Attributes.GetNamedItem("ows_Title").Value);
        Console.WriteLine("Order #: " +
          item.Attributes.GetNamedItem("ows_Order_x0020_Number").Value);

        string folderName = item.Attributes.GetNamedItem("ows_Title").Value;
        XmlNode queryOptions = doc.CreateElement("QueryOptions");
```

LISTING 22.3   Continued

```
        queryOptions.InnerXml =
            "<Folder>" + folderName + "</Folder>";
        XmlNode viewFields = doc.CreateElement("ViewFields");
        viewFields.InnerXml =
            "<FieldRef Name=\"ID\"/>" +
            "<FieldRef Name=\"OrderItem\"/>" +
            "<FieldRef Name=\"SKU\"/>";
        XmlNode subItems = listService.GetListItems(
          "Hierarchy Demo", "", null, viewFields, "0", queryOptions, "");

        int x = 0;
        foreach (XmlNode subItem in
          subItems.SelectNodes("//*[local-name()='row']"))
        {
            if (x > 0)
            { // skip the first row, since thats the containing folder
                Console.WriteLine(
                    string.Format("\tItem {0}: {1}",
                    subItem.Attributes.GetNamedItem("ows_OrderItem").Value,
                    subItem.Attributes.GetNamedItem("ows_Title").Value));
                Console.WriteLine("\tSKU: " +
                    subItem.Attributes.GetNamedItem("ows_SKU").Value);
            }
            x++;
        }
    }
    Console.ReadLine();
}
}
}
```

The preceding code produces output that looks like the following (assuming you have created some sample Order folders and Order Items contained within them):

```
Order: First Order
Order #: 1001.00000000000
        Item 1.00000000000000: MP3 Player
        SKU: MP3100
```

As you can see, the folder/item paradigm is extremely powerful when coupled with the parent/child pattern for storing and retrieving hierarchical data and could potentially be one of the most powerful new features in Microsoft Office SharePoint 2007 beside the Business Data Catalog for using SharePoint as a data back end.

Working with Revision Control

In previous versions of SharePoint, the ability to track changes to a list item was limited only to document library lists. With MOSS, you can now track revisions to any list item in any list. In addition, instead of simple numerical revision numbers, MOSS 2007 supports major and minor version numbers. This section shows you how the Lists Web Service has been updated to include support for revision control.

One of the revision control methods, `GetVersionCollection`, retrieves a list of changes to a specific field within a list item in a given list. The method call:

```
XmlNode versions =
  listService.GetVersionCollection("Updated List Title", "4", "Title");
```

yields the following XML:

```
<Versions xmlns="http://schemas.microsoft.com/sharepoint/soap/">
<Version Title="Title Changed Again Again Again"
  Modified="6/26/2006 3:21:44 AM" />
<Version Title="Title Changed Again Again"
  Modified="6/26/2006 3:21:20 AM" />
<Version Title="Title Changed Again"
  Modified="6/26/2006 3:21:08 AM" />
<Version Title="Title Changed!"
  Modified="6/26/2006 2:38:16 AM" />
</Versions>
```

Note that because you are looking purely at the change in one field over time, there is no revision number included, as the revision number applies to the entire list item and not just one field.

If you use the `GetListItemChanges` method on the Lists Web Service, you can get a list of changes made to list items since a given date. This provides you a field called `ows_owshiddenversion` that shows the item version.

Although the version control story for the Lists Web Service is certainly not as fleshed out as it could be, it's a useful start. As always, if you find functionality that is provided in the application programming interface (API) but is not exposed well or at all through a web service, you can write your own web service that is tailored specifically to your needs. In this case, you might consider writing a web service that provides a more robust version control querying system.

Querying List Data

So far, you have seen how to get list data and list items based on unique identification strings. This section shows you how you can use a CAML query to filter the results of a `GetListItems` operation.

Adding Web References

You have to be extremely careful when adding web references to your Visual Studio 2005 projects. You cannot rely on the web reference system to give you the URL you want. For example, an attempt to reference http://lab/sitedirectory/research/_vti_bin/lists.asmx often results in a reference to http://lab/_vti_bin/lists.asmx. This is obviously not the site you were attempting to reference. This is why the service URL is manually set at runtime in all of the samples throughout this chapter.

You can do more than just filter using CAML queries—you can sort as well. For a full list of what's available through CAML queries and a reference on the syntax for building such queries, consult the SharePoint Software Development Kit (SDK) documentation. The following few lines of code illustrate both sorting and filtering:

```
win2k3r2lab.Lists listService = new GetListItemsQuery.win2k3r2lab.Lists();
listService.Credentials =
    new System.Net.NetworkCredential("Administrator", "password");
listService.Url = "http://win2k3r2lab/sitedirectory/research/_vti_bin/lists.asmx";

XmlDocument doc = new XmlDocument();

XmlElement query = doc.CreateElement("Query");
query.InnerXml =
    "<OrderBy>" +
        "<FieldRef Name=\"Title\"/>"+
    "</OrderBy>"+
    "<Where>" +
        "<Eq>" +
            "<FieldRef Name=\"First_x0020_Name\"/>" +
            "<Value Type=\"Text\">Bob</Value>"+
        "</Eq>"+
    "</Where>";

XmlNode results =
  listService.GetListItems("Updated List Title", "", query, null, "0", null, "");
Console.WriteLine(results.OuterXml);

foreach (XmlNode item in results.SelectNodes("//*[local-name()='row']"))
{
    Console.WriteLine(
        string.Format("{0} : {1}",
        item.Attributes.GetNamedItem("ows_Title").Value,
        item.Attributes.GetNamedItem("ows_Full_x0020_Name").Value));
}
Console.ReadLine();
```

The output from the preceding code looks like this (alphabetically sorted by item title, showing only those items whose first name is "Bob"):

```
This is a new item : string;#Jones, Bob
Title Changed Again Again Again : string;#Jones, Bob
```

Note that the format of the calculated string isn't just simple output: It uses a special syntax where the data type of the calculated field is displayed, then the ";#" delimiter, followed, finally, by the actual field data.

Working with Views

Views are an incredibly powerful complement to lists within SharePoint. Views allow administrators to display, sort, and filter data in multiple different ways, and personal views can even allow individual users to create their own views on public data. This section of the chapter shows you how you can manipulate and query views using the Views Web Service.

Creating a View

To create a view, you need to know the name of the list that will act as the source for the view, as well as the fields you want displayed in the view, and the query you want to produce the view's output. The following code produces a new view containing only items that have a First Name column containing the value Bob. This view only shows the Last Name and Title columns.

```
win2k3r2lab.Views viewService = new ViewDemo.win2k3r2lab.Views();
viewService.Credentials =
  new System.Net.NetworkCredential("Administrator", "password");
viewService.Url =
  "http://win2k3r2lab/sitedirectory/research/_vti_bin/views.asmx";


XmlDocument doc = new XmlDocument();
XmlNode viewFields = doc.CreateElement("ViewFields");
viewFields.InnerXml =
    "<FieldRef Name=\"Last_x0020_Name\"/>" +
    "<FieldRef Name=\"ows_Title\"/>";
XmlNode query = doc.CreateElement("Query");
query.InnerXml =
    "<Where>" +
        "<Eq>" +
            "<FieldRef Name=\"First_x0020_Name\"/>"+
            "<Value>Bob</Value>" +
        "</Eq>" +
    "</Where>";
viewService.AddView(
    "Updated List Title",
```

```
"Bob Items",
viewFields,
query,
null,
"HTML",
false);
```

Deleting a View

Deleting a view is pretty simple. All you need is the name of the list and the name of the view, as follows:

```
viewService.DeleteView("Updated List Title", "Bob Items");
```

Getting View Collections and Details

To obtain the list of views available for a given list, simply issue the following method call:

```
XmlNode viewCollection = viewService.GetViewCollection("List Name");
```

This returns an XML node called Views that contains a list of views. The following lists some of the important attributes on each child View node:

- ▶ Name—The name of the view (GUID)
- ▶ DisplayName—The friendly name of the view
- ▶ DefaultView—A Boolean indicating whether the view is the current default for the list
- ▶ Url—A direct link to the view (does not include server name)
- ▶ ImageUrl—An icon for the view

Summary

The Lists Web Service is one of the most frequently used web services within SharePoint. This chapter has provided you with an in-depth look at some of the tremendous power available at the fingertips of developers using the Lists Web Service and the Views Web Service. Using code samples in this chapter, you can create lists, update list items, query lists and list items, create views, and much more.

CHAPTER 23

Using the Meeting Workspace Web Service

IN THIS CHAPTER

▶ Overview of Meeting Workspaces

▶ Managing Meeting Workspaces

▶ Managing Meetings

▶ Managing Meeting Attendance

▶ Accessing Meeting Workspace Lists

The Meeting Workspace Web Service is one of the many powerful and extremely useful web services made available to developers. This web service is provided by Windows SharePoint Services (WSS), so you do not need access to a portal server to utilize this web service.

This chapter provides you with an overview of Meeting Workspaces, including a walk-through of creating a sample Meeting Workspace site that will be used in the code samples throughout the chapter. After you have a sample Meeting Workspace up and running, this chapter shows you all of the things that you can accomplish using the Meeting Workspace Web Service.

Overview of Meeting Workspaces

Meeting Workspaces were introduced to solve a very specific problem that exists within virtually any workplace, whether you work in Information Technology (IT), Management, Development, Marketing, or anywhere else. Just about everyone has been in the situation where they send out a meeting request and they include a quick agenda in the body of the request. Some people see the agenda, others don't. Worse—when the agenda changes, you have to resend the request to everyone after modifying the body of the message request. Even worse is that there is no way for you to track the responsibilities of each attendee—you can just see who's going to show up from the Scheduling tab in Microsoft Outlook. All of this leads to a very unsatisfying meeting experience. There is no collaboration, no defined meeting workflow, no central place to store meeting minutes, meeting presentation materials, agendas, task lists, and other data related to a meeting that must be tracked. The Meeting Workspace provides this central location of collaboration in which meeting attendees and organizers can collaborate, share information, publish pertinent documents, and even record crucial meeting decisions on the website.

Creating a Meeting Workspace Site

To create a Meeting Workspace site that will be used in the samples throughout the rest of this chapter, first open a browser window to the Microsoft Office SharePoint Server (MOSS) 2007 portal home page. In the case of the screenshots in this chapter, that is http://win2k3r2lab. Complete the following steps to create a new team collaboration site and a Meeting Workspace underneath it:

1. Click the Site Actions button.

2. Click the Create Site link.

3. Call the new site Research Team.

4. Select the standard template.

5. Set the uniform resource locator (URL) name of the site to research.

6. Make sure that, after the site is created, you are looking at the Research Team home page.

7. Click the Site Actions button.

8. Click the Create Site button.

9. Call the new site Defect Tracking Vendor Analysis.

10. Select defecttracking as the URL for the new site.

11. Click the Meetings tab in the template selection area and then choose Decision Meeting Workspace.

12. After being created, you should have a Meeting Workspace that looks very much like the one shown in Figure 23.1. Go ahead and add some sample data to mimic the data shown in the screenshot.

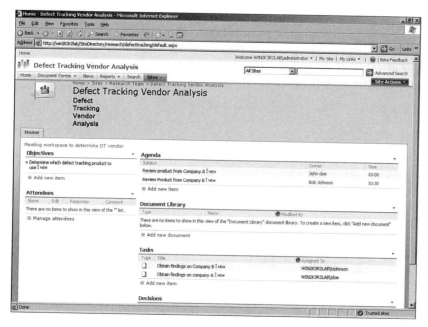

FIGURE 23.1   A sample Meeting Workspace.

Managing Meeting Workspaces

The tasks you just completed to manually create a Meeting Workspace can be done programmatically through the web service. In addition to creating Meeting Workspaces, you can delete them, modify their details, and get a list of all Meeting Workspaces. This can be extremely useful and powerful if you want to integrate Meeting Workspace functionality into other systems within your enterprise, such as automated scheduling software, or if you want to enhance the existing integration between Outlook 2007 and SharePoint 2007.

This section walks you through creating a Windows Forms application that manages SharePoint 2007 Meeting Workspaces.

Listing Available Meeting Workspaces

Before working on listing Meeting Workspaces, you need an application to work with. Create a new Windows Forms application called WorkspaceManager and add a web reference to the following URL: http://[your server]/ research/_vti_bin/meetings.asmx.

Name the reference research. It doesn't matter which meetings.asmx service you reference because the URL is dynamically entered in the application anyway. Next, drag a text box named parentsiteUrl and a list view named workspaceList onto the form. Set the view's mode to "Detail". You also need a button with the text Load Workspaces somewhere on the form. Add the following code to the button's event handler:

```
private void button1_Click(object sender, EventArgs e)
{
    research.Meetings meetingWs = new research.Meetings();
    meetingWs.Credentials = new System.Net.NetworkCredential(
        "Administrator", "password");
    meetingWs.Url = parentsiteUrl.Text;
    XmlNode resultsNode = meetingWs.GetMeetingWorkspaces(false);
    workspaceList.Items.Clear();

    foreach (XmlNode workspaceNode in resultsNode.ChildNodes)
    {
        ListViewItem lvi = new ListViewItem();
        lvi.Text = workspaceNode.Attributes["Title"].Value;
        lvi.SubItems.Add(workspaceNode.Attributes["Url"].Value);
        workspaceList.Items.Add(lvi);
    }
}
```

Obviously, you need to change the user credentials and URL to match your system. If you followed the directions at the beginning of the chapter and created a sample Meeting Workspace, your form should look very similar to the one shown in Figure 23.2 when you run the application and click the Load Workspaces button.

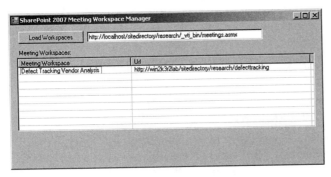

FIGURE 23.2   List of Meeting Workspaces on a SharePoint site.

Creating a Workspace

Creating a workspace is a fairly simple process. The only thing that can be difficult is that you must specify the site template name when creating the workspace. Unfortunately, you can't simply specify "Meeting Workspace" or "Decision Meeting Workspace" when creating the workspace. Instead, you need to specify the internal template name as defined in the SharePoint Extensible Markup Language (XML) files. To save you the trouble of sifting through the XML files, Table 23.1 lists the template name and configuration number of each type of Meeting Workspace.

TABLE 23.1   Meeting Workspace Template Names and Configurations

Template	Configuration	Description
MPS	0	Basic Meeting Workspace. Contains: Objectives, Attendees, Agenda, and Document Library.
MPS	1	Blank Meeting Workspace, nothing preconfigured.
MPS	2	Decision Meeting Workspace. Contains: Objectives, Attendees, Agenda, Document Library, Tasks, and Decisions.
MPS	3	Social Meeting Workspace. Contains: Attendees, Directions, Image/Logo, Things to Bring, Discussions, Picture Library. Excellent for SharePoint User group organization!
MPS	4	Multipage Meeting Workspace. Contains: Objectives, Attendees, Agenda, and two blank pages for whatever is required.

To create a new Meeting Workspace, you specify the template name, a pound sign, and the configuration number. So, to create a new Multipage Meeting Workspace, you would pass the string MPS#4 as a parameter to the CreateWorkspace method.

Now that you have access to the most important piece of information required to create workspaces, you can add an Add Workspace button to the form in the sample application. Add the following code to the event handler for the Click event:

```
private void newWorkspaceButton_Click(object sender, EventArgs e)
{
    research.Meetings meetingsWs = new WorkspaceManager.research.Meetings();
    meetingsWs.Credentials = new System.Net.NetworkCredential(
        "Administrator", "password");
    meetingsWs.Url = parentsiteUrl.Text;

    research.TimeZoneInf tzi = new WorkspaceManager.research.TimeZoneInf();
    // modify timezone data as you see fit..
    XmlNode results = meetingsWs.CreateWorkspace(
        "New Workspace", "MPS#0", 1033,
        tzi);
    MessageBox.Show(
        "New workspace created. Reload Workspaces to see new workspace.");
}
```

Run the application and add a new workspace (it could take as long as 30 seconds to create the new workspace depending on your lab environment) and then reload the workspace list. You should see a form that looks similar to the one shown in Figure 23.3.

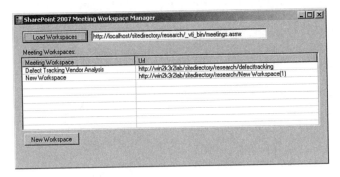

FIGURE 23.3   Adding multiple workspaces.

Deleting a Workspace

Given that you use the parent, or container, site to enumerate the list of available workspaces and to create new workspaces, you might think that you use the same parent site to delete a workspace. To delete a Meeting Workspace, *the web reference must actually refer to the Meeting Workspace to be deleted.* For example, if you were going to delete the Meeting Workspace tempWorkspace from the parent site Research, you might set the URL of your web reference to http://[servername]/ Research/tempWorkspace/_vti_bin/meetings.asmx to delete the tempWorkspace Meeting Workspace.

To add the "Delete" functionality to the existing Windows Forms application, simply add a new button to the interface called deleteWorkspaceButton and set its text to "Delete Workspace." The following code shows an event handler for this button that deletes the workspace indicated by the currently selected list view item:

```
private void deleteWorkspaceButton_Click(object sender, EventArgs e)
{
    if (workspaceList.SelectedItems.Count == 0) return;

    ListViewItem selectedWorkspace = workspaceList.SelectedItems[0];
    if (selectedWorkspace != null)
    {
        if (MessageBox.Show("Are you sure you want to delete this workspace?",
            "Delete Workspace", MessageBoxButtons.YesNo) ==
            DialogResult.Yes)
        {
```

```
        research.Meetings meetingsWs =
          new WorkspaceManager.research.Meetings();
        meetingsWs.Credentials =
          new System.Net.NetworkCredential("Administrator", "password");
        meetingsWs.Url =
          selectedWorkspace.SubItems[1].Text + "/_vti_bin/meetings.asmx";
        meetingsWs.DeleteWorkspace();
        selectedWorkspace.Remove();
        MessageBox.Show("Workspace deleted.");
      }
    }
}
```

The parameterless method, `DeleteWorkspace`, is responsible for deleting the workspace data and the provisioned SharePoint site.

Changing Workspace Details

The only detail you can change of a Meeting Workspace that you can change with the Meeting Workspace Web Service (as opposed to direct site management) is the title of the workspace. You do this using the `SetWorkspaceTitle` method. After adding a new `TextBox` called `renameTitle` and a button called `renameWorkspaceButton`, create an event handler that looks like the following code to make use of the `SetWorkspaceTitle` method:

```
private void renameWorkspaceButton_Click(object sender, EventArgs e)
{
    if (workspaceList.SelectedItems.Count == 0) return;

    ListViewItem selectedWorkspace = workspaceList.SelectedItems[0];
    if (selectedWorkspace != null)
    {
        research.Meetings meetingsWs = new WorkspaceManager.research.Meetings();
        meetingsWs.Credentials =
            new System.Net.NetworkCredential("Administrator", "password");
        meetingsWs.Url = selectedWorkspace.SubItems[1].Text + "/_vti_bin/
➥meetings.asmx";
        meetingsWs.SetWorkspaceTitle(renameTitle.Text);
        selectedWorkspace.Text = renameTitle.Text;
    }
}
```

The new user interface, showing a recently renamed Meeting Workspace, should look similar to the one illustrated in Figure 23.4.

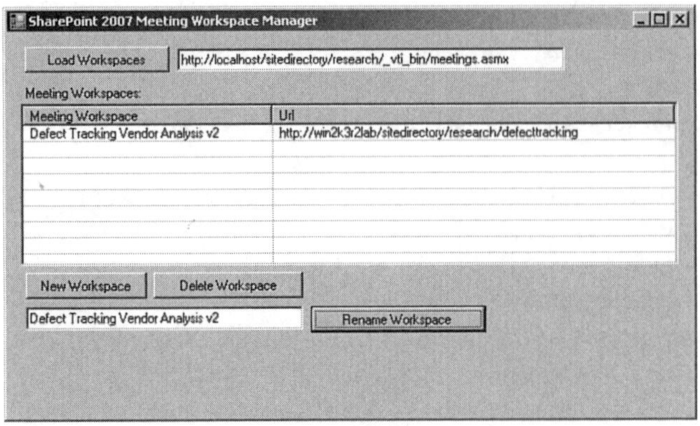

FIGURE 23.4   Renaming a Meeting Workspace.

Managing Meetings

Meeting management can be tricky if you haven't spent a lot of time working with meetings and Meeting Workspaces as an end user or an administrator within MOSS. This section shows you how to use the Meetings Web Service to create, remove, update, and restore meetings for a given Meeting Workspace.

Creating Meetings

Creating a new meeting is a process that might be confusing at first. A lot of developers assume that if they create a meeting within a Meeting Workspace that a new calendar entry is created on the parent site. This isn't the case. What happens is a new `instance` of the Meeting Workspace is created given the new start and end dates. You can duplicate this by creating multiple meetings through the SharePoint graphical user interface (GUI) on the parent site and associating all of them with the same Meeting Workspace. It is important to note that even though the Meeting Workspace itself remains the same, all list data changes with each instance. This allows the user to hold multiple meetings concerning the same topic and have each meeting have its own agenda, attendee list, and so on. If the meeting is associated with a calendar entry, the Meeting Workspace header will contain a Go to Calendar link. You can switch between meetings within a Meeting Workspace with a navigational control on the left side of the site.

Add a context menu to the `ListView` control from the sample you have been building throughout this chapter with a new item called Add Meeting. This menu adds a new meeting to the selected workspace by opening up a dialog box (a form you should create called `MeetingDetails`) and using the values from the dialog box as parameters to the `AddMeeting` method, as shown in the following code:

```
private void addMeetingToolStripMenuItem_Click(object sender, EventArgs e)
{
    if (workspaceList.SelectedItems.Count == 0) return;
```

```
ListViewItem selectedWorkspace = workspaceList.SelectedItems[0];
MeetingDetails newMeeting = new MeetingDetails();
newMeeting.Text = "New Meeting";

if (newMeeting.ShowDialog() == DialogResult.OK)
{
    // create new meeting, confirmed.

    research.Meetings meetingsWs = new WorkspaceManager.research.Meetings();
    meetingsWs.Credentials =
        new System.Net.NetworkCredential("Administrator", "password");
    meetingsWs.Url =
        selectedWorkspace.SubItems[1].Text + "/_vti_bin/meetings.asmx";
    meetingsWs.AddMeeting(
        "",
        System.Guid.NewGuid().ToString(),
        0,
        DateTime.Now.ToUniversalTime(),
        newMeeting.Title,
        newMeeting.Location,
        newMeeting.StartDate.ToUniversalTime(),
        newMeeting.EndDate.ToUniversalTime(), false);
}
}
```

You don't have to use a globally unique identifier (GUID) for the ID of the meeting, but if you have a Meeting Workspace that will have quite a few meetings, you might just find it convenient to use GUIDs for the meeting identifiers.

Another way that you can create a meeting is through the use of the `AddMeetingFromiCal` method. This method creates a new meeting based on information contained in an Internet Calendar (iCal) file. To use this method, simply locate the iCal file you want to use, load it into a string, and pass it to the `AddMeetingFromICal` method, as follows:

```
meetingsWs.AddMeetingFromICal("", iCalText);
```

NOTE

You must be careful with authentication when using web services. Everything in SharePoint is done with regard to a specific user. Therefore, when your application attempts to create a meeting, it is doing so as the authenticated user. This means that if you attempt to supply an email address for the organizer, your code is essentially indicating that it is an authorized delegate for that user to create meetings. The caveat here is that if the currently authenticated user is not actually an authorized delegate, security issues and even runtime exceptions can occur. If you aren't sure what to do, just leave the organizer field as an empty string to use the email address of the currently authenticated user.

23

Removing Meetings

Removing a meeting is just a matter of getting the unique ID of an existing meeting and supplying it to the RemoveMeeting method on the Meetings Web Service. Unfortunately, you can't use the Meetings Web Service to iterate through the list of meetings associated with Meeting Workspace. For that, you need to use the Lists Web Service (discussed in Chapter 22, "Using the Lists Web Service") to obtain the list items from a special list called Meeting Series. The following code snippet obtains the list of all meetings stored within a Meeting Workspace site:

```
XmlDocument doc = new XmlDocument();
XmlNode queryNode = doc.CreateElement("Query");
XmlNode viewfieldsNode = doc.CreateElement("ViewFields");
XmlNode queryOptionsNode = doc.CreateElement("QueryOptions");
researchLists.Lists lists = new WorkspaceManager.researchLists.Lists();
lists.Url =
  "http://win2k3r2lab/sitedirectory/research/defecttracking/_vti_bin/lists.asmx";
lists.Credentials =
  new System.Net.NetworkCredential("Administrator", "password");
XmlNode results =
    lists.GetListItems("Meeting Series", "",
        queryNode, viewfieldsNode, "0", queryOptionsNode, "");
```

Table 23.2 contains a cheat sheet of some of the more important XML attribute names (columns) that are returned as part of the hidden Meeting Series list. For a complete list, you can look at the list specification XML or just examine the XML node returned in the preceding method call.

TABLE 23.2   Meeting Series Columns

Attribute/Column	Description
ows_fRecurrence	Indicates the recurrence type of the meeting.
ows_EventDate	Indicates the start date of the meeting.
ows_EndDate	Indicates the end date of the meeting.
ows_UniqueId	Contains the list item unique ID that is common to all SharePoint lists.
ows_EventUrl	Links to the host calendar. This does not link to the individual meeting itself.
ows_EventUID	Indicates the string that is passed to the method calls for remove, update, and restore. Keep in mind that although GUIDs were used as samples in this chapter, the format for this field is arbitrary. For example, the following lines both represent valid values for this column: b1caff06-d7df-4ef0-804a-d9f08acb8a5b
	STSTeamCalendarEvent:List:
	➥{4AE0FCBD-73A9-41B8-903A-8E921AC0A4E3}:Item:1
	The second line represents the default meeting associated with a Meeting Workspace when it is first created.

After you have the unique ID of the meeting, the method call to remove a meeting looks like this:

```
XmlNode node = meetingsWs.RemoveMeeting(instanceId, meetingGuid, 0,
DateTime.Now.ToUniversalTime(), cancelMeeting);
```

`instanceId` is the instance of the meeting (0 for recurring or first instance, 1 or higher for additional instances) and `cancelMeeting` is a Boolean value indicating whether the meeting should be deleted entirely or just disconnected from the workspace.

Keep in mind that you *cannot* remove meetings (instances) from Meeting Workspaces using the user interface; it can only be done programmatically via the application programming interface (API) or through web services.

23

Updating Meetings

Updating an existing meeting requires the same information as deleting an existing meeting. You must supply the unique ID of the meeting and the updated information such as the new title, description, location, and start and end dates, as shown in the following code snippet:

```
XmlNode resultsNode = meetingsWs.UpdateMeeting(0, meetingGuid,
 DateTime.Now.ToUniversalTime(), meetingSubject.Text, meetingLocation.Text,
 meetingStart.ToUniversalTime(), meetingEnd.ToUniversalTime(), false);
```

Remember that the only way to get at the list of meetings associated with a Meeting Workspace is through the SharePoint API or the Lists Web Service. The `false` at the end of the parameter list indicates that the dates are in the standard Gregorian calendar format.

Instead of having to manually specify the meeting information in explicit parameters, you can pass the meeting information in iCal (Internet Calendar) format to the web service. iCal data is often found in email attachments containing meeting invites and in many common email clients and personal information managers. To update a meeting using iCal information, simply load the iCal file into a single string and pass it to the `UpdateMeetingFromICal` method as follows:

```
meetingsWs.UpdateMeetingFromICal(iCalText, ignoreAttendees);
```

iCal data can contain information about event attendees as well. By passing the Boolean flag `ignoreAttendees`, you can indicate whether you want SharePoint to process the attendee data contained within the iCal file. If you have an iCal file that already contains precise attendee information, you can have SharePoint parse through that rather than having your code do it manually, which is definitely a time-saver.

Restoring Meetings

The `RestoreMeeting` method restores a previously removed meeting and reestablishes the link between the meeting and the Meeting Workspace. The code to restore a meeting is quite simple because it only requires the unique ID (in this chapter you have been using GUIDs) of the meeting itself:

```
XmlNode result = meetingsWs.RestoreMeeting(meetingGuid);
```

Managing Meeting Attendance

Attendee responses are specific to an instance of a Meeting Workspace, or rather, they belong to a specific meeting and not to the entire workspace as a whole. When you are setting the attendee response, you need to supply the *recurrence* identifier of the appropriate workspace instance, the unique identifier of the meeting, and the email address of the attendee.

To see how to set the attendee acceptance status (Accepted, Declined, or Tentative), first add a new `ListView` to the existing form. This one will be called `meetingList` and will be populated with the list of meetings belonging to the currently selected Meeting Workspace. Set the `SelectedIndexChanged` event handler of the `workspaceList` control to the following code (the `GetListItems` call should look familiar):

```
private void workspaceList_SelectedIndexChanged(object sender, EventArgs e)
{
    if (workspaceList.SelectedItems.Count == 0) return;

    ListViewItem selectedWorkspace = workspaceList.SelectedItems[0];

    XmlDocument doc = new XmlDocument();
    XmlNode queryNode = doc.CreateElement("Query");
    XmlNode viewfieldsNode = doc.CreateElement("ViewFields");
    XmlNode queryOptionsNode = doc.CreateElement("QueryOptions");
    researchLists.Lists lists = new WorkspaceManager.researchLists.Lists();
    lists.Url = selectedWorkspace.SubItems[1].Text + "/_vti_bin/lists.asmx";
    lists.Credentials =
        new System.Net.NetworkCredential("Administrator", "password");
    XmlNode results =
        lists.GetListItems("Meeting Series", "",
        queryNode, viewfieldsNode, "0", queryOptionsNode, "");

    meetingList.Items.Clear();
    foreach (XmlNode meeting in results.SelectNodes("//*[local-name()='row']"))
    {
        ListViewItem lvi = new ListViewItem();
        lvi.Text = meeting.Attributes.GetNamedItem("ows_Title").Value;
```

```
            lvi.SubItems.Add(meeting.Attributes.GetNamedItem("ows_Location").Value);
            lvi.SubItems.Add(meeting.Attributes.GetNamedItem("ows_EventUID").Value);
            meetingList.Items.Add(lvi);
        }
    }
```

Obviously, in a production application you wouldn't keep instantiating the service and setting credentials; that would be something that would be done once per application load.

Now create a new context menu strip called `meetingContextMenu`, associate it with the `meetingList` control, and add a Set Attendee action with the following click event handler:

```
private void setAttendeeToolStripMenuItem_Click(object sender, EventArgs e)
{
    if (workspaceList.SelectedItems.Count == 0) return;
    ListViewItem selectedWorkspace = workspaceList.SelectedItems[0];
    if (meetingList.SelectedItems.Count == 0) return;
    ListViewItem selectedMeeting = meetingList.SelectedItems[0];

    research.Meetings meetingsWs = new WorkspaceManager.research.Meetings();
    meetingsWs.Credentials =
        new System.Net.NetworkCredential("Administrator", "password");
    meetingsWs.Url =
    selectedWorkspace.SubItems[1].Text + "/_vti_bin/meetings.asmx";

    meetingsWs.SetAttendeeResponse("someone@example.com",
        0,
        selectedMeeting.SubItems[2].Text,
        0,
        DateTime.Now.ToUniversalTime(),
        DateTime.Now.ToUniversalTime(),
➥WorkspaceManager.research.AttendeeResponse.responseDeclined);
}
```

Anytime the new context menu item is clicked, it tells SharePoint that the attendee someone@example.com (that is the email address of the administrator on the lab machine used in this example) has declined that particular meeting. If you are working with multiple meetings created for a single Meeting Workspace by the application in this chapter, you will be able to switch between the various meetings and see how the attendee status has only been modified for *one instance of a meeting and not all instances within the Meeting Workspace.*

Accessing Meeting Workspace Lists

Chapter 22 showed you the mechanics of working with lists of data contained within SharePoint using the Lists Web Service, so that code isn't rehashed here. However, Meeting Workspaces do have their own custom list types with their own custom fields; Tables 23.3 through 23.6 provide a helpful quick reference of some of the more commonly used columns. Remember that when you get this data as XML via the Lists Web Service, the column names contain the ows_ prefix.

TABLE 23.3   Agenda Fields

Column	Description
Owner	The owner of the particular agenda line item.
Notes	Notes about the agenda line item.
Time	The time at which the agenda item should occur. Even though the name and description of this field indicates a time stamp, it is actually just a free-form text field.

TABLE 23.4   Decision Fields

Column	Description
Contact	The name of the person to contact regarding a given decision.
Status	The status of the decision.
Title	Every SharePoint list has a Title field. This field indicates the short description/name of the decision that must be made.

TABLE 23.5   Objective Fields

Column	Description
Objective	A string indicating the objective to be persued for the given Meeting Workspace instance

TABLE 23.6   "Things to Bring" Fields

Column	Description
Title	The name/short description of the item to bring.
Comment	A comment about the item to be brought to the meeting.
Owner	The person responsible for bringing the item. Note that this is free-form text and not a lookup into the user table.

Summary

Meeting Workspaces are a powerful feature of Microsoft Office SharePoint Server (MOSS). They provide a centralized location around which meeting collaboration and information sharing can take place. They provide a central location for document storage, specialized list management, and even calendar integration with Microsoft Outlook. This chapter showed you how your client applications—whether those applications are Windows Forms, Windows Presentation Foundation (WPF), or ASP.NET applications—can harness the power of Meeting Workspaces and meetings through the Meetings Web Service (`meetings.asmx`). Finally, you also saw that you can combine the power of the Meetings Web Service with the utility of the Lists Web Service to exert complete control over the entire Meeting Workspace experience through web services.

When you run the samples in this chapter, make sure to change the URLs of the services and of the SharePoint server to match that of your own environment. You need either a local copy of MOSS installed or access to a copy of it over the network.

23

CHAPTER 24

Working with User Profiles and Security

IN THIS CHAPTER

▶ What's New with User Profiles in MOSS 2007

▶ Working with User Profiles

▶ Working with the User Group Service

Identity is quite often at the top of the priority list for intranet and Internet applications, even if it is agreed that anonymous users will have access. For system administrators (and, potentially, compliance investigators) to know which users made changes to the system, and when they made the changes, the system needs to keep track of who is using it.

In addition to keeping track of which users are on the system, Microsoft Office SharePoint Server (MOSS) needs to give administrators the ability to control and secure access to the system through user groups and permissions. This chapter shows you how to use the User Groups Web Service, the User Profile Web Service, and how to work with security remotely via web services.

What's New with User Profiles in MOSS 2007

Microsoft Office SharePoint Server (MOSS) 2007 provides many enhancements to user profiles over previous versions as well as additional functionality above and beyond the functionality provided by Windows SharePoint Services v3.0. The following is a list of just a few of the enhancements and additions that have been made to user profile support in MOSS:

▶ **Enhanced audience support**—Profiles and profile data can be used to selectively display pieces of a profile to specific users or groups of users.

▶ **Multivalued profile property support**—Profiles now support the notion of multivalued data. This means that a single profile property can contain an array of values.

▶ **Relationships among users are deduced in a social networking manner**—MOSS uses implicit and explicit links among users to compute a "social distance" factor as well as display colleagues and profiles from related users.

▶ **Property-level security controls**—Each individual profile property now has the ability to be secured individually. Users can control who sees what information on their profile, and administrators have larger scope control over profile property visibility.

▶ **Per-site property extensions**—Individual sites can extend user profile properties that are only visible to that site, providing an extremely powerful platform for extension and user customization and personalization.

Working with User Profiles

If you don't have local access to the SharePoint object model and you want to access and manipulate user profiles, you can use the User Profile Web Service. This web service can be found at http://[server]/_vti_bin/userprofileservice.asmx. This web service is a portal-scoped web service that works with the MOSS (not Windows SharePoint Services [WSS]) user profile data store.

Table 24.1 provides a list of methods available on the User Profile Web Service.

TABLE 24.1   User Profile Web Service Methods

Method	Description
AddColleague	Adds a colleague to a user in a given group with a specified privacy level; privacy can be set as: Contacts, Manager, NotSet, Organization, Private, or Public
AddLink	Adds a published uniform resource locator (URL) to a user profile in a given group with a specified privacy level
AddMembership	Adds a mail group membership information record to a user profile
AddPinnedLink	Adds an ungrouped link to a user profile
CreateMemberGroup	Creates a group membership record
CreateUserProfileByAccountName	Creates a new user profile based on an account (remember that domain accounts and profiles are separate)
GetCommonColleagues	Gets common colleagues for the supplied account; returns an array of MembershipData
GetCommonManager	Gets the manager for the supplied account
GetCommonMemberships	Returns the list of membership groups to which the specified account belongs

TABLE 24.1   Continued

Method	Description
GetInCommon	Returns an `InCommonData` instance that contains all common data for the user: Memberships, Colleagues, and Manager
GetPropertyChoiceList	Returns the list of acceptable property values for a given property name
GetUserColleagues	Gets an array of `ContactData` instances, one for each colleague; provides more personal information than `GetCommonColleagues`
GetUserLinks	Returns an array of `QuickLinkData` (name, url, group, privacy, and so on) instances representing the user's links
GetUserMemberships	Returns an array of `MembershipData` based on the account name supplied
GetUserPinnedLinks	Returns an array of `PinnedLinkData` instances corresponding to the user's ungrouped (pinned) links
GetUserProfileByGuid	Retrieves a user profile (an array of `PropertyData`) based on the user's globally unique identifier (GUID)
GetUserProfileByIndex	Retrieves a user profile by the profile index
GetUserProfileByName	Retrieves a user profile by name
GetUserProfileSchema	Retrieves the schema for the user profile, including all custom properties and SharePoint-specific properties
ModifyUserPropertyByAccountName	Supplies an array of `PropertyData` instances for the given user account name
RemoveColleague	Removes a colleague from a user profile
RemoveLink	Removes a standard link from a user profile
RemoveMembership	Removes a group membership from a user profile
RemovePinnedLink	Removes a pinned (ungrouped) link from a user profile
UpdateColleaguePrivacy	Updates the privacy/visibility of a given colleague for a given user profile
UpdateLink	Updates an existing link
UpdateMembershipPrivacy	Updates an existing membership group's privacy status
UpdatePinnedLink	Takes a `PinnedLinkData` instance to be updated for the given user profile

All of the methods relating to commonalities among profiles, such as `GetInCommon` or `GetCommonManager`, deal with the new social networking features inherent in MOSS 2007, such as the concept of "social distance" and implicit and explicit linking of user profiles through common links.

There are a lot of methods on the User Profile Service, some of which are more commonly used than others. One of the most common reasons why client applications consume the MOSS User Profile Service is to read profile properties.

To see how to write code that will examine profile properties, take a look at the code in Listing 24.1. This is the code for the main form of a Windows Forms application. The user of the application supplies an account name in a text box and then clicks a button to retrieve all of the profile properties (stored as name:value pairs) for that user account. The profile properties are then added to a list view on the main form.

LISTING 24.1   Retrieving User Profile Properties

```
using System;
using System.Collections.Generic;
using System.ComponentModel;
using System.Data;
using System.Drawing;
using System.Text;
using System.Windows.Forms;
using Profiles.win2k3r2lab1;

namespace Profiles
{
public partial class Form1 : Form
{
private win2k3r2lab.UserProfileService userProfiles;
private win2k3r2lab1.UserProfileChangeService userProfileChange;

public Form1()
{
    InitializeComponent();

    userProfiles = new Profiles.win2k3r2lab.UserProfileService();
    userProfiles.Url =
      "http://win2k3r2lab/_vti_bin/userprofileservice.asmx";
    userProfiles.Credentials =
      System.Net.CredentialCache.DefaultCredentials;
    userProfileChange = new Profiles.win2k3r2lab1.UserProfileChangeService();
    userProfileChange.Url =
      "http://win2k3r2lab/_vti_bin/userprofilechangeservice.asmx";
    userProfileChange.Credentials =
      System.Net.CredentialCache.DefaultCredentials;
}

private void loadButton_Click(object sender, EventArgs e)
{
```

LISTING 24.1   Continued

```
win2k3r2lab.PropertyData[] properties =
    userProfiles.GetUserProfileByName(accountName.Text);
propertyList.Items.Clear();
foreach (win2k3r2lab.PropertyData propertyData in properties)
{
    ListViewItem lvi = new ListViewItem();
    lvi.Text = propertyData.Name;
    StringBuilder sb = new StringBuilder();
    foreach (win2k3r2lab.ValueData value in propertyData.Values)
    {
        sb.AppendFormat("{0} ", value.Value);
    }
    lvi.SubItems.Add(sb.ToString());
    propertyList.Items.Add(lvi);
}

accountChangesButton.Enabled = true;
}

private void accountChangesButton_Click(object sender, EventArgs e)
{
    win2k3r2lab1.UserProfileChangeDataContainer changes =
        userProfileChange.GetUserAllChanges(accountName.Text);
    ChangeLogViewer changeViewer = new ChangeLogViewer(changes);
    changeViewer.ShowDialog();
}
}
}
```

When this application runs and loads a valid user profile, the main form looks like the one shown in Figure 24.1.

One thing you might have noticed from the code in Listing 24.1 is that the application actually has two references to web services. The first reference is to the User Profile Web Service, whereas the second is a reference to the User Profile Change Web Service. The latter provides methods for querying the change log as it pertains to user profiles.

The sample application has a button on the main form that loads a second form called ChangeLogViewer. The form is invoked by retrieving a UserProfileDataChangeContainer instance from the user profile change service:

```
win2k3r2lab1.UserProfileChangeDataContainer changes =
    userProfileChange.GetUserAllChanges(accountName.Text);
ChangeLogViewer changeViewer = new ChangeLogViewer(changes);
```

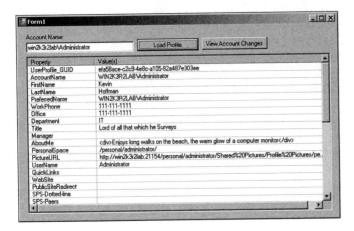

FIGURE 24.1   User profile properties.

The code for this form is shown in Listing 24.2.

LISTING 24.2   Code to Display Changes to a User Profile

```
using System;
using System.Collections.Generic;
using System.ComponentModel;
using System.Data;
using System.Drawing;
using System.Text;
using System.Windows.Forms;

using Profiles.win2k3r2lab1;

namespace Profiles
{
public partial class ChangeLogViewer : Form
{
private UserProfileChangeDataContainer _changeLog;

public ChangeLogViewer(UserProfileChangeDataContainer changeLog)
{
    InitializeComponent();

    _changeLog = changeLog;

    tokenLabel.Text = "Change Token : " + changeLog.ChangeToken;

    foreach (UserProfileChangeData change in changeLog.Changes)
    {
```

LISTING 24.2 Continued

```
        ListViewItem lvi = new ListViewItem();
        lvi.Text = change.EventTime.ToString();
        lvi.SubItems.Add(change.ChangeType.ToString());
        lvi.SubItems.Add(change.PropertyName);
        lvi.SubItems.Add(change.Value == null ? "null" : change.Value.ToString());

        changeLogView.Items.Add(lvi);
    }
}
}
}
```

Although the preceding code samples are far from paragons of good Windows Forms
application design, they do illustrate one of the most common use cases for the user
profile services—obtaining user profile properties and a list of changes made to those
properties over time. A sample of the user profile change log output is shown in Figure
24.2.

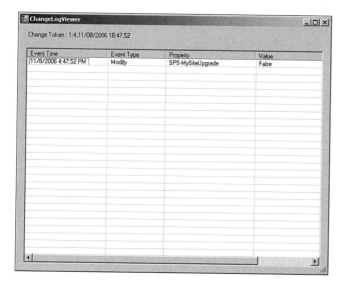

FIGURE 24.2 User profile change history.

Table 24.2 shows the methods available on the User Profile Change Web Service, which
can be accessed at http://[MOSS root]/_vti_bin/userprofilechangeservice.asmx.

TABLE 24.2   User Profile Change Web Service Methods

Method	Description
GetAllChanges	Retrieves a list of all changes to all user profiles, limited only by the systemwide change log depth setting
GetChanges	Gets all changes made to all user profiles since the given change token and matching the given user profile change query
GetCurrentChangeToken	Returns a string representing the current change token in the change log for user profiles
GetUserAllChanges	Gets a list of all changes made to a specific user's profile
GetUserChanges	Works the same as GetChanges but limited by a user account name
GetUserCurrentChangeToken	Gets the current change token for the given user

Change tokens are mentioned quite a bit in Table 24.2. A change token is really nothing more than a string representing the last moment in time that a change took place. These tokens are useful in retrieving all changes that have taken place *since* that token occurred. If you were to examine the internals of SharePoint's change audit log, you would see that every change is associated with a change token.

A change token is a delimited string with the following parts in the following order:

▶ Version number

▶ A number indicating the change scope: 0 – Content Database, 1 – site collection, 2 – site, 3 – list.

▶ GUID representing the scope ID of the change token

▶ Time (in UTC) when the change occurred

▶ Number of the change relative to other changes

If you have access to the SharePoint object model, you can use the SPChangeToken class for dealing with change tokens. The form displayed in Figure 24.2 displays the change token associated with the set of changes displayed on that form.

Working with the User Group Service

The User Group Web Service has a fairly obvious purpose—it provides access to read and manipulate groups, roles, and group and role memberships. See Table 24.3 for a list of User Group Web Service methods. The User Group Web Service is a WSS-provided service. As such, you connect to the service at the site collection level.

All of the operations performed by the User Group Web Service are done with regard to the site collection to which the client was bound. For example, operations on server/ siteA/_vti_bin/usergroup.asmx will take place in an entirely different scope than methods called on server/siteB/_vti_bin/usergroup.asmx.

TABLE 24.3   User Group Web Service Methods

Method	Description
AddGroup	Adds a group to the current site collection
AddGroupToRole	Adds the indicated group to the given role definition
AddRole	Adds a role to the site collection
AddRoleDef	Adds a role definition to the site collection
AddUserCollectionToGroup	Adds a list of users indicated by an Extensible Markup Language (XML) fragment to the indicated group
AddUserCollectionToRole	Adds a list of users (XML fragment) to the given role definition
AddUserToGroup	Adds a single user to a group
AddUserToRole	Adds a single user to a role definition
GetAllUserCollectionFromWeb	Gets a collection of all defined users (users with explicit permissions) in the website
GetGroupCollection	Gets information about the list of groups defined on the current website
GetGroupCollectionFromRole	Gets a list of groups assigned to the given role
GetGroupCollectionFromSite	Gets a list of groups defined within the given site collection
GetGroupCollectionFromUser	Gets a list of groups to which a given user has been assigned
GetGroupCollectionFromWeb	Gets a list of groups defined within a given website
GetGroupInfo	Returns details about a given group
GetRoleCollection	Gets a list of roles defined within the current website
GetRoleCollectionFromGroup	Gets a list of role definitions to which the indicated group belongs
GetRoleCollectionFromUser	Gets a list of role definitions to which the user has been assigned by virtue of his/her group memberships
GetRoleCollectionFromWeb	Gets a collection of role definitions defined within the given website
GetRoleInfo	Gets detailed information about the given role
GetRolesAndPermissionsFor-CurrentUser	Returns roles and permission mask information for the given user on the current site
GetRolesAndPermissionsFor-Site	Returns roles and permission mask information for the given user on the indicated site
GetUserCollection	Gets user detail information (for example, id, login name, display name) based on an XML node query of user details
GetUserCollectionFromGroup	Gets a list of users that belong to the given group
GetUserCollectionFromRole	Gets a list of users that have the given role
GetUserCollectionFromSite	Gets a list of users from the given site collection
GetUserCollectionFromWeb	Gets a list of users from the given website

24

TABLE 24.3   Continued

Method	Description
GetUserInfo	Gets detailed user information based on the login name of a given user
GetUserLoginFromEmail	Gets the login name for a user based on their email address
RemoveGroup	Removes the given group from the current site collection
RemoveGroupFromRole	Removes the given group from the specified role
RemoveRole	Removes the specified role from the site collection
RemoveUserCollectionFromGroup	Removes a list of users from a given group
RemoveUserCollectionFromRole	Removes a list of users from a given role
RemoveUserCollectionFromSite	Removes a list of users from a given site collection
RemoveUserFromGroup	Removes a single user from a group
RemoveUserFromRole	Removes a single user from a role
RemoveUserFromSite	Removes a single user from a site collection
RemoveUserFromWeb	Removes a single user from a website
UpdateGroupInfo	Updates group details
UpdateRoleDefInfo	Updates role definition information (such as name and permission mask)
UpdateRoleInfo	Updates role definition information (such as name and permission mask)
UpdateUserInfo	Updates user details (display name, notes, email address) for the user with the specified login name

To illustrate how to use the User Group Web Service to obtain a list of groups on a given site as well as enumerate the list of security principles contained within those groups, this chapter includes a sample written using the Windows Presentation Foundation (WPF; part of the .NET Framework 3.0). Don't worry if you're not familiar with WPF; this sample makes extensive use of the monostate (see *Agile Principles, Patterns, and Practices in C#* [ISBN: 0131857258], pg. 331) pattern, so all you need to worry about is how to populate a business object with data from the web service and WPF takes care of the rest.

The code in Listing 24.3 shows the code for the main window of the WPF application. It simply populates an object model and lets WPF's powerful data-binding capabilities handle the rest. Make sure that you modify the web service URL and credentials to suit your own environment.

LISTING 24.3   Code-behind for a XAML Window Bound to Data from the User Group Web Service

```
using System;
using System.Collections.Generic;
using System.Text;
using System.Windows;
using System.Windows.Controls;
```

LISTING 24.3   Continued

```
using System.Windows.Data;
using System.Windows.Documents;
using System.Windows.Input;
using System.Windows.Media;
using System.Windows.Media.Imaging;
using System.Windows.Shapes;
using System.Xml;


namespace EnumUsersAndGroups
{
/// <summary>
/// This application populates two lists. The left-side list is a list of all
/// groups on the site. As the user clicks a group on the left, the list of users
/// belonging to that group is displayed on the right.
/// </summary>

public partial class Window1 : System.Windows.Window
{
private win2k3_splab.UserGroup _groupService;

public Window1()
{
InitializeComponent();
try
{
    _groupService = new EnumUsersAndGroups.win2k3_splab.UserGroup();
    _groupService.Credentials = new System.Net.NetworkCredential
➥("Administrator", "password");

    XmlNode groupNode = _groupService.GetGroupCollectionFromSite();
    AppModel model = new AppModel();
    foreach (XmlNode group in groupNode.ChildNodes[0].ChildNodes)
    {
        SecurityGroup sg = new SecurityGroup();
        sg.GroupName = group.Attributes["Name"].Value;
        model.Groups.Add(sg);
    }
}
catch (Exception ex)
{
    System.Diagnostics.Debug.WriteLine(ex.ToString());
}
}
```

LISTING 24.3   Continued

```
public void groupList_SelectionChanged(object sender, RoutedEventArgs e)
{
try
{
    SecurityGroup sg = (SecurityGroup)groupList.SelectedItem;
    AppModel model = new AppModel();
    model.Users.Clear();
    XmlNode userNode = _groupService.GetUserCollectionFromGroup(sg.GroupName);
    System.Diagnostics.Debug.WriteLine(userNode.InnerXml);
    foreach (XmlNode user in userNode.ChildNodes[0].ChildNodes)
    {
        SecurityUser newUser = new SecurityUser();
        newUser.UserName = user.Attributes["Name"].Value;
        newUser.Email = user.Attributes["Email"].Value;
        model.Users.Add(newUser);
    }
}
catch (Exception ex)
{
    System.Diagnostics.Debug.WriteLine(ex.ToString());
}
}
}
}
```

Figure 24.3 shows an example of this application running on Windows Vista.

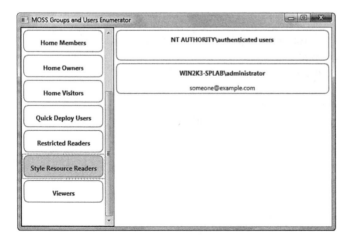

FIGURE 24.3   WPF data binding to data from the User Group Web Service.

Summary

This chapter illustrated how to work with user profiles, user profile changes, and change history, as well as how to access and manipulate user groups, roles, and group and role memberships. Knowing the difference between roles, groups, group and role memberships, user profiles and user profile changes, and how to programmatically access all of that functionality remotely via web services will add even more tools to your ever-growing arsenal of potential SharePoint development solutions.

24

CHAPTER 25

Using Excel Services

IN THIS CHAPTER

▶ Introduction to Excel Services

▶ Excel Services Architecture

▶ Using the Excel Services Web Service

▶ Creating a Managed Excel Services User-Defined Function

Excel Services is just one of many new and powerful Shared Services that are part of Microsoft Office SharePoint Server (MOSS) 2007. Using Excel Services, users can centrally store important Microsoft Excel documents and expose their calculations, functionality, and data to other users of SharePoint through Web Parts and through a web service. This chapter provides you with an in-depth look at this powerful new feature, its impact on business operations, Business Intelligence, and how you can interact with Excel Services as a developer.

Introduction to Excel Services

In virtually every organization, there are people who work with Excel. Excel enables individuals to create charts from data contained in a spreadsheet, link data in a spreadsheet with relational data in a database such as SQL Server 2005, and much more. In addition to storing data and rendering data-driven charts and graphs, Excel has a powerful formula language that enables it to perform extremely complex calculations. These calculations enable information workers to do everything from create expense reports that dynamically calculate the amount of refund due an employee to perform extremely complex calculations on sets of data taken as a snapshot from a back-end database. The key feature that Excel provides isn't simply the ability to create formulas that operate on data; it is the fact that Excel enables information workers *with no programming language skills* to perform these calculations.

The problem with Excel stems from the fact that, while immensely powerful, an Excel spreadsheet is still just a simple file on a disk. When people attempt to share spreadsheets, collaborate on the data contained within the spreadsheets, and utilize the formulas and automatic calculations contained within a spreadsheet at the enterprise level—things get ugly quick.

What happens all too often in this situation is that the Excel spreadsheet becomes cumbersome. The spreadsheet is often retired and enormous, lengthy, and costly custom development projects are started to replace the Excel spreadsheet with a so-called better solution. The problem is that these solutions are the domain of programmers, and the information workers, managers, analysts, and other Excel users are then at the mercy of the application built by developers. If a formula needs to be changed, or some analytical rules need to be changed, more custom code might have to be written. The speed, flexibility, and ability of Excel to change formulas on the fly disappears and is replaced by the slow, cumbersome development life cycle of an enterprise-scale software product.

The solution to this problem is Excel Services. Excel Services is one of the new Shared Services that are part of SharePoint 2007 and it extends the functionality of Excel spreadsheets into the enterprise, allowing the functionality of the spreadsheets to be shared at the enterprise level without requiring custom programming, expensive software development projects, or even knowledge of a programming language.

Excel Services provides three main features: workbook management, Centralized Application Logic, and Business Intelligence enablement. All of these features and how Excel Services enables them are discussed in this section.

Workbook Management

Instead of managing the nightmare of having multiple versions of the same workbook spread throughout an organization on multiple machines, Excel Services allows for central workbook management. A single, trusted author can be given the rights to make changes to the workbook, which are then made visible to all clients utilizing the shared version of the workbook. Workbooks working against snapshots of back-end data can then be provided to multiple users in read-only fashion to protect the underlying data source while still providing enterprise-scope functionality for analytics, graphing, and charting.

Centralized Application Logic

Instead of spending a lot of time and money converting a workbook into a complex custom application, the application logic contained within a workbook can be maintained in Excel Services and provided to the entire enterprise in a secure, reliable, and scalable fashion. Excel Services can handle hundreds of simultaneous requests for the same piece of data from within a workbook, and will dynamically provide the results of cell calculations. For example, the custom logic embedded in a time sheet workbook can be hosted in Excel Services and provided to client applications. Any time the time sheet rules and formulas need to change, the single workbook can be modified by the trusted author without requiring expensive and time-consuming code changes.

Business Intelligence

Business Intelligence portals provide central, unified access to summary information obtained from data warehouses. This summary information includes report cards and score cards. A score card is essentially a list of Key Performance Indicators (KPI) that graphically display whether a particular aspect of the data is performing within desired thresholds. Using a workbook on a portal page via Excel Web Access (the architecture of Excel Services is discussed in detail in the next section), data supporting the score cards and KPIs can be displayed using charts, graphs, or even raw data. Moreover, administrators can configure the interactivity level of the hosted workbook such as defining read-only cell ranges and indicating which portions of the Excel user interface are displayed. This is an unbelievably powerful feature that provides functionality that required extensive custom programming or integration of third-party products in previous versions of SharePoint.

Excel Services Architecture

Excel Services contains three different components: Excel Web Access, Excel Calculation Services, and Excel Web Services. This section illustrates what each component does and how the components interact. A diagram of the Excel Services architecture is shown in Figure 25.1.

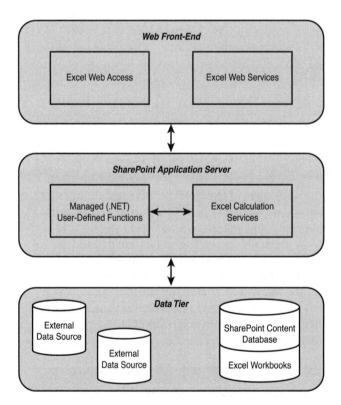

FIGURE 25.1   Excel Services architecture.

Excel Web Access

Excel Web Access (EWA) is the portion of Excel Services that is visible to the end user. EWA is a Web Part that can render workbooks on a SharePoint Web Part page. There are dozens of configurable options, including the ability to set how interactive the workbook will be when displayed on a page. In addition to specifying how interactive the rendered workbook will be, you can also specify which columns and rows to display, as well as how much of the Excel graphical user interface (GUI) to render, such as the toolbar.

Figure 25.2 shows a sample of the Excel Web Access Web Part on a portal home page. In this screenshot, interactivity has been disabled on the Web Part.

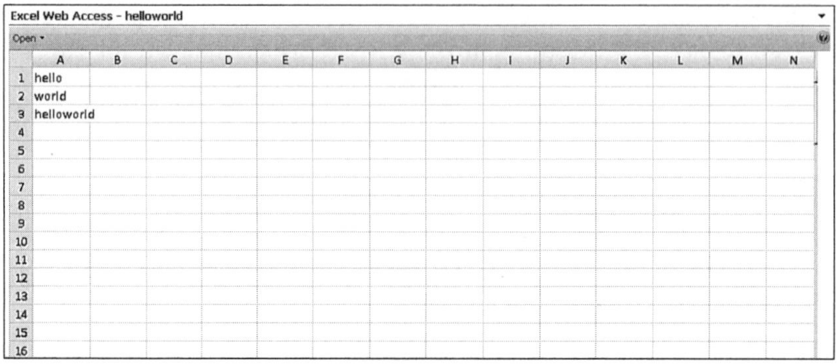

FIGURE 25.2   The Excel Web Access Web Part.

Excel Calculation Services

Excel Calculation Services (ECS) is the workhorse of the Excel Services feature suite. ECS is responsible for loading a workbook at the request of a client in a session unique to that client. After being loaded, ECS can do things like refresh snapshots of external data and dynamically perform calculations. Changes made during the session are maintained for the duration of the session but are discarded when the session is completed. For example, a client application opens a workbook and enters in the total hours worked on a project. The workbook dynamically calculates the amount to charge the client for that project based on the input. While the session is open, the client application can interrogate the cell containing the bill amount. When the application is done utilizing ECS, the session can be terminated and the workbook will be unloaded.

NOTE

It is important to realize that Excel Services is not a means by which end users can make and save changes to Excel workbooks. Those changes can be made through SharePoint libraries and the Excel client itself. Excel Calculation Services is responsible for refreshing snapshot data in the workbook and running calculations in the workbook. It does not allow you to make permanent changes to a cell's value.

Excel Web Services

Excel Web Services is essentially a front end to Excel Calculation Services. By using the web service, developers can create code that can remotely open Excel workbooks, input values, perform calculations, and obtain results. All of this is done utilizing the fully scalable architecture of Excel Services and will work in a farm scenario. The next section focuses specifically on consuming the Excel Services Web Service.

Using the Excel Services Web Service

You will find the Excel Services Web Service at the portal level. The uniform resource locator (URL) for the web service is http://[server]/_vti_bin/ExcelService.asmx.

The Excel Services Web Service provides the methods described in Table 25.1. Keep in mind that you can either use a numeric, zero-based ordinal indexing mechanism for indicating cells and ranges, or you can use the Excel standard "A1" notation where you indicate cells based on their letter column and numeric row, such as E5 or A1:A7.

TABLE 25.1   Excel Services Web Service Methods

Method	Description
Calculate	Calculates formulas in the workbook or within a specified numeric range of cells
CalculateA1	Calculates formulas in the workbook or within a specified range of cells indicated by Excel "A1" notation
CalculateWorkbook	Calculates the entire workbook, optionally only recalculating formulas affected by changed cells
CancelRequest	Cancels the most recent request if it is still pending
CloseWorkbook	Closes the workbook and shuts down the active session
GetApiVersion	Gets version data on Excel Web Services
GetCell	Gets a dynamically calculated value from a cell within a workbook specified by numeric coordinates
GetCellA1	Gets a dynamically calculated value from a cell within a workbook specified using Excel "A1" coordinates
GetRange	Gets calculated values from an open book within the range indicated by numeric coordinates
GetRangeA1	Gets calculated values from an open book within the range indicated by "A1" coordinates
GetSessionInformation	Obtains information on the active session
GetWorkbook	Gets the raw bytes representing the active workbook within the current session
OpenWorkbook	Opens an Excel workbook and creates a new Excel Calculation Services (ECS) session
Refresh	Causes the workbook to reload data from external sources, if applicable
SetCell	Sets the value in a cell indicated by numeric coordinates

25

TABLE 25.1   Continued

Method	Description
SetCellA1	Sets the value in a cell indicated by "A1" coordinates
SetRange	Sets the values in a range indicated by numeric coordinates
SetRangeA1	Sets the values in the range indicated by "A1" coordinates

Setting Excel Services Trusted Locations

To provide a secure environment for Excel Services, Excel Services does not allow a work-book to be loaded by Excel Web Access, Excel Web Services, or Excel Calculation Services unless that workbook resides in a trusted location.

Trusted locations are configured through Excel Services settings and allow you to define the security settings for a workbook location as well as settings dictating data refresh behavior and whether a workbook in that location can pull data from external sources.

To add a trusted location to Excel Services, first open the SharePoint Central Administration page (you can reach this from the Start menu on the server as the port number for the administration site varies from installation to installation). Next, go to Application Management and then Shared Services. Finally, click Trusted File Locations within Excel Services. From there, you can click the Add Trusted File Location link, which can be a Universal Naming Convention (UNC) or a URL. For example, if you create a document library at the portal level called Excel Files, the trusted location URL might be: http://[server]/Excel Files/.

Canonical "Hello World" Sample, Excel Services Style

To see the Excel Services Web Service in action, you need to put an Excel workbook into a trusted location. Following the steps in the preceding section, create a new document library called Excel Files and make it a trusted location.

Next, create a new Excel 2007 spreadsheet. Set the contents of cell A1 to "hello" and the contents of cell A2 to "world". Set the contents of cell A3 to a formula that concatenates the contents of cell A1 and A2. Figure 25.3 shows this workbook inside Excel.

Save the workbook to the document library created earlier and you are now able to utilize this workbook within Excel Services because the document library is an ECS-trusted location.

Create a new C# console application in Visual Studio 2005 and add a web reference to the ExcelService.asmx Web Service on your development server. (This will also work on a Virtual PC testing server if you're short on hardware.) Name the web reference ES. Modify the Program.cs file in the console application so that it matches the code shown in Listing 25.1. To get the fully qualified URL to the Excel spreadsheet that you will need for the following code, you can simply right-click the filename in the document library and choose Properties.

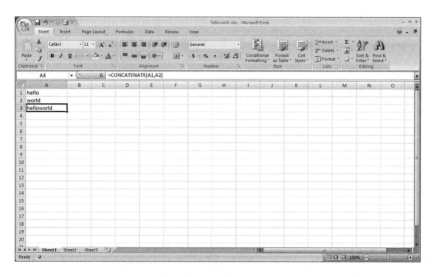

FIGURE 25.3   A "hello world" workbook.

LISTING 25.1   ExcelServicesHelloWorld Console Application

```
using System;
using System.Collections.Generic;
using System.Text;
using ExcelServicesHelloWorld.ES;

namespace ExcelServicesHelloWorld
{
class Program
{
static void Main(string[] args)
{
    ExcelService excel = new ES.ExcelService();
    excel.Credentials =
        new System.Net.NetworkCredential("Administrator", "password");
    Status[] stati;
    string sessionId =
        excel.OpenWorkbook("http://win2k3r2lab/Excel Files/helloworld.xlsx",
        "en-US", "en-US", out stati);

    object o = excel.GetCellA1(sessionId, "Sheet1", "A3", true, out stati);
    Console.WriteLine("Formula-generated string from Excel services: {0}",
        (string)o);

    // change A1
```

LISTING 25.1   Continued

```
    excel.SetCellA1(sessionId, "Sheet1", "A1", "goodbye ");
    o = excel.GetCellA1(sessionId, "Sheet1", "A3", true, out stati);
    Console.WriteLine(
      "Formula-generated string from Excel services after modification: {0}",
      (string)o);

    excel.Dispose();
    Console.ReadLine();


  }
 }
}
```

Obviously, you'll want to change the server name and credentials to match your development environment. When you run the application, you will see the following output:

```
Formula-generated string from Excel services: helloworld
Formula-generated string from Excel services after modification: goodbye world
```

An important thing to note with this code sample is that the actual workbook on the
server did not change. Each session within ECS gets its own private copy of the workbook
to use. When a client application makes changes, those changes are made to the session
and not to the actual Excel file stored in the trusted location. This allows hundreds of
different people to use the same shared workbook for calculation without running into
each other's data. Of course, this only works when you open the spreadsheet through the
SharePoint link rather than downloading the file.

Also note that with every web service method call after the initial call to Openworkbook,
the string sessionId is passed as a parameter. This is what allows Excel Calculation
Services to keep calculation sessions separate while providing calculation services for
multiple clients for the same workbook at the same time.

Developing a Real-World Excel Services Client Application

Although it might be instructive to see how to use the Excel Web Service to concatenate
two strings, it isn't exactly practical. In more common usage scenarios, an Excel spreadsheet developer will define multiple named ranges that will be used as input parameters
to the workbook. A client application will then supply values for the input ranges and
read values from the output ranges and can even save a copy of the workbook maintained
within the ECS session to disk.

A more practical example of using the web service might be to have a client application
interface with a shared workbook that manages compensation amounts for mileage trav-
eled on company business.

To create the shared spreadsheet for this example, create a workbook in an Excel 2007 spreadsheet that has a named range called `MileageValues` (this range contains 15 cells in this example). Also, another named range called `PaybackAmounts` should be created positioned alongside the first range. Finally, another range should be created called `TotalPayback` that contains the sum total of all reimbursements for company travel.

If you don't want to create this spreadsheet yourself, you can use the `mileage_expense.xlsx` file that comes with this chapter's code. A screenshot of this spreadsheet is shown in Figure 25.4.

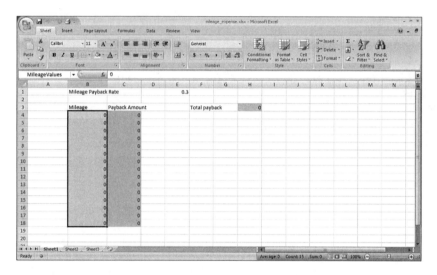

FIGURE 25.4   A shared spreadsheet with multiple named ranges.

Using the steps detailed earlier in this chapter, add the `mileage_expense.xlsx` spreadsheet to your trusted document library.

Create a new console application called `MileageExpenseClient`, add a web reference to the Excel Web Service called `excelService`, and change the `Program.cs` file so that it contains the code in Listing 25.2.

LISTING 25.2   Reading/Writing Ranges and Saving Temporary Workbooks

```
using System;
using System.Collections.Generic;
using System.Text;
using MileageExpenseClient.excelService;
using System.IO;


namespace MileageExpenseClient
{
```

LISTING 25.2   Continued

```
class Program
{
static void Main(string[] args)
{
excelService.ExcelService ews = new ExcelService();
ews.Credentials = new System.Net.NetworkCredential("Administrator",
    "password");

// open the workbook
Status[] stati;

string sessionId =
    ews.OpenWorkbook("http://win2k3r2lab/Excel Files/mileage_expense.xlsx",
    "en-US", "en-US", out stati);

// set the range of values for the mileage traveled
object[] rangeValues = new object[] { new object[] { 15 },
    new object[] { 9 },
    new object[] { 21 },
    new object[] { 18 },
    new object[] { 35 },
    new object[] { 72 },
    new object[] { 64 },
    new object[] { 90 },
    new object[] { 13 },
    new object[] { 18 },
    new object[] { 21 },
    new object[] { 30 },
    new object[] { 91 },
    new object[] { 15 },
    new object[] { 21 },
};
stati = ews.SetRangeA1(sessionId, "Sheet1", "MileageValues",
        rangeValues);

// now take a look at the total calculated compensation for mileage traveled.
object[] totalPaybackRows =
    ews.GetRangeA1(sessionId, "Sheet1", "TotalPayback", false, out stati);
object[] totalPayback = (object[])totalPaybackRows[0];

byte[] workbookBytes =
    ews.GetWorkbook(sessionId, WorkbookType.FullSnapshot, out stati);

FileStream fs = new FileStream(@"C:\MileageExpenseSnapshot.xlsx", FileMode.Create);
```

LISTING 25.2   Continued

```
fs.Write(workbookBytes, 0, workbookBytes.Length);
fs.Close();

Console.WriteLine("Total amount due employee : {0:C}", (double)totalPayback[0]);
Console.ReadLine();
}
}
}
```

There is a lot going on in this sample. The first thing that differs from the "hello world" sample is the creation of a new jagged object array called rangeValues. All range-based operations on the Excel Web Service deal with jagged arrays. The first dimension of the jagged array is the list of rows in the given range. Each row, also a jagged array, is the list of cells contained within that row. So, to fill a vertical range of single-cell rows, you need to create an array of 15 single-element jagged arrays, as shown in the preceding code sample.

Next, the sample uses the GetWorkbook method to obtain the raw bytes of the workbook. The data retrieved is determined by the WorkbookType enumeration, which can contain the following values:

▶ FullSnapshot—This workbook type returns a snapshot of the entire Excel spreadsheet file.

▶ FullWorkbook—This workbook type returns a snapshot of the indicated workbook only.

▶ PublishedItemsSnapshot—This workbook type returns a snapshot of only the published objects in the file.

> **NOTE**
>
> One thing to remember when working with ranges is that the array you supply to set a range must be the same size as the range within the workbook. You can supply null values or other placeholder values to indicate a lack of data, but if your range contains 15 rows, you need to supply a 15-element jagged array, even if the subarrays don't contain any elements.

All range operations work with jagged arrays, so when you retrieve a range from a workbook, the values are also contained within a jagged array—even if the range contains only a single cell.

When you call GetRange or GetRangeA1, the result is an object array. Each element in this array is a jagged array representing the cells within that row. In this case, the range "TotalPayback" was a single cell. A single cell range is a single-element jagged array that

25

contains a single-element object array. Because an object array can contain any kind of element, you have to specifically typecast each element of the outermost object array as object[] to get the actual values.

Figure 25.5 shows the MileageExpenseSnapshot.xlsx spreadsheet retrieved from the session. Note that all of the values within the input range have been specified, and all calculations were performed.

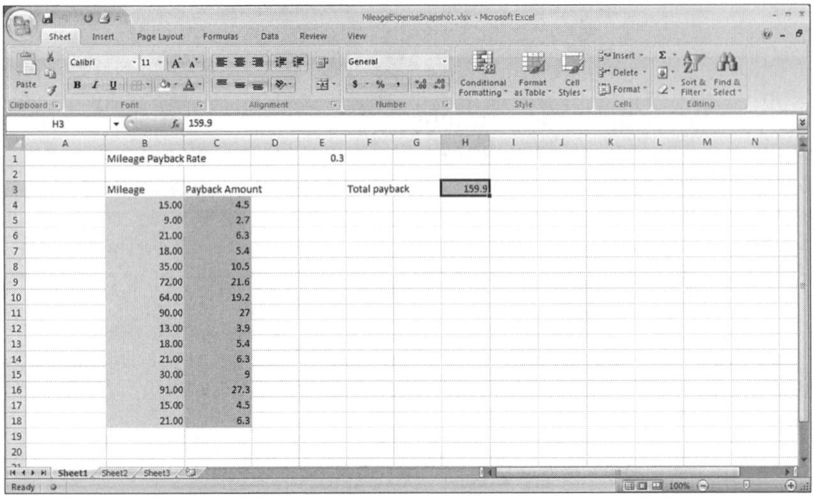

FIGURE 25.5   A workbook snapshot retrieved from the Excel Web Service.

When looking at the workbook snapshot, it is important to remember that the raw workbook saved from the GetWorkbook method call *has no formulas or calculations contained in it*. It is, quite literally, a snapshot of what the workbook *looked like* at the moment the workbook was retrieved. This is done by design and is extremely useful for client applications that want to allow users to fill in data, perform calculations, and then retrieve printable or viewable results.

Creating a Managed Excel Services User-Defined Function

The ability for programmers and information workers to create extremely powerful scripts directly within Excel using Visual Basic for Applications (VBA) has always been a major factor in Excel's appeal. With VBA, the Excel users could allow their workbooks to access Component Object Model (COM) objects, read data from external sources, and perform complex conditional logic that would be too cumbersome to perform within an Excel calculation formula.

With Excel Services, you can create your own user-defined functions (UDFs). However, instead of being limited to a loosely typed scripting language like VBA, users can create UDFs in C#.

The creation of a UDF is very simple, and might seem familiar if you have created stored procedures in SQL Server 2005. To start with, you will need to locate the `Microsoft.Office.Excel.Server.Udf.dll` Assembly. By default, this Assembly can be found at `[drive:]\Program Files\Common Files\Microsoft Shared\web server extensions\12\ISAPI`.

Create a new Class Library project in C# called `ExcelUDFLibrary` and add a reference to the Excel UDF library. The process of creating the UDF itself is quite simple. All you need to do is create a class and decorate it with the `UdfClassAttribute` code attribute, and decorate each method within that class that will be used as a UDF with the `UdfMethod` attribute.

Take a look at the code in Listing 25.2 that illustrates an extremely simple user-defined function provided for Excel Services. Keep in mind that UDF libraries belong to the SharePoint installation and not to a specific workbook, so you can create libraries that can be used by multiple workbooks.

LISTING 25.2   A Sample Excel Services UDF

```
using System;
using System.Collections.Generic;
using System.Text;
using Microsoft.Office.Excel.Server.Udf;

namespace ExcelUDFLibrary
{
[UdfClass]
public class SampleUDFClass
{
    // supply the methods for your UDF here.

    [UdfMethod]
    public string GetStringFromService()
    {
        using (localhost.Service localSvc =
➥new ExcelUDFLibrary.localhost.Service())
        {
            return localSvc.GetString();
        }
    }
}
}
```

In the preceding example, there is a web reference to a web service hosted on the local machine that provides a single test method called `GetString`. This illustrates the real power of Excel Services: Within a UDF, you can do virtually anything that the .NET Framework can do, and provide that functionality to a centrally hosted workbook. Further, UDFs invoked from within an Excel calculation in a hosted workbook are also invoked when the workbook is accessed via Excel Web Services, giving the developer unprecedented power from within a simple workbook.

There are a few restrictions. Obviously, you will not want your code to do anything that requires interaction with the console or Windows interface such as opening dialog boxes, creating Windows Forms, and so forth. Second, you are limited in the data types that can be used because Excel Services has to convert the data contained within the Excel spreadsheet to something that can be read by the .NET Framework, and vice versa.

The following is a list of the data types that can be passed as parameters to an Excel Services UDF:

- ▶ Numeric data types, such as integer, decimal, double, float, long, and so on
- ▶ String
- ▶ Boolean
- ▶ Array of object
- ▶ DateTime

In addition to these types, the return value of UDF methods can include data of type `System.Object` including the value `null`.

After your UDF library is created, you need to deploy it to the physical SharePoint 2007 server machine because Excel Services does not allow remotely located UDF libraries.

Copy the file to any location you want; just remember the location because you will need it when configuring Excel Services next.

After the file is copied, open the Shared Services Administration page and select Excel Services. Within the Excel Services Administration page, select the User-Defined Function Assemblies option. Add a new UDF library to the list, making sure to provide the local file-system location of the library and select the `File path` option. After the UDF library has been configured within Excel Services, your UDF maintenance screen should look similar to the one shown in Figure 25.6.

You're almost done. The only thing left to do is to create an Excel workbook that utilizes this new user-defined function and then place that workbook in an Excel Services trusted location like the one created at the beginning of this chapter.

To use the new UDF, just invoke it in an Excel formula within a cell in the workbook:

```
=GetStringFromService()
```

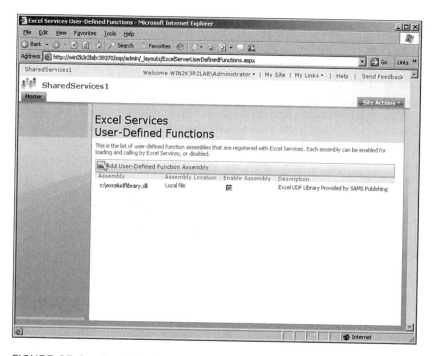

FIGURE 25.6   Excel Services User-Defined Functions library administration.

When Excel evaluates this formula offline, the text #NAME? appears within the cell. This normally tells the Excel user that there was a problem with the name of a function call in a formula. You can safely ignore this message because the UDF will be evaluated when the workbook is placed inside Excel Services.

When you upload the new workbook to a trusted location, any cells using UDFs configured within SharePoint will automatically evaluate them properly. Because the workbook is now managed by Excel Services, you can access the value of the dynamically calculated cell either through Excel Web Services, or through Excel Web Access, as shown in Figure 25.7.

Excel Web Access - udfdemo					
Open ▾					
	A	B	C	D	E
1	GetString:	This string came from a web service.			
2					
3					

FIGURE 25.7   A workbook invoking a C# UDF hosted in Excel Services.

Summary

Excel Services is an incredibly powerful new Shared Service that is part of Microsoft Office SharePoint Server 2007. It enables organizations to take calculations and business logic that used to be difficult to propagate and share and place them in a central location. From there, any number of clients can create a session against that shared workbook, enter input, perform calculations, read calculated values, and even obtain their own copy of the static workbook output. Using Excel Web Services, developers can attach their application front end to the powerful shared business logic contained within the Excel Services back end, enabling new application models and allowing for the reuse of existing investment and business logic.

This chapter showed you how to configure Excel Services trusted locations, place workbooks in those locations, and begin working with the shared workbooks programmatically using Excel Web Services. Microsoft has created an immensely powerful tool that seems only limited by the creativity and imagination of developers.

CHAPTER 26

Working with the Web Part Pages Web Service

IN THIS CHAPTER

▶ Overview of the Web Part Pages Web Service

▶ Adding and Updating Web Parts

▶ Querying Web Part Pages

If you have used Microsoft Office SharePoint Server (MOSS) for more than five minutes, you have encountered Web Part pages. Any page within SharePoint that renders Web Parts is a Web Part page—a page that builds on top of the ASP.NET 2.0 Web Part functionality by adding SharePoint-specific features on top.

You can choose to manipulate these pages programmatically via the object model or via the Web Part Pages Web Service. This chapter deals with the latter, providing you with information on how to use this web service to query and manipulate Web Parts on Web Part pages.

Overview of the Web Part Pages Web Service

The Web Part Pages Web Service can be accessed at http://[server]/[site]/_vti_bin/webpartpages.asmx. This web service provides facilities for querying and manipulating Web Parts on Web Part pages within the site to which the client is connected. Table 26.1 provides an overview of the methods available on this web service.

TABLE 26.1   Web Part Pages Web Service Methods

Method	Description
AddWebPart	Adds a new Web Part to a Web Part page
AddWebPartToZone	Adds a Web Part to a Web Part page inside the given zone
AssociateWorkflowMarkup	Associates a workflow markup configuration file with the Web Part page
ConvertWebPartFormat	Converts the Web Part format
DeleteWebPart	Deletes a Web Part from the page
ExecuteProxyUpdates	Executes the update data contained in the input string
FetchLegalWorkflowActions	Returns a string containing the list of valid workflow actions, as defined in the Actions File Schema
GetAssemblyMetaData	Returns metadata for the given Assembly in a string format
GetBindingResourceData	Gets data for the given binding resource
GetCustomControlList	Gets the custom control list for the site
GetDataFromDataSourceControl	Gets data from the given Extensible Markup Language (XML) containing the data source control description and query information
GetFormCapabilityFrom-DataSourceControl	Gets form capabilities (string) from the given data source control XML
GetSafeAssemblyInfo	Returns an XmlNode containing the safe Assembly information for the site
GetWebPart	Gets the XML data for a dynamic Web Part
GetWebPart2	Gets the XML data for a dynamic Web Part, specifying a web service behavior
GetWebPartCrossPage-Compatibility	Gets connection information for all parts on the given page and compatibility information of the Web Part with all the targets on the page; useful for determining to which parts a given Web Part can connect
GetWebPartPage	Gets a string containing the Web Part page and requires the client to specify whether it supports Windows SharePoint Services (WSS) v2.0 or WSS v3.0 Web Parts
GetWebPartPageConnectionInfo	Provides connection information for all Web Parts on the given page and compatibility information
GetWebPartPageDocument	Provides detailed information on the Web Part page as well as all parts on that page and properties for each Web Part zone
GetWebPartProperties	Gets an XML node that contains all Web Parts on a page and their associated properties
GetWebPartProperties2	Gets a list of all Web Parts on a page and their associated properties; allows client to specify WSS v2.0 or WSS v3.0 behavior
GetXmlDataFromDataSource	Gets XML data from the given data source provider

TABLE 26.1   Continued

Method	Description
`RemoveWorkflowAssociation`	Removes all workflow association objects on the list defined by a specific value in the workflow configuration file
`RenderWebPartForEdit`	Returns an XML fragment containing Web Part properties and a Hypertext Markup Language (HTML) rendering of the Web Part described in the XML input
`SaveWebPart`	Saves changes to a Web Part
`SaveWebPart2`	Saves changes to a Web Part, optionally including a change to the type itself
`ValidateWorkflowMarkup-AndCreateSupportObjects`	Creates a workflow task list

As with all web services within SharePoint, any client code connecting to the web service needs to provide valid credentials to access the service both for discovery and for runtime execution.

Adding and Updating Web Parts

Adding Web Parts to Web Part pages is unfortunately somewhat of an ugly looking process. To add a Web Part to a Web Part page, you need to provide an Extensible Markup Language (XML) fragment representing the entire Web Part and all of its properties as input to the `AddWebPart` or `AddWebPartToZone` methods. Thankfully, the element names for the Web Part XML fragment have a fairly straightforward relationship to the configurable properties within the Web Part tool pane on a SharePoint site.

Listing 26.1 shows some code that uses the `AddWebPart` method to add a new Web Part to a page. The Web Part is a content editor part and the XML fragment also contains the value for the Web Part's `Content` property. The XML fragment defines the content for the Web Part. Those of you used to doing low-level SharePoint administration will recognize the XML fragment from Web Part definitions found in XML files on the SharePoint server in the templates directory.

LISTING 26.1   Adding a Web Part to a Web Part Page

```
using System;
using System.Collections.Generic;
using System.Text;

namespace AddWebParts
{
class Program
{
static void Main(string[] args)
{
```

LISTING 26.1   Continued

```
win2k3r2lab.WebPartPagesWebService webPartSvc =
    new AddWebParts.win2k3r2lab.WebPartPagesWebService();

webPartSvc.Credentials=
    System.Net.CredentialCache.DefaultCredentials;

string newPartXml =
        "<?xml version=\"1.0\" ?>\n" +
        "<WebPart xmlns:xsd=\"http://www.w3.org/2001/XMLSchema\""+
        " xmlns:xsi=\"http://www.w3.org/2001/XMLSchema-instance\""+
        " xmlns=\"http://schemas.microsoft.com/WebPart/v2\">\n" +
        "<Title>Content Editor Web Part</Title>\n  " +
        "<FrameType>Default</FrameType>\n  " +
        "<Description>Use for formatted text, tables, and images." +
        "</Description>\n  " +
        "<IsIncluded>true</IsIncluded>\n  " +
        "<ZoneID>Header</ZoneID>\n  " +
        "<PartOrder>1</PartOrder>\n  " +
        "<FrameState>Normal</FrameState>\n  " +
        "<Height />\n  " +
        "<Width />\n  " +
        "<AllowRemove>true</AllowRemove>\n  " +
        "<AllowZoneChange>true</AllowZoneChange>\n  " +
        "<AllowMinimize>true</AllowMinimize>\n  " +
        "<IsVisible>true</IsVisible>\n  " +
        "<DetailLink />\n  " +
        "<HelpLink />\n  " +
        "<Dir>Default</Dir>\n  " +
        "<PartImageSmall />\n  " +
        "<MissingAssembly />\n  " +
        "<PartImageLarge>/_layouts/images/mscontl.gif</PartImageLarge>\n  " +
        "<IsIncludedFilter />\n  " +
        "<Assembly>Microsoft.SharePoint, Version=12.0.0.0, Culture=neutral, " +
            "PublicKeyToken=71e9bce111e9429c</Assembly>\n  " +
        "<TypeName>Microsoft.SharePoint.WebPartPages.ContentEditorWebPart
➥</TypeName>\n  " +
        "<ContentLink " +
            "xmlns=\"http://schemas.microsoft.com/WebPart/v2/
➥ContentEditor\" />\n  " +
        "<Content "+
            "xmlns=\"http://schemas.microsoft.com/WebPart/v2/
➥ContentEditor\"><![CDATA["+
            "<P>Content created <b><i>programmatically</b></i></P>" +
          "]]></Content>\n  " +
        "<PartStorage "+
```

LISTING 26.1   Continued

```
            "xmlns=\"http://schemas.microsoft.com/WebPart/v2/
➥ContentEditor\" />\n</WebPart>";

Guid newPartGuid =
    webPartSvc.AddWebPart(
        "http://win2k3r2lab/budget test site/default.aspx", newPartXml,
        AddWebParts.win2k3r2lab.Storage.Shared);

Console.WriteLine("Added a new part with guid {0} to default.aspx",
    newPartGuid.ToString());

Console.ReadLine();

}
}
}
```

The XML format for the Web Part as well as a very similar sample can be found online in the Windows SharePoint Services (WSS) Software Development Kit (SDK) on MSDN, so don't worry if you don't have the format memorized.

After executing the code in Listing 26.1, the page in question has been modified to include a new Web Part, as shown in Figure 26.1.

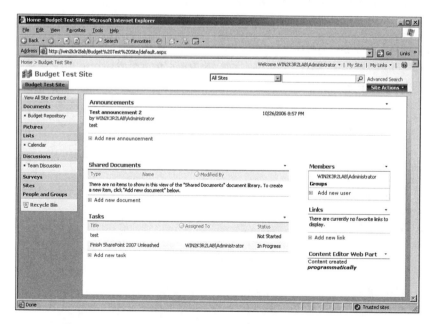

FIGURE 26.1   Rendered page after adding a Web Part programmatically.

Similarly, the act of saving changes to a Web Part must be done using an XML fragment that is passed to the SaveWebPart method, as shown in Listing 26.2.

LISTING 26.2   Updating an Existing Web Part

```
using System;
using System.Collections.Generic;
using System.Text;

namespace SavePart
{
class Program
{
static void Main(string[] args)
{
Guid partGuid = new Guid("{e4db1683-4723-455b-acaf-64ded220dc80}");

win2k3r2lab.WebPartPagesWebService partSvc =
    new SavePart.win2k3r2lab.WebPartPagesWebService();
partSvc.Credentials =
    System.Net.CredentialCache.DefaultCredentials;

string partXml =
    "<?xml version=\"1.0\" ?>\n" +
    "<WebPart xmlns:xsd=\"http://www.w3.org/2001/XMLSchema\" "+
    " xmlns:xsi=\"http://www.w3.org/2001/XMLSchema-instance\"" +
    " xmlns=\"http://schemas.microsoft.com/WebPart/v2\">\n" +
    "<Title>Content Editor Web Part</Title>\n   " +
    "<FrameType>Default</FrameType>\n   " +
"<Description>Use for formatted text, tables, and images.</Description>\n   " +
"<IsIncluded>true</IsIncluded>\n   " +
"<ZoneID>Header</ZoneID>\n   " +
"<PartOrder>1</PartOrder>\n   " +
"<FrameState>Normal</FrameState>\n   " +
"<Height />\n   " +
"<Width />\n   " +
"<AllowRemove>true</AllowRemove>\n   " +
"<AllowZoneChange>true</AllowZoneChange>\n   " +
"<AllowMinimize>true</AllowMinimize>\n   " +
"<IsVisible>true</IsVisible>\n   " +
"<DetailLink />\n   " +
"<HelpLink />\n   " +
"<Dir>Default</Dir>\n   " +
"<PartImageSmall />\n   " +
"<MissingAssembly />\n   " +
```

LISTING 26.2   Continued

```
"<PartImageLarge>/_layouts/images/mscontl.gif</PartImageLarge>\n  " +
"<IsIncludedFilter />\n  " +
"<Assembly>Microsoft.SharePoint, Version=12.0.0.0, Culture=neutral,
➥PublicKeyToken=71e9bce111e9429c</Assembly>\n  " +
"<TypeName>Microsoft.SharePoint.WebPartPages.ContentEditorWebPart</TypeName>\n  " +
"<ContentLink xmlns=\"http://schemas.microsoft.com/WebPart/v2/
➥ContentEditor\" />\n  " +
"<Content " +
"xmlns=\"http://schemas.microsoft.com/WebPart/v2/ContentEditor\">" +
"<![CDATA[" +
"<P>Content <B><i><u>modified</b></i></u> programmatically.</P> "+
"]]></Content>\n  " +
"<PartStorage xmlns=\"http://schemas.microsoft.com/WebPart/v2/
➥ContentEditor\" />\n</WebPart>";

partSvc.SaveWebPart(
    "http://win2k3r2lab/budget test site/default.aspx",
    partGuid,
    partXml,
    SavePart.win2k3r2lab.Storage.Shared);
}
}
}
```

26

Other than the tedious and unfortunate XML manipulation that must take place to add and update Web Parts, the other thing that can catch developers unaware is that you must specifically have the globally unique identifier (GUID) of the Web Part being modified to save changes. You can obtain the GUID either by maintaining a reference to it after initial creation, or by querying the Web Part page in any number of ways, some of which are illustrated later in the chapter.

Figure 26.2 shows two content editor Web Parts, one was created using the web service and the other was created and modified using the web service.

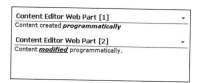

FIGURE 26.2   Rendered output after modifying an existing Web Part.

Querying Web Part Pages

There is a wealth of information that can be obtained from the Web Part Pages Web Service, including information on individual Web Parts, Web Part connection data, properties for all Web Parts on a page, and even information on Assembly metadata and the list of trusted Assemblies installed. This section shows you a few of the methods available on the Web Part Pages Web Service for enumerating Web Parts and querying information.

Using the GetWebPart Method

The GetWebPart method obtains property details for an individual Web Part contained on a Web Part page and returns that information in the form of a string that can be read into an XML document. Some methods on this web service return strings, whereas others return XmlNode instances. Being aware of the inconsistency in design of the web service up front makes it a little easier to use. Listing 26.3 shows how to use the GetWebPart method.

LISTING 26.3   Calling the GetWebPart Method

```
using System;
using System.Collections.Generic;
using System.Text;
using System.Xml;

namespace GetWebPart
{
class Program
{
static void Main(string[] args)
{
    Guid partGuid = new Guid("{e4db1683-4723-455b-acaf-64ded220dc80}");

    win2k3r2lab.WebPartPagesWebService partSvc =
        new GetWebPart.win2k3r2lab.WebPartPagesWebService();
    partSvc.Credentials =
        System.Net.CredentialCache.DefaultCredentials;

    string x = partSvc.GetWebPart(
        "http://win2k3r2lab/budget test site/default.aspx",
        partGuid,
        GetWebPart.win2k3r2lab.Storage.Shared);

    XmlDocument doc = new XmlDocument();
    doc.LoadXml(x);
```

LISTING 26.3   Continued

```
    foreach (XmlNode node in doc.DocumentElement.ChildNodes)
    {
        if (node.LocalName.ToLower() == "content")
        {
            Console.WriteLine(node.InnerXml);
        }
    }

    Console.ReadLine();
}
}
}
```

When the preceding code is executed, the following output is shown, which contains the contents of the Content node:

```
<![CDATA[<P>Content <B><i><u>modified</b></i></u> programmatically.</P> ]]>
```

Getting Safe Assembly Details

Safe Assemblies are Assemblies indicated as "safe" by various configuration files used by SharePoint. For more information on what constitutes a Safe Assembly and Assembly security within SharePoint, consult a SharePoint administration guide or *Microsoft SharePoint 2007 Unleashed* (Sams, ISBN: 0672329476). The following code snippet illustrates how to call the GetSafeAssemblyInfo method and interpret the results:

```
win2k3r2lab.WebPartPagesWebService partSvc =
    new GetSafeAssembly.win2k3r2lab.WebPartPagesWebService();
partSvc.Credentials =
    System.Net.CredentialCache.DefaultCredentials;

XmlNode safeNode = partSvc.GetSafeAssemblyInfo();
foreach (XmlNode assemblyNode in safeNode)
{
    Console.WriteLine(assemblyNode.Attributes["Name"].Value);
    Console.WriteLine(assemblyNode.Attributes["FullName"].Value);
    Console.WriteLine("---");
}
```

Figure 26.3 shows the output from the preceding code.

26

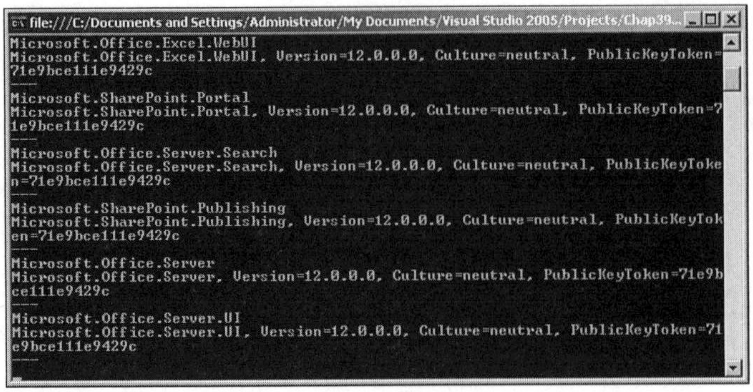

FIGURE 26.3   Safe Assembly output.

Summary

This chapter provided some examples of how you can write code that will remotely query and manipulate Web Parts within Web Part pages, a key component of SharePoint's content management capabilities.

CHAPTER 27

Using the Business Data Catalog Web Services

IN THIS CHAPTER

▶ Overview of the Business Data Catalog

▶ Using the Business Data Catalog Web Service

▶ Using the BDC Field Resolver Web Service

The Business Data Catalog (BDC) is an incredibly power-ful feature of Microsoft Office SharePoint Server (MOSS) 2007 that connects native SharePoint data such as lists and Web Parts to data stored in external Line of Business (LOB) systems. This chapter provides you with an overview of the BDC and illustrates the different ways in which your code can interact with BDC-related web services.

Overview of the Business Data Catalog

As you saw in Chapter 10, "Integrating Enterprise Business Data," and Chapter 11, "Creating Business Data Applications," the Business Data Catalog is made up of metadata that describes an external Line of Business appli-cation that either exposes functionality via a web service or stores data in a relational database.

The BDC allows SharePoint administrators to access and view LOB data, and it allows developers to write code against the BDC model so that their code will work against *any* external entities.

Chapters 11 and 12 referred to several concepts inherent to the BDC:

- ▶ **LOB systems and system instances**—The LOB system is the top level in the BDC hierarchy. It is a container of entities and related metadata.

- ▶ **Entities**—An entity can be represented by a row in a table or a single result from a web service. Examples of entities shown in Chapters 11 and 12 include customers, bugs, bug issues, products, and order items.

▶ **Methods**—Methods are actions that can be performed against an entity that are either Structured Query Language (SQL) queries or invocations of web service methods.

▶ **Finders**—A Finder is a specific type of method that can be used to locate individual entities or groups of identities either by specific identifiers or by wildcard matches.

One thing that developers might find disappointing about the BDC Web Service is that you cannot use it to make changes to the catalog. There are no methods on either of the BDC Web Services that will let you upload new metadata files or modify existing metadata. That said, the ability to query the contents of the BDC and use the Field Resolver Web Service is extremely useful to developers. The next two sections illustrate how to use the BDC Web Service and the Field Resolver Web Service.

Using the Business Data Catalog Web Service

The Business Data Catalog Web Service is a service provided by MOSS, not by Windows SharePoint Services (WSS) v3.0. As a result, the service is located at the root level of a portal site, for example, http://server/_vti_bin/businessdatacatalog.asmx. Note that in many configurations of SharePoint, the web services themselves reside in a different Internet Information Services (IIS) web application and on a different port number than the rest of the SharePoint installation, for example, http://server:1122/_vti_bin/ businessdatacatalog.asmx or, using host headers, http://services.server.company.com/ _vti_bin/businessdatacatalog.asmx.

At the top level of the hierarchy of metadata contained within the BDC is the LOB system instance. Thankfully, the developers of the new BDC Web Service decided to return structured data instead of free-form Extensible Markup Language (XML). As a result, obtaining the list of LOB system instances returns an array of `LobSystemInstanceStruct` structs. The properties of this struct are shown in Table 27.1.

TABLE 27.1   `LobSystemInstanceStruct` Properties

Property	Description
id	The numeric identifier of the system instance
lcids	An array of locale identifiers for which the LOB system instance is applicable
lobSystemId	The numeric identifier of the LOB system to which this instance belongs
localizedNames	An array of localized names for the LOB system instance
name	The name of the instance
propertyNames	An array of property names for the instance
propertyTypes	An array of property types; the indices for property types match with the property names and property values
propertyValues	An array of property values of type `System.String`

The code in Listing 27.1 shows a set of sample code that connects to the BDC Web Service, provides default credentials, and returns a list of LOB system instances as well as the properties associated with each LOB system instance.

LISTING 27.1   Enumerating LOB Systems

```
using System;
using System.Collections.Generic;
using System.Text;
using EnumInstances.win2k3r2lab;

namespace EnumInstances
{
class Program
{
static void Main(string[] args)
{
    BdcWebService bdc = new BdcWebService();
    bdc.Credentials = System.Net.CredentialCache.DefaultCredentials;

    win2k3r2lab.LobSystemInstanceStruct[] instances =
      bdc.GetLobSystemInstances();
    foreach (LobSystemInstanceStruct lobInstance in instances)
    {
        Console.WriteLine("{0} - {1}", lobInstance.lobSystemId,
          lobInstance.name);
        for (int x = 0; x < lobInstance.propertyValues.Length; x++)
        {
            Console.Write("\t{0} : {1}", lobInstance.propertyNames[x],
                lobInstance.propertyValues[x]);
            Console.WriteLine();
        }
    }
    Console.ReadLine();
}
}
}
```

Figure 27.1 shows the output of the console window when the preceding code is executed.

27

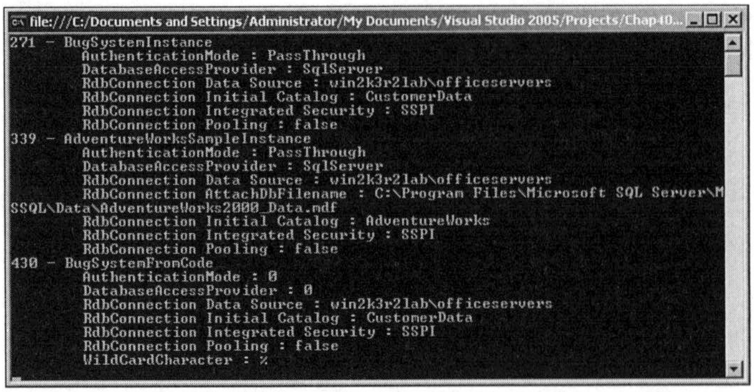

FIGURE 27.1   Enumerating LOB instances and properties.

Below each LOB system instance in the metadata hierarchy are the entities. Entities are returned from the web service in the form of an array of `EntityStruct` structs. The `EntityStruct` struct has the same member names and types as the `LobSystemInstanceStruct` struct. Listing 27.2 contains sample code that enumerates through the list of entities that belong to a given LOB system instance and the properties associated with that entity.

Note that to invoke the `GetEntitiesForLobSystemInstance` method, you need to supply the numeric identifier for the LOB system instance. You can figure out the ID for the LOB system instance by examining the `id` property of the `LobSystemInstanceStruct` struct returned by the web service. In the sample shown in Listing 27.2, the ID supplied is that of the AdventureWorks sample instance.

LISTING 27.2   Enumerating Entities and Associated Properties

```
using System;
using System.Collections.Generic;
using System.Text;
using GetEntities.win2k3r2lab;

namespace GetEntities
{
class Program
{
static void Main(string[] args)
{
    BdcWebService bdc = new GetEntities.win2k3r2lab.BdcWebService();
    bdc.Credentials = System.Net.CredentialCache.DefaultCredentials;

    // on my machine, lob system ID is 339, lob system instance is 340
    EntityStruct[] entities = bdc.GetEntitiesForLobSystemInstance(340);
    foreach (EntityStruct entity in entities)
```

LISTING 27.2   Continued

```
    {
        Console.WriteLine(entity.name);
        for (int x = 0; x < entity.propertyNames.Length; x++)
        {
            Console.WriteLine("\t{0} : {1}", entity.propertyNames[x],
                entity.propertyValues[x]);
        }
    }

    Console.ReadLine();
}
}
}
```

When the preceding code is compiled and executed against the Adventure Works sample BDC application, it produces output like that shown in Figure 27.2.

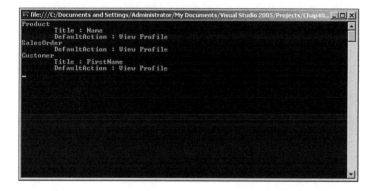

FIGURE 27.2   Enumerating entities and associated properties.

One of the types of metadata that resides below the entity level in the BDC is the method. A method is an action that can be performed on an action (though methods cannot be directly invoked via the BDC Web Service). You can use the GetMethodsForEntity and the GetMethodInstancesForEntity methods to return method and method instance structures. Table 27.2 contains a list of the properties on the MethodStruct structure.

TABLE 27.2   MethodStruct Properties

Property	Description
entityId	The ID of the entity to which the method applies
Id	The ID of the method itself
isStatic	A Boolean value indicating whether the method is static

TABLE 27.2   Continued

Property	Description
lcids	An array of integers containing the list of locale identifiers for which the method is applicable
localizedNames	An array of strings containing the localized names of the method
Name	The name of the method
propertyNames	The names of the method's properties
propertyTypes	The names of the types of each method property
propertyValues	The data value for each method property

Table 27.3 contains a list of properties on the MethodInstanceStruct structure.

TABLE 27.3   MethodInstanceStruct Properties

Property	Description
Id	The numeric identifier of the method instance
Lcids	The array of locale IDs for the method instance
localizedNames	The array of localized names for the method instance
methodId	The numeric identifier of the method to which this method instance belongs
methodInstanceType	The MethodInstanceType of the method instance: Finder, GenericInvoker, IdEnumerator, Scalar, SpecificFinder, ViewAccessor
Name	The name of the method instance
propertyNames	The array of property names
propertyTypes	The array of property types for the method instance
propertyValues	The array of property values for the method instance
returnTypeDescriptorId	The ID of the type descriptor for the return type of the method

Listing 27.3 shows a sample of enumerating methods and method instances for each entity within a BDC application.

LISTING 27.3   Enumerating Methods and Method Instances

```
using System;
using System.Collections.Generic;
using System.Text;
using EntityMethods.win2k3r2lab;

namespace EntityMethods
{
class Program
{
static void Main(string[] args)
```

LISTING 27.3   Continued

```
{
    BdcWebService bdc = new BdcWebService();
    bdc.Credentials = System.Net.CredentialCache.DefaultCredentials;

    EntityStruct[] entities = bdc.GetEntitiesForLobSystemInstance(340);
    foreach (EntityStruct entity in entities)
    {
        MethodStruct[] methods = bdc.GetMethodsForEntity(entity.id);
        Console.WriteLine("Entity: {0}", entity.name);
        foreach (MethodStruct method in methods)
        {
            Console.WriteLine("\tMethod {0} : {1}", method.id, method.name);
        }
        MethodInstanceStruct[] methodInstances =
            bdc.GetMethodInstancesForEntity(entity.id);
        foreach (MethodInstanceStruct methodInstance in methodInstances)
        {
            Console.WriteLine("\tMethod Instance {0} : {1}", methodInstance.id,
                methodInstance.name);
        }

    }

    Console.ReadLine();
}
}
}
```

27

When the preceding code is compiled and executed, the output resembles that of the
output shown in Figure 27.3.

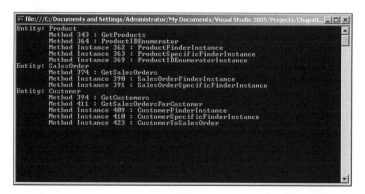

FIGURE 27.3   Enumerating methods and method instances.

Below the method level in the hierarchy, there are method filter descriptors, which can be retrieved and enumerated much like the rest of the metadata illustrated so far in this chapter. Listing 27.4 shows how to do this.

LISTING 27.4   Enumerating Filter Descriptors for a Method

```
using System;
using System.Collections.Generic;
using System.Text;
using FilterDescriptors.win2k3r2lab;

namespace FilterDescriptors
{
class Program
{
static void Main(string[] args)
{
    BdcWebService bdc = new BdcWebService();
    bdc.Credentials = System.Net.CredentialCache.DefaultCredentials;

    FilterDescriptorStruct[] filterDescriptors =
        bdc.GetFilterDescriptorsForMethod(394);
    foreach (FilterDescriptorStruct filter in filterDescriptors)
    {
        Console.WriteLine(filter.name);
        for (int x = 0; x < filter.propertyNames.Length; x++)
        {
            Console.WriteLine("\t{0} ({1}) : {2}", filter.propertyNames[x],
                filter.propertyTypes[x],
                filter.propertyValues[x]);
        }
    }
    Console.ReadLine();
}
}
}
```

When the preceding code is compiled and executed, the output resembles the following snippet:

```
ID
        Comparator (System.String) : Equals
Name
```

Using the BDC Field Resolver Web Service

Although you might not be able to directly execute methods against the entities within
the BDC using web services, you can make use of the BDC Field Resolver Web Service to
retrieve a list of fields and their associated values for a given entity.

Just like with the BDC Web Service, the BDC Field Resolver Web Service is provided by
MOSS. You can access it via the uniform resource locator (URL) http://server:port/
_vti_bin/bdcfieldsresolver.asmx.

The code in Listing 27.5 illustrates how to enumerate the fields and values associated with
a given entity.

LISTING 27.5   Using the BDC Field Resolver Web Service

```
using System;
using System.Collections.Generic;
using System.Text;
using FieldResolver.win2k3r2lab;

namespace FieldResolver
{
class Program
{
static void Main(string[] args)
{
    BDCFieldsResolver resolver = new BDCFieldsResolver();
    resolver.Credentials = System.Net.CredentialCache.DefaultCredentials;

    ResolveResult result = resolver.Resolve(
        "AdventureWorksSampleInstance",
        "Customer", "1", "FirstName:LastName");

    Console.WriteLine(result.Status.ToString());
    if (result.Status == ResolveStatus.MultipleMatch ||
        result.Status == ResolveStatus.UniqueMatch)
    {
        foreach (FieldRecord fr in result.Results)
        {
            Console.WriteLine("{0}:{1}", fr.FieldName,
                fr.Value);
        }
    }

    result = resolver.Resolve(
        "AdventureWorksSampleInstance",
        "Product",
```

LISTING 27.5 · Continued

```
        "12",
        "Name:ListPrice:ProductNumber");
    Console.WriteLine();
    Console.WriteLine(result.Status.ToString());
    if (result.Status == ResolveStatus.MultipleMatch ||
        result.Status == ResolveStatus.UniqueMatch)
    {
        foreach (FieldRecord fr in result.Results)
        {
            Console.WriteLine("{0}:{1}", fr.FieldName,
                fr.Value);
        }
    }

    Console.ReadLine();

}
}
}
```

The Resolve method takes the following arguments:

▶ systemInstance—The name (not numeric ID) of the LOB system instance in which the value should be resolved

▶ entity—The name of the entity being resolved (for example, Customer, Product)

▶ valueToResolve—The identifier value of the entity to be resolved

▶ fieldNames—A *colon-delimited* string of field names to resolve into values

You might have noticed that the field names passed to the Resolve method for the second example don't have spaces contained in them. That is because the actual names of the fields must be passed into the method, not the descriptions. You can get at the names of the fields easily if you were the one who developed the BDC application, or you can simply query the BDC application Registry using the object model or using the web service discussed earlier in this chapter.

When the preceding code is compiled and executed against the AdventureWorks sample BDC application, the output looks similar to the following:

```
UniqueMatch
FirstName:Jon
LastName:Yang

UniqueMatch
```

```
Name:Mountain-500 Black, 52
ListPrice:539.9900
ProductNumber:BK-M18B-52
```

Summary

The Business Data Catalog is an integral part of the new Microsoft Office SharePoint Server 2007. It allows developers and end users to access data contained within remote Line of Business systems, creating an environment of integration and aggregation that was previously painstaking and costly to develop manually. This chapter provided illustrations of how to interact with the BDC using two BDC web services: the BDC Web Service and the BDC Field Resolver Web Service.

27

CHAPTER 28

Using the Workflow Web Service

IN THIS CHAPTER

▶ Overview of Workflows in SharePoint 2007

▶ Introduction to the Workflow Web Service

▶ Performing Workflow Tasks with the Web Service

With the release of Microsoft Office SharePoint Server (MOSS) 2007 comes the integration of the Windows Workflow Foundation into the product. This chapter provides you with an overview of how the Workflow Foundation has been integrated into SharePoint and, more important, how to utilize a subset of SharePoint's workflow functionality remotely via the Workflow Web Service.

This chapter contains an overview of how the Workflow Foundation is integrated within SharePoint, an introduction to the Workflow Web Service, and extensive code samples illustrating how to remotely access and manipulate workflows via the web service.

Overview of Workflows in SharePoint 2007

The Windows Workflow Foundation (WF) was released as part of the .NET Framework 3.0 distribution, which also included the Windows Communication Foundation and the Windows Presentation Foundation. The .NET Framework 3.0 works on Windows XP SP2, Windows Server 2003, and Windows Vista. The workflow capabilities of MOSS 2007 are provided by the .NET Framework 3.0 running on Windows Server 2003.

The WF is a powerful runtime that provides applications with the ability to dynamically model workflows. This modeling ability extends from design time to runtime by providing a facility for applications to instantiate and manage WF programs as well as store and retrieve workflow state. The true power of the WF lies in its bookmarking nature. A WF program is a tree of activities that, by and large, execute asynchronously. WF programs are resumable and reentrant. This means that any given workflow can last for a few minutes or a few months. The lifetime of a workflow is unrelated to the lifetime of the process managing it. This key fact is essential to understanding how to properly deal with SharePoint workflows whether you're working with them using the object model or the web service.

Introduction to the Workflow Web Service

The Workflow Web Service allows client applications not residing on a SharePoint server to integrate with SharePoint workflows. This web service publishes methods that allow for the querying and manipulation of tasks/to-dos for a given item, as well as the ability to query the list of open workflows for an item and even to start a new workflow for an item.

This web service is used by Microsoft Office 2007 clients to determine whether a document being opened has any workflow tasks associated with it, as well as allowing individuals to move the workflow forward by altering the tasks.

TABLE 28.1   Workflow Web Service Methods

Method	Description
AlterToDo	Modifies a task item associated with a particular item's workflow
ClaimReleaseTask	Assumes or releases ownership of a given workflow task item
GetTemplatesForItem	Gets the list of workflow templates available for a given item
GetToDosForItem	Gets the list of tasks associated with a given item (filtered by calling user credentials!)
GetWorkflowDataForItem	Gets the workflow Extensible Markup Language (XML) data associated with a given item
GetWorkflowTaskData	Gets workflow task data for an item
StartWorkflow	Starts a new workflow

The rest of this chapter provides an overview of each of the web service methods as well as some code examples that illustrate how to invoke the various methods.

Performing Workflow Tasks with the Web Service

Many of SharePoint's web services are notorious for reading and writing seemingly unformatted blocks of Extensible Markup Language (XML) without much help as far as determining the format of the data. Unfortunately, the Workflow Web Service is just as difficult—with good reason. Many of the tasks associated with a workflow require the transmission of data *specific to that workflow*. In other words, the format of the parameters to several method calls change depending on whether you are working on an Approval workflow, a Feedback workflow, or a custom workflow created in Visual Studio 2005 or Microsoft Office SharePoint Designer.

Getting Workflow Data for an Item

If you want to retrieve every bit of possible information related to an item in a list, you can use the GetWorkflowDataForItem method on the Workflow Web Service. This method returns an XML node containing an enormous amount of information. You should note two important things about this method:

▶ The information returned varies depending on the credentials of the caller.

▶ You must refer to the item by its full uniform resource locator (URL), not by its item ID.

The code in the following sample illustrates how to invoke this method and save the resulting XML in a file on disk. Note that the URL of the web service is going to be the workflow.asmx file beneath the _vti_bin directory of the site in question.

```
using System;
using System.Collections.Generic;
using System.Text;
using GetWorkflowData.win2k3_splab;
using System.Xml;
using System.IO;

namespace GetWorkflowData
{
class Program
{
static void Main(string[] args)
{
    Workflow wfService = new Workflow();
    wfService.Credentials =
        new System.Net.NetworkCredential("Administrator", "password",
➥"win2k3-splab");
    XmlNode dataNode = wfService.GetWorkflowDataForItem(
        "http://win2k3-splab/teamsample/shared documents/test document.docx");
    Console.WriteLine(dataNode.InnerXml);

    StreamWriter sw = File.CreateText(@"out.xml");
    sw.WriteLine(dataNode.OuterXml);
    sw.Close();

    Console.ReadLine();
}
}
}
```

28

Figure 28.1 shows the XML produced by the preceding code as viewed by Microsoft Internet Explorer.

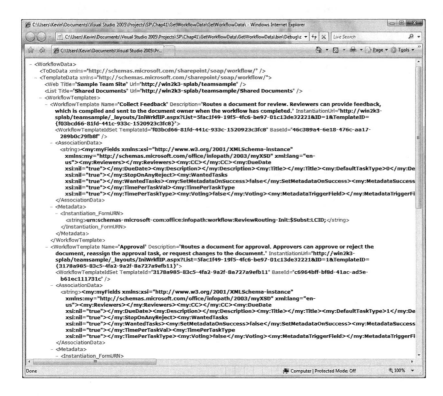

FIGURE 28.1   Output XML after obtaining workflow data for an item.

Getting To-Dos for an Item

When someone opens a document in Microsoft Word (or Microsoft Excel, or any other Office 2007 product) from a SharePoint server, the Office client performs a check to see if the user opening the document has any tasks associated with that item. If they do have tasks, those tasks are displayed below the Ribbon. The method used by the Office client to determine the tasks associated with a given item is GetToDosForItem and is illustrated in the console application shown in Listing 28.1.

LISTING 28.1   Obtaining a List of To-Dos for an Item

```
using System;
using System.Data;
using System.Collections.Generic;
using System.Text;
using GetToDos.win2k3_splab;
```

LISTING 28.1   Continued

```
using System.Xml;
using System.IO;

namespace GetToDos
{
class Program
{
static void Main(string[] args)
{
    Workflow wfService = new Workflow();
    wfService.Url = "http://win2k3-splab/teamsample/_vti_bin/workflow.asmx";

    wfService.Credentials =
      new System.Net.NetworkCredential("Juser", "joe", "win2k3-splab");

    XmlNode resultNode = wfService.GetToDosForItem(
        "http://win2k3-splab/teamsample/shared documents/Test document.docx");
    DataSet ds = new DataSet();
    ds.ReadXml(new StringReader(resultNode.InnerXml));

    DataTable workflowTodos = ds.Tables["row"];
    foreach (DataRow row in workflowTodos.Rows)
    {
        foreach (DataColumn col in workflowTodos.Columns)
        {
            Console.WriteLine("{0} : {1}", col.ColumnName, row[col]);
        }
        Console.WriteLine("---");
    }
    Console.ReadLine();
}
}
}
```

It is important to note that this method returns only those to-do items that are *assigned to the calling user*. In the preceding example, the calling user was a local user named "Juser" with a password of "joe". The following output shows that "Joe User" has a single to-do item assigned to him for the item Test document.docx.

```
ows_ContentTypeId : 0x01080100C9C9515DE4E24001905074F980F9316000E459211789B2064B
BE30AC2B14BCA923
ows_Title : Please review Test document
ows_Priority : (2) Normal
ows_Status : Not Started
```

28

ows_AssignedTo : 16;#WIN2K3-SPLAB\juser
ows_Body : Please take a look at this document and supply your feedback as soon
as you get a chance. Thanks!
ows_StartDate : 2007-01-20 16:49:29
ows_DueDate : 2007-01-31T05:00:00+00:00
ows_WorkflowLink : http://win2k3-splab/teamsample/Shared Documents/Test document
.docx, Test document
ows_WorkflowName : Collect Feedback
ows_TaskType : 0
ows_FormURN : urn:schemas-microsoft-com:office:infopath:workflow:ReviewRouting-R
eview:$Subst:LCID;
ows_HasCustomEmailBody : 0
ows_SendEmailNotification : 1
ows_Completed : 0
ows_WorkflowListId : {5FAC1F49-19F5-4FC6-BE97-01C13DE32221}
ows_WorkflowItemId : 1
ows_AllowChangeRequests : True
ows_AllowDelegation : True
ows_BodyText : Please take a look at this document and supply your feedback as s
oon as you get a chance. Thanks!
ows_ContentType : Office SharePoint Server Workflow Task
ows_ID : 1
ows_Modified : 2007-01-20 13:49:31
ows_Created : 2007-01-20 13:49:31
ows_Author : 1;#WIN2K3-SPLAB\administrator
ows_Editor : 1073741823;#System Account
ows_owshiddenversion : 1
ows_WorkflowVersion : 1
ows__UIVersion : 512
ows__UIVersionString : 1.0
ows_Attachments : 0
ows__ModerationStatus : 0
ows_LinkTitleNoMenu : Please review Test document
ows_LinkTitle : Please review Test document
ows_SelectTitle : 1
ows_Order : 100.000000000000
ows_GUID : {D973BD64-F641-4BE0-80CA-363BD9CFA545}
ows_WorkflowInstanceID : {30852AE8-BFF1-46BE-9346-D82FDD2DCCB3}
ows_FileRef : 1;#teamsample/Lists/Tasks/1_.000
ows_FileDirRef : 1;#teamsample/Lists/Tasks
ows_Last Modified : 1;#2007-01-20 13:49:31
ows_Created Date : 1;#2007-01-20 13:49:31
ows_FSObjType : 1;#0
ows_PermMask : 0x1b03c4312ef
ows_FileLeafRef : 1;#1_.000

```
ows_UniqueId : 1;#{99191889-0358-4C65-86C3-50AE79292813}
ows_ProgId : 1;#
ows_ScopeId : 1;#{BE00F3F6-3F2D-4736-B953-61C217CD6ABC}
ows__EditMenuTableStart : 1_.000
ows__EditMenuTableEnd : 1
ows_LinkFilenameNoMenu : 1_.000
ows_LinkFilename : 1_.000
ows_ServerUrl : /teamsample/Lists/Tasks/1_.000
ows_EncodedAbsUrl : http://win2k3-splab/teamsample/Lists/Tasks/1_.000
ows_BaseName : 1_
ows__Level : 1
ows__IsCurrentVersion : 1
ows_MetaInfo_vti_versionhistory : 19a6e6a9342744d69c85078c66ddbf44:1
ows_MetaInfo_WorkflowCreationPath : f03bcd66-81fd-441c-933c-1520923c3fc8;
ows_TaskListId : 19a6e6a9-3427-44d6-9c85-078c66ddbf44
ows_EditFormURL : http://win2k3-splab/teamsample/_layouts/WrkTaskIP.aspx?ID=1&Li
st=19a6e6a9-3427-44d6-9c85-078c66ddbf44
data_Id : 0
---
```

Modifying To-Do Items

To modify task items, you must use the `AlterToDo` method. If you have had any experience with the SharePoint object model, it might help to know that this web service method is essentially a front end for the `AlterTask` method on the `SPWorkflow` class. This method takes the following parameters:

- ▶ `item`—A string containing the full URL to the item that is the source of the workflow, for example, the document list item (*not* the task item!)

- ▶ `todoId`—The integer ID of the task item

- ▶ `todoListId`—The globally unique identifier (GUID) of the list in which the task item resides

- ▶ `taskData`—The XML node indicating the task data to be sent to the web service

It is important to note that the `taskData` parameter is actually an XML serialization of a hash table in the following format:

```
<Data>
    <Name>Value</Name>
    <Name>Value</Name>
    ...
</Data>
```

28

The XML submitted to the web service is converted into a hash table and then passed to the AlterTask method of the SPWorkflowTask class. For more information on that method, consult the SharePoint Software Development Kit (SDK).

Claiming or Releasing Tasks

Occasionally, client applications might want to provide the ability for users to assume responsibility for workflow tasks, or they might want to be able to release responsibility for a workflow tasks. To do this, a single method has been provided for both actions: ClaimReleaseTask. You must supply the full URL of the item that spawned the workflow, as well as the numeric ID of the task item and the GUID of the task list. Finally, by supplying a value of false for the bClaimRelease parameter, the task will be released. Supplying a value of true will claim the task for the user whose credentials were supplied to the web service.

Getting Templates for an Item

If your code needs to know what templates are available to start new workflows for a given item, you can use the GetTemplatesForItem method. When you supply the full URL of the item as the parameter to this method, you will receive an XML node in return that contains the list of templates that can be used to start a workflow for the item.

The following code snippet shows how to invoke this method:

```
using System;
using System.Collections.Generic;
using System.Text;
using GetTemplates.win2k3_splab;
using System.Xml;

namespace GetTemplates
{
class Program
{
static void Main(string[] args)
{
    Workflow wfService = new Workflow();
    wfService.Credentials =
        new System.Net.NetworkCredential("Administrator", "password",
        "win2k3-splab");
    XmlNode results = wfService.GetTemplatesForItem(
        "http://win2k3-splab/teamsample/shared documents/Test document.docx");

    Console.WriteLine(results.OuterXml);
    Console.ReadLine();
}
}
}
```

When this code is executed, it produces a rather large XML node, some of which is shown in Figure 28.2.

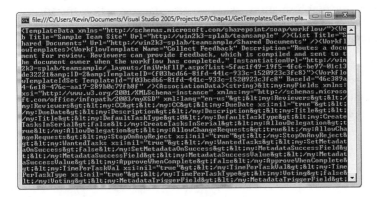

FIGURE 28.2   XML template data for an item.

Getting Workflow Task Data

This method works like the other methods that retrieve information related to an individual task and an item for which an active workflow exists. To get the resulting XML node for this method, you need to supply the full URL to the source item (for example, http://server/site/library/document.docx), the numeric ID of the task item, and the GUID of the list in which the task item exists.

Starting a Workflow

After you know the full URL of the item, and the GUID of the workflow template you want to start (possibly obtained through a method call to GetTemplatesForItem), you just need to supply the parameters to the workflow and call StartWorkflow to create a new workflow for the item.

Like many other methods, the final parameter to the StartWorkflow method (workflowParameters) is an XML node that contains a hash table of name/value pairs that seed the workflow with the input parameters. You can determine these parameters by looking at the workflow files, which should be especially easy if you were the author of the workflow you are activating.

28

Summary

The Workflow Web Service provides client applications on remote machines with the ability to access workflow template information, workflow task data, workflow instance information, and even to remotely start workflows. The format of the web service is designed such that it can be used by any workflow, which also makes the web service a little difficult to use.

One alternative to accessing the web service directly using generic methods might be to create your own web service that is tailored specifically to the workflow you are accessing, which might make the task of consuming the service from a client easier.

CHAPTER 29

Working with Records Repositories

IN THIS CHAPTER

▶ Overview of Records Repositories

▶ Using Records Repositories

▶ Creating Your Own Records Repository

One of the main driving factors for corporations to adopt centralized document management solutions beyond version control is compliance and auditing. Virtually every industry these days has requirements on document management that often dictate that certain documents be placed in a read-only repository that can be audited at a later date. This chapter provides an overview of how Microsoft Office SharePoint Server (MOSS) facilitates such compliance and how you can both consume and create your own records repository.

Overview of Records Repositories

Records repositories are covered in this section of the book because they are facilitated almost entirely through the use of the Official File Web Service. SharePoint provides a default implementation of the Official File Web Service in the file officialfile.asmx. This file doesn't do any good unless you access it through the relative uniform resource locator (URL) of a SharePoint website created from the Records Center site definition.

When a SharePoint web application has been configured to link to an external records repository, the name of the records repository appears on the Send To submenu for individual documents within any site in that web application's site collection.

As mentioned earlier, you can configure a web application to send files to a SharePoint Records Center site, or to a web service that you developed on your own, provided your web service's definition matches what SharePoint is looking for.

Using Records Repositories

This section of the chapter provides an overview of how to use records repositories within SharePoint, as well as how to write code that consumes the Official File Web Service.

Using the Records Center Site Definition

When you create a new site, there is a site definition called Records Center on the Enterprise tab. When this site is provisioned, it creates a default document library called `Unclassified Records`. This document library serves as the default location for submitted records. In a real-world scenario, your Records Center site might have multiple rules for record routing and multiple document libraries that serve as possible destinations for records.

To add record routing rules, you just need to add items to the Record Routing list. You can also temporarily place record storage on hold by adding items to the Holds list.

By default, SharePoint does not enable the drop-down menu item that allows an item to be sent to a Records Center site because the default installation does not include an instance of this site definition.

The first step toward using a records repository is to open the SharePoint 3.0 Central Administration site and go to Application Management. About halfway down the page on the right is a link called Records Center. When you click this link, you will be given a chance to configure the link to a records center *for all sites and site collections within that web application*. It is extremely important to note that you can only have one records center defined for each web application in a SharePoint installation.

Figure 29.1 shows a screenshot of the Configure Connection to Records Center screen.

This screen allows you to turn on or off access to an external records center and to supply the URL for the records center. The URL for the records center *must be the full URL of the records center website followed by* `_vti_bin/officialfile.asmx`.

To get the Official File Web Service within the Records Center site to work, you either need to enable anonymous access or you need to make sure that the identity of the application pool of the *submitting* application has *contribute* access to the destination document library.

When the Records Center site is provisioned, a site group called "Web Service Submitters for Records" preceded by the name of the records center is created. For example, if you have a Records Center site called "SEC Compliance," then there will be a site group named "SEC Compliance Web Service Submitters for Records." Any identity that needs to be able to submit to the web service needs to be a member of this group.

After the link to the Official File Web Service has been established, there will be a new item on the Send To submenu on every document contained in every site within the application's site collections, as shown in Figure 29.2.

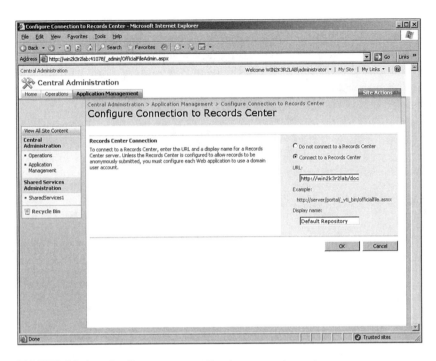

FIGURE 29.1   Configure a connection to a records center.

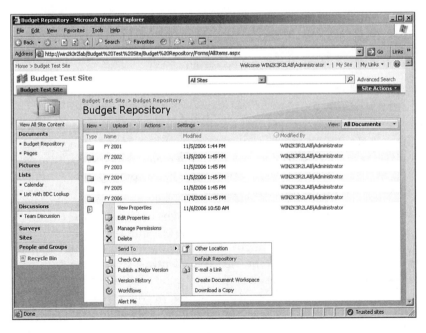

FIGURE 29.2   Send To menu after configuring a records center destination.

When the file has been submitted to the repository, its filename is modified so that it is guaranteed to be unique and the file and its metadata information are stored in a folder under the document library indicated by the routing rule. Figure 29.3 shows a sample of the metadata information that was submitted to the records repository along with the simple text file from Figure 29.2.

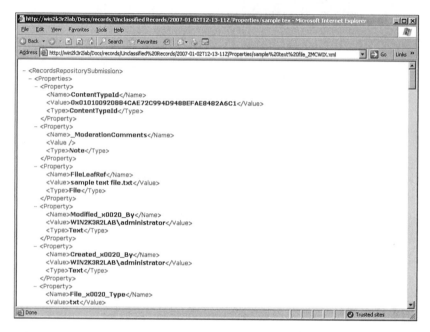

FIGURE 29.3   Metadata information stored in a records repository.

Using a Custom Records Center

Using a custom records center should provide the exact same end-user experience as using a Records Center site provided by SharePoint. When you (or some other developer) have provided an `officialfile.asmx` Web Service with all of the required methods (discussed later in this chapter), you should be able to submit files to the custom repository using the Send To menu just as you would with a Records Center site.

If you already have compliance procedures in place, you might not want to use the Records Center site. Many companies use document storage facilities that are far more secure than the Records Center site or they might use facilities provided by UNIX operating systems. In this case, you might want to provide your own web service that deals with the persistence of documents and their metadata. Keep in mind that the Records Center site provides more functionality than just the web service—it provides read-only access to the vault of stored documents and metadata as well as a web-based administration console for routing rules.

Submitting Files via Workflows

One way in which records repositories are made even more powerful is through the use of workflows. One of the activity types that is predefined within the SharePoint 2007 workflow system is the `SendToRecordRepository` activity. When you include this activity in a document workflow, it will send the document to the document repository defined for the web application in which the workflow is running.

This enables some extremely powerful and robust compliance and document storage scenarios. One example might be an enhanced approval workflow. After all of the involved parties have approved the document, you could design the workflow so that the document is automatically submitted to the records center just before the workflow completes.

Programmatically Submitting Files Using the `SPFile` Class

The `SPFile` class has a method that provides a convenient means of submitting a file to a records repository. The method name is `SendToOfficialFile`, and it can take one or two string arguments:

- ▶ `recordSeries`—Indicates the record series for the file
- ▶ `additionalInformation (out)`—Provides for additional information text, including the URL of the page used to supply values for missing properties

Listing 29.1 illustrates how to use the SharePoint object model to locate an individual instance of the `SPFile` class and then submit that file to the defined records repository.

LISTING 29.1   Submitting Files Programmatically via the `SPFile` Class

```
using System;
using System.Collections.Generic;
using System.Text;
using Microsoft.SharePoint;

namespace SPFileSubmit
{
class Program
{
static void Main(string[] args)
{
    SPSite site = new SPSite("http://win2k3r2lab");
    SPWeb budgetWeb = site.AllWebs["Budget Test Site"];
    SPDocumentLibrary budgetFiles =
      (SPDocumentLibrary)budgetWeb.Lists["Budget Repository"];

    SPFile fileToSubmit =
      budgetFiles.RootFolder.Files[
```

29

LISTING 29.1   Continued

```
        "http://win2k3r2lab/budget test site/budget repository/test document.docx"];
    string additionalInfo;
    fileToSubmit.SendToOfficialFile(out additionalInfo);
    Console.WriteLine("File " + fileToSubmit.Url +
        " submitted to official file:\n{0}",
        additionalInfo);

    Console.ReadLine();
}
}
}
```

One extremely common use for the SendToOfficialFile method is in responding to
events. Responding to events such as file check-ins, file uploads, and modifications, you
can automatically submit files to the defined records repository without requiring manual
intervention by the user.

Querying an Official File Web Service

The Official File Web Service contains a few methods that can be used to interrogate it.
You can obtain the list of routing rules and information on the official file server, as
shown in Listing 29.2.

LISTING 29.2   Querying the Official File Web Service

```
using System;
using System.Collections.Generic;
using System.Text;
using consume_records.win2k3r2lab;

namespace consume_records
{
class Program
{
    static void Main(string[] args)
    {
        RecordsRepository records = new RecordsRepository();
        records.Url = "http://win2k3r2lab/docs/records/_vti_bin/officialfile.asmx";
        records.Credentials = System.Net.CredentialCache.DefaultCredentials;
        string serverInfo = records.GetServerInfo();
        Console.WriteLine(serverInfo);

        string recordRouting = records.GetRecordRoutingCollection();
        Console.WriteLine(recordRouting);
```

LISTING 29.2   Continued

```
        Console.ReadLine();
    }
}
}
```

The output of the preceding code will look similar to the following text when run against a default Records Center site:

```
<ServerInfo><ServerType>Microsoft.Office.Server</ServerType>
<ServerVersion>Microsoft.Office.OfficialFileSoap,
  Version=12.0.0.0, Culture=neutral,
 PublicKeyToken=71e9bce111e9429c</ServerVersion>
</ServerInfo>
<RecordRoutingCollection>
<RecordRouting><Name>Unclassified Records</Name>
<Description>This Record Routing is an example that stores records submitted to
➡the Records Center in the &quot;Unclassified Records&quot;
➡document library.</Description>
<Default>True</Default>
<Location>Unclassified Records</Location>
<Mappings></Mappings></RecordRouting>
</RecordRoutingCollection>
```

As you can see from the preceding Extensible Markup Language (XML) fragment, the default implementation of the Records Center site contains a document library called Unclassified Records that is the default location for all submitted files. You can define custom routing paths for individual content types and you can define alternate mappings and destinations by adding items to the Record Routing list in the Records Center site.

Creating Your Own Records Repository

Creating your own records repository either from scratch or as a front for an existing records repository already in use within your organization involves creating an implementation of the Official File Web Service.

The Official File Web Service exposes the methods discussed in the following sections.

SubmitFile

This method accepts an array of bytes containing the raw file, as well as additional metadata information. It returns an XML fragment containing information pertinent to the file submission. The following is a list of parameters to the SubmitFile method:

▶ fileToSubmit—An array of bytes containing the raw contents of the file being submitted.

▶ properties—An array of `OfficialFileProperty` objects. In any implementation of this web service, the `OfficialFileProperty` class must have the following public string fields: `Name`, `Other`, `Type`, `Value`.

▶ recordSeries—The name of the record routing type of the file being submitted. If this doesn't match any routing type on file, the default routing type will be used.

▶ sourceUrl—A string containing the fully qualified URL of the file being submitted.

▶ userLoginName—The name of the user submitting the file.

GetServerInfo

This method queries information about the records repository server. It returns an XML string that has the following structure (the values returned in this sample are from the MOSS 2007 server):

```
<ServerInfo>
<ServerType>Microsoft.Office.Server</ServerType>
<ServerVersion>Microsoft.Office.OfficialFileSoap,
Version=12.0.0.0,    Culture=neutral, PublicKeyToken=71e9bce111e9429c
</ServerVersion>
</ServerInfo>
```

Summary

Microsoft Office SharePoint Server 2007 provides a comprehensive solution for document management, document version control, and document warehousing and vaulting through the Records Center site definition and the Official File Web Service. This chapter provided you with an overview of how to use the Records Center site definition, how to consume the Official File Web Service, and what you need to do to create your own Official File Web Service.

CHAPTER **30**

Additional Web Services

IN THIS CHAPTER

▶ Using the Spell Checker Web
Service

▶ Using the Alerts Web Service

▶ Using the Versions Web
Service

This section of the book has gone into a lot of detail regarding many of the web services that expose and extend the functionality of Microsoft Office SharePoint Server (MOSS). This chapter provides an overview of a few remaining web services that the authors feel are important enough to warrant attention in this book but that aren't large enough to fit in their own chapter.

This chapter provides an overview of the Spell Checker Web Service, the Alerts Web Service, and the Versions Web Service.

Using the Spell Checker Web Service

The Spell Checker Web Service is one of the services that SharePoint provides that is extremely useful, can add a lot of useful functionality to any application, and is also one of the most underrated services in the entire SharePoint web services arsenal.

You can find the service at the root of a MOSS web application, for example, http://server/_vti_bin/spellcheck.asmx. This service has a single method called SpellCheck that examines an array of strings and returns a set of results indicating where all of the spell-checking failures have occurred in each of the strings.

These results can be used when implementing a rich text editor with the offset information being provided by the service allowing the client application to highlight misspelled words.

The code in Listing 30.1 illustrates how to invoke the SpellCheck method and render the results from the method call.

LISTING 30.1   Using the Spell Checker Web Service

```csharp
using System;
using System.Collections.Generic;
using System.Text;
using Spellcheck.win2k3_splab;

namespace Spellcheck
{
class Program
{
static void Main(string[] args)
{
    SpellingService spellSvc = new SpellingService();
    spellSvc.Credentials =
      new System.Net.NetworkCredential(
      "Administrator", "password", "win2k3-splab");
    SpellCheckResults results =
        spellSvc.SpellCheck(
        new string[] {"Teh quik brown fxo",
            "ran over the lzy dog"},
            1033,
            false);

    foreach (SpellingErrors spellErrors in results.spellingErrors)
    {
        Console.WriteLine("Spelling error set:");
        foreach (FlaggedWord flaggedWord in spellErrors.flaggedWords)
        {
            Console.WriteLine("\tWord '{0}' at offset {1} within string failed
            {2}",
                flaggedWord.word, flaggedWord.offset,
                flaggedWord.type.ToString());
        }
        Console.WriteLine();
    }

    Console.ReadLine();
}
}
}
```

The output of the application will look similar to the output shown in Figure 30.1.

FIGURE 30.1   Using the Spell Checker Web Service.

The Spell Checker Web Service works without regard for relative site context, so it can be used within your own custom web applications, custom Web Parts, and even within your smart client or Windows Presentation Foundation (WPF)/Vista applications.

Using the Alerts Web Service

The Alerts Web Service works relative to the site from which it was accessed. This means that the information available to the Alerts Web Service from http://server/site1/_vti_bin/ alerts.asmx is not the same data that is available from http://server/site2/_vti_bin/alerts. asmx. The main purpose of the Alerts Web Service is to retrieve the alerts that *belong to the calling user*. In other words, the credentials supplied for the web service call are the same credentials used to identify the user requesting his alerts.

Fortunately, the Alerts Web Service is one of the few SharePoint services that returns structured data instead of Extensible Markup Language (XML) nodes or XML strings. To keep things interesting, the sample shown in Listings 30.2 and 30.3 is actually some Extensible Application Markup Language (XAML) for a WPF application and its associated code-behind. This not only shows the power of WPF data binding, but also how amazingly helpful it is when web services return structured data instead of free-form XML chunks.

Don't worry if you don't understand all of the finer details of the data binding—the point is that you can consume these web services from any application from a console application to a web application to a WPF application.

30

LISTING 30.2   Window1.xaml for an Alerts Viewing Application

```xml
<Window x:Class="ViewAlerts.Window1"
  xmlns="http://schemas.microsoft.com/winfx/2006/xaml/presentation"
  xmlns:x="http://schemas.microsoft.com/winfx/2006/xaml" _____
  Title="ViewAlerts" Height="300" Width="300"
  xmlns:local="clr-namespace:ViewAlerts"
  xmlns:svc="clr-namespace:ViewAlerts.spserver"
  >
<Window.Resources>
  <DataTemplate x:Key="DeliveryChannel">
    <Border>
      <StackPanel>
        <TextBlock Text="{Binding Path=Address}"/>
        <TextBlock Text="{Binding Path=Frequency}" />
      </StackPanel>
    </Border>
  </DataTemplate>
  <DataTemplate x:Key="AlertItem">
    <Border>
      <StackPanel>
        <TextBlock Text="{Binding Path=AlertForUrl}"/>
        <TextBlock Text="{Binding Path=Title}"/>
        <TextBlock Text="{Binding Path=EventType}"/>
        <ListBox
            ItemsSource="{Binding Path=DeliveryChannels}"
            ItemTemplate="{StaticResource DeliveryChannel}">
        </ListBox>
      </StackPanel>
    </Border>
  </DataTemplate>

</Window.Resources>
<Grid x:Name="MainGrid">
  <Grid.RowDefinitions>
    <RowDefinition Height="40"/>
    <RowDefinition Height="40"/>
    <RowDefinition Height="40"/>
    <RowDefinition Height="40"/>
    <RowDefinition Height="*"/>
  </Grid.RowDefinitions>
  <Grid.ColumnDefinitions>
    <ColumnDefinition Width="150"/>
    <ColumnDefinition/>
  </Grid.ColumnDefinitions>
```

LISTING 30.2   Continued

```
<Label VerticalAlignment="Center" Grid.Column="0" Grid.Row="0">Server Name:
➥</Label>  <TextBlock Grid.Column="1" Text="{Binding Path=AlertServerName}"
   Grid.Row="0" VerticalAlignment="Center"/>

<Label VerticalAlignment="Center" Grid.Column="0" Grid.Row="1">Server Type:
➥</Label>
<TextBlock Grid.Column="1" Grid.Row="1"
  Text="{Binding Path=AlertServerType}" VerticalAlignment="Center"/>

<Label VerticalAlignment="Center" Grid.Column="0" Grid.Row="2">Server URL:
➥</Label>
<TextBlock Grid.Column="1" Grid.Row="2"
  Text="{Binding Path=AlertServerUrl}" VerticalAlignment="Center"></TextBlock>

<Label VerticalAlignment="Center" Grid.Column="0" Grid.Row="3">
➥Management URL:</Label>
<TextBlock Grid.Column="1" Grid.Row="3"
  Text="{Binding Path=AlertsManagementUrl}" VerticalAlignment="Center"/>

<ListBox Grid.ColumnSpan="2" Grid.Row="4"
  ItemsSource="{Binding Path=Alerts}" ItemTemplate="{StaticResource AlertItem}">

</ListBox>
</Grid>
</Window>
```

The code in Listing 30.3 invokes the GetAlerts method and sets the data context of the main grid to the returned value. WPF takes care of the rest.

LISTING 30.3   Window.xaml.cs for an Alerts Viewing Application

```
using System;
using System.Collections.Generic;
using System.Text;
using System.Windows;
using System.Windows.Controls;
using System.Windows.Data;
using System.Windows.Documents;
using System.Windows.Input;
using System.Windows.Media;
using System.Windows.Media.Imaging;
using System.Windows.Shapes;
```

30

LISTING 30.3   Continued

```
using ViewAlerts.spserver;


namespace ViewAlerts
{
/// <summary>
/// Interaction logic for Window1.xaml
/// </summary>

public partial class Window1 : System.Windows.Window
{

public Window1()
{
    InitializeComponent();

    Alerts alerts = new Alerts();
    alerts.Url = "http://win2k3-splab/teamsample/_vti_bin/alerts.asmx";
    alerts.Credentials =
      new System.Net.NetworkCredential(@"Administrator", "password",
      "win2k3-splab");
    AppModel model = new AppModel();
    AlertInfo alertInfo = alerts.GetAlerts();
    System.Diagnostics.Debug.WriteLine("Found " +
      alertInfo.Alerts.Length.ToString() + " alerts.");

    MainGrid.DataContext = alertInfo;

}
}
}
```

When you run the application in Listings 30.2 and 30.3 on Windows Vista, the result looks similar to the screenshot in Figure 30.2. It isn't tremendously pretty now, but with a few cleverly placed styles, it could be made into a professional looking application.

FIGURE 30.2   Viewing alerts and alert details.

Using the Versions Web Service

The Versions Web Service is another extremely powerful and often underrated web service. It gives developers the ability to query the version history of a given file. This is extremely powerful considering the new enhanced support within SharePoint for major and minor versions, workflows, and so on.

The version information returned from the web service not only gives you the version history of the file, but it provides you the uniform resource locator (URL) through which you can access *previous versions of the file*. This web service is one of the only places that SharePoint exposes that kind of information to the developer.

The code in Listing 30.4 shows how to use the Versions Web Service.

LISTING 30.4   Using the Versions Web Service

```
using System;
using System.Xml;
using System.Collections.Generic;
using System.Text;
using VersionsService.win2k3_splab;

namespace VersionsService
{
class Program
{
```

LISTING 30.4   Continued

```csharp
static void Main(string[] args)
{
    Versions vService = new Versions();
    vService.Url = "http://win2k3-splab/teamsample/_vti_bin/versions.asmx";
    vService.Credentials =
        new System.Net.NetworkCredential("Administrator", "password",
➥"win2k3-splab");
    XmlNode xmlVersions = vService.GetVersions(
        @"shared documents/test document.docx");

    XmlNode resultNode = xmlVersions.ChildNodes[3];
    foreach (XmlAttribute attribute in resultNode.Attributes)
    {
        Console.WriteLine("\t{0} : {1}", attribute.Name, attribute.Value);
    }

    Console.WriteLine("\n----");
    resultNode = xmlVersions.ChildNodes[4];
    foreach (XmlAttribute attribute in resultNode.Attributes)
    {
        Console.WriteLine("\t{0} : {1}", attribute.Name, attribute.Value);
    }
    Console.ReadLine();
}
}
}
```

When you compile and run the console application from Listing 30.4, the output should look similar to the output shown in Figure 30.3.

FIGURE 30.3   Using the Versions Web Service.

Summary

This chapter provided an overview of a few of the remaining web services not covered by previous chapters. SharePoint provides an incredible extension point and integration point for applications through its object model and through its extensive web service support. The Spell Checker, Alerts, and Versions Web Services are just a few of the many important web services available to SharePoint developers.

Index

A

accessing
    document libraries, 84
    Feature collections, 26
    lists, 206-209
        BDC data in, 59-62
        item values, 53
    site collection information, 41
    web information, 45
activating Features, 25, 29-30
Add Reference dialog box, 19
Add( ) method
    EventReceivers collection, 77
    Solutions collection, 32
    SPFeatureDefinitionCollection class, 31
    SPMeeting class, 103
AddCollegue( ) method, 308
Added property (SPSolution class), 33
AddGroup( ) method, 315
AddGroupToRole( ) method, 315
adding
    Assemblies to GAC, 181
    Global Assembly Cache, 236
    JavaScript to Web Parts, 204
    record routing rules, 370
    setup projects, 235
    Web controls to Web Parts, 199
    Web Custom Controls, 166
    Web Parts to Web Part pages, 339-341
    web references, 287
    user profiles to groups, 145
AddLink( ) method, 308
AddMeeting( ) method, 298
AddMeetingFromiCal( ) method, 299
AddMembership( ) method, 308
AddPinnedLink( ) method, 308
AddRole( ) method, 315
AddRoleDef( ) method, 315
AddUserCollectionToGroup( ) method, 315
AddUserCollectionToRole( ) method, 315
AddUserToGroup( ) method, 315
AddUserToRole( ) method, 315
AddWebPart( ) method, 338
AddWebPartToZone( ) method, 338
AddWorkflowAssociation( ) method, 55
AdventureWorks SQL database, 113
AfterProperties property
  (SPItemEventProperties class), 74
AfterUrl property (SPItemEventProperties
  class), 74

agenda fields (Meeting Workspaces), 304
alerts, viewing, 379-382
Alerts property (SPWeb class), 42
Alerts Web Service, 379-382
AlertTemplate property (SPList class), 48-49
AllowAnonymousAccess property (SPWeb class), 42
AllowContentTypes property (SPList class), 48
AllowDeletion column (lists), 275
AllowDeletion property (SPList class), 48
AllowEveryoneViewItems property (SPList class), 48
AllowMultiResponse property (UpdateList( ) method), 278
AllowMultiResponses column (lists), 275
AllowMultiResponses property (SPList class), 48
AllowRssFeeds property
    SPList class, 48
    SPSite class, 36
    SPWeb class, 42
AllowUnsafeUpdates property
    SPSite class, 36
    SPWeb class, 42
AllProperties property (SPWeb class), 42
AllUsers property (SPWeb class), 42
AllWebs property (SPSite class), 36
AlternateCssUrl property (SPWeb class), 42
AlternateHeader property (SPWeb class), 42
AlterTask( ) method, 365
AlterToDo( ) method, 360
AnonymousPermMask column (lists), 274
AnonymousState property (SPWeb class), 42
APIs (Application Programming Interfaces)
    BDC administration, 121-123
    BDC runtime, 124
        data access, 126-131
        direct method execution, 131-132
        metadata, querying, 124-126
AppearanceEditorPart control, 174
applications
    alerts viewing, 379-382
    BDC, configuring, 111-114
    console
        creating, 21-22
        deploying, 22-23
    ExcelServicesHelloWorld, 326-328
    Feature Enumerator, 29
    list items, 281-282
    ListRetriever, 276-277
    photo album browser, 267-272
    reading/writing ranges and saving
        temporary workbooks, 329-332

    remote, 18
    server, 17-18
    web
        hierarchy, 36
        site collections, listing, 35
    Windows Forms
        DocLibPicker.cs, 89-90
        Form1.cs, 86-88
ApplyTheme( ) method, 44
ApplyWebTemplate( ) method, 44
approval workflows, 148
Approve( ) method, 94
approving files, 94
architecture (Excel Services), 323
    Calculation Services, 324
    Web Access, 324
    Web service, 325
        hello world example, 326-328
        methods, 325-326
        multiple named ranges client application
            example, 328-329
        reading/writing ranges and saving temporary workbooks application, 329-332
        trusted locations, configuring, 326
ASP.NET
    server controls
        building, 166-168
        extending, 168-172
        saving to ViewState, 170-172
        user controls, compared, 163-166
    user/server control integration, 184
    Web Parts
        accessing lists, 206-209
        attributes, 194-195
        connected. See connected Web Parts
        controls, 173
        creating, 178-181
        debugging, 234
        design mode, 177
        entering data into lists, 210
        functionality, 197
        HelloWorld example, 179-180
        importing, 188
        integration, 174
        JavaScript, adding, 204
        layout, 197
        managing, 175-176
        postbacks, 203
        properties, 191-196
        providers, 217
        rendering in browsers, 199

SharePoint integration, 185-188
SharePoint Web Parts, compared, 185
SimpleLoanCalculator, 192-194
SQLExecute example, 197-203
System.Web.dll file reference, 178
template, 198-199
testing, 181-183
third-party tools, 183
time sheet list example, 205
Timesheet Entry Web Part example
  listing, 210-213
updating lists, 209-215
web controls, adding, 199
zones, 178
assemblies
adding to GAC, 181
PublicKeyToken, retrieving, 186
references, testing, 21-22
strong naming, 180
AssociateWorkflowMarkup( ) method, 338
associations
BDC entities, 110
workflows, 150
Attachments property (SPListItem class), 51
attendance (meetings), 302-303
attendee responses (meetings), 105
attributes
ConnectionConsumer, 223
ConnectionProvider, 220
Web Part properties, 194-195
Audit property
SPFolder class, 86
SPList class, 48
SPListItem class, 51
SPSite class, 36
SPWeb class, 42
authentication
BDC, 110-111
web services, 299
AuthenticationMode property (SPWeb class), 42
Author column (lists), 274
Author property
SPFile class, 84
SPWeb class, 42
**AvailableContentTypes property (SPWeb
class), 42**

B

BackColor property (TextBox class), 168
BaseTemplate property (SPList class), 48

Basetype column (lists), 274
BaseType property (SPList class), 48
batch file for installation, 158-159
BDC (Business Data Catalog), 59, 109, 347
administration API, 121-123
applications, 111-114
authentication, 110-111
benefits, 111
columns in custom lists, 118-119
compatible web services, 132
disadvantages, 111
entities, 110
  actions, 117-118
  associations, 110
  enumerating, 350-351
  finding, 117, 126-132
  methods, 110
Field Resolver Web Service, 355-356
fields, enumerating, 355-356
filter descriptors, enumerating, 354
ID enumerators, 110
Line of Business system
  enumerating, 349
  properties, 348
lists, 59-62
metadata, querying, 124-126
methods
  enumerating, 352-353
  instances, 351
overview, 347-348
relational data, exposing, 133
runtime API, 124
  data access, 126-131
  direct method execution, 131-132
  metadata, querying, 124-126
Web Parts, 114-116
Web Service, 348
  entities, enumerating, 350-351
  filter descriptors, enumerating, 354
  Line of Business systems, 348-349
  methods, 351-353
**BeforeProperties property
  (SPItemEventProperties class), 74**
**BeforeUrl property (SPItemEventProperties
  class), 74**
BehaviorEditorPart control, 174
binary representations (files), 94
breakpoints (Web Parts), 231-233
BreakRoleInheritance( ) method
SPList class, 55
SPListItem class, 57

btnExecuteSQL control, 202
building
    BDC compatible web services, 132
    consumer Web Parts, 221-223
    document library explorer, 86
        DocLibPicker.cs, 89-90
        Form1.cs, 86-88
    provider Web Parts, 217
        data interface, 218
        Web Part, creating, 21-220
    server controls, 166-168
    workflows, 150
        designing forms, 151-153
        modeling, 153-155
        typical roadmap, 150
built-in style sheets, 213
Business Data Actions Web Part, 114
Business Data Catalog. See BDC
Business Data Item Builder Web Part, 115
Business Data Item List Web Part, 114
Business Data Item Web Part, 114
Business Data Related List Web Part, 115

C

Calculate( ) method (Excel Services Web
  Services), 325
CalculateA-1( ) method (Excel Services Web
  Service), 325
CalculateWorkbook( ) method (Excel Services
  Web Service), 325
calendar events, 105
CAML (Collaborative Application Markup
  Language), 5
    comparison operators, 6
    FieldRef extraction utility, 7-8
    list items, querying, 8-11, 62-64, 287-288
    queries, creating, 6
    U2U CAML Query Builder, 11
Cancel( ) method, 104
Cancel property
    SPItemEventProperties class, 74
    SPListEventProperties class, 71
CancelRequest( ) method, 325
CanCreateDwsUrl( ) method, 242
CanReceiveEmail property (SPList class), 48
CatalogZone control, 173, 178
CatchAccessDeniedException property (SPSite
  class), 36
CertificationDate property (SPSite class), 36

change log query for user profiles, 140-142
change tokens (user profiles), 314
CheckedOutBy property (SPFile class), 84
CheckedOutDate property (SPFile class), 84
CheckForPermissions( ) method, 38
CheckIn( ) method, 91, 94
CheckInComment property (SPFile class), 84
checking in/out files, 91-94
CheckOut( ) method, 91, 94
CheckOutExpires property (SPFile class), 84
CheckOutStatus property (SPFile class), 84
CheckSubWebAndList( ) method, 257
child/parent relationships (lists), 64
    content types, creating, 65
    hierarchical, traversing, 66-67
choice list properties (user profiles), 144
claiming workflow tasks, 366
ClaimReleaseTask( ) method, 360, 366
classes
    document libraries, 84
    ExpandingTextBox, 170
    Features, 26
    GenericWebPart, 184
    ListMetaLogger, 72-73
    MembershipManager, 145
    object model, 16
    ProfilePropertyCollection, 143
    SPChangeToken, 314
    SPContext, 21
    SPEventReceiverBase, 70
    SPFarm, 27-29
    SPFeatureDefinitionCollection, 31
    SPFile
        CheckIn( ) method, 91
        CheckOut( ) method, 91
        methods, 94
        properties, 84-85
        SaveBinary( ) method, 93
        submitting files to records repositories,
          373-374
    SPFolder
        methods, 94
        properties, 86
    SPItemEventProperties, 74
    SPItemEventReceiver, 69
    SPList
        enumerating lists, 50-51
        methods, 55
        properties, 48-50
    SPListEventProperties, 71
    SPListEventReceiver, 70

SPListItem
   list contents, viewing, 52
   list item values, accessing, 53
   methods, 57
   properties, 51
   Update method, 214
SPMeeting, 99
   Add( ) method, 103
   Cancel( ) method, 104
   LinkWithEvent( ) method, 105
   SetAttendeeResponse( ) method, 105
   Update( ) method, 104-105
SPSite, 35-36
   accessing site collection information, 41
   creating site collections, 39-41
   Features property, 27
   instance of, creating, 27-29
   methods, 38
   properties, 36-38
   updating site collections, 42
SPSiteCollection, 35-36
SPSolution, 32
   deploy methods, 34
   properties, 33
SPWeb, 36, 42
   accessing webs information, 45
   creating webs, 44-45
   Delete method, 99
   Features property, 27
   methods, 44
   properties, 42-43
   updating webs, 46
SPWebApplication, 35-36
SPWebPartManager, 185
SPWorkflow, 365
TextBox, 166
UserProfileManager, 135, 143
WebControl, 166
WebPart, 185
WebPartManager
   static connection properties, 224
   Web Parts, connecting, 223
WebPartZone, 185
Close( ) method
   SPSite class, 38
   SPWeb class, 44
CloseWorkbook( ) method, 325
coding workflows, 155-156
Collaborative Application Markup Language.
  See CAML

collections
   EventReceivers, 77
   Features, 26
   Solutions, 32
   SPFeaturePropertyCollection, 30
columns
   custom BDC lists, 118-119
   lists, 274-275
   Meeting Series, 300
comparison operators (CAML), 6
Compatibility( ) method, 338
compiling setup projects, 237
compliance. See records repositories
configuring
   BDC applications, 111-114
   development environment, 18-19
      local, 19-20
      remote, 20-21
   domain-level trusts, 151
   Excel Services trusted locations, 326
   feature.xml file, 156-157
   install.bat file, 158-159
   Records Center connections, 370
   setup projects, 236
   workflow.xml file, 157
ConfirmUsage( ) method, 38
connected Web Parts
   connecting, 223-226
   consumers, 221-223
   providers, 217-220
ConnectionConsumer attribute (SetCustomer( )
   method), 223
ConnectionProvider attribute (GetCustomerID( )
   method), 220
console applications
   creating, 21-22
   deploying, 22-23
consumer Web Parts, 221-226
ConsumerConnectionPoint property
   (WebPartManager class), 224
ConsumerID property (WebPartManager
   class), 224
ContainingDocumentLibrary property (SPFolder
   class), 86
Contains element, 6
ContainsCasPolicy property (SPSolution class), 33
ContainsGlobalAssembly property (SPSolution
   class), 33
ContainsWebApplicationResource property
   (SPSolution class), 33

content types
    creating, 65
    event receivers, deploying, 81
    hierarchical list items, querying, 283-285
    Order Item, 65
    Order Parent, 65
ContentDatabase property (SPSite class), 36
ContentType property (SPListItem class), 51
ContentTypes property
    SPList class, 48
    SPWeb class, 42
ContentTypesEnabled property (SPList class), 48
Context property (SPItemEventProperties
    class), 74
controls
    server, 184
        ASP.NET integration, 184
        building, 166-168
        extending, 168-172
        saving to ViewState, 170-172
        user controls, compared, 163-166
    SQLExecute Web Part, 202
    user
        ASP.NET integration, 184
        information collection user control, 164-
            165
        server controls, compared, 163-166
    Web Part, 173
        adding, 199
        CatalogZone, 178
        WebPartManager, 175-176
        WebPartZones, 178
Convert( ) method, 94
converting files, 94
ConvertWebPartFormat( ) method, 338
Copy( ) method, 57
CopyDestinations property (SPListItem class), 51
copying files/folders, 94
CopyTo( ) method, 94
core objects, 207
CorrelationToken property, 155
Create( ) method, 143
Create New Item interface, 210
Create, Retrieve, Update, and Delete (CRUD), 274
CreateChildControls( ) method, 199, 202-203
Created column (lists), 274
Created property
    SPList class, 48
    SPWeb class, 42
CreateDws( ) method, 242
CreateMemberGroup( ) method, 308
CreateNewFolder( ) method, 257, 263-264

CreateUserProfile( ) method, 143
CreateUserProfileByAccountName( ) method, 308
CRUD (Create, Retrieve, Update, and Delete), 274
Current property (SPContext object), 207
CurrentChangeToken property
    SPList class, 48
    SPSite class, 36
CurrentUser( ) method, 315
CurrentUser property (SPWeb class), 43
CurrentUserId property (SPItemEventProperties
    class), 74
CustomerID property (ISelectedCustomer inter-
    face), 218
customizing. See modifying

D

data entry (lists), 210
DataSourceControl( ) method, 338
DateRangesOverlap element, 6
deactivating Features, 29-30
DeadWebNotificationCount property (SPSite
    class), 37
debugging Web Parts, 229-230
    breakpoints, setting, 231-233
    common SharePoint server, 234
    development workstations, 229-230
    local SharePoint server, 234
    Visual Studio 2005, 230-231
    Web Part library, compiling, 231
    without SharePoint or WSS, 233
decision fields (Meeting Workspaces), 304
DeclarativeCatalogPart control, 174
DefaultItemOpen property (SPList class), 48
DefaultView property (SPList class), 48
DefaultViewUrl column (lists), 274
DefaultViewUrl property (SPList class), 48
Delete( ) method
    Imaging Web Service, 257, 263
    SPFile class, 94
    SPFolder class, 94
    SPList class, 55
    SPListItem class, 57
    SPSite class, 38
    SPWeb class, 44, 99
DeleteWebPart( ) method, 338
DeleteWorkspace( ) method, 297
deleting
    Document Workspaces, 243-244, 248
    Feature definitions, 31
    files, 94

folders, 94
images, 263
list items, 56-57, 281-282
lists, 53-55
Meeting Workspaces, 296-297
meetings, 104, 300-301
Solutions, 32
views, 289
Deny( ) method, 94
denying files, 94
Deploy( ) method, 34
Deployed property (SPSolution class), 33
DeployedServers property (SPSolution class), 33
DeployedWebApplications property (SPSolution class), 33
deploying
   console application, 22-23
   event receivers
      content types, 81
      Features, 77-79
      programmatically, 77
   Solutions, 34
   Web Parts, 235
      compiling setup project, 237
      configuring setup project, 236
      MSI-based, 235
      setup projects, adding, 235
   workflows, 156-159
DeploymentState property (SPSolution class), 33
Description column (lists), 274
Description property
   SPList class, 48
   SPWeb class, 43
   UpdateList( ) method, 278
designing workflow forms, 151-153
development environment
   configuring, 18-19
   local, 19-20
   remote, 20-21
Direction column (lists), 274
Direction property
   SPList class, 48
   UpdateList( ) method, 278
DisplayName property (SPListItem class), 51
Dispose( ) method, 38
DocLibPicker.cs Windows Forms application, 89-90
DocTemplates property (SPWeb class), 43
DocTemplateUrl column (lists), 274
document libraries
   accessing, 84
   classes, 84

documents, 84
explorer, building, 86
   DocLibPicker.cs, 89-90
   Form1.cs, 86-88
overview, 83
SPFile class, 84-85
SPFolder class, 86
uploading documents, 84
Document Workspaces
   creating, 242-244
   data, retrieving, 244-246
   deleting, 243-244
   document ID storage, 251-252
   folders, 248
   metadata, retrieving, 246-247
   overview, 241
   URLs, validating, 242
   users, managing, 253
documents
   uploading to document libraries, 84
   versioning, 91-93
DoesUserHavePermissions( ) method
   SPList class, 55
   SPListItem class, 57
   SPSite class, 38
domain-level trusts, 151
Download( ) method, 257, 262
downloading images to picture libraries, 262
DraftVersionVisibility property (SPList class), 48

E

ECS (Excel Calculation Services), 324
Edit in DataSheet interface, 210
EditorZone control, 174
elements
   Contains, 6
   DateRangesOverlap, 6
   Eq, 6
   FieldRef, 6-8
   Geq, 6
   IsNotNull, 6
   IsNull, 6
   Leq, 6
   Lt, 6
   Neq, 6
Elements.xml file, 78-79
EmailAlias column (lists), 275
EmailAlias property (SPList class), 48
EmailInsertsFolder column (lists), 275
EnableAssignedToEmail property (UpdateList( ) method), 278

EnableAttachments column (lists), **275**
EnableAttachments property
   SPList class, 49
   UpdateList( ) method, 278
EnableFolderCreation property (SPList class), **49**
EnableMinorVersions property (SPList class), **49**
EnableMinorVersoin column (lists), **275**
EnableModeration column (lists), **275**
EnableModeration property
   SPList class, 49
   UpdateList( ) method, 278
EnableVersioning column (lists), **275**
EnableVersioning property
   SPList class, 49
   UpdateList( ) method, 278
entities
   BDC, 110
      actions, 117-118
      associations, 110
      finding, 117, 126-132
      methods, 110
   LOB, enumerating, 350-351
EntityStruct struct, **350**
enumerating
   Feature definitions lists, 27-29
   Features, 27-29
   fields, 355-356
   filter descriptors, 354
   Line of Business systems, 349
   lists, 48-51
      contents, 51-53
      item values, 53
   LOB system entities, 350-351
   methods, 352-353
   picture libraries, 258
   Solutions, 32-33
Eq element, **6**
ErrorMessage property
   SPItemEventProperties class, 74
   SPListEventProperties class, 71
Event property (SPList class), **49**
EventReceivers collection, **77**
EventReceivers property
   SPFile class, 85
   SPWeb class, 43
events
   calendar, 105
   handlers, 69
   lists, 71, 75
   receivers
      creating, 70
      deploying, 77-81
      lists, 70-76

EventSinkAssembly column (lists), **275**
EventSinkClass column (lists), **275**
EventSinkData column (lists), **275**
EventType property
   SPItemEventProperties class, 74
   SPListEventProperties class, 71
EWA (Excel Web Access), **324**
Excel Services
   application logic, 322
   architecture, 323-325
   business intelligence, 322
   Calculation Services (ECS), 324
   overview, 322
   user-defined functions, creating, 332-335
   user-defined libraries, 334
   Web Services, 325
      hello world example, 326-328
      methods, 325-326
      multiple named ranges client application
         example, 328-329
      reading/writing ranges and saving tem-
         porary workbooks application, 329-332
      trusted locations, configuring, 326
   workbook management, 322
Excel Web Access (EWA), **324**
ExcelServicesHelloWorld application, **326-328**
ExecuteProxyUpdates( ) method, **338**
Exists( ) method, **38**
Exists property
   SPFile class, 85
   SPFolder class, 86
expanding TextBox control listing, **169-170**
ExpandingTextBox class, **170**
extending server controls, **168-172**
extracting fields from lists, **7-8**

F

Feature definitions, **30**
   compared, 27
   deleting, 31
   enumerating, 27-29
   installing, 31
   properties, 30-31
Feature Enumerator application, **29**
Feature.xml file, **78, 156-157**
FeatureDefinitions property (SPFarm class), **27**
FeatureId column (lists), **274**
Features
   activating/deactivating, 25, 29-30
   classes, 26
   collections, accessing, 26

defined, 25
enumerating, 27-29
packaging, 26
properties, 30-31
Features property
SPSite class, 27, 37
SPWeb class, 27, 43
FetchLegalWorkflowActions( ) method, 338
Field property (SPListEventProperties class), 71
FieldAdded event, 71
FieldAdding event, 71
FieldDeleted event, 71
FieldDeleting event, 71
**FieldName property (SPListEventProperties
class), 71**
FieldRef element, 6
FieldRef extraction utility, 7-8
fields (lists), 7-8
Fields property
SPList class, 49
SPListItem class, 51
FieldUpdated event, 71
FieldUpdating event, 71
**FieldXml property (SPListEventProperties
class), 71**
File property (SPListItem class), 51
files
approving, 94
binary representation, 94
checking in/out, 91-94
converting, 94
copying, 94
deleting, 94
denying, 94
Elements.xml, 78-79
feature.xml, 78, 156-157
install.bat, 158-159
moving, 94
Program.cs, 21-22
publishing, 94
restoring to checked-in state, 94
saving, 94
sending to Recycle Bin, 94
submitting to records repositories, 373-374
System.Web.dll, 178
taking offline, 94
transform states, 94
updating, 94
workflow.xml, 157
Files property
SPFolder class, 86
SPWeb class, 43

filters
descriptors, 354
Finders, 128-129
lists, 287-288
FindDwsDoc( ) method, 251
finding BDC entities, 117
direct method execution, 131-132
filter Finders, 128-129
specific Finders, 126-128
wildcard Finders, 130-131
Flags column (lists), 274
Folder property (SPListItem class), 51
folders
copying, 94
deleting, 94
Document Workspace, 248
Global Assembly Cache, 236
moving, 94
picture libraries, 263-264
sending to Recycle Bin, 94
updating, 94
Folders property
SPList class, 49
SPWeb class, 43
Form1.cs Windows Forms application, 86-88
Forms property (SPList class), 49

G

GenericWebPart class, 184
Geq element, 6
GetAlerts( ) method, 381
GetAllChanges( ) method, 314
GetAllUserCollectionFromWeb( ) method, 315
GetApiVersion( ) method, 325
GetAssemblyMetaData( ) method, 338
GetBindingResourceData( ) method, 338
GetCatalog( ) method
SPSite class, 38
SPWeb class, 44
GetCell( ) method, 325
GetCellA1( ) method, 325
GetChanges( ) method
SPList class, 55
SPWeb class, 44
User Profile Web Change Web Service, 314
GetCommonColleagues( ) method, 308
GetCommonManager( ) method
MembershipManager class, 145
User Profile Web Service, 308

GetCommonMemberships( ) method
   MembershipManager class, 145
   User Profile Web Service, 308
GetConversionState( ) method, 94
GetConvertedFile( ) method, 94
GetCurrentChangeToken( ) method, 314
GetCustomControlList( ) method, 338
GetCustomerID( ) method, 220
GetCustomListTemplates( ) method, 38
GetCustomWebTemplates( ) method, 38
GetDataFromDataSourceControl( ) method, 338
GetDocDiscussions( ) method, 44
GetDwsData( ) method, 244-246
GetDwsMetaData( ) method, 246-247
GetFile( ) method, 44
GetFolder( ) method, 44
GetFormCapabilityFrom( ) method, 338
GetGroupCollection( ) method, 315
GetGroupCollectionFromRole( ) method, 315
GetGroupCollectionFromSite( ) method, 315
GetGroupCollectionFromUser( ) method, 315
GetGroupCollectionFromWeb( ) method, 315
GetGroupInfo( ) method, 315
GetInCommon( ) method, 309
GetItemById( ) method, 55
GetItemByUniqueId( ) method, 55
GetItems( ) method, 55
GetItemsByIds( ) method, 257, 260
GetItemsXMLData( ) method, 257, 260
GetList( ) method, 44
GetListFromUrl( ) method, 44
GetListItem( ) method, 44
GetListItems( ) method, 257-258
GetListsOfType( ) method, 44
GetPropertyChoiceList( ) method, 309
GetRange( ) method, 325
GetRangeA1( ) method, 325
GetRecycleBinItems( ) method
   SPSite class, 38
   SPWeb class, 44
GetRecycleBinStatistics( ) method, 38
GetRoleCollection( ) method, 315
GetRoleCollectionFromGroup( ) method, 315
GetRoleCollectionFromUser( ) method, 315
GetRoleCollectionFromWeb( ) method, 315
GetRoleInfo( ) method, 315
GetRolesAndPermissionsFor( ) method, 315
GetSafeAssemblyInfo( ) method, 338, 345
GetServerInfo( ) method, 376
GetSessionInforamtion( ) method, 325
GetSiteData( ) method, 44

GetTemplatesForItem( ) method, 360, 366
GetToDosForItem( ) method, 360
GetUsageData( ) method, 44
GetUserAllChanges( ) method, 314
GetUserChanges( ) method, 314
GetUserColleagues( ) method, 309
GetUserCollection( ) method, 315
GetUserCollectionFromGroup( ) method, 315
GetUserCollectionFromRole( ) method, 315
GetUserCollectionFromSite( ) method, 315
GetUserCollectionFromWeb( ) method, 315
GetUserCurrentChangeToken( ) method, 314
GetUserInfo( ) method, 316
GetUserLinks( ) method, 309
GetUserLoginFromEmail( ) method, 316
GetUserMemberships( ) method, 309
GetUserPinnedLinks( ) method, 309
GetUserProfileByGuid( ) method, 309
GetUserProfileByIndex( ) method, 309
GetUserProfileByName( ) method, 309
GetUserProfileSchema( ) method, 309
GetView( ) method, 55
GetWebPart( ) method, 338, 344
GetWebPart2( ) method, 338
GetWebPartCrossPage( ) method, 338
GetWebPartPage( ) method, 338
GetWebPartPageConnectionInfo( ) method, 338
GetWebPartPageDocument( ) method, 338
GetWebPartProperties( ) method, 338
GetWebPartProperties2( ) method, 338
GetWebTemplates( ) method, 38
GetWorkbook( ) method, 325
GetWorkflowDataForItem( ) method, 360
GetWorkflowTaskData( ) method, 360
GetXmlDataFromDataSource( ) method, 338
Global Assembly Cache
   assemblies, adding, 181
   folders, adding, 236
   verifying, 237
groups
   security principles, enumerating, 316-318
   User Group Web Service, 315-316
   user profiles, adding, 145
Groups property (SPWeb class), 43
gvResults control, 202

H

HasPublishedVersion property (SPListItem
   class), 51
HasUniqueScopes column (lists), 275

hello world Excel Services example, 326-328
HelloWorld Web Part, 179-180
HelloWorldSequentialWorkflow Assembly
    features.xml file, 156-157
    install.bat file, 158-159
    workflow designer, 155
    workflow.xml file, 157
Hidden column (lists), 275
Hidden property
    SPList class, 49
    UpdateList method, 278
hierarchical list items, querying, 283-285
hierarchy
    lists, 64-67, 206
    site collections, 36
    web applications, 36
    websites, 36
HostHeaderIsSiteName property (SPSite class), 37
HTML (Hypertext Markup Language), 213

I

IconUrl property (SPFile class), 85
ID enumerators, 110
ID property
    SPListItem class, 51
    SPSolution class, 33
    SPWeb class, 43
    WebPartManager class, 224
IDs
    document ID storage, 251-252
    picture library images, retrieving, 260
IISAllowsAnonymous property (SPSite class), 37
images (picture libraries)
    deleting, 263
    downloading, 262
    photo browser example, 266-272
    renaming, 263
    retrieving from
        IDs, 260
        lists, 258-260
        XML data, 260-261
    uploading, 261-262
ImageUrl column (lists), 274
ImageUrl property (SPList class), 49
Imaging Web Service, 256-257, 266-272
Impersonating property (SPSite class), 37
ImportCatalogPart control, 174
importing Web Parts, 188
InDocumentLibrary property (SPFile class), 85

InfoPath, 152
information collection user control, 164-165
install.bat file, 158-159
installing
    Feature definitions, 31
    Solutions, 32
    WF templates, 147-148
instances (workflows), 150
interfaces
    Create New Item, 210
    Edit in DataSheet, 210
    IPostBackDataHandler, 170-172
    ISelectedCustomer, 218-220
    provider Web Part data interface, 218
IPostBackDataHandler interface, 170-172
ISelectedCustomer interface, 218-220
IsIRMed property (SPFile class), 85
IsNotNull element, 6
IsNull element, 6
IsRootWeb property (SPWeb class), 43
IsWebPartPackage property (SPSolution class), 33
Item property
    SPFile class, 85
    SPFolder class, 86
ItemAdded event, 75
ItemAdding event, 75
ItemAttachmentAdded event, 75
ItemAttachmentAdding event, 75
ItemAttachmentDeleted event, 75
ItemAttachmentDeleting event, 75
ItemCheckedIn event, 75
ItemCheckedOut event, 75
ItemCheckingIn event, 75
ItemCheckingOut event, 75
ItemCount column (lists), 274
ItemCount property (SPList class), 49
ItemDeleted event, 75
ItemDeleting event, 75
ItemFileConverted event, 75
ItemFileMoved event, 75
ItemFileMoving event, 75
items (lists)
    creating, 56-57, 281-282
    deleting, 56-57, 281-282
    event receivers, creating, 73-76
    events, 75
    filtering, 287-288
    hierarchical
        querying, 283-285
        traversing, 66-67

querying, 62-64
retrieving, 275-277
revision control, 286
updating, 56-57, 281-282
values, accessing, 53
Items property (SPList class), 49
ItemUncheckedOut event, 75
ItemUncheckingOut event, 75
ItemUpdated event, 75
ItemUpdating event, 75

J–K

JavaScript, 204

KPIs (Key Performance Indicators), 322

L

Language property (SPWeb class), 43
LastContentModifiedDate property (SPSite class), 37
LastDeleted column (lists), 274
LastItemDeletedDate property (SPList class), 49
LastItemModifiedDate property (SPList class), 49
LastOperationDetails property (SPSolution class), 33
LastOperationEndTime property (SPSolution class), 33
LastOperationResult property (SPSolution class), 33
LastSecurityModifiedDate property (SPSite class), 37
layout (Web Parts), 197
LayoutEditorPart control, 174
lblError control, 202
Length property (SPFile class), 85
LengthByUser property (SPFile class), 85
Leq element, 6
Level property (SPFile class), 85
libraries
document
accessing, 84
classes, 84
explorer, building, 86-90
overview, 83
SPFile class properties, 84-85
SPFolder class properties, 86
uploading documents, 84

picture, 94, 255-256
deleting images, 263
downloading images, 262
enumerating, 258
folders, creating, 263-264
Imaging Web Service, 256-257
photo browser example, 266-272
renaming images, 263
retrieving images, 258-261
uploading images, 261-262
Unclassified Records, 370, 375
user-defined, 334
Line of Business systems
entities, 350-351
enumerating, 349
properties, 348
LinkWithEvent( ) method, 105
.List object, 207
List property (SPListEventProperties class), 71
ListId property
SPItemEventProperties class, 74
SPListEventProperties class, 71
listings
alerts viewing application, 379-382
BDC
data in lists, accessing, 60
Field Resolver Web Service, 355-356
metadata, querying, 125
consumer Web Part, 221-222
document library explorer
DocLibPicker.cs, 89-90
Form1.cs, 86-88
Document Workspaces
creating/deleting, 243-244
document ID storage, 251-252
Elements.xml file, 78-79
Excel Services user-defined functions example, 333-334
ExcelServicesHelloWorld application, 326-328
expanding TextBox control, 169-170
feature.xml file, 78, 156-157
Features and Feature Definitions, enumerating, 27-29
filter descriptors, enumerating, 354
finding BDC entities
direct method execution, 131-132
filter Finders, 128-129
specific Finders, 127-128
wildcard Finders, 130-131
GetDwsData method, 244-245

HelloWorld Web Part, 179-180
information collection user control, 164-165
install.bat file, configuring, 158-159
IPostBackDataHandler interface
  implementation, 170-172
Line of Business systems, 349-351
list items
    creating/deleting, 281-282
    event receiver, 72-76
    hierarchical, querying, 284-285
    hierarchical, traversing, 66
    manipulation, 54-56
    querying, 62-63
    updating, 281-282
    values, accessing, 53
ListRetriever application, 276-277
LOB system and entity, creating, 122-123
Meeting Workspaces, creating, 98
meetings, creating, 102-103
methods, enumerating, 352-353
numeric textbox server control, 167-168
Official File Web Service, querying, 374
photo album browser application, 267-272
Program.cs file for testing Assembly
  references, 21-22
provider Web Part, 219-220
reading/writing ranges and saving
  temporary workbooks, 329-332
SDK sample DWS utility methods, 249-250
SimpleLoanCalculator Web Part, 192-194
Spell Checker Web Service, 378
SQLExecute Web Part, 199-202
submitting files to records repositories with
  SPFile class, 373
Timesheet Entry Web Part, 210-213
user profiles
    change history, 312-313
    change log query, 140-142
    properties, retrieving, 137-138, 310-311
    retrieving, 136-137
versioning example, 91-93
Versions Web Service, 383
Web Parts
    adding to Web Part pages, 339-341
    connecting, 225-226
    debugging, 230-231
    list access, 208-209
    Manager, 175-176
    pages, querying, 344-345
    template, 198-199
    updating, 342-343

workflow tasks, retrieving, 362-363
workflow.xml file, configuring, 157
WPF data binding to data from User Group
  Web Service, 316-318
ListItem property (SPItemEventProperties
  class), 74
ListItemId property (SPItemEventProperties
  class), 74
ListItems property (SPListItem class), 51
ListMetaLogger class, 72-73
ListPictureLibrary( ) method, 257-258
ListRetriever application, 276-277
lists
    accessing, 206-209
    BDC
        custom, columns, 118-119
        data, accessing, 59-62
    columns, 274-275
    contents, viewing, 51-53
    creating, 53-55
    data entry, 210
    deleting, 53-55
    enumerating, 48-51
    events, 71
        handlers, 69
        receivers, 70-73
    fields, extracting, 7-8
    hierarchy, 206
    items
        creating, 56-57, 281-282
        deleting, 56-57, 281-282
        event receivers, creating, 73-76
        events, 75
        filtering, 287-288
        hierarchical, querying, 283-285
        hierarchical, traversing, 66-67
        querying, 62-64
        retrieving, 275-277
        revision control, 286
        updating, 56-57, 281-282
        values, accessing, 53
    lookup data, 58
    managing, 47
    manipulation listing, 54
    Meeting Series, 100-101
    Meeting Workspaces, 100, 304
    parent/child relationships
        content types, creating, 65
        creating, 64
        hierarchical list, traversing, 66-67
    picture library images, retrieving, 258-260

querying, 8-11
retrieving, 275-277
schema changing code, testing, 279
schemas, 277
Site Feature, 79
templates, 80
updating, 53-55, 209-210-215
  cautions, 214
  data entry functionality, 213
  Lists Web Service, 278-281
  Timesheet Entry Web Part example, 210-213
views, 289
Web Part property values, selecting, 195-196
Lists property
SPList class, 49
SPWeb class, 43
Lists Web Service, lists, 273
creating, 281-282
deleting, 281-282
filtering, 287-288
hierarchical, querying, 283-285
retrieving, 275-277
revision control, 286
updating, 278-282
ListTemplates property (SPWeb class), 43
ListTitle property
SPItemEventProperties class, 74
SPListEventProperties class, 71
LoadPostBackData( ) method, 170-172
LOB system and entity, creating, 122-123
LobSystemInstanceStruct structure properties, 348
local development environment, 19-20
Locale property (SPWeb class), 43
lookup data (lists), 58
Lt element, 6

M

MajorVersion property (SPFile class), 85
MajorVersionLimit column (lists), 275
MajorVersionLimit property (SPList class), 49
MajorwithMinorVersionLimit column (lists), 275
MajorWithMinorVersionsLimit property (SPList class), 49
MakeFullUrl( ) method, 38
managing
Document Workspace users, 253
Excel workbooks, 322

lists, 47
Web Parts, 175-176
MasterUrl property (SPWeb class), 43
Meeting Series columns, 300
Meeting Series list, 100-101
Meeting Workspaces, 291
available, listing, 293-294
creating, 97-98, 295-296
deleting, 296-297
details, modifying, 297
lists, 100
Meeting Series list, 100-101
meetings
  attendance, 302-303
  attendee responses, 105
  calendar events, linking, 105
  creating, 102-104, 298-299
  deleting, 104, 300-301
  lists, 304
  modifying, 104
  restoring, 302
  updating, 301
sites, creating, 292
templates, 295
meetings
attendance, 302-303
attendee responses, 105
calendar events, linking, 105
creating, 102-104, 298-299
deleting, 104, 300-301
lists, 304
modifying, 104
recurring, 101
restoring, 302
updating, 301
MembershipManager class
GetCommonManager( ) method, 145
GetCommonMemberships( ) method, 145
metadata
BDC, 124-126
Document Workspace, 246-247
methods
Add( )
  EventReceivers collection, 77
  Solutions collection, 32
  SPFeatureDefinitionCollection class, 31
  SPMeeting class, 103
AddMeetingFromiCal( ), 299
AlterTask( ), 365
BDC entities, 110
Cancel( ), 104
CanCreateDwsUrl( ), 242

CheckIn( ), 91
CheckOut( ), 91
ClaimReleaseTask( ), 366
Create( ), 143
CreateChildControls( ), 199, 202-203
CreateDws( ), 242
CreateUserProfile( ), 143
ddMeeting( ), 298
Delete( ), 99
DeleteWorkspce( ), 297
Deploy( ), 34
enumerating, 352-353
Excel Services Web Service, 325-326
FindDwsDoc( ), 251
GetAlerts( ), 381
GetCommonManager( ), 145
GetCommonMemberships( ), 145
GetCustomerID( ), 220
GetDwsData( ), 244-246
GetDwsMetaData( ), 246-247
GetSafeAssemblyInfo( ), 345
GetServerInfo( ), 376
GetTemplatesForItem( ), 366
GetWebPart( ), 344
Imaging Web Service, 256
instance structures (BDC), 351
LinkWithEvent( ), 105
LoadPostBackData( ), 170-172
PostBacks( ), 170-172
RaisePostDataChangedEvent( ), 170-172
Remove( ), 32
RemoveDwsUser( ), 253
RemoveMeeting( ), 300
Render( )
    ExpandingTextBox class, 170
    Web Parts, 199
Resolve( ), 356
RestoreMeeting( ), 302
Retract( ), 34
SaveBinary( ), 93
SendToOfficialFile( ), 373
SetAttendeeResponse( ), 105
SetCustomer( ), 223
SetWorkspaceTitle( ), 297
SpellCheck( ), 378
SPFile class, 94
SPFolder class, 94
SPList( ), 55
SPList class, 55
SPListItem class, 57
SPSite class, 38
SPWeb class, 44

StartWorkflow( ), 367
SubmitFile( ), 375
Update( )
    SPListItem class, 214
    SPMeeting class, 104-105
UpdateList( ), 278
UpdateMeetingFromICal( ), 301
User Group Web Services, 315-316
User Profile Web Change Web Service,
    312-314
User Profile Web Services, 308-309
Web Part Pages Web Service, 337-339
MethodStruct structure, 351
Microsoft Office SharePoint Server (MOSS), 15
Microsoft.Office.Server namespace, 16
Microsoft.SharePoint namespace, 16
MinorVersion property (SPFile class), 85
MobileDefaultViewUrl property (SPList class), 49
modeling workflows, 153-155
Modified column (lists), 274
modifying
    list data, 213-215
    Meeting Workspace details, 297
    meetings, 104
    records centers, 372
    user profiles, 140
    Web Parts. *See also* properties, Web Parts
        JavaScript, adding, 204
        postbacks, 203
        rendering in browsers, 199
        SQLExecute example, 199-203
        template, 198-199
        web controls, 199
    workflow tasks, 365-366
ModifyUserPropertyByAccountName( )
    method, 309
MOSS (Microsoft Office SharePoint Server), 15
MoveTo( ) method, 94
moving files/folders, 94
MSI-based Web Part deployment, 235
MulitpleDataList column (lists), 275
MultipleDataList property
    SPList class, 49
    UpdateList( ) method, 279
multivalued properties, 144

N

Name column (lists), 274
Name property
    SPFile class, 85
    SPFolder class, 86

SPListItem class, 51
SPSolution class, 33
SPWeb class, 43
naming images, 263
Navigation property (SPWeb class), 43
Neq element, 6
NoCrawl property (SPList class), 49
Northwind database, 219-220
numeric textbox server control, 167-168

O

object models
   applications on the server, developing, 17-18
   BDC
      administration, 121-123
      runtime. See BDC, runtime API
   classes, 16
   console application
      creating, 21-22
      deploying, 22-23
   document libraries support, 84
   Features
      activating/deactivating, 29-30
      classes, 26
      collections, accessing, 26
      enumerating, 27-29
      Feature definitions, 27-31
      properties, 30-31
   namespaces, 16
   remote applications, developing, 18
   Solutions
      deleting, 32
      deploying, 34
      enumerating, 32-33
      installing, 32
   user profiles
      change log history query, 140-142
      common data, retrieving, 145-146
      creating, 143
      groups, adding, 145
      modifying, 140
      properties, 143-144
      property retrieval, 137-139
      retrieving, 135-137
   Web Parts, developing, 18
objective fields (Meeting Workspaces), 304
objects
   core, 207
   .List, 207
   .Site, 207

SPContext, 207-209
SPFeatureProperty, 30
SPQuery, 7
.Web, 207
Official File Web Service
   querying, 374-375
   record repositories, creating, 375-376
   Records Center, 370
offline files, 94
OpenBinary( ) method, 94
OpenWeb( ) method, 38
OpenWorkbook( ) method, 325
Order Item content type, 65
Order Parent content type, 65
Ordered column (lists), 275
Ordered property (UpdateList( ) method), 279
Owner property (SPSite class), 37

P

packaging Features, 26
PageCatalogPart control, 174
parent/child relationships (lists), 64
   content types, creating, 65
   hierarchical list, traversing, 66-67
ParentFolder property
   SPFile class, 85
   SPFolder class, 86
ParentList property (SPListItem class), 51
ParentListId property (SPFolder class), 86
ParentWeb property
   SPFolder class, 86
   SPList class, 49
   SPWeb class, 43
ParentWebUrl property (SPList class), 49
Passthrough authentication mode (BDC), 110
Personalization attribute, 194
photo album browser application, 267-272
photos. See images
picture libraries, 94, 255-256
   enumerating, 258
   folders, creating, 263-264
   images
      deleting, 263
      downloading, 262
      renaming, 263
      retrieving, 258-261
      uploading, 261-262
   Imaging Web Service, 256-257
   photo browser example, 266-272
Port property (SPSite class), 37

PortalMember property (SPWeb class), **43**
PortalName property (SPWeb class), **43**
PortalSubscription property (SPWeb class), **43**
PortalUrl property
   SPSite class, 37
   SPWeb class, 43
postbacks (Web Parts), **203**
PostBacks( ) method, **170-172**
posting data back to servers, **170-172**
PresenceEnabled property (SPWeb class), **43**
ProfilePropertyCollection class, **143**
profiles (user)
   change history, 312-313
   change log history query, 140-142
   choice list properties, 144
   common data, retrieving, 145-146
   creating, 143
   groups, adding, 145
   modifying, 140
   new features, 307-308
   properties
      creating, 143-144
      multivalued properties, 144
      retrieving, 137-139, 310-311
   retrieving, 135-137
   User Profile Web Service, 308-309
   value separators for properties, 144
Program.cs file, **21-22**
properties
   BackColor, 168
   ConsumerConnectionPoint, 224
   ConsumerID, 224
   CorrelationToken, 155
   Current, 207
   CustomerID, 218
   Feature definitions, 30-31
   FeatureDefinitions, 27
   Features, 27, 30-31
   ID, 224
   Line of Business system instance, 348
   list updatable, 278
   LobSystemInstanceStruct structure, 348
   MethodStruct structure, 351
   Properties, 30
   ProviderID, 224
   Sites, 35
   Solutions, 32
   SPFile class, 84-85
   SPFolder class, 86
   SPItemEventProperties class, 74
   SPList class, 48-50

SPListEventProperties, 71
SPListItem class, 51
SPSite class, 36-38
SPSolution class, 33
SPWeb class, 42-43
user profiles
   choice list, 144
   creating, 143-144
   multivalued, 144
   retrieving, 137-139, 310-311
   value separators, 144
Web Parts, 191-195
   attributes, 194-195
   selecting from lists, 195-196
   SimpleLoanCalculator example, 192-194
WebApplication, 22
Properties property
   SPFeaturePropertyCollection collection, 30
   SPFile class, 85
   SPFolder class, 86
   SPListItem class, 51
   SPSolution class, 33
PropertiesXml property (SPList class), **49**
property bags, **30**
PropertyGridEditorPart control, **174**
Protocol property (SPSite class), **37**
provider Web Parts, **217**
   connecting with consumer Web Parts,
      223-226
   data interface, 218
   Web Part, creating, 218-220
ProviderID property (WebPartManager class), **224**
ProxyWebPartManager control, **173**
PublicKeyToken, **186**
Publish( ) method, **94**
publishing files, **94**

Q

queries (CAML)
   creating, 6
   lists, 8-11, 287-288
   U2U CAML Query Builder, 11
querying
   BDC metadata, 124-126
   list items, 62-64, 283-285
   Official File Web Service, 374-375
   Web Part pages, 344-345

How can we make this index more useful? Email us at indexes@samspublishing.com

R

RaisePostDataChangedEvent( ) method, 170-172
RdbCredentials authentication mode (BDC), 110
ReadLocked property (SPSite class), 37
ReadOnly property (SPSite class), 37
ReceiverData property
    SPItemEventProperties class, 74
    SPListEventProperties class, 71
record routing rules, adding, 370
Records Center
    connections, configuring, 370
    files, submitting, 373-374
    modifying, 372
    Official File Web Service
        linking, 370
        querying, 374-375
    record routing rules, 370
    site definition, 370
records repositories
    creating, 375-376
    files, submitting, 373-374
    metadata information storage example, 372
    Official File Web Service, 374-375
    overview, 369
    Records Center
        connections, configuring, 370
        files, submitting, 373-374
        modifying, 372
        Official File Web Service, 370, 374-375
        record routing rules, 370
        site definition, 370
recurring meetings, 101
Recycle Bin, 94
Recycle( ) method, 94
RecycleBin property
    SPSite class, 37
    SPWeb class, 43
references
    Assembly, 21-22
    System.Web.dll file, 178
Refresh( ) method, 325
relational data, exposing, 133
RelativeWebUrl property
    (SPItemEventProperties class), 74
releasing workflow tasks, 366
remote applications, developing, 18
remote development environment, 20-21
Remove( ) method, 32
RemoveColleague( ) method, 309
RemoveDwsUser( ) method, 253

RemoveGroup( ) method, 316
RemoveGroupFromRole( ) method, 316
RemoveLink( ) method, 309
RemoveMeeting( ) method, 300
RemoveMembership( ) method, 309
RemovePinnedLink( ) method, 309
RemoveRole( ) method, 316
RemoveUserCollectionFromGroup( ) method, 316
RemoveUserCollectionFromRole( ) method, 316
RemoveUserCollectionFromSite( ) method, 316
RemoveUserFromGroup( ) method, 316
RemoveUserFromRole( ) method, 316
RemoveUserFromSite( ) method, 316
RemoveUserFromWeb( ) method, 316
RemoveWorkflowAssociation( ) method, 339
Rename( ) method, 257
renaming images, 263
Render( ) method
    ExpandingTextBox class, 170
    Web Parts, 199
RenderAsHtml( ) method, 55
RenderWebPartForEdit( ) method, 339
RequireCheckout column (lists), 275
Resolve( ) method, 356
RestoreMeeting( ) method, 302
restoring
    files, 94
    meetings, 302
Retract( ) method, 34
retrieving
    commonalities among user profiles, 145-146
    Document Workspace data, 244-247
    list items, 275-277
    picture library images
        IDs, 260
        lists, 258-260
        XML data, 260-261
    task data, 367
    user profile properties, 135-139, 310-311
    workflows
        data, 361-362
        tasks, 362-365
        templates, 366-367
RevertToSelf authentication mode (BDC), 110
revision control (lists), 286
RootFolder column (lists), 274
RootFolder property
    SPList class, 50
    SPWeb class, 43
RootWeb property (SPSite class), 37

S

Safe Assemblies, 345
SaveAsTemplate( ) method
    SPList class, 55
    SPWeb class, 44
SaveBinary( ) method, 93-94
SaveWebPart( ) method, 339
SaveWebPart2( ) method, 339
saving
    files, 94
    server controls to ViewState, 170-172
schemas (lists), 277
SchemaXml property (SPList class), 50
ScopeId column (lists), 275
SearchDocuments( ) method, 44
SearchListItems( ) method, 44
SearchServiceInstance property (SPSite
    class), 37
SecondaryContact property (SPSite class), 37
security groups, 316-318
SelfServiceCreateSite( ) method, 38
SendToLocation column (lists), 275
SendToLocationName property (SPList class), 50
SendToLocationUrl property (SPList class), 50
SendToOfficialFile( ) method, 373
server controls
    ASP.NET integration, 184
    building, 166-168
    extending, 168-172
    saving to ViewState, 170-172
    user controls, compared, 163-166
ServerRedirected property (SPFile class), 85
ServerRelativeUrl property
    SPFile class, 85
    SPFolder class, 86
    SPSite class, 37
    SPWeb class, 43
servers
    applications on, developing, 17-18
    posting data back to, 170-172
ServerTemplate column (lists), 274
services
    Excel, 322
        application logic, 322
        architecture, 323
        business intelligence, 322
        Excel Calculation Services, 324
        Excel Web Access, 324
        hello world example, 326-328
        multiple named ranges client application
            example, 328-329

        reading/writing ranges and saving tem-
            porary workbooks application, 329-332
        trusted locations, 326
        user-defined functions, creating, 332-335
        user-defined libraries, 334
        web service, 325-326
        workbook management, 322
    web. See web services
SetAttendeeResponse( ) method, 105
SetCell( ) method, 325
SetCellA1( ) method, 326
SetCustomer( ) method, 223
SetRange( ) method, 326
SetRangeA1( ) method, 326
setup projects, adding, 235
SetWorkspaceTitle( ) method, 297
Sharepoint 2007 SDK template, 148
ShowUser column (lists), 275
ShowUser property (UpdateList( ) method), 279
SimpleLoanCalculator Web Part, 192-194
Single Sign-On authentication mode (BDC), 110
site collections
    creating, 39-41
    defined, 35
    hierarchy, 36
    information, accessing, 41
    listing, 35
    SPSite class, 36-38
site context console application
    creating, 21-22
    deploying, 22-23
Site Feature list, 79
Site( ) method, 315
.Site object, 207
Site property (SPWeb class), 43
SiteId property
    SPItemEventProperties class, 74
    SPListEventProperties class, 71
SiteLogoUrl property (SPWeb class), 43
sites
    Document Workspace, 241
        creating, 242-244
        data, retrieving, 244-246
        deleting, 243-244
        document ID storage, 251-252
        folders, 248
        metadata, retrieving, 246-247
        URLs, validating, 242
        users, managing, 253
    Meeting Workspaces, 291
        available, listing, 293-294
        creating, 292
        details, modifying, 297

Sites property (SPWebApplication class), 35
SmartPart, 183
SolutionFile property (SPSolution class), 33
SolutionId property (SPSolution class), 33
Solutions
    deleting, 32
    deploying, 34
    enumerating, 32-33
    installing, 32
Solutions collection, 32
Solutions property, 32
SourceLeafName property (SPFile class), 85
SourceUIVersion property (SPFile class), 85
SPChangeToken class, 314
SPContext class, 21
SPContext object, 207
    Current property, 207
    referencing timesheet list, 208-209
SPElementDefinition class, 26
Spell Checker Web Service, 377-379
SpellCheck( ) method, 378
SPEventReceiverBase class, 70
SPFarm class
    FeatureDefinitions property, 27
    instance of, creating, 27-29
SPFeature class, 26
SPFeatureCollection class, 26
SPFeatureDefinition class, 26
SPFeatureDefinitionCollection class, 31
SPFeatureDependency class, 26
SPFeatureProperty class, 26
SPFeatureProperty objects, 30
SPFeaturePropertyCollection class, 26
SPFeaturePropertyCollection collection, 30
SPFeatureScope class, 26
SPFile class
    methods, 91-94
    properties, 84-85
    submitting files to records repositories,
        373-374
SPFolder class
    methods, 94
    properties, 86
SPItemEventProperties class, 74
SPItemEventReceiver class, 69
SPList class
    lists, enumerating, 50-51
    methods, 55
    properties, 48-50
        AlertTemplate, 48-49
        AllowContentTypes, 48

AllowDeletion, 48
AllowEveryoneViewItems, 48
AllowMultiResponses, 48
AllowRssFeeds, 48
Audit, 48
BaseTemplate, 48
BaseType, 48
CanReceiveEmail, 48
ContentTypes, 48
ContentTypesEnabled, 48
Created, 48
CurrentChangeToken, 48
DefaultItemOpen, 48
DefaultView, 48
DefaultViewUrl, 48
Description, 48
Direction, 48
DraftVersionVisibility, 48
EmailAlias, 48
EnableAttachments, 49
EnableFolderCreation, 49
EnableMinorVersions, 49
EnableModeration, 49
EnableVersioning, 49
Event, 49
Fields, 49
Folders, 49
Forms, 49
Hidden, 49
ImageUrl, 49
ItemCount, 49
Items, 49
LastItemDeletedDate, 49
LastItemModifiedDate, 49
Lists, 49
MajorVersionLimit, 49
MajorWithMinorVersionsLimit, 49
MobileDefaultViewUrl, 49
MultipleDataList, 49
NoCrawl, 49
ParentWeb, 49
ParentWebUrl, 49
PropertiesXml, 49
RootFolder, 50
SchemaXml, 50
SendToLocationName, 50
SendToLocationUrl, 50
Title, 50
Version, 50
Views, 50
WorkflowAssociations, 50

SPListEventProperties class, 71
SPListEventReceiver class, 70
SPListItem class
   lists
      contents, viewing, 52
      values, accessing, 53
   methods, 57
   properties, 51
   Update method, 214
SPMeeting class, 99
   Add( ) method, 103
   Cancel( ) method, 104
   LinkWithEvent( ) method, 105
   SetAttendeeResponse( ) method, 105
   Update( ) method, 104-105
SPQuery object, 7
SPSite class, 35-36
   Features property, 27
   instance of, creating, 27-29
   methods, 38
   properties, 36-38
      AllowRssFeeds, 36
      AllowUnsafeUpdates, 36
      AllWebs, 36
      Audit, 36
      CatchAccessDeniedException, 36
      CertificationDate, 36
      ContentDatabase, 36
      CurrentChangeToken, 36
      DeadWebNotificationCount, 37
      Features, 37
      HostHeaderIsSiteName, 37
      IISAllowsAnonymous, 37
      Impersonating, 37
      LastContentModifiedDate, 37
      LastSecurityModifiedDate, 37
      Owner, 37
      Port, 37
      PortalUrl, 37
      Protocol, 37
      ReadLocked, 37
      ReadOnly, 37
      RecycleBin, 37
      RootWeb, 37
      SearchServiceInstance, 37
      SecondaryContact, 37
      ServerRelativeUrl, 37
      SyndicationEnabled, 37
      UpgradeRedirectedUri, 37
      Url, 37
      Usage, 37

      WebApplication, 38
      WorkflowManager, 38
      WriteLocked, 38
      Zone, 38
   site collections
      creating, 39-41
      information, accessing, 41
      updating, 42
SPSiteCollection class, 35-36
SPSolution class, 32
   deploy methods, 34
   properties, 33
SPWeb class, 36, 42
   Delete( ) method, 99
   Features property, 27
   methods, 44
   properties, 42-43
   webs
      creating, 44-45
      information, accessing, 45
      updating, 46
SPWebApplication class, 35-36
SPWebPartManager class, 185
SPWorkflow class, 365
SQLExecute Web Part, 197
   controls, 202
   CreateChildControls event, 202-203
   listing, 199-202
   postbakcs, 203
starting workflows, 367
StartWorkflow( ) method, 360, 367
Status property
   SPItemEventProperties class, 74
   SPListEventProperties class, 71
StorageManagementInformation( ) method, 38
strong naming Assemblies, 180
stsadm.exe command, 79
style sheets, 213
SubFolders property (SPFolder class), 86
SubmitFile( ) method, 375
SyndicationEnabled property (SPSite class), 37
System.Web.dll file, 178

T

TakeOffline( ) method, 94
tasks
   claiming, 366
   data, retrieving, 367
   modifying, 365-366
   releasing, 366
   retrieving, 362-365

Tasks property (SPListItem class), 51
templates
    lists, 80
    Meeting Workspaces, 295
    Web Custom Control, 166
    web IDs, 40-41
    Web Parts, 198-199
    WF, 147-148
    workflow, 149, 366-367
testing
    Assembly references, 21-22
    schema changing code for lists, 279
    Web Parts, 181-183
TextBox class, 166
Theme property (SPWeb class), 43
things to bring fields (Meeting Workspaces), 304
ThumbnailSize column (lists), 274
time sheet list example, 205
    accessing, 206-209
    data entry, 210
    hierarchy, 206
    updating, 209-215
TimeCreated property (SPFile class), 85
TimeLastModified property (SPFile class), 85
Timesheet Entry Web Part example, 210-213
Title column (lists), 274
Title property
    SPFile class, 85
    SPList class, 50
    SPListItem class, 51
    SPWeb class, 43
    UpdateList( ) method, 279
tools
    FieldRef extraction, 7-8
    third-party Web Parts, 183
    U2U CAML Query Builder, 11
    Web Parts, 183
TotalLength property (SPFile class), 85
transform states, 94
trusts (domain-level), configuring, 151
txtSQL control, 202

U

U2U CAML Query Builder, 11
UIVersion property (SPFile class), 85
UIVersionLabel property (SPFile class), 85
Unclassified Records library, 370, 375
UndoCheckOut( ) method, 94
uniform resource locators (URLs), 242
UniqueID parameter, 220

UniqueId property
    SPFile class, 85
    SPFolder class, 86
    SPListItem class, 51
UnPublish( ) method, 94
Update( ) method
    SPFile class, 94
    SPFolder class, 94
    SPList class, 55
    SPListItem class, 57, 214
    SPMeeting class, 104-105
    SPWeb class, 44
UpdateColleaguePrivacy( ) method, 309
UpdateGroupInfo( ) method, 316
UpdateLink( ) method, 309
UpdateList( ) method, 278
UpdateMeetingFromICal( ) method, 301
UpdateMembershipPrivacy( ) method, 309
UpdateOverwriteVersion( ) method, 57
UpdatePinnedLink( ) method, 309
UpdateRoleDefInfo( ) method, 316
UpdateRoleInfo( ) method, 316
UpdateUserInfo( ) method, 316
updating
    files, 94
    folders, 94
    lists, 53-57, 209-215
        cautions, 214
        data entry functionality, 213
        Lists Web Service, 278-282
        Timesheet Entry Web Part example,
            210-213
    meetings, 301
    site collections, 42
    Web Parts, 342-343
    webs, 46
UpgradeRedirectUrl property (SPSite class), 37
Upload( ) method, 257, 262
uploading
    documents to document libraries, 84
    images to picture libraries, 261-262
Url property
    SPFile class, 85
    SPFolder class, 86
    SPListItem class, 51
    SPSite class, 37
    SPWeb class, 43
URLs (uniform resource locators), 242
Usage property (SPSite class), 37
user controls
    ASP.NET integration, 184
    information collection user control, 164-165
    server controls, compared, 163-166

User Group Web Service
    methods, 315-316
    WPF data binding, 316-318
user groups
    security principles, enumerating, 316-318
    User Group Web Service, 315-316
User Profile Web Change Web Service, 312-314
User Profile Web Service
    methods, 308-309
    user profile properties, retrieving, 310-311
user profiles
    change history, 312-313
    change log history query, 140-142
    common data, retrieving, 145-146
    creating, 143
    groups, adding, 145
    modifying, 140
    new features, 307-308
    properties
        choice list, 144
        creating, 143-144
        multivalued, 144
        retrieving, 137-139
        value separators, 144
    properties, retrieving, 310-311
    retrieving, 135, 137
    User Profile Web Service, 308-309
user-defined functions, 332-335
user-defined libraries, 334
UserDisplayName property
    SPItemEventProperties class, 74
    SPListEventProperties class, 71
UserLoginName property
    SPItemEventProperties class, 74
    SPListEventProperties class, 71
UserProfileManager class, 135, 143
utilities. See tools

V

ValidateWorkflowMarkupAndCreateSupport-
    Objects( ) method, 339
validating Document Workspace URLs, 242
value separators (properties), 144
VBA (Visual Basic for Applications), 332-335
verifying Global Assembly Cache, 237
versioning, 91
    checking files in/out, 91
    example, 91-93
Version column (lists), 274
Version property (SPList class), 50

Versionless property (SPItemEventProperties
    class), 74
Versions property
    SPFile class, 85
    SPListItem class, 51
Versions Web Service, 383-384
views
    alerts, 379-382
    built-in style sheets, 213
    creating, 288-289
    deleting, 289
    list contents, 51-53
    list of, 289
    user profile changes, 312-313
Views property (SPList class), 50
Views Web Service, views, 288-289
ViewState of server controls, 170-172
Visual Basic for Applications (VBA), 332-335
Visual C# 2005 Express Edition download, 18
Visual Studio 2005
    Extensions for Windows Workflow
        Foundation, 148
    Web Parts, debugging, 230-231
    web references, adding, 287
    workflows, modeling, 153-155

W

web applications
    hierarchy, 36
    site collections, 35
Web Custom Controls, 166
.Web object, 207
Web Part pages
    querying, 344-345
    Safe Assemblies, 345
    Web Parts
        adding, 339-341
        updating, 342-343
    Web Service
        adding Web Parts, 339-341
        methods, 337-339
        Safe Assemblies, 345
        Web Part pages, querying, 344-345
        updating Web Parts, 342-343
Web Parts
    adding to Web Part pages, 339-341
    BDC, 114-116
    connecting, 223-226
    consumers, 221-223

controls, 173
   CatalogZone, 178
   WebPartManager, 175-176
   WebPartZones, 178
creating, 18, 178-181
debugging, 229-230
   breakpoints, setting, 231-233
   common SharePoint server, 234
   development workstations, 229-230
   local SharePoint server, 234
   Visual Studio 2005, 230-231
   Web Part library, compiling, 231
   without SharePoint or WSS, 233
deploying, 235
   compiling setup project, 237
   configuring setup project, 236
   MSI-based, 235
   setup projects, adding, 235
design mode, 177
functionality, 197
HelloWorld example, 179-180
importing, 188
integration, 174
JavaScript, adding, 204
layout, 197
library, compiling, 231
lists
   accessing, 206-209
   data entry, 210
   updating, 209-215
managing, 175-176
postbacks, 203
properties, 191-195
   attributes, 194-195
   selecting from lists, 195-196
   SimpleLoanCalculator example, 192-194
providers, 217-220
rendering in browsers, 199
SharePoint, 185-188
SQLExecute example, 197
   controls, 202
   CreateChildControls event, 202-203
   listing, 199-202
   postbacks, 203
System.Web.dll file reference, 178
template, 198-199
testing, 181-183
third-party tools, 183
time sheet list example, 205-206
Timesheet Entry Web Part example listing,
   210-213

updating, 342-343
web controls, adding, 199
zones, 178
Web property
   SPListEventProperties class, 71
   SPListItem class, 51
web references, adding, 287
web services
   Alerts, 379-382
   authentication, 299
   BDC, 348
      compatible, 132
      entities, enumerating, 350-351
      Field Resolver, 355-356
      filter descriptors, enumerating, 354
      Line of Business systems, 348-349
      methods, 351-353
   Document Workspace
      data, retrieving, 244-246
      folders, 248
      metadata, retrieving, 246-247
   Excel Services, 325
      hello world example, 326-328
      methods, 325-326
      multiple named ranges client application
         example, 328-329
      reading/writing ranges and saving
         temporary workbooks applications,
         329-332
      trusted locations, configuring, 326
   Imaging, 256-257, 266-272
   Lists, 273
      creating list items, 281-282
      deleting list items, 281-282
      filtering, 287-288
      querying hierarchical list items, 283-285
      retrieving lists/list items, 275-277
      revision control, 286
      updating, 278-282
   Official File
      querying, 374-375
      record repositories, creating, 375-376
      Records Center, 370
   Spell Checker, 377-379
   User Group
      methods, 315-316
      WPF data binding, 316-318
   User Profile
      methods, 308-309
      user profile properties, retrieving,
         310-311

User Profile Web Change, 312-314

Versions, 383-384

Views, 288-289

Web Part Pages

adding Web Parts, 339-341

methods, 337-339

querying, 344-345

Safe Assemblies, 345

updating Web Parts, 342-343

Workflow

methods, 360

starting workflows, 367

tasks, 362-367

templates, retrieving, 366-367

workflow data, retrieving, 361-362

Visual C# 2005 Express Edition

download, 18

web template IDs, 40-41

WebApplication property (SPSite class), 22, 38

WebBrowsable attribute, 194

WebControl class, 166

WebDescription attribute, 194

WebDisplayName attribute, 194

WebFullUrl column (lists), 275

WebId column (lists), 275

WebId property (SPListEventProperties class), 71

WebImageHeight column (lists), 274

WebImageWidth column (lists), 274

WebPart class (SharePoint versus ASP.NET), 185

WebPartConnection Collection Editor, 223

WebPartManager class

static connection properties, 224

Web Parts, connecting, 223

WebPartManager control, 173-176

WebPartZone class, 185

WebPartZone control, 173

webs

creating, 44-45

information, accessing, 45

SPWeb class, 42-43

updating, 46

Webs property (SPWeb class), 43

websites

AdventureWorks SQL database, 113

hierarchy, 36

Sharepoint 2007 SDK, 148

SmartPart, 183

U2U CAML Query Builder download, 11

Visual Studio 2005 Extensions for Windows Workflow Foundation template, 148

WebUrl property

SPItemEventProperties class, 74

SPListEventProperties class, 71

WelcomePage property (SPFolder class), 86

WF (Windows Workflow Foundation), 147, 359

templates, installing, 147-148

Workflow Web Service

methods, 360

tasks, 365-367

templates, retrieving, 366-367

workflow data, retrieving, 361-362

workflows, starting, 367

wildcard Finders, 130-131

Windows Forms applications

DocLibPicker.cs, 89-90

Feature Enumerator, 29

Form1.cs, 86-88

Windows Presentation Foundation (WPF), 316

Windows SharePoint Services (WSS), 15

Windows Workflow Foundation. See WF

WindowsCredentials authentication mode (BDC), 111

WinForms applications

creating, 21-22

deploying, 22-23

workbooks (Excel). See also Excel Services

application logic, 322

business intelligence, 322

hello world example, 326-328

managing, 322

multiple named ranges client application example, 328-329

reading/writing ranges and saving temporary workbooks application, 329-332

Workflow Web Service

methods, 360

tasks

claiming, 366

data, retrieving, 367

modifying, 365-366

releasing, 366

retrieving, 362-365

templates, retrieving, 366-367

workflows

data, retrieving, 361-362

starting, 367

workflow.xml file, 157

WorkflowAssociations property (SPList class), 50

WorkflowId column (lists), 275

WorkflowManager property (SPSite class), 38

workflows
approval, 148
associations, 150
batch file for installation file, 158-159
building, 150
coding, 155-156
data, retrieving, 361-362
deploying, 156-159
feature.xml file, 156-157
forms, designing, 151-153
HelloWorldSequentialWorkflow Assembly
   features.xml file, 156-157
   install.bat file, 158-159
   workflow designer, 155
   workflow.xml file, 157
instances, 150
modeling, 153-155
starting, 367
submitting files to records repositories, 373
support, 153
tasks
   claiming, 366
   data, retrieving, 367
   modifying, 365-366
   releasing, 366
   retrieving, 362-365
templates, 149, 366-367
Web Service, 360
workflow.xml file, 157
Workflows property (SPListItem class), 51
WorkflowTemplates property (SPWeb class), 43
workspaces
Document
   creating, 242-244
   data, retrieving, 244-246
   deleting, 243-244
   document ID storage, 251-252
   folders, 248

metadata, retrieving, 246-247
overview, 241
URLs, validating, 242
users, managing, 253
Meeting, 291
   attendee responses, 105
   available, listing, 293-294
   calendar events, linking, 105
   creating, 97-98, 295-296
   creating meetings, 102-104, 298-299
   deleting, 296-297
   deleting meetings, 104, 300-301
   details, modifying, 297
   lists, 100, 304
   meeting attendance, 302-303
   Meeting Series list, 100-101
   modifying meetings, 104
   restoring meetings, 302
   sites, creating, 292
   templates, 295
   updating meetings, 301
WPF (Windows Presentation Foundation), 316
WriteLocked property (SPSite class), 38
WriteRssFeed method (SPList class), 55
WriteSecurity column (lists), 274
WSS (Windows SharePoint Services), 15

X–Z

XML data, 260-261
Xml property (SPListItem class), 51

Zone property
   SPItemEventProperties class, 74
   SPSite class, 38
zones (Web Parts), 178

THIS BOOK IS SAFARI ENABLED

INCLUDES FREE 45-DAY ACCESS TO THE ONLINE EDITION

The Safari® Enabled icon on the cover of your favorite technology book means the book is available through Safari Bookshelf. When you buy this book, you get free access to the online edition for 45 days.

Safari Bookshelf is an electronic reference library that lets you easily search thousands of technical books, find code samples, download chapters, and access technical information whenever and wherever you need it.

TO GAIN 45-DAY SAFARI ENABLED ACCESS TO THIS BOOK:

- Go to **http://www.samspublishing.com/safarienabled**
- Complete the brief registration form
- Enter the coupon code found in the front of this book on the "Copyright" page

If you have difficulty registering on Safari Bookshelf or accessing the online edition, please e-mail customer-service@safaribooksonline.com.

UNLEASHED

Unleashed takes you beyond the basics, providing an exhaustive, technically sophisticated reference for professionals who need to exploit a technology to its fullest potential. It's the best resource for practical advice from the experts, and the most in-depth coverage of the latest technologies.

Microsoft® SharePoint 2007 Unleashed
ISBN: 0672329476

OTHER UNLEASHED TITLES

Microsoft BizTalk Server 2006 Unleashed
ISBN: 0672329255

Microsoft Exchange Server 2007 Unleashed
ISBN: 0672329204

Microsoft Expression Blend Unleashed
ISBN: 067232931X

Microsoft ISA Server 2006 Unleashed
ISBN: 0672329190

Microsoft Office Project Server 2007 Unleashed
ISBN: 0672329212

Microsoft Operations Manager 2005 Unleashed
ISBN: 067232928X

Microsoft Small Business Server 2003 Unleashed
ISBN: 0672328054

Microsoft Visual C# 2005 Unleashed
ISBN: 0672327767

Microsoft Visual Studio 2005 Unleashed
ISBN: 0672328194

VBScript, WMI and ADSI Unleashed
ISBN: 0321501713

Windows Communication Foundation Unleashed
ISBN: 0672329484

Windows PowerShell Unleashed
ISBN: 0672329530

Windows® Presentation Foundation Unleashed
ISBN:0672328917

ASP.NET 2.0 Unleashed
ISBN:0672328232

SAMS

www.samspublishing.com